Sunday Baseball

ALSO BY CHARLIE BEVIS

*Mickey Cochrane: The Life of a
Baseball Hall of Fame Catcher*
(McFarland, 1998)

Sunday Baseball

*The Major Leagues' Struggle to Play
Baseball on the Lord's Day, 1876–1934*

CHARLIE BEVIS

McFarland & Company, Inc., Publishers
Jefferson, North Carolina, and London

LIBRARY OF CONGRESS CATALOGUING-IN-PUBLICATION DATA

Bevis, Charlie, 1954–
Sunday baseball: the major leagues' struggle to play baseball on the Lord's day, 1876–1934 / Charlie Bevis.
p.   cm.
Includes bibliographical references and index.

ISBN 0-7864-1564-9 (softcover : 50# alkaline paper)

1. Baseball—Social aspects—United States. 2. Sports—United States—Religious aspects. 3. Civil religion—United States. I. Title: Major leagues' struggle to play baseball on the Lord's day, 1876–1934. II. Title.
GV867.6.B48   2003   796.357'64'0973—dc21   2002156687

British Library cataloguing data are available

©2003 Charlie Bevis. All rights reserved

No part of this book may be reproduced or transmitted in any form or by any means, electronic or mechanical, including photocopying or recording, or by any information storage and retrieval system, without permission in writing from the publisher.

Cover image: ©2003 PhotoSpin

Manufactured in the United States of America

McFarland & Company, Inc., Publishers
Box 611, Jefferson, North Carolina 28640
www.mcfarlandpub.com

To my mother, for instilling in me the concept
that I could accomplish anything if I set my mind to it

Contents

Preface	1
1. Ball Players Arrested for It	5
2. National League Disliked It	24
3. American Association Loved It	34
4. St. Louis and Brooklyn Exulted in It	51
5. Sabbatarians Hated It	75
6. National League Embraced It	101
7. Cleveland Attempted It	116
8. American League Liked It	135
9. Brooklyn Used Subterfuge to Do It	152
10. New York Wanted It	174
11. Philadelphia Experimented with It	200
12. Boston Finally Got It	214
13. Bribery Scandal Soiled It	228
14. Philadelphia at Last Adopted It	246
15. Legacy of Sunday Baseball	261
Appendix A—Sunday Baseball Firsts in the Major Leagues	271
Appendix B—Significant Court Decisions on Sunday Baseball	275
Appendix C—Massachusetts Ballot Initiative, 1928	292
Notes	293
Bibliography	309
Index	311

Preface

My interest in Sunday baseball came about by happenstance, the result of frustration in one research endeavor that led to the exploration of another topic.

Originally, I set out to explore a history of the New England League, to blend the on-field exploits of this minor league with the economic events in the textile and shoe industries that forever changed the mill cities in which the league operated. From its first season in 1885 to its final days in 1949, the New England League operated sporadically and never seemed to hold together for any appreciable length of time. The 1920s were a particularly difficult time for the New England League, during a period that many consider to be The Golden Age of Sport.

The basic reason for the league's tribulations during such an affluent time was that its teams couldn't play baseball games on Sunday. State laws in Massachusetts, Maine, and New Hampshire then prohibited professional baseball games on the Lord's Day.

Claude Davidson, the enterprising New England League president, was a prominent proponent, along with the Boston Braves management, for a ballot referendum to get the Sunday baseball issue before the Massachusetts voters, since the state legislature resisted passing a law to legalize professional baseball games on Sunday. As late as 1920, baseball games played by amateurs on Sunday had also been illegal in Massachusetts.

Sunday baseball opponents foiled the initial effort to get the referendum on the 1926 ballot. While the measure was overwhelmingly approved in the 1928 election, it came too late to save the New England League, which barely lasted one more season before disbanding once again. The new law nearly came too late to save the Boston Braves team, whose owners also suffered through an embarrassing set of public hearings in 1929 over allegations of bribery to win approval from the Boston City Council for a permit to play Sunday games at Braves Field.

An interesting side note to baseball history, I initially thought, which encouraged me to find out more about Sunday baseball. There was almost nothing available on the topic, I found, as there was no assembled body of knowledge on the topic. Several pages in Harold Seymour's seminal works on baseball history and a few paragraphs in David Voigt's classic work (although nearly impossible to locate since the topic was mal-indexed as "Baseball, Sunday") were about it for readily available knowledge. There were no comprehensive writings on Sunday baseball among the many secondary sources on baseball history. What I had read, though, intrigued me to find out more.

As I dug into the topic, I uncovered a wealth of interesting developments in how Sunday baseball had impacted the growth of the major leagues. First of all, Massachusetts wasn't alone in prohibiting baseball on Sunday; at one time it was illegal in many states. There were also numerous bizarre incidents that occurred at Sunday games, not the least of which were the games that were halted when the local constabulary arrested the ball players for participating in baseball games on the Lord's Day. Then there were the ballparks that were only used on Sunday, in places designed to evade the Sunday laws, and the one-game road trips that ball clubs made to other cities just to play a game on Sunday.

The topic became more fascinating as the research became more challenging. Combing through the microfilm of the long-defunct *Sporting Life* publication yielded a plethora of information on Sunday baseball—the only obstacle was digging it out issue by issue. Because *Sporting Life* was based in Philadelphia, a bastion of Sunday decorum, it seemed to have a firmer grasp on Sunday baseball issues and report on them in much greater detail than did *The Sporting News*, which was based in St. Louis, a city considered "wide open" when it came to Sunday issues. *Baseball Magazine* had a few articles on Sunday baseball and there were a couple of articles in academic history journals. Local newspapers also contained abundant colorful accounts of the many Sunday baseball incidents, once you knew what dates to look for.

I hope you will share my thrill that a thorough compilation and analysis of the Sunday baseball topic is now available. Sunday baseball is a fascinating part of baseball history and one that has been nearly lost for future generations to comprehend how it helped to advance the development of the game.

My interest in the Sunday baseball topic was definitely piqued in October 2001 when my son Scott pitched in a fall baseball tournament near my hometown. The third-round game was slated for Sunday morning October 7. I brought my mom, then 80 years old, to the game so that she could see her grandson pitch a few innings in the sunny, but chilly autumnal weather.

It turned out to be a memorable day for several reasons. With a peewee football game being played just beyond right field, Scott pitched well in the initial innings. I happened to mention to my mom that 85 years ago it wouldn't have been legal for Scott to pitch on Sunday in Massachusetts. She then told me stories about how her mother enforced a strict Sunday when she was growing up in the 1920s. She and her sisters had to walk several miles to church and when they returned from services, it was a rigid "day of rest." They could barely do anything, not even sew.

Suddenly, the loud speaker at the football game blared an announcement that the United States had invaded Afghanistan to hunt down terrorist leader Osama bin Laden to atone for the World Trade Center suicide bombings that had transpired just a month earlier. Somehow who won or who lost the baseball game then seemed far less important.

Scott's team lost that baseball game, an interminable 16-inning contest that no team seemed to want to win. I took my mom home after

Author's son, Scott Bevis, pitching in an amateur Sunday baseball game in Massachusetts during 2001. While now perfectly legal, if the game had been contested before 1920, the ball players would have been arrested for violating the Massachusetts law that prohibited playing sports on Sunday. (Author's collection)

the third inning and stopped to buy a newspaper and coffee on my way back to the baseball game, driving by several churches in the process. In the tenth inning, I went out for sandwiches, as many stores were open for business. I imagined how different times must have been 85 years earlier when almost no activity would have been visible on a Sunday morning, except people like my mother walking to church, and how if my son's baseball game were played back then, the police likely would have stopped the game and perhaps even arrested him.

That day spurred me to complete my research on Sunday baseball and prepare the manuscript that resulted in this book.

For their assistance in retrieving numerous roles of microfilm, I wish to thank the staffs at the Boston Public Library, the Worcester Public Library, the New York State Library in Albany, and the Library of Congress in Washington D.C. I especially want to thank the Society for American Baseball Research in Cleveland for its mail-order microfilm lending service, which more easily made available issues of *Sporting Life*. The SABR staff was terrific in responding to my requests.

Extra thanks go to Cheryl Laugherty at the Birchard Public Library in Fremont, Ohio for going out of her way to retrieve a newspaper article on an 1893 train wreck that occurred nearby, which injured several ball players en route to Chicago to play in a one-game Sunday series. The staff at the National Baseball Library in Cooperstown was also very helpful, especially letting me peruse the original volumes of the *New York Clipper*. The feel of century-old newspaper (even with white gloves on) really makes history come alive.

Several SABR members were particularly helpful in securing hard-to-locate information for the book. Thanks to Karen Koziara, Bill Gagliano, Eric Weiss, James Beck, and Anthony Papalas.

Appreciation is due several co-workers at my day job who helped out with various aspects of the book. Thanks to Art MacPherson, Lisa Campbell, and Kirk Cupp. And thanks to Gavin Quill for his continuing inspiration to finish the manuscript.

Many thanks go to my family for putting up with me during my research and writing efforts, which with every book seems to take at least double the effort originally projected. Extra-special thanks to my wife Kathie and our children Scott and Kelly. Also thanks to our dog Kris, who contributed subtle support through his many hours lying next to my chair while I pounded away at the keyboard of our computer.

Chapter 1

BALL PLAYERS ARRESTED FOR IT

"Sunday baseball" long ago evaporated as a term in our sports vocabulary.

During the period 1876–1934, though, the term had a very real context in then-current sports lexicon. Sunday baseball described the once unusual phenomenon of men playing baseball on a day many considered sacred in the belief that the Lord had set it aside as a "day of rest" to observe the Sabbath.

Men playing baseball on Sunday—a once peculiar, and often illegal, event—has been transformed into such a common occurrence today that a specific phrase to describe the activity is no longer necessary.

One hundred years ago, though, Sunday baseball was a polarizing expression among people living on the East Coast, and during the preceding 25 years that polarization had extended across the entire nation.

We take for granted today that major league baseball can be played on Sunday without interference by our government. The right to play baseball on Sunday, though, was not so easily ordained as an inalienable right among the populace. Groups on both sides of the issue, to play or not play sports on Sunday, harbored strong opinions about the justification of their positions.

The issue was fought both figuratively in court and literally on the baseball field. Numerous players and managers, in addition to team owners, suffered the indignity of police arrest to help further the cause to legally play baseball on the Lord's Day. Many of these arrests occurred on the ball field in front of thousands of onlookers.

Indianapolis, Indiana, was the site of the first arrests for alleged violations of Sunday laws by ball players participating in a major league baseball game. In May 1884, players of both the visiting Cincinnati team and the home Indianapolis team were arrested in the days following their Sunday, May 18, game in the American Association, then a major league, for "desecration of the Sabbath."[1]

The first on-field arrests happened in an American Association game in Columbus, Ohio, on June 22, 1884. After the fifth inning of the game between Columbus and Brooklyn, three constables appeared on the field and arrested three Brooklyn players and six Columbus players. "There were 3,000 people on the ground and a riot was imminent," one writer recounted the scene of the arrests. "It was finally agreed that if they would let the game go on, all would go with them to justice's office after the game."[2]

Players both famous and obscure were arrested in the quest by Sabbatarian organizations, which promoted strict observance of Sunday as a day of rest, to eliminate Sunday baseball.

Future Hall of Famers such as Cap Anson, Jesse Burkett, and Mike Kelly were all arrested for playing Sunday baseball. Anson was arrested in Chicago in 1895, Burkett in Cleveland in 1897, while Kelly was arrested several times for his Cincinnati team's Sunday play in 1891. Among the more obscure major leaguers arrested for playing baseball on Sunday were Cub Stricker, second baseman for Cleveland in 1887; Fred Carroll, catcher for Columbus in 1884; Charlie Abbey, outfielder for Washington in 1897; John Reilly, first baseman for Cincinnati in 1889; and Fred Jacklitsch, catcher for Brooklyn in 1904. Several dozen more players could also be listed.

For the most part, team owners escaped the long arm of the law. One early exception was the 1887 arrest of St. Louis president Chris Von der Ahe at the scheduled July 10 game with Baltimore. After Von der Ahe was acquitted at his trial, Sabbatarian groups focused attention on the arrest of ball players to make their point.

On-field confrontations between Sabbatarians and baseball spectators were sometimes contentious.

At Rochester in 1890, in the third inning of the July 20 American Association game, a justice of the peace accompanied by several constables and members of the Law and Order Society marched onto the diamond in single file and ordered players to stop the game. They may have underestimated the intensity of the club's followers though.

"As the players came in, spectators began to pour out upon the diamond and shout derisively at the officers," the *Rochester Herald* described the scene. "Here and there a cushion seat went flying through the air and the crowd surged thicker and thicker." While it appeared a fight would ensue, Rochester manager Pat Powers stepped in and convinced the constabulary that if they'd let the game continue, then the players would report the next day to the justice's office. The justice, "deeming discretion the better part of valor, accepted the terms and departed."[3]

Another uneasy situation occurred in the outskirts of Cincinnati in 1889, in the fourth inning of the August 25 game. "When the squad of bluecoats marched through the park gate they were vigorously cheered by the spectators, most of them laboring under the impression that the minions of the law had come to preserve order and put the crowd back," the *Cincinnati Enquirer* reported. The police had come, though, to arrest the players in the game, not to move the standing-room crowd farther from the diamond. In the resulting confusion, spectators swarmed the field, allowing several players to escape the grasp of the police.[4]

Once arrested, typically one player would be selected to stand trial, with the result of that case to apply to all the arrested ball players. Sometimes the legal proceedings had humorous elements.

After juries acquitted the popular Mike "King" Kelly several times following the Cincinnati team's arrests in 1891, the prosecutor instead put pitcher Willie Mains on trial. The jury deliberated five hours and beyond midnight when it seemed stymied at 11–1 for acquittal of Mains. A juror named A. E. Higbee, a man who avowedly "devoted himself to religion more than base ball on Sunday," was the lone juror holding out for a guilty verdict. On the 15th ballot, Higbee finally changed his vote and the jury rendered a verdict of not guilty for Mains. Kelly was acquitted at another trial after a Baptist preacher, holding out for a guilty verdict, switched his vote to acquit Kelly.[5]

Walt Wilmot was put on trial in January 1896 after the June 23, 1895, arrests of the Chicago team at its West Side Grounds. Wilmot was found not guilty, after the prosecution's case was undermined upon the revelation that the one of the witnesses "had sold seats on his rear shed to persons wishing to view the ball game in progress on the eventful Sunday." The witness, Edward Thompson, claimed that the case was about "the peace and quiet of the West Side Sabbath," and not whether he "had accumulated any wealth in this connection."[6]

A few players gained everlasting legal fame when court cases were pursued up to the state supreme court or became legal precedents.

Jack Powell, a Cleveland pitcher, was one of the 18 ball players arrested at the May 16, 1897, Sunday game at Cleveland's League Park. "Arrangement has been made with the authorities whereby only one man will of necessity appear. This will be Powell, who was put in the game yesterday and assigned to first base," the *Cleveland Plain Dealer* reported. "Powell will know a whole lot about baseball law when it is finished."[7]

Powell was found guilty in the trial, but upon appeal, Judge Walter

CLEVELAND, S.

SUNDAY BALL.

Judge Ong Decides That It Can be Played Here.

Law Prohibiting It Declared Unconstitutional.

Base Ball Playing Not a Crime.

Neither Can It be Called Immoral, According to the Decision, So the Law is Unconstitutional — The Judgment of the Police Court Reversed in the Case of John Powell of the Cleveland Baseball Club — President Robison Much Pleased Over the Result.

Cleveland Plain Dealer headline in 1897 declaring "Base Ball Playing Not a Crime" after Judge Ong overturned the guilty verdict of Jack Powell for playing baseball on Sunday for the Cleveland club in the National League. The Ohio Supreme Court later reversed the decision.

Ong overturned Powell's conviction. Ong determined that the Sunday law under which Powell was arrested violated Powell's constitutional guarantee of personal liberty and therefore the law was unconstitutional. The *Cleveland Plain Dealer* trumpeted the decision in the headline "Base Ball Playing Not a Crime."[8]

The case was not over yet, though, as the prosecution appealed Judge Ong's decision to the Ohio Supreme Court. On April 19, 1898, the Ohio Supreme Court ruled in *State v. Powell* that the Sunday law was constitutional and overturned the decision of Judge Ong. The court ruled that the legislature had the power "to adopt all such wholesome laws as may be necessary to promote the peace, health, and well-being of society. Laws fixing regularly recurring days of rest from all secular pursuits, such as our Sunday laws, are of this character, and do not violate the personal liberty of the individual."[9]

Ed Poole had a rather short major league pitching career, including just one year with the Brooklyn team in 1904, but his impact in New York legal circles lasted many years. Poole was arrested on April 24, 1904, for pitching the game that Sunday against Philadelphia. Justice William Gaynor found Poole innocent of violating the Sunday law in that game. District Attorney John Clarke prosecuted the Sunday ball playing again, though, with arrests at the May 29 game between Brooklyn and New York, in which Poole was once again pitching. This time, the prosecution got its arguments straight.

"In the case of Rath and others which were recently before me on the writ of habeas corpus, the complaint was simply that the defendants played a game of baseball on Sunday. The complaint presented nothing but the case of ordinary private games of baseball on Sunday which are not prohibited by the statute," Gaynor wrote in his opinion in the case of *People*

1. Ball Players Arrested for It

v. Poole. "The present case is different. The complaint is of a public game of baseball, i.e., of a game to which the public were invited, and to which an admission fee was charged. Is such a game prohibited by the statute? I think it is."[10]

People v. Poole was an often quoted legal precedent as New York wrestled over the ensuing 15 years with the issue of legalizing baseball on Sunday.

The arrest of ball players was increasingly seen as not being the root of the Sunday baseball issue, since team owners were the ones most concerned with the ability to stage Sunday games. Wholesale arrests of all the players in a Sunday game were stopped, with just certain players designated for arrest to pursue the case against the owners.

Sometimes volunteers were recruited for the arrests. That was the situation with Frank Roth, the first Philadelphia batter in the April 24, 1904, Sunday game in Brooklyn that led to the People v. Poole case. Hugh Duffy had been scheduled to be the first Philadelphia batter, but Roth volunteered to have the arrest made on him rather than the 37-year-old Duffy.

By the turn of the century, arrests for Sunday baseball play began to be viewed with less seriousness and often with some frivolity.

At the May 16, 1897, arrests in Cleveland that precipitated State v. Powell, the players were ushered into the police station and "then the stately Lieut. Herman Felhaber, with a new filled fountain pen in his hand, marched to the registration window, laid violent hands upon the blotter, and called: 'Step up, gentlemen, and get your tickets. You will have a full half hour before the main circus in the large tent commences.' [He then] booked Umpire Hurst." Burkett was the first ball player to be booked and was "to all outward appearances, far from unhappy. He smiled and talked pleasantly with the lieutenant, and seemed to relish the entire proceeding as an 18-karat joke."[11]

In the final attempt to legitimatize Sunday baseball in Brooklyn without legislative action, the last arrests of major league ball players were made on June 17, 1906. By this time, Sunday baseball arrests had reached the stage of a farce, as volunteers were solicited from both teams to be arrested at the beginning of the game. "Mal Eason of the Brooklyns and Chic Fraser of the Reds displayed marked bravery (published by special request of the press agent) in stepping forward and volunteering to become martyrs," the Brooklyn Daily Eagle remarked in jest.[12]

The Cincinnati team had a little fun with picking which player would be the first batter and therefore subjected to arrest. Manager Ned Hanlon had originally picked Charlie Chech, a little-used pitcher, to be the first batter. Chech, though, pleaded off on the assignment. Hanlon then offered

$25 to any Cincinnati player to substitute. Fraser, a regular pitcher, volunteered to become an "arrestee for hire."[13]

"Fraser displayed the proper diffidence at the crucial moment. It was seen that he faltered somewhat in his farcical attempt to avoid hitting the two balls pitched by Eason and the act was somewhat strained because of the delay on the part of Captain Baldwin and his plain clothes men in responding to their cues," the *Brooklyn Daily Eagle* continued its humorous report on the arrests. "However, the police finally entered L.C. upon the stage—beg pardon, diamond—as the chief villains. They were properly hissed at by the assembled populace, showing that their parts were in capable hands."[14]

Since later Sunday baseball battles were fought mostly in the legislature rather than the courts, it wasn't until 1917 that further arrests were made for Sunday games. In New York City, the three major league teams had decided to hold Sunday benefits for World War I–related charities, skirting the Sunday law by positioning a "free" baseball game to follow a paid sacred concert at the ballpark.

The Yankees hosted the first Sunday benefit at the Polo Grounds on June 17 without incident. Following the July 1 benefit game at Ebbets Field in Brooklyn, though, president Charlie Ebbets and manager Wilbert Robinson were arrested for violating the Sunday law. As the Brooklyn arrests worked their way through the court system, the New York Giants played a benefit game on August 19 with the Cincinnati Reds. The following day, the managers of the two teams, John McGraw and Christy Mathewson, were arrested for violating the Sunday law.

While the Sabbatarians might have survived the publicity favoring Sunday baseball that arose from the Ebbets trial in Brooklyn, the arrest of Mathewson—a former star pitcher for the Giants, hero to many New Yorkers, and avowed abstainer from playing baseball on Sunday when he was a player—was considered an action way over the top.

"It is my opinion that there was no infraction of any statute. Playing ball on the first day of the week, when not amounting to any serious interruption of the repose and religious liberty of the community, is not a violation of this section [of the law]," Magistrate Francis McQuade commented upon the release of McGraw and Mathewson. "There is not a scintilla of evidence of any one in the vicinity being disturbed. Instead of McGraw and Mathewson being summoned here to answer a charge of this kind, the public owes to each of them a vote of the highest commendation for lending their services gratis to this patriotic cause."[15]

The arrest of Mathewson and McGraw, and their rapid acquittal (Ebbets and Robinson were found guilty in their trial), was the last Sunday baseball arrest of an on-field participant in a major league game.

It wasn't, however, the last court appearance for the Sunday baseball cause. While no arrests were made at the August 22, 1926, test game in Philadelphia, the Pennsylvania attorney general initiated a lawsuit against the Philadelphia Athletics for a Sunday law violation. The Athletics appealed all the way to the Pennsylvania Supreme Court, which ruled that professional Sunday baseball was indeed illegal in the state.

What caused all these arrests and court proceedings over the exhibition of a baseball game on Sunday?

Blame it on the Puritans and their quest for religious freedom. To understand the motivation of our country's forefathers, one must go back all the way to Biblical days and the Fourth Commandment that states:

> Keep the Sabbath day to sanctify it, as the Lord thy God hath commanded thee. Six days shalt thou labor and do thy work. But the seventh day is the Sabbath of the Lord thy God.

While the Jewish religion continues to consider the Sabbath to be the seventh day of the week, or Saturday, the Christian religions believe that the Old Testament of the Bible shifted the Sabbath from the seventh day to the first day, or Sunday. Thus, Sunday became the Lord's Day, a day free from labor, or more simply, a day of rest.

Constantine decreed the first secular law recognizing Sunday as a day of rest in 321 A.D. By the Middle Ages, the importance of the Sunday Sabbath day began to wane in Europe as medieval Sundays took on a riotous atmosphere with feasts, dances, and fairs taking place in churchyards and ales and food consumed in large quantities by the participants. This festive attitude toward Sunday became known in America as the "Continental Sabbath."

To many people, there was nothing inconsistent between the Continental Sabbath and the Fourth Commandment. "The Fourth Commandment forbids work and it forbids nothing else. It requires rest, and it requires nothing else. There is no suggestion in this commandment of any religious service, no suggestion of any prohibition of innocent and healthful recreation," Lyman Abbott opined on Sunday observance. "The day is, indeed, a day to be kept holy to the Lord, but holiness to the Lord is not inconsistent with festivity and rejoicing."[16]

It was the Puritans in England in the 15th century that took exception to anything other than a strictly religious Sunday observance, in contrast to the practice of many Englishmen. In 1618, King James I enumerated lawful Sunday recreation in the *Book of Sports*. This Anglican contradiction to strict Sabbath observance was too much for the Puritan commitment to pure Sabbatarianism and they soon left England to head across the ocean to the shores of what would become the United States.

Religious freedom, that staple grammar school explanation for why the Puritans journeyed here, was in reality the freedom to practice restrictive religious interpretations. The Puritans regarded the *Book of Sports* as an endorsement of sin and they identified sports with the overreaching power of both the Anglican hierarchy and English aristocracy, which they considered as an inseparable combination. To the Puritans, "church and state were almost convertible terms; or rather the state was simply the secular arm of spiritual power."[17]

Puritan opposition to sporting activities, not just on Sunday but during any day of the week, became part of the American ethos. It wasn't as simple as the Puritans merely disliking amusements; they had their reasons.

Being among the first settlers, the harsh conditions required the Puritans to continually work. "Merely to keep alive in a land which to their inexperience was cruel and inhospitable demanded all their energy," Foster Rhea Dulles wrote in *A History of Recreation*. Starvation, disease, and attacks by the natives among other dangers were constant perils. There was no time for amusements since there was one basic fact in the colonies—"if the settlers did not direct all their energy to their work, they could not hope to survive."[18]

In addition to the realities of living in the colonies, the Puritans also brought with them their negative perspective on English sports. The term *sport* to the Puritans meant "ball games and bloody contests." They did approve of other "sports" like hunting, fishing, and martial competitions, since these activities "fit comfortably into Puritan ideology: productive, useful, despoiling no one, they were a natural part of life."[19]

Puritans disdained ball games because, in England, class status rigidly segregated ball games. Tennis and bowling were popular among nobility, gentry, and wealthy merchants, with royal decrees forbidding all others from playing these games. Soccer (known as football in England) was the sport of English peasantry, which Puritans associated with pagan ritual and low-class criminality, since the games "as a matter of course produced disabling injuries and great property damage."[20]

With their middle-class ideals, the Puritans held contempt for both the upper and lower classes in English society, an attitude that fostered their intense dislike for ball games in the New World.

Blood sports pitted humans against animals or animals against animals in contests that were designed to at least inflict injury if not death. "They involved outright cruelty or even torture," Bruce Daniels wrote in his book *Puritans at Play: Leisure and Recreation in Colonial New England*. "In bear-baiting and bull-baiting, for example, people teased and then killed the animals in front of cheering crowds." Blood sports also included the more benign boxing and horse racing.[21]

This Puritan attitude toward sport gave rise to the oft-repeated contention that "Puritans forbade bear-baiting, not because of the pain it caused the bear, but because of the pleasure it afforded the spectators." More appropriately, the Puritans felt "it religious to pray and irreligious to play."[22]

Puritans denounced sports and other amusements such as dancing not so much to suppress merriment but rather because they failed "a basic test for all recreations of being moderate and useful." Among the reasons that Puritans opposed sports were sports were frivolous and wasted time; sports did not refresh the body as good recreation should; sporting contests usually led to gambling; and more sporting activities took place on Sunday than any other day of the week, which encouraged people to defile the Sabbath. The contempt for ball sports, therefore, was rooted in the "inevitable ancillary evils that accompanied ball playing and from the historical evils associated with it in England."[23]

"Puritan life was to be a totality, a society with no seams," Daniels concluded in *Puritans at Play*, which turned out to be the dark side of the Puritan restraint on sports.

> Leisure and recreation posed a special threat to the ideal of a unity of experience. Play suspended the normal rules of life and substituted its own rules, which allowed violence, deception, destructive competition, even outright lying. Play mocked the community and its moral standards. And, most horrifying of all, formal play had its own rituals, which competed with social rituals for loyalty and time.[24]

This was the backdrop to the development of Sunday laws in this country, which created the contentious atmosphere in 1876–1934 surrounding the issue of playing major league baseball on Sunday.

Initially, the New England colonies didn't pass laws governing ball games and blood sports, since public distaste for them served to limit the activities. As more non–Puritans arrived as settlers, though, laws became necessary to restrict sports and amusements on the one day of the week that people might find the time to participate in them—Sunday.

"Along with many other long-lived customs, the Puritans brought a strict form of Sunday observance to the New World that influenced how other British North American colonies developed their own blend of Sunday regulations," Alexis McCrossen wrote in *Holy Day, Holiday: The American Sunday*. "Sunday laws—known as "blue laws" because of the supposed color of paper on which they were published in colonial Connecticut—emerged out of widely shared respect for Sunday. Both law and custom set the day apart from the rest of the week."[25]

The first Sunday law in Massachusetts was established in 1650. A harsher law was passed in 1671, which included the possibility of being put to death for playing a ball game:

> That whoever shall profane the Lord's day, by doing unnecessary servile work, by unnecessary travailing, or by sports and recreations, he or they that so transgress, shall forfeit for every such default forty shillings, or be publicly whipped. But if it clearly appears that the sin was proudly, presumptuously and with a high hand committed, such a person therein despising and reproaching the Lord, shall be put to death or grievously punished at the judgment of the court.[26]

Over time, as immigrants of more diverse backgrounds arrived, the hard line of the Puritan Sunday faded, although the Sunday laws didn't disappear. Sunday laws were adopted in most of the colonies and also in the new territories as settlers moved west.

Sunday laws were accepted, or at least tolerated, as long as the United States had an agrarian economy, where there was a clear line between six days of work and one day of rest, and citizens were mostly of English ancestry. That began to change in the mid–19th century when the Industrial Revolution occurred and immigrants from other European countries arrived on our shores.

The Industrial Revolution immutably changed life. Urban areas replaced rural ones as centers of influence and immigrant workers dominated city dwellings, bringing with them a different perspective on Sunday—the Continental Sabbath.

"This new threat to Puritan tradition and practice seemed to grow in proportion to the tide of Europeans reaching our shores and to the commercialization of society," John Betts wrote in *America's Sporting Heritage*. "As ministers and their congregations became increasingly concerned, local laws were passed to prohibit ball games and other sports as well as to close the theater and the saloon."[27]

"In an industrializing society still dependent on armies of agricultural laborers, Sunday stood in opposition to relentless work for the majority of nineteenth century Americans," McCrossen wrote in *Holy Day, Holiday: The American Sunday*. "The six working days blended into one unit—the workweek—in contrast to Sunday, the day of rest."[28]

The average workweek in 1830 was six days of more than 12 hours each day, according to author Witold Rybczynski of *Waiting for the Weekend*. The workday shortened to about 11 hours by 1850, but the workweek at the turn of the century was still typically at least six days of 10-hour workdays.[29]

Sunday was the day of rest for working people, and just about everyone else except for clergymen. How "rest" was best utilized, however, differed between locales in the east and the west.

By the 1870s, many cities west of the Allegheny Mountains, especially those dominated by immigrants from Germany and other European countries, observed a Continental Sabbath where people participated in festivities and sporting events.

St. Louis was a western city considered "wide open" on Sunday, in contrast to the more decorous stance of eastern cities such as New York, Boston, and Philadelphia where the American Sunday of church attendance and quiet reflection reigned. "Everybody that was not sick was out in the sunshine, in the streetcars, at the beer gardens, or 'on the road'," the *St. Louis Globe-Democrat* remarked in a "Sunday in St. Louis" article in the 1870s. "Every living horse in this city was employed in creating dust on some one of the favorite avenues. The road houses were patronized to the complete satisfaction of their managers."[30]

In the early 1880s, the concept of "rest" was beginning to be redefined in eastern states, as suggested in the *Atlantic Monthly* article "The New Sunday."

> The day has been regarded, heretofore, so exclusively from its religious side that important social and sanitary conditions have been quite overlooked. It still remains the fact that "the Sabbath was made for man, not man for the Sabbath." The foremost point is that it shall continue to be a day of rest. This alone furnishes the opportunity for its higher uses. But it can never again be a day of rest in the old Puritan sense, nor can it be regarded by all sorts of people as God's time in a special sense. Modern society in our great centers is so constituted that Sunday is the only day when rest, recreation, and education can be generally attended to; and the wider and deeper interests of human life, as they are now understood, demand that the day shall be used for a great variety of purposes, which more or less entail labor upon a few.[31]

The first shift in Sunday attitude was that "rest" could be used for educational purposes. Libraries were one of the first institutions to open on Sunday. The trustees of the Boston Public Library debated Sunday opening for 14 years before finally opening on February 9, 1873. Museums were another source of educational "rest" where trustees hotly contested Sunday openings. The Metropolitan Museum of Art in New York City finally opened on May 31, 1891, after two decades of debate. By 1900, newspapers publishing Sunday editions were fairly common.[32]

Parks, with their grass lawns and tree-shaded areas, were also well used for Sunday strolls and general relaxation. Parks sprung up outside urban areas in more rural locations to cater to Sunday crowds. This led to the Sunday excursion, where people would travel by carriage or horse-drawn streetcar for no other reason than to enjoy the trip.

Soon, however, the fresh air and quiet of the parks gave way to noisy picnics, abuse of alcoholic beverages, and eventually loud and bawdy amusements. Coney Island outside of Brooklyn was a lightning rod for all that was bad about Sunday amusements, which created not only noise (which could often be a breach of peace under the law) but also gave rise to other illegal ventures such as gambling and more sordid activities.

This gradual shift in Sunday attitude from rest used for education to rest used for amusements (including baseball) was the breaking point for many eastern Sabbatarian groups, who loathed the eastward progress of the Continental Sabbath. The fact that Sunday baseball in eastern states during the 1880s was often played at makeshift ball fields at Sunday resorts, many times amid a carnival atmosphere, did not help the acceptance of Sunday baseball for the long haul.

Rest for greater intellectual and physical well-being might have been acceptable for some Sabbatarians at this time, but rest used for leisure purposes was patently over the line. After 1889, Sabbatarians thus greatly resisted the playing of Sunday baseball as they did many expansions of "rest" on Sunday, including the expenditure of government money for Sunday openings of the 1893 Chicago World's Fair (the Columbian Exposition). Sabbatarians feared that Sunday baseball would be an opening wedge to "open" Sundays like those in St. Louis, Chicago, and Milwaukee that had legal openings of theater, poolrooms, and saloons.

"Work and rest remained in opposition until after the end of the nineteenth century, but as leisure matured into a separate sphere, its distinction from rest lost clarity," McCrossen wrote in *Holy Day, Holiday: The American Sunday*. "If leisure was not work, was it rest?" The conflicts over Sunday observance created a third sphere between those of work and rest—leisure. Sunday baseball was able to take advantage of the emergence of leisure as another identifiable element of life.[33]

Sabbatarians shifted their attitude toward Sunday observance away from the religious elements and concentrated their efforts on the more socially acceptable facets of labor and noise, which courts in the 20th century could more easily defend as the basis for Sunday laws.

While work hours were shortening in length by 1900, it was the widening gap in social status that spurred more liberal thinking to fortify the leisure revolution. The industrialists that had changed how America worked, creating an urban industrial climate at the expense of the country's rural heritage, had begun to eviscerate the middle class, especially the clergy.

"The clergy were probably the most conspicuous losers from the status revolution," Richard Hofstadter wrote in *The Age of Reform: From Bryan to FDR*. "They not only lost ground in all the outward ways, as most middle-class elements did, but were also hard hit in their capacity as moral and intellectual leaders by the considerable secularization that took place in American society and intellectual life in the last three decades of the nineteenth century."[34]

The shrinking influence of the middle class created two primary effects: either the middle class joined the liberal forces seeking change in how society interacted with the powerful industrial corporations or they steadfastly clung to their conservative viewpoints.

Neither perspective was particularly helpful to the Sunday baseball cause, however. Progress in legalizing professional Sunday baseball in eastern states moved at an excruciatingly slow pace in the 20th century, as the fairly rapid spread of Sunday baseball in western cities in the 1880s and 1890s failed to impact eastern acceptance.

Liberals, or "progressives" as they were known in those days, had many other ills to tackle before they could actively advocate Sunday baseball. Progressive principles included a desire to enlarge democracy (secret ballot, referendum, women's suffrage), to have government protect the public interests (curb corporate abuses and provide social services), and to improve social justice (prevent child labor, shorten work hours, improve work conditions). Progressives also tended to support prohibition laws, which furthered their cause more than Sunday baseball did.

Teddy Roosevelt, U.S. president from 1901 to 1909, was a well-known progressive. Yet during his terms in Washington, Roosevelt did little if anything to try to influence the passage of Sunday baseball legislation in his native state of New York, where he had previously served as governor. Progressive politicians in Detroit and Cleveland were not overly helpful to the development of Sunday baseball in their cities. Cleveland mayor Tom Johnson, a progressive on many issues, actually worked to stop Sunday baseball from occurring in Cleveland. It was only after Johnson's death in 1911 that Sunday baseball finally could be played within the Cleveland city limits.

The rock-bound conservatives, refusing to change to respond to different social mores, just fought harder to try to preserve the world as it once was. These were, for the most part, the Sabbatarians of the 20th century. They continued to hold clout in politics and therefore were able to hold out to prohibit Sunday baseball much longer than they might have if working people had been able to accumulate political power at a faster rate.

Sabbatarians "feared that the gradual separation of ideas about rest from religion, along with the pervasive presence of leisure, threatened the unique nature of Sunday," McCrossen wrote. "Their efforts, however, served only to establish that periodic rest from work was necessary, not that Sunday should remain the day of rest or that it was the only time to rest, or that rest was different from leisure."[35]

Even the labor argument wore thin. "Many Americans refused to equate baseball with manual labor, believing that baseball games and other amusements enhanced, rather than endangered, Sunday's position as a day of rest."[36]

American workers surely wanted Sunday baseball, since it was their only chance to see a baseball game given the six-day workweek. The only problem was that American workers lacked the organizational and political power to change the laws to make Sunday baseball a reality. Like the progressives, workers also had more pressing issues to tackle that impacted the six days they worked before they could push for activities on the seventh day when they did not work.

The Saturday half-holiday became more common in the early years of the 20th century and the eight-hour workday became a reality in 1907 with print compositors. The first five-day factory workweek was enacted at a New England spinning mill in 1908 to accommodate Jewish workers that observed a Saturday Sabbath. Henry Ford reduced daily hours in his automobile factories in 1914 from nine to eight hours, and in 1926 closed them Saturday to create a five-day workweek too.[37]

The popularity of the automobile and the moving-picture show from 1900 to 1920 created greater demand for leisure time and amusements to fulfill that time. By the 1920s, Sabbatarians generally recognized leisure and exercise as "legitimate" Sunday activities, even if involving some degree of work (adopting the "servile" interpretation of "labor," not simply any type of work). But they drew the line at overt commercialization of Sunday. Amateur baseball on Sunday was okay for the most part, but not professional; semi-pro games where pass-the-hat collections were undertaken remained a gray area.

Despite all the publicity that baseball owners were doing social good by staging ball games on Sunday so working people could attend games, it *was* all about money. When working people filled ballparks, they not coincidentally filled the owners' pockets with money. Polar positions on Sunday baseball thus developed "as either a force for moral good or as a dangerous subversion of religious values."[38]

Sportswriters often cooperated with baseball owners to promote the game. "They proved to post–Victorian Americans that attending ball games was not a waste of time, but an enjoyable and useful leisure activity," historian Steven Riess wrote. "Baseball was viewed as an edifying institution which taught traditional nineteenth century frontier qualities, such as courage, honesty, individualism, patience, and temperance as well as certain contemporary values like team work."[39]

Baseball was cast as an indigenous American game, perpetuated by the Doubleday-Cooperstown mythology, which had originated in the countryside and typified the rural values that had shaped American society and made it so great. "Two principal functions ascribed to baseball were that it would teach children traditional American values and that it would help newcomers assimilate into the dominant WASP culture through their participation in the sport's rituals," Riess wrote. Baseball fostered the ideology "through the rituals of spectatorship and by providing heroes and role models for youngsters."[40]

What better way to perpetuate the ideology of baseball than through attending ball games on Sunday, the only day that parents and their children could realistically attend the games.

Continuing improvements in economic prosperity, transportation, and communication (especially the advent of radio) helped to turn leisure into recreation and put additional pressure on legislators to permit professional Sunday baseball.

"Opponents of Sunday baseball defended their position doggedly. They denied that baseball offered relaxation, and as for getting fresh air, a good walk was better," historian Harold Seymour wrote. "They viewed the cursing and brawling that accompanied games as tending to lessen respect for the Sabbath. As one of them put it, a person 'did not get a glimpse of God in a frenzied crowd.'"[41]

Sabbatarians also did a great job convincing legislators in eastern states to forestall liberalization of Sunday baseball laws, using arguments ranging from jingoism against immigrants to outright political blackmail.

It was the "local option" concept, however, that ultimately did in the Sabbatarians. Advocates of Sunday baseball never could secure a "pure" legislative solution that impacted a major league city, but rather needed to settle for laws that permitted individual localities to decide whether or not they wanted to approve Sunday baseball.

Local option was a technique often used to prevent the spread of Sunday showings of moving pictures. Legislatures would pass a law permitting movies on Sunday only if local governments in cities and towns granted approval. Very often, cities and towns did not approve of Sunday moving-picture shows. Politicians loved the local-option technique, since it enabled them to say "yes, you can have it" to appease the liberal element, but yet say "no, you don't have to have it" to their constituents who likely opposed the idea.

Sunday baseball, though, was overwhelmingly approved in cities that hosted major league teams, while many rural areas declined to authorize such activities, once voters did finally obtain the chance to vote on the issue.

Pennsylvania was the last state where major league baseball was played to grudgingly approve a Sunday baseball law, which naturally contained a local option provision. Philadelphia voters overwhelmingly approved the Sunday baseball question at the ballot box (370,858 to 57,740), as did Pittsburgh and most large cities. Many rural communities voted against the measure. As late as 1969, the town of Elmer, Pennsylvania, still prohibited Sunday baseball by even amateur players, preventing a team of 16-year-olds from scheduling Sunday home games at the local ball field.[42]

In 1934, all 16 major league teams could finally play home games on Sunday. But at the same time, Sunday was losing its special status as the only day of rest during the week. The weekend as we know it today was increasingly part of the calendar for working people.

"In the end, what finally consolidated the two-day weekend was not altruism or activism or, paradoxically, prosperity; it was the Great Depression," Rybczynski wrote in *Waiting for the Weekend*. "Shorter hours came to be widely regarded as a remedy for unemployment—people would work less, but more people would have jobs." New Deal legislation also legally mandated a 40-hour workweek at regular pay, with overtime payable after those hours.[43]

By 1940, the eight-hour day and five-day workweek were customary. Following the end of World War II, the five-day workweek and two-day weekend became a fixture of post-war American life. With most workers now able to see a ball game on Saturday, as well as during the week due to the rapid rise of night baseball, Sunday baseball lost its special status as the only time that workers could see a ball game. Soon, the term faded from existence.

Sunday baseball has a rich history at the major league level, which is examined in the following chapters of this book. First, a brief backdrop of how Sunday baseball fit into the development of the game.

In 1846, the Knickerbocker Club and Alexander Cartwright, the architect of the modern game, played baseball on the Elysian Fields in Hoboken, New Jersey—a future bastion of Sunday baseball playing. The Knickerbockers were gentlemen and wouldn't think of playing baseball on Sunday. It would have been unseemly to do so.

While the Knickerbockers didn't play ball on Sunday, neither did most teams. Since working people toiled six days a week, for 12 to 14 hours a day, only the upper echelon of society could generally afford the time to participate in baseball Monday through Saturday.

None of the important "firsts" in baseball history occurred on a Sunday. The first recorded game between two teams of Knickerbockers was played on a Tuesday (October 7, 1845) while the first "real" baseball game between the Knickerbockers and the New York Nine, a 23–1 Knickerbocker victory, was played on a Friday (June 19, 1846). The first game with an admission charge was played on July 20, 1858, which was a Tuesday. The famous "grand match for the championship of the United States" between the Atlantics of Brooklyn and the Mutuals of New York on August 3, 1865, watched by 15,000 spectators, was played on a Thursday.

As the competitive nature of the game increased, some clubs began to unofficially pay their best players in order to field a better team. After the Civil War, professionals were finally recognized, since many clubs had paid players "under the table" or compensated them in other ways.

It was the 1868 recognition by the National Association of Base Ball Players of two categories of players—amateur and professional—that gave rise to the first possibility of a professional baseball game played on a Sunday. Because most of the professional teams were located on the East Coast, like the Atlantics and the Mutuals, the first baseball game on a Sunday where professionals participated most likely occurred in a midwestern city around 1868.

Sunday baseball in St. Louis was played at Grand Avenue Park by independent teams as early as 1868. According to testimony at the 1887 Sunday baseball trial of St. Louis Browns president Chris Von der Ahe, Grand Avenue Park "has been used as a base ball park since 1868, and base ball has been played there on Sunday afternoons between the hours of 3 and 6 o'clock since that time." Charles Turner, a witness at the trial, said he "had seen hundreds of games on Sunday" in the 18 years since Grand Avenue Park had been built.[44]

The 1869 Cincinnati Red Stockings were the first baseball club to openly pay all its players a salary. The Red Stockings, although hailing from a city with many of its citizens steeped in the Continental Sabbath, played no games on Sunday during its storied undefeated season of 1869. Harry Wright, the team's captain, was a strict believer in Sabbath observance.[45]

As the first structural confederation of professional baseball clubs, the National Association of Professional Base Ball Players (NAPBBP) was formed in 1871. The NAPBBP was the first major league, of sorts, although it is not recognized as such due to its haphazard scheduling. With nearly all the NAPBBP clubs situated in eastern cities where Sunday baseball was illegal, matches were played exclusively Monday through Saturday.

During the National Association's first three years of existence, there were only sporadic instances of western teams—Rockford and Fort Wayne in 1871, Cleveland in 1871–72, and Chicago in 1871. Chicago burst back on the scene in 1874, with moderate success on the playing field. Three more strong midwestern independent teams joined Chicago in the National Association in 1875—St. Louis Brown Stockings, St. Louis Red Stockings, and the Westerns from Keokuk, Iowa.

The additional of the two St. Louis teams for the 1875 season began to change the stance toward Sunday baseball at the highest professional level.

In joining the National Association, the St. Louis Brown Stockings and the St. Louis Red Stockings both had to forsake regular Sunday games that they had played for several years "as the championship code prevents contests for the pennant being played on Sunday." In order to generate revenue to meet rising expenses, the Red Stockings soon skirted this rule.[46]

On Sunday, May 16, the Red Stockings defeated the Elephants 18–10 at Red Stocking Park on Compton Avenue, and two weeks later on May 30 a picked nine representing the Empires defeated the Red Stockings 15–12. Both these games were played against local St. Louis teams. On Sunday, May 23, though, the Red Stockings played an exhibition game with the Keokuk team of the National Association. "Fully two thousand spectators were in attendance at Compton Park yesterday and they went away perfectly delighted with the magnificent display which they had witnessed," the *St. Louis Globe-Democrat* reported of the 7–1 St. Louis victory over Keokuk.[47]

By the end of June, the Washington team in the National Association was on its last financial legs. After Washington lost 6–3 to the Brown Stockings on Saturday, June 26, in St. Louis, the Red Stockings played Washington the next day and defeated the visitors 3–0. Both the Red Stockings and Washington, along with Keokuk, soon left the National Association following the renegade Sunday game played on June 27, 1875.

St. Louis may have had different thoughts regarding Sunday baseball than eastern clubs, even the Chicago club, but the Brown Stockings drew large crowds to its games at Grand Avenue Park.

William Hulbert, president of the Chicago club in the National Association, had ambitions for professional baseball under different conditions than NAPBBP play. To counter anticipated trouble from the eastern clubs that controlled the National Association, Hulbert worked with St. Louis team representatives to draw up a constitution for the new league and lined up support from strong independent teams in Cincinnati and Louisville.

On February 2, 1876, the National Association of Professional Base

Ball Clubs was born. While only one word among the seven words in the organization's title had changed from its National Association of Professional Base Ball Players origins—"Clubs" rather than "Players"—the substitute term signified the change in power that would direct professional baseball at its highest athletic level in the coming years.

Chapter 2

NATIONAL LEAGUE DISLIKED IT

While it is clear the National League of Professional Base Ball Clubs finally sanctioned Sunday baseball in 1892, the early history of banning Sunday baseball in the National League is much more obscured.

The years 1876, 1878, and 1880 are all cited in various sources as the year that the National League banned Sunday baseball. Since the National League actually outlawed Sunday baseball in a three-stage process, each of these dates is partially correct. For its inaugural season in 1876 the National League did not, in fact, prohibit the playing of Sunday games. Those games merely did not count in the standings.

It is commonly understood, and recounted in many summaries of National League history, that Sunday baseball games were banned as part of an objective "to make base ball playing respectable and honorable." Respectability was certainly one of the constitutional objectives of "the League," as the organization was referred to in its formative years to create an air of superiority. Prohibiting Sunday games, however, was not one of the first steps initiated to accomplish that objective.

Passages in many respected baseball histories relating to the 1876 organizing activities are technically not accurate due to the choice of verb, including "Sunday games were forbidden" and "League leaders ordered member clubs to ban Sunday games."[1]

Historian Harold Seymour put the Sunday issue more correctly when he wrote in his book *Baseball: The Early Years* that "the league frowned on Sunday games." Another historian more appropriately characterized the earliest Sunday policy as "the league eschewed Sunday ball."[2]

When codified in the League's Constitution, the concept of "frowned" and "eschewed" was buried in Article XIII, Section 1, and it read simply as "No game played on Sunday shall count in the championship series."[3]

2. National League Disliked It

There was just a 70-game schedule of championship games in 1876, with each club to play each other ten times, with games slated for three days a week (Tuesday, Thursday, and Saturday). This left ample time to schedule other games to supplement the club revenues that could be garnered from paying customers to 35 games on the home grounds.

Where legally permitted, Sunday exhibition contests were lucrative, drawing anywhere from two to three times the number of spectators that attended a game during the other six days.

The Sunday issue was moot, though, in most eastern cities in 1876, such as the four League clubs playing in Boston, Hartford, New York, and Philadelphia. In eastern states, Sunday amusements were almost universally prohibited by law, if not by actual practice of the majority of the population that subscribed to the Sunday day of rest philosophy.

Eastern teams played exhibition games outside of the regular League schedule, but not on Sundays.

It was in the western cities of the League—Chicago, Cincinnati, Louisville, and St. Louis—where Sunday contests were often staged by the local non-professional teams. Sunday games were important to several League members as a source of revenue to help make ends meet, particularly St. Louis and Louisville, which Hulbert had courted to help defuse eastern politics to establish the new league. Revenue from Sunday games was particularly needed to offset the enormous expense associated with travel to eastern cities for the championship pennant.

The "frowning" on Sunday baseball in the initial National League constitution was geared to the high moral standard favored by Hulbert, head of the Chicago club and organizer of the League's transformation from its predecessor loose confederation, the NAPBBP. While the constitutional language stopped short of an outright prohibition on Sunday games, the text did help appease the middle-class, church-going public that the League was trying to attract as patrons to its games.

While Hulbert may have desired to flatly prohibit Sunday games at the outset, and totally appease the middle-class audience that was naturally predisposed to a ban on Sunday games, Hulbert had bigger issues to contend with before he could act more squarely on the Sunday issue. He needed to tighten up the loose scheduling, contend with the selling of liquor at certain locales, and stop the gambling that led to player misdeeds.

Commenting on the February 2, 1876, organizing meeting of the League, the *New York Clipper* remarked that what was needed was "to put a stop to the growing abuses connected with their [the professional] class of the baseball fraternity, the most prominent of which is the evil of fraudulent play in the form of 'hippodroming' or the 'selling' or 'throwing' of games for betting purposes, practiced by knavish members of the club-teams and countenanced by still worse club officials."[4]

The *New York Clipper*, a weekly entertainment newspaper, was one of the very few publications that carried more than box scores in the early days of the League before more extensive baseball coverage became more readily available in *Sporting Life* and *The Sporting News* in 1883 and 1886, respectively.

Neither the *Clipper* nor the *Chicago Tribune*, the hometown newspaper of Hulbert and the other primary source of baseball news, carried one word about Sunday games in their extensive articles about the February 2 meeting at the Grand Central Hotel in New York City, which established the ground rules for the upcoming 1876 season.

In its article "The Diamond Squared: An Honest Base-Ball Association Born into the World," the *Tribune* wrote, "The present Association [of professional players] has been proved powerless to properly govern the games, because it had been run by unscrupulous men, who had been willing to resort to any meannesses to compass their ends." The article went on to say, "It was the idea of the promoters of the plan to make an association of sufficient character to make it an object to get into it and to behave well in order to stay in."[5]

While these words may have inferred a prohibition of Sunday games, for the first two years of the League's existence, the only formal stance on Sunday games was that they didn't count toward the League championship.

Scheduling was the first of the "honesty" issues to be resolved by the League. When the Mutual club of New York and the Athletic club of Philadelphia both failed to make their last road trips in the initial 1876 season to play the circuit's western teams (claiming they needed to save money), the League expelled both teams. Since each team represented one of the country's major population centers, the expulsion was a gutsy move.

Gambling was tackled in 1877, when Louisville was found to have four players that had thrown ball games. The players—Jim Devlin, Al Nichols, George Hall, and Bill Craver—as well as the Louisville team were expelled from the League that fall.

Then there was the St. Louis team, also expelled after the 1877 season. The Brown Stockings blatantly played exhibition games on Sunday, with Hulbert's tacit approval via the wording of the League's constitution. While they were only exhibition games, these Sunday matches eventually led to the League's first actual stipulations against Sunday games. It wasn't so much the Sunday games played by St. Louis that irked Hulbert, but rather the persistency that St. Louis lost any exhibition game.

Action to stifle Sunday games probably would not have occurred as quickly as the 1878 season had the League teams faired better in the exhibition games they played during the 1877 season, not just Sunday games, against the presumed lower caliber teams that did not hold League membership.

In 1877, the League had a less than admiral record versus the non–League competition, losing nearly 40 percent of its games against the top ten "lower level" teams from the other organized leagues. Of the 143 games played against this competition in 1877, League teams won only 87 games and lost 56 games.[6]

The Lowell club of Lowell, Massachusetts, was a particular thorn in the side of League teams in 1877. Lowell was not affiliated with either of the two organized leagues outside the National League, the League Alliance or the International Association. Instead, it was a member of a loose confederation in the New England Association.

Lowell won 11 of 18 games played against League clubs in 1877, to the extent of splitting eight games with League champion Boston. Lowell also defeated Sunday-playing St. Louis in two games, both played in Lowell during interludes between the St. Louis matches with Boston.[7]

On June 20, Lowell defeated the Brown Stockings 3–0 at the Fair Grounds in Lowell, as Curry Foley yielded just five hits (all one-base hits) to St. Louis batters. Joe Blong, the St. Louis pitcher, gave up only four hits to Lowell, but ten errors committed by the St. Louis defenders provided little support to Blong.

"Everybody interested in the Lowell base ball nine has reason to be proud over their splendid playing yesterday, when they defeated the celebrated St. Louis team by the humiliating score of 3 to 0," the *Lowell Courier* reported. "The joy of the spectators knew no bounds, and the home players were heartily congratulated. The St. Louis nine crept into their wagon and were quietly driven away."[8]

By nearly anyone's perspective, except the local non–League team and its fans, this was bad publicity for the League. The fact that St. Louis lost regularly to non–League teams was bad enough, but the club's desire to play games on Sunday (even though originally countenanced by Hulbert) pushed the limit and resulted in its expulsion from the League.

St. Louis had a $4,000 debt, "which the club tried to retire by playing Sunday games," Tom Melville wrote in *Early Baseball and the Rise of the National League*. It was "a move that didn't seem to help its financial situation but apparently so outraged other League clubs that Hulbert was convinced St. Louis was 'dead past resurrection' by the season's close."[9]

By 1877, baseball on Sunday was an accepted occurrence in St. Louis, as local teams played nearly every Sunday at both Grand Avenue Park and

Red Stocking Park. The Brown Stockings team in the League often played Sundays just across the Mississippi River in West Bellville, Illinois, but these games attracted only a few hundred spectators. For example, on July 7, the Brown Stockings played at West Bellville in front of just 500 spectators.[10]

To pay off its debts, the Brown Stockings scheduled stronger teams for Sunday games at Grand Avenue Park. On June 10, the Brown Stockings defeated the League's Cincinnati team 12–9. "That Sunday ball playing is popular in St. Louis was evidenced by the crowd—estimated at 2,000—which was present at Grand Avenue Park yesterday afternoon to witness the game between the Cincinnati and St. Louis clubs," the *St. Louis Globe-Democrat* reported.[11]

The revenue power of Sunday baseball was demonstrated at the June 10 game, as the size of the Sunday crowd was double that of the average attendance at a Brown Stocking game during the workweek. In another Sunday event on July 22, the Brown Stockings defeated Syracuse of the International Association, 3–1.

In addition to the expulsion of Louisville and St. Louis from the League at its annual meeting that fall on December 5, there were also a number of constitutional changes enacted. Most of these changes involved games played with non–League clubs during the championship season that ran from May 1 to October 1 and seemed designed to remedy replication of the less-than-stellar results of the just-concluded 1877 season.

No games could be played with non–League clubs on the grounds of a League club. Games could be played on the grounds of the non–League club, but the non–League club had to provide a $100 guarantee and 50 percent of gross receipts if they exceeded $200. Non–League clubs also had to pay $50 if the game was rained out.

All these conditions relating to "off day" games were disincentives for non–League clubs to schedule League clubs for exhibition games. The changes were made to enhance the appearance of League teams as top-drawer baseball as well as to subjugate the inferior competition to League rules.

An additional disincentive to scheduling exhibition games was the constitutional change that added a Section 6 to Article V to provide a severe penalty to Sunday play, and thus officially "prohibit" Sunday games:

> If any club shall take part in any game of ball on Sunday, or if it shall fail to immediately expel any man under contract with it for taking part in such game as player, umpire or scorer; then, and in either of these cases, the club shall forfeit its membership in the League.[12]

From newspaper reports, the Sunday-playing clause seemed to be an afterthought, or at least not designed to rectify a substantial problem. The *New York Clipper* focused on the impact to games with non–League clubs, with just one paragraph relating to the new Sunday rule. The *Chicago Tribune* curtly reported, "Sunday playing was effectively settled by the adopting [of] an article of the constitution that any League club or player taking part in a Sunday game was thereby expelled."[13]

The new clause more forcibly prohibiting Sunday games was mostly a moot point by December 1877. Both the St. Louis and Louisville clubs, the most likely to host a Sunday game, had been ejected from the League.

In theory, Milwaukee and Indianapolis, two new clubs in the League in 1878, might have played Sunday baseball. But the new sanctions limiting non–League games would have been sufficient to limit playing opportunities outside the championship season. Hulbert had snuck the Sunday clause into the constitution to satisfy other concerns.

Indeed, both Milwaukee and Indianapolis lasted just one season in the National League as financial woes took an early and heavy toll on the two franchises. For the 1879 season, the League enticed Syracuse and Buffalo to join it and thus abandon the International Association, hoping to kill off that circuit. It also admitted Troy, New York, and Cleveland to expand the league to eight teams.

Syracuse lasted just one season and was replaced by Worcester, Massachusetts, for the 1880 season. Worcester was one of the smaller cities in the League, but it would have a large role to play in the ultimate resolution of Sunday baseball policy in the League.

Cincinnati became embroiled in League politics due to the leasing of its ball grounds to the local Buckeyes team for games on Sunday. That action eventually led to Cincinnati's expulsion from the League.

By 1880, Hulbert had successfully steered the League through the turbulent waters of professional baseball during that era, at a time when economic conditions in the country were not all that prosperous. With the League on the brink of finally achieving financial success, Hulbert took up the cudgel to wage a campaign to rid the League of what he considered the evils of Sunday games and on-premise liquor sales.

It's not certain which of these evils Hulbert disliked more, though it seems certain that he didn't dislike them personally, but rather simply pursued a campaign of their riddance to serve a business purpose. "Base-ball ... is supported by a class of people by whom these practices [liquor and Sunday games] are regarded as an abomination," Hulbert once wrote.[14]

Indeed, Cincinnati president Justin Thorner, following his club's expulsion, said he couldn't understand the action since "the League president loved his whisky as well as any man."[15]

Cincinnati, though, had become quite overt in its use of both beer and Sunday games to support its club finances. This overtness led to its downfall. Cincinnati officials thought Hulbert's proposals to ban liquor sales and rental of grounds to Sunday-playing amateur teams would reduce club revenues by nearly $3,000.[16]

An article published in the *Worcester Spy* brought the Cincinnati issue to light among all the clubs in the League. With Hulbert in Worcester to watch the Chicago-Worcester series in July, the *Worcester Spy* reported on July 23 that it was probable that legislation to prevent the sale of liquor and "the use of grounds for any purpose Sunday" would be introduced at the next meeting of the League. While Cincinnati and Buffalo were the only League cities where the sale of beer was allowed at games, "the Cincinnati grounds are also used for Sunday games, the legislation of some time ago, by which this was to be prevented, not being general enough in provisions to prevent it."[17]

"It has been demonstrated that League nines can exist without the receipts from Sunday games, or the sale of beer on the grounds during other games," the article in the *Worcester Spy* continued. "If there is any good reason why Cincinnati should continue its questionable custom, it is yet to be advanced."

Hulbert, who seemed to be behind the printing of this article in the Worcester newspaper, appeared to use the Worcester team to further his own agenda to rid the League of the Cincinnati club. Worcester was clearly a weak sister in the League, an exception having been made to award the city a League franchise in 1880 since it didn't meet the requirement for a population of 75,000. At the opening game of the Chicago series in Worcester on July 21, only 567 persons attended the contest at the Worcester Fair Grounds to see the league-leading Chicago club.

The *Worcester Spy* had printed a gushing article about Hulbert two weeks earlier, at the tail end of a western road trip that a week earlier had stopped in Chicago. Worcester lost all three games in the Chicago series, but the team saw what big-time baseball was all about when 4,000 persons attended the Chicago-Worcester game on Saturday, June 26.

"President Hulbert of the Chicago club is the best posted man in the country on all matters pertaining to baseball and the business management of clubs," the *Worcester Spy* proclaimed. "To him more than all other base ball authorities put together is the public indebted for the respectability of the game as played by professionals."[18]

Cincinnati did in fact rent out its grounds for Sunday games played by the Buckeyes, a local amateur team. Every Sunday in June and July, the Buckeyes played at the Cincinnati Base Ball Grounds. On Sunday, July 4, the Buckeyes defeated a picked nine 5–0 before 1,500 spectators. The Boston team of the National League was in town that day awaiting the holiday game with Cincinnati to be played on Monday, July 5, since the 4th fell on a Sunday in 1880, perhaps adding some fuel to the fire of the *Worcester Spy* article.

On July 29, the *Cincinnati Enquirer* printed a reply to the charges in the *Worcester Spy* article. Among other things, the newspaper questioned Worcester's place in the League ("Worcester's attendance at games this season has not paid the visiting teams' hotel and railroad bills") and claimed beer sales and Sunday rentals were necessary for Cincinnati to turn a profit.

"Puritanical Worcester is not liberal Cincinnati by a jugful, and what is sauce for Worcester would be wind for the Queen City," the *Cincinnati Enquirer* expounded. "Beer and Sunday amusements have become a popular necessity in Cincinnati. Deprive Cincinnati people of the privilege of getting beer during a game of ball and 50 percent of the attendance will cease. Why, you unsophisticated young man, we drink beer in Cincinnati as freely as you used to drink milk, and it is not a mark of disgrace either. If the League doesn't want Cincinnati in its circuit, it will do as the *Spy* man suggests."[19]

The last statement seemed to go to the heart of the issue. Hulbert did not want Cincinnati in the League, not strictly because of the beer and Sunday games, but more so because the Cincinnati club opposed the reserve clause that was just gaining a foothold in the League.

In August, the *Chicago Tribune* rebuked the *Cincinnati Enquirer* in a lengthy essay for saying that the League must not interfere with Sunday games or beer peddling. "Severity should be displayed toward Sunday games on League Club grounds," the *Chicago Tribune* demanded. "Such games are a fraud upon visiting clubs in that they attract to the Sunday play visitors who would otherwise go to a Monday game, and surfeit and destroy the appetite of the community for base-ball." At the end of the *Tribune* article, the newspaper added further rebuke (and what appeared to be the true underlying reason for all the trouble) for the *Cincinnati Enquirer* having declared that "the five-player agreements providing for reservation by each Club must be forever abolished."[20]

Unlike St. Louis that did not dispute its coming expulsion from the League after the 1877 season, Cincinnati wanted to stay in the League. To handle the Cincinnati situation, Hulbert scheduled a special League meeting on October 4, 1880, at the Osborne House in Rochester, New York. At the meeting, H. T. Root of the Providence club presented the following agreement for consideration:

> The subscribing clubs of the National League of Professional Base Ball Clubs hereby pledge themselves to vote at the annual meeting of the League, to be held in December 1880, for the following amendment to the Constitution of the League:
>> Insert in Section 7, Article 5, after the words "if any club shall take part in any game of ball on Sunday," the following, "or shall allow any game of ball to be played on its grounds on Sunday."
>
> We further pledge ourselves to vote at the annual meeting ... for an amendment to the League Constitution that will, under penalty of forfeiture of membership in the League, prohibit the sale of every description of malt, spirituous or vinous liquors upon its grounds, nor in any building owned or occupied by it.[21]

The agreement was signed by seven League clubs—Chicago, Providence, Boston, Cleveland, Buffalo, Troy, and Worcester. William Kennett, representing Cincinnati at the meeting, refused to sign. On the next day, October 5, the meeting was adjourned to the following day to give Cincinnati a chance to rethink its position. When the Cincinnati club did not change its stance, the following preamble and resolution were adopted when the meeting resumed on October 6:

> Whereas, the Cincinnati Base Ball Association has failed to respond in a satisfactory manner to the inquiries relative to its intentions regarding observance of the rules, agreements and requirements of the League.
> Resolved: That the position of the Cincinnati Association in the National League of Professional Base Ball Clubs be, and is hereby declared, vacated.[22]

"So Cincinnati was expelled for past acts which the league intended to prohibit in the future," Seymour wrote in *Baseball: The Early Years*. "The Constitution of the United States might ban ex post facto laws, but the National League could and did use them with a vengeance."[23]

At the December 8 annual meeting in New York City, as reported by the *New York Clipper*, "After the roll-call, the first business acted upon was the selection of a club to fill the place of the withdrawn Cincinnati Club." The paper then went on to report that an amendment to the constitution was adopted that increased the number of penalties in which forfeiture of membership was concerned. One of these was "a prohibition of any match game on League grounds on Sunday."[24]

This action to take effect for the 1881 season was the third step in the absolute prohibition of Sunday baseball in the early days of the National League.

Beer or Sunday games were not, of course, the real reasons for Cincinnati's expulsion from the league. "The real reason appears to be that the Cincinnati president, William Kennett, unique among the magnates, was vigorously opposed to the reserve clause," Lee Allen wrote in a 1965 book, *The National League Story: The Official History*. "It was Hulbert, fighting for the reserve clause, who most wanted Cincinnati out of the league and he enlisted the aid of the Worcester, Troy, Providence, and Cleveland clubs. The liquor business was then used as a smoke screen."[25]

Allen also related an amusing story about Cincinnati writer O. P. Caylor and his response to the moral indignation of Hulbert in expelling Cincinnati.

"We respectfully suggest that while the League is in the missionary field, having eliminated beer and Sunday games from the Cincinnati grounds, they turn their attention to Chicago and prohibit the admission to the Lake Street grounds of the great number of prostitutes who patronize the game up there."[26]

What caused the Cincinnati exit from the National League after the 1880 season was immaterial to the Sunday baseball issue. Sunday baseball was caught in the crossfire of other issues influencing the game at the time and wound up being a victim.

The decisions to expel St. Louis, Louisville, and Cincinnati from the National League, some of which involved Sunday baseball, would come back to haunt the League for many years to come.

"By all means form an anti–League Association, with Cincinnati, St. Louis, and a few other villages as members," the *Chicago Tribune* joked in another August 1880 article. "The League would be glad to get rid of some dead wood."[27]

What was a humorous proposition to the Chicago writer was a great idea to several other people.

Chapter 3

AMERICAN ASSOCIATION LOVED IT

While the National League formalized its stance against Sunday baseball in the fall of 1880 with an amendment to its constitution, 18 months later Sunday baseball would become a cornerstone of the first league to compete head-on with the National League—the American Association.

Cincinnati's forced withdrawal from the League after the 1880 season, ostensibly in part for its Sunday-related activities, was an indirect factor in the establishment of the American Association. More important were the previous banishments enacted by the League, the 1876 eviction of the Mutual and Athletic clubs representing New York and Philadelphia, respectively, and the 1877 ousting of the St. Louis and Louisville franchises for their transgressions that season.

Looking to resurrect a professional team in Cincinnati, baseball writer O. P. Caylor began to shepherd some tentative movements that had arisen to form a league that would challenge the National League monopoly. After Caylor organized a meeting in Pittsburgh that demonstrated interest from all the larger populated, non–League cities, the second-league movement gained momentum and culminated in the formation of the American Association at a November 2, 1881, meeting at Cincinnati's Gibson House hotel.

The platform was thus born to regularly play baseball on Sunday at its highest athletic ability.

Sunday baseball was one of three canons that differentiated the Association from the League. The other two were the ability to serve liquor at the ball grounds and to have the lowest priced ticket cost 25 cents.

"Since the money backing several of the Association teams—most notably St. Louis, Louisville, and Cincinnati—came from the brewers, the vote carried to play games on Sunday in cities where the law permitted and to sell spirits to spectators," David Nemec wrote in *The Beer and Whisky*

League, a book named after the derisive term used by detractors to refer to the Association during its playing days.¹

While most of the Association's detractors focused on the liquor issue, the Association was also taken to task for its Sunday games.

"For giving its members the right to decide themselves the question of Sunday baseball, the Association was denounced by its rival as immoral and corrupt. But such epithets were soon muted by the whirring of Sunday turnstiles in Association towns," historian David Voigt wrote in *American Baseball*. Harry Wright, for one, thought "the money from Sunday games didn't justify the moral struggle." Wright argued that the big Sunday crowds merely siphoned off attendance from Friday, Saturday, and Monday games and "in the long run failed to raise annual figures enough to warrant engaging in legal and moral controversies."²

Many people would adopt Wright's attendance argument over the years. But it failed to take into account a larger issue.

With the three-pronged philosophy of the Association, baseball could appeal to the average working man, a distinct departure from the League's stated mission to appeal to the "better classes." With quarter ball played on Sunday, the average working person now had the opportunity to watch a professional baseball game several times a year on other than the Decoration Day (now Memorial Day) and Fourth of July holidays. Labor Day would become a third holiday when some states recognized it as a holiday in the late 1880s; it became a national holiday in 1894.

Hulbert sent a series of letters to Association president Denny McKnight in which he criticized the "Cincinnati plan" of Sunday games, cheap admission fees, and on-premise liquor sales. "You cannot afford to bid for the patronage of the degraded," Hulbert told McKnight, adding that any and all attempts to justify these policies on the basis of financial expediency or club autonomy were simply the "rankest fallacies."³

Although the plan was to have Association teams in both New York and Philadelphia, the New York representatives wouldn't commit to join. The Association then signed on Brooklyn as an alternative to New York, since Brooklyn was then the third largest city in the country (Brooklyn was then a separate city from New York, before it was annexed in 1898). The New York strategy fell apart in March, however, when Brooklyn also bailed out. Baltimore was signed up as a replacement team on short notice.

With clubs in six large metropolitan areas—Baltimore, Cincinnati, Louisville, Philadelphia, Pittsburgh, and St. Louis—the Association began play on May 2.

Hulbert died just before the Association season began. If he had lived into the early years of the Association's competition with the League,

Hulbert's continued advocacy against Sunday baseball and beer sales in his role as League president may have eventually thwarted the Association's success. Hulbert's successors were not nearly as influential as he was, however, and the Association was able to flourish—along with Sunday baseball.

Despite the furor over Sunday baseball, only two of the six founding clubs of the Association actually played home games on Sunday—St. Louis and Louisville—although the other four teams exercised little hesitation to play Sunday baseball on the road. As the only clubs playing at their own grounds on Sunday, St. Louis and Louisville each played nine Sunday games in the inaugural 80-game 1882 season.

St. Louis already had experienced success with Sunday games the year before, attracting large crowds as an independent non–League team. Sunday games with cross-town rival St. Louis Red Stockings attracted 5,000 persons on both July 24 and July 31 (the Browns won both). On August 14, the Browns defeated the Cincinnati Buckeyes 12–4 before "one of the largest crowds ever seen on a St. Louis ball field." Spectators were 25 feet deep cordoned off in the outfield.[4]

The fact that Cincinnati didn't play Sunday baseball at its home grounds in 1882 lends further credence to the belief that Hulbert ousted Cincinnati from the National League due to its resistance to the reserve clause. Cincinnati was also the last of the six Association clubs to play Sunday games on the road in 1882, indicating a degree of concern for its home patronage if the club did indeed participate in a game on the Lord's Day.

The first major league game played on Sunday that counted in the league standings occurred on May 7, 1882, when St. Louis traveled to Louisville to play the Eclipse club. The home team was victorious, as Eclipse defeated St. Louis 10–3.

"Base ball usually draws a large attendance on Sunday, but the assemblage at Eclipse Park yesterday was the largest that ever looked upon the sport in this city," the *Louisville Courier-Journal* reported. "The crowd lined the entire grounds and settled on the fences and out-houses like a swarm of bees. The place had a decidedly Fourth-of-July appearance. There was hardly room for the players, and a rule had to be made giving a batsman two bases for losing the ball in the crowd."[5]

Tony Mullane pitched well for Eclipse, yielding just four hits to St. Louis. Eclipse collected 16 hits, three each by Dan Sullivan and Denny Mack, while batting star Pete Browning (of the Louisville slugger legend fame) had two hits.

Not every team in those days adopted its home city as the name of its team. The team based in Louisville, Kentucky, was then known as the Eclipse club, not the Louisville Eclipses. In fact, three of the original six teams in the Association were better known for their club names than the cities in which they played their home games.

Besides Eclipse from Louisville, there was the Athletic club from Philadelphia and the Allegheny club from the Pittsburgh area. Actually, the Allegheny club played in the city of Allegheny, Pennsylvania, adjacent to Pittsburgh on the north side. In the early 1880s, Allegheny was among the 25 largest cities in the country. The city lost its separate identity in 1907 when Allegheny became part of Pittsburgh through annexation.

While modern-day baseball publications usually list these teams by their city affiliations, contemporary reporting of events, including league standings, almost always listed the club name rather than the city name (a convention also followed in this book). By the time of the Association-League merger in 1891, teams were universally known by their city locations (although not all had club names).

Baseball was also spelled as two words, "base ball," for much of the 19th century and for several years into the 20th century before it contracted to one word (quotes in this book use the spelling convention in the actual publication).

On June 4, St. Louis held its opening Sunday game, defeating the Allegheny club 7–3 before a crowd of 8,000 despite threatening weather. St. Louis drew large crowds to its Sunday games at Sportsman's Park, topped by the 9,500 spectators that witnessed the August 6 game with Cincinnati, the eventual champion that year in the Association.

The two eastern teams, Baltimore and the Athletic club, played their initial Sunday road games at Louisville on June 4 and June 18, respectively. Including the inaugural game with St. Louis on May 7, Eclipse won its first three Sunday games at Eclipse Park as the club edged Athletic 2–1 on June 4 and slammed Baltimore 11–1 on June 18.

Because Louisville had about one-third the population of St. Louis, the Eclipse club drew fewer spectators for its Sunday games than did St. Louis. The largest crowd at Eclipse Park in 1882 was less than half the largest at Sportsman's Park, numbering 4,500 for the August 13 game with the Athletic club.

Cincinnati made its Sunday debut in a one-day journey to Louisville for a July 2 game with the Eclipse club, prior to a return match on the Fourth of July holiday the following Tuesday. Louisville finally lost on a Sunday as Cincinnati's Harry McCormick outdueled Mullane for a 2–1 victory.

"The gathering at the grounds was an exemplary one," the *Cincinnati Enquirer* reported. "It represented over 4,000 people and a more orderly or impartial one could not be wished for. They applauded visiting and local players alike, and there was not a bit of blackguardism let loose during the nine innings."[6]

Cincinnati would win four of five Sunday games in 1882 en route to the Association pennant that year, winning the flag handily with a 55–25 record.

Financially, the Association was a success, as hefty Sunday crowds helped to offset the 25-cent standard admission fee.

"Taken together, all these income sources—25 cent tickets, Sunday games, and liquor sales—provided most American Association clubs with an exceptionally strong cash flow," Melville wrote in *Early Baseball and the Rise of the National League*. "By mid-season, Pittsburgh had reportedly cleared $2,700 while the Athletics, by that same time, had grossed over $50,000. Cincinnati ended their first season so flush with cash the club was able to pay off its guarantor notes ahead of schedule."[7]

Seeing the success of the Association in 1882, the League began to settle its disagreements with the competition through a peace discussion in February 1883. Eventually, these meetings would result in the first National Agreement, a formal document that outlined how the leagues would co-exist.

For the 1883 season, both the League and the Association expanded into the vacant New York market, which was also the most highly populated city in the country. The Association invited the Metropolitan club to join it, while the League ousted the Troy franchise to make room for a team in New York. Interestingly, John Day owned both New York teams, which would lead to some skullduggery in future years. The League also ousted the Worcester franchise to allow for a team in Philadelphia, the country's second-largest city, in order to re-establish relations with both the #1 and #2 population centers in the country.

The Association expanded from six to eight teams for the 1883 season, adding a team in Columbus, Ohio, in addition to its expansion with the Metropolitan club in New York.

Columbus, although much smaller in population than New York, added a third Sunday-playing city to the Association. Columbus opened its Sunday play on May 6 at Recreation Park entertaining the St. Louis club. They lost 9–1. "Four thousand were present and greatly disappointed over the exhibition of their favorites," *Sporting Life* reported, as Columbus made just six hits off St. Louis pitcher Jumbo McGinnis and committed nine errors in the field.[8]

Results were little better the following Sunday, when defending champion Cincinnati traveled north to Columbus for a May 13 game and triumphed 7–0. "Over 5,000 disgusted Columbus citizens saw the Columbus

3. American Association Loved It

club endeavor to play ball last Sunday against the champions," as Columbus garnered seven hits and made five errors in the field.[9]

Neighbors of Recreation Park weren't fond of Sunday baseball, though, and introduced a petition to the Columbus City Council to prohibit it, complaining that Sunday baseball:

> Violates the feelings and wishes of a great majority of citizens residing in this community by disturbing their peace and quiet on the day of rest; by bringing an uproarious throng of non-residents into our midst; by demoralizing our youth in leading them contrary to the teachings of their parents and religious instructors; by crowding out of the street cars those returning from or going to divine service at such hours; and in all these diverse and other ways cast odium upon our community as a place of residence.[10]

The City Council passed a Sunday ordinance during a Columbus road trip. When the club returned in late June, it attempted to relocate its scheduled July 1 Sunday game with Baltimore from Recreation Park to a farm at Reese's Station on the Schioto Valley road. At the last moment, the Columbus club was "reluctantly compelled to abandon the scheme as Mr. Reese refused to let them have the ground for fear of interference from the township authorities, so the game was reluctantly abandoned."[11]

Pressure mounted on the council to repeal the ordinance after the July 1 game was postponed to the following Tuesday. On that Monday evening, the Sunday ordinance was repealed, permitting the July 8 game with the Metropolitan club to go on as planned at Recreation Park.

Metropolitan had already demonstrated its ability to attract a crowd. The club's initial Sunday game at St. Louis on June 17 drew a record 15,000 spectators, as pitcher Tim Keefe lost the battle with McGinnis in a 7–5 St. Louis victory.

When Sunday, July 8, arrived, wet weather did as well. With paying customers still arriving at the gate at Recreation Park despite the rain, the Columbus owners pushed forth with the game. Columbus prevailed 6–4 over Metropolitan, even though the "grounds were in a wretched condition and unfit for play on account of the heavy rains. But rather than disappoint the 3,000 persons who came out, the game was played."[12]

Despite the Sunday play, Columbus had the lowest attendance in the Association in 1883, averaging just 1,000 people to its games. When Columbus had journeyed to St. Louis for its May 20 Sunday contest, the club witnessed how successful Sunday baseball was in a city where many of its citizens subscribed to the Continental Sabbath. The May 20 game attracted about 10,000 spectators, more than double the usual attendance for a Sunday game at Recreation Park in Columbus.

Sunday baseball really blossomed in St. Louis during 1883. St. Louis attracted almost one-quarter million spectators during the 1883 season, nearly doubling its 1882 attendance figure in a slightly longer 1883 campaign. Of the one million people who attended games in all eight Association cities in 1883, St. Louis pulled in 25 percent of the total attendance in the Association.

Having a competitive team was one reason. The Browns challenged for the pennant, which the Athletic club eventually captured by a slim one-game margin, finishing in second place with a 65–33 record. The Sunday game on September 23 between the Browns and the Athletic club, a week before the season ended, attracted 16,800 to Sportsman's Park, a new Association attendance record. The crowd went away disappointed, though, as the Browns lost to the Athletic club 9–2.

Playing its games in a fun facility was even a bigger reason for the big attendance numbers.

Sportsman's Park has oft been described as "a saloon with a baseball attachment." One of its features was a bar behind the top row of the grandstand, "where patrons could stand with one foot on the rail and drink beer, wine, or whisky by the glass while watching action on the field." Vendors in white aprons also worked the aisles of the seating area and "the more sedentary could watch the game from the beer garden in the right field corner. Balls hit into the beer garden were in play, requiring outfielders to wade through patrons to dig them out."[13]

Sportsman's Park was also fitted with lawn bowling, handball courts, and other recreation areas that patrons could use when bored with baseball. Later, after the team's glory years were past, a "shoot the chutes" water slide, horse racing, and other less lofty recreational pursuits were added to Sportsman's Park to keep patrons coming through the turnstiles.

Chris Von der Ahe, the self-described "boss president," was the owner of the St. Louis club." To some historians, Von der Ahe was "a lucky beer garden owner who moved into baseball to sell more beer, and when his team began winning, took on what for him was the ludicrous role of baseball genius." The less kind have styled Von der Ahe "half-genius and half-buffoon." Others say he "found it expedient to dress and act and talk like a buffoon, but he was really a shrewd rat."[14]

Two successes that Von der Ahe is universally credited with are hiring Charlie Comiskey to run the baseball club (to the extent that Von der Ahe had the smarts to defer baseball matters to his talented manager) and the rise of Sunday baseball.

"Knowing how much St. Louisans loved the leisureways of the Continental Sabbath, he offered them his formula of cheap baseball in extra-large Sunday doses, and with offerings of beer, horse races, and fireworks," David Voigt wrote about Von der Ahe in *American Baseball*. "This broadened concept of a baseball spectacle quickly turned the St. Louis franchise from a weak sister to a baseball bonanza." Von der Ahe claimed a $70,000 profit for the 1883 season, a very large sum of money in the 19th century.[15]

With such evident financial success as St. Louis showed in Association, the League signed the National Agreement with the Association (and the newly acknowledged "minor" league, the Northwestern League) on October 27, 1883, to bring some stability to professional baseball. Part of this stability was the reserve clause, which bound players to the baseball clubs for life and consequently severely restricted their salary negotiation ability.

The financial success of the American Association also encouraged wealthy young St. Louis millionaire Henry Lucas to establish a third major league, the Union Association, in 1884. Lucas hoped to capitalize on player resentment over the reserve clause formalized in the National Agreement by having Union Association clubs not reserve players for any time period beyond the terms of their current contracts.

While the new league existed for only that one brief season in 1884, the establishment of the Union Association helped to further the expansion of Sunday baseball in several ways.

The Union Association failed ultimately because three major leagues consisting of 28 teams proved too much baseball supply for the existing spectator demand. Seven of the initial eight Union teams overlapped franchises in existing League and Association cities, the lone exception being Altoona, Pennsylvania. In fact, there was a Philadelphia club in all three leagues, as the Keystones of the Union competed for customers with the Athletic club of the Association and the yearling League entry, later to be known as the Phillies.

Three of the eight Union clubs had designs to play Sunday baseball on their home grounds, rivaling the trio of Association clubs that hosted games in 1883 on the Lord's Day. With the Association expanding to 12 teams for the 1884 season to try to thwart the success of the Union, the addition of an Indianapolis club to the Association made it a foursome for Sunday play in 1884.

Lucas, who doubled as league president and owner of the St. Louis Maroons club, definitely had his sights on the big Sunday crowds that Von der Ahe's Browns had attracted to its Association games in St. Louis. Lucas built his own playing grounds with a seating capacity of 10,000. His quest for glory backfired, though, when his strong team outclassed the entire league. The Maroons began the season with 21 straight wins and cruised to a 91–19 record in a first place finish absurdly ahead of the remaining field.

The Maroons attracted a full house for its first Sunday game on April 20, defeating Chicago 7–2 in six innings as the 10,000 spectators sat through the cold and drizzle. "At least 6,000 occupied uncovered seats," the *St. Louis Globe-Democrat* reported, "and all sat through a six-inning contest apparently cheerful if not grateful for having an opportunity to see the game."[16]

With few competitive games the rest of the season, however, the crowds stayed away from Union Park in droves. The Maroons averaged 2,000 per game for their 55 home gates, but were attracting just hundreds to its games by the end of the season. The Maroons' dominance of the highly imbalanced talent distribution in the Union Association only served to increase attendance at the competing St. Louis baseball venue, where the Browns challenged again for the American Association pennant.

On May 4, a crowd of 10,000 entered Sportsman's Park to see the Browns defeat Toledo 4–0. Sunday baseball would soon become most identified with the St. Louis Browns and Sportsman's Park.

The second Union club to change the Sunday baseball landscape was the Cincinnati club, which had managed to grab the lease on the Bank Street Grounds used by the Association team in 1882 and 1883. The second act of audacity by the Cincinnati Unions was to schedule Sunday games at the Bank Street Grounds, an action that the Association team had averred from doing in its first two years of play.

On April 27, 1884, the Cincinnati Unions played the first major league game on Sunday in the city of Cincinnati, defeating Chicago 4–3 before a gathering of 2,000.

In order to keep its customers, who'd otherwise flock to the Union games not only on Sunday but also on other days of the week, the Association team scheduled its first Sunday home game for May 11, openly challenging the cross-town rivals who were also playing that day.

The Cincinnati Unions defeated Baltimore 7–6 in the May 11 game at Union Athletic Park, the former Bank Street Grounds. In the Association game that day, Toledo defeated Cincinnati 3–2 at the abandoned brickyard that the team had relocated to after losing out on the lease for the Bank Street Grounds. The former brickyard was the team's home for the next 80 years, transforming into League Park, Palace of the Fans, Redland Field, and eventually Crosley Field.

One other noteworthy aspect of the May 11 Association game was the appearance of Fleet Walker as the Toledo catcher. Walker, one of the few black players to appear in the major leagues before the color line was instituted, would become embroiled in a courtroom battle the following year over the right to play baseball on Sunday.

Without the Union Association club pushing Sunday play in Cincinnati, it no doubt would have been several more years before Sunday baseball transpired in Cincinnati.

All three Sunday-hosting Union teams played on May 11, hoping to get a jump on their intra-city rivals in the League and the Association. The Chicago Unions played the first major league game on Sunday in Chicago that day, since the League's White Stockings continued to staunchly oppose Sunday play even with Albert Spalding heading the club after Hulbert's death. Before a crowd of 3,000, the Chicago Unions defeated the Keystones of Philadelphia 3–2 in the Chicago Sunday opener. The winning pitcher was "One Arm" Daily, who would go on to register 483 strikeouts in the 1884 Union season, a major league record for right-handed pitchers that has never been eclipsed.

Although the Unions scheduled Sunday games for the first 10 weeks of the season, it wasn't enough to make the league viable. St. Louis and Cincinnati were two of just five teams that finished the Union Association season among the original eight teams. Altoona was the first to disband, folding in late May after just 25 games, which included an April 27 Sunday game in St. Louis.

Kansas City, located 250 miles west of St. Louis and in 1884 still on the edge of the Wild West, replaced Altoona and had no compunction against Sunday baseball. The first of seven Sunday games in Kansas City was played on July 27. St. Louis rode herd on the overmatched Kansas City club 9–4, which would stumble to a humbling 16–63 record as a replacement for Altoona.

In August, Philadelphia dropped back to two major league teams when the Keystones disbanded and Chicago became a one-team city again when its Unions transferred to Pittsburgh. Neither Pittsburgh nor the Wilmington Quicksteps that replaced the Keystones played Sunday baseball either home or on the road; both teams also disbanded in mid–September. Milwaukee and St. Paul, two teams from the recently failed Northwestern League, were enticed to finish out the schedules of Pittsburgh and Wilmington.

Milwaukee became a fifth Union club to play Sunday baseball on its home grounds, as its heavily concentrated German population was accustomed to the Continental Sabbath and had few reservations with Sunday baseball. In the waning weeks of the Union schedule, Milwaukee played the first of three Sunday games on September 28 against the National club of Washington, en route to a perky 8–4 record as a replacement team in the Union.

Another Sunday baseball first occurred in September when the Boston Unions played the first Sunday game by a Boston major league team on September 28 at Kansas City.

Playing its home games in the bastion of Puritan resistance to Sunday amusements, Boston was the only club among the original eight members of the Union Association that declined to play Sunday games on the road. By September, however, with all its remaining games away from home and a serious question of whether there'd be a second Union season in 1885, Boston decided to play on the final four Sundays of the 1884 season.

Kansas City defeated Boston 6–1 on September 28, in the Boston club's Sunday debut before 5,000 spectators in the westernmost outpost in the three major leagues. Boston defeated Milwaukee 3–1 on October 5 and lost to Cincinnati 11–5 on October 12.

As the 1884 season headed to a close, Sunday became a way for the Union clubs to help make up for the season's financial setback. All eight clubs played on October 5 and October 12, the first time that all teams of a major league played on the Lord's Day.

In its final Sunday appearance on October 19, Boston defeated champion St. Louis 5–0 before 8,000 spectators at Union Park. Dupee Shaw pitched and batted Boston to victory. In the pitcher's box, Shaw yielded just four hits to the Maroons. At the bat in the fourth inning with three men on base, Shaw "hit for two bases" a serve from Charlie Sweeney, scoring two with a third run scoring on a wild throw.[17]

The most significant Sunday baseball development in the American Association during the 1884 season was the rise of organized opposition to Sunday baseball.

Having seen Association teams reap a financial reward from Sunday baseball in 1882 and 1883, and witnessing Sunday play for the first time in Chicago and Cincinnati in 1884 through Union games, Sabbatarian groups tried to stop the playing of Sunday baseball. These first Sabbatarian efforts were lodged in Columbus and Indianapolis.

With professional Sunday baseball having debuted in Cincinnati on April 27, signaling its spread to a major city east of St. Louis, the Sabbatarian influences began to gather steam to try to stop its further expansion as well as to curtail its tolerance where it was already played.

On May 18, the Indianapolis club in the Association inaugurated Sunday baseball in that city when Cincinnati defeated the home club 5–1 before 4,000 spectators.

Indianapolis owners were wise enough to schedule the contest not at the club's regular site, Athletic Park, but rather outside the city boundaries at Bruce Grounds in Broad Ripple to try to avoid prosecution for playing

Sunday baseball. Indianapolis thus became the first major league club to employ the technique of using a Sunday-only ball grounds to play its Sabbath games.

"The first Sunday game of base ball in this city took place yesterday at the new grounds on the extension of College Avenue, just beyond the city limits," the *Indianapolis Journal* reported. "The crowd was so large that they could not be seated, although there was capacity for nearly 3,000. The Wabash ran three crowded trains, and there were private conveyances by the score, while many walked. Contrary to general expectation, there was no interference on the part of the officers of the law, although it is understood that the players and other attaches will be filed against to-day for desecration of the Sabbath."[18]

Both the Cincinnati and Indianapolis teams were arrested in the days following the May 18 game. The charge was violating a law specifying that it was "unlawful for any person over the age of 14 to pursue his usual avocation upon the Sabbath day."[19]

"These arrests were made to-day, not from a spirit of malicious prosecution, but because I believe the matter should be settled one way or the other," Sheriff Hess told the *Indianapolis Journal*. "If the Indianapolis club is to be prevented from playing Sunday games here, they should know it at once, and if they are allowed to play they should know that also. Personally, I believe there are a great many things here that will do a great deal more injury to the morals of the community than these Sunday games of ball will if they are conducted in an orderly manner. The crowds out there will keep men and boys away from the saloons and from getting drunk down town. My jail list from the Mayor's Court yesterday shows that the game on Sunday had that effect, for it was not half as large as last week."[20]

Cincinnati had already prepared a defense based on a prior case "that baseball is simply a sport and not an avocation."[21]

Nothing ever became of the Sunday baseball arrests, as Indianapolis went on to play its May 25 game against the Eclipse club and then nine more Sunday games that season at Bruce Grounds.

Sunday baseball kept the club afloat financially, as nearly half the team's total season attendance of 50,000 came from these 11 Sunday games. The other 44 games at Athletic Park were sparsely attended, averaging a little over 500 persons a game. In the end, the Sunday games weren't enough to save the Indianapolis team, and it went under at the end of the 1884 season.

Sabbatarians were more successful in Columbus the following month. While Columbus played its first two Sunday games of 1884 unimpeded, its June 22 game with Brooklyn was another matter.

With the Columbus Law and Order League intent upon shutting down Sunday baseball in the city, as a violation of the law that prohibited common labor on Sunday, a citizens' committee was formed to try to arrange an agreement with the Columbus ball club to discontinue Sunday games.

"Sunday base ball means in the near future Sunday horse racing, Sunday excursions, Sunday theaters, Sunday operas, Sunday cock fights and the like," W. G. Deshler of the citizens' committee voiced. "If Sunday arrests can't be made for such things then all those who like such things will make our Sundays saturnalias far ahead of those of old Rome in which to do evil. It is the very popularity and fascination of the game of base ball among our young people which makes it the more insidious as a precursor to things greatly worse if this is allowed on Sunday."[22]

The committee issued its report early in the week before the scheduled June 22 game. "There is a disposition on the part of the committee not to prosecute the Columbus Club for games already scheduled on Sunday," which would result in forfeits. The report suggested that the June 22 and June 29 games be allowed to proceed if future Sunday games would be canceled. Owners of the Columbus team scoffed at the suggested compromise.[23]

In the sixth inning of the June 22 game, three constables appeared on the field and arrested three Brooklyn players (Adonis Terry, Oscar Walker, and Bill Greenwood) and six Columbus players (pitcher Cannonball Morris, catcher Fred Carroll, and infielders Jim Field, Pop Smith, John Richmond, and Willie Kuehne). The constables were not warmly received, as the "spectators opened upon them with hisses and yells of 'fire them out!' and 'throw them over the fence!'" as the game was delayed 20 minutes.[24]

"There were 3,000 people on the ground and a riot was imminent," reported *Sporting Life*. "It was finally agreed that if they would let the game go on, all would go with them to the justice's office after the game closed." Columbus defeated Brooklyn by an 8–2 score.[25]

What an introduction to Sunday baseball for the Brooklyn club, for the Columbus game was the team's first game ever played on the Lord's Day. Back home, a *New York Times* editorial chastised the concept of Sunday baseball:

> The "pulling" of two teams of base-ball players at Columbus yesterday for violating the Sunday law is one of the many incidents which show how widely the social and moral standards of the West are coming to differ from those in the East. For no Eastern state, not even in this city, which Bostonians and Philadelphians like to call a foreign encampment, would

such an incident be possible. It is possible that the persistent agitation against Puritanical Sunday laws which has been carried on in the interest of beer has had its effect in producing a popular contempt for the Sunday laws in general. The case of base-ball, however, is on a very different footing from the case of beer. A man may plausibly maintain that beer is necessary to him, but no man can say that it is necessary for him to see or to play a game of base-ball on Sunday. Moreover, beer may be consumed quietly and without offense to those who disbelieve in the drinking of beer on Sunday, while a base-ball match on Sunday is a public scandal to all people who believe in the religious obligation of Sunday.[26]

The arrested Columbus and Brooklyn players went before Judge Fritchey and signed $100 bonds to appear for trial on Tuesday, June 24. On Monday, club president Chittenden and directors of the Columbus club were also arrested. Chittenden demanded an immediate trial at his hearing, "for he sprang to his feet and in an excited and vehement manner announced that he would not give bail and demanded that civil cases should give way to those of a criminal character."[27]

Of course, baseball was not the only labor performed on Sunday in Columbus. "The president of the base ball club says this is a death-blow to the game in Columbus, as it cannot be supported without the Sunday games," *Sporting Life* reported. "As a retaliatory measure, the Columbus management states that cases against the Consolidated Road running its street cars on Sunday will be prosecuted under the same law and also intimates that warrants will be sworn out tomorrow against the State Journal Company to stop its issue of a Monday morning newspaper, as the principal part of the work has to be done on Sunday. It is also rumored that some of the most prominent saloon keepers will be arrested under the same law."[28]

Columbus was the first club to invoke the Sunday baseball defense of casting aspersions on other Sunday-permitted activities, particularly the ability to serve liquor in saloons. Sunday baseball proponents, however, would find the liquor interests to be tough competition over the next 20 years.

At the June 24 hearing, the Brooklyn players were arraigned first and Terry, Walker, and Greenwood all pleaded not guilty. "Manager Doyle was desirous this morning of having his men enter pleas of guilty, but was prevailed upon by the Columbus club men not to do so," the *Columbus Dispatch* reported. "[Doyle] said he lived in a State where people had to obey such laws."[29]

On Wednesday, June 25, Pop Smith of the Columbus team was bound over to the Common Pleas Court for a fine of $50, rendering a slim chance that Columbus would prevail on the Sunday baseball issue. The club used the case of catcher Fred Carroll, who was next on the docket, to elevate the proceedings by contesting the legality of the arrests. They tried to argue that the arrests on Sunday were illegal, since the law provided that no person shall be arrested on Sunday except in cases of treason, felony, or breach of peace.

Carroll's case was transferred to Common Pleas Court where Judge Wylie heard the case. It was decided that if Judge Wylie ruled against the Columbus club, then the team would abandon Sunday baseball. On June 27, the Law and Order League presented its case that the arrests were legal, and on June 28 Judge Wylie concurred with the Law and Order League. "The decision received with evident marks of satisfaction by the Law and Order people," the *Columbus Dispatch* noted in its article "Judge Wylie Decides the Arrest of Base Ball Players on Sunday to be Legal."[30]

"From these sections it is argued that an arrest on Sunday for the misdemeanor of playing base ball on that day contrary to the statute, cannot lawfully be made," Judge Wylie wrote in his ruling on the Carroll case. "We have a chapter called 'Offenses against public peace.' It is contended that Carroll's offense is not within this class, and therefore the arrest is illegal. Assault and battery, robbery and rape are not there either, but it is neither law nor logic to conclude they are not breaches of the peace. Section 5459 does not say breach of the public peace. It is simply 'a breach of the peace;' any breaking, any peace ... This clause, in my judgement means indictable misdemeanor."[31]

Columbus management briefly debated an appeal to the Ohio Supreme Court, but "as that Court has adjourned until September, there seems nothing left for the ball players to do but to forego the scheduled Sunday games in Columbus." On Saturday afternoon, June 28, Columbus hammered out an agreement with the citizens' committee as Mayor Walcott issued an order "to have the police force in readiness to preserve the peace and back up the law and order people" at the June 29 game. The directors of the Columbus club agreed to "hereby order that no Sunday games be played by our ball club in Columbus after June 29, 1884, and it is further ordered that no Sunday games be allowed at Recreation Park by any base ball club after Sunday, June 29, 1884."[32]

Fred Carroll, the defendant in the Common Pleas Court hearing before Judge Wylie, was one of the earliest players to hail from California. He was a catcher for eight major league seasons from 1884 to 1891 and was perhaps best known as the battery mate of pitcher Ed "Cannonball" Morris. Carroll teamed with Morris for seven of those eight seasons and both were part of the Columbus arrests in 1884 for playing Sunday baseball.[33]

Carroll compiled a lifetime batting average of .284 for his major league service, though he did better in his post-major-league days in the California League. Carroll, who often played winter ball in California during his major league days in the east, batted .315 in his three seasons in the California League.

Since Carroll was a California native (born in Sacramento) and California was the first state to rescind its Sunday laws in 1883, Carroll seemed to be a natural candidate to be the defendant in the first major Sunday baseball legal confrontation.

The June 29 Sunday game in Columbus went on as agreed. The Metropolitan club defeated Columbus 4–3 as Keefe pitched a six-hitter for the New Yorkers and Tom Esterbrook collected four hits, including a pair of two-base hits, and scored three runs.

Fred Carroll was one of several Columbus ball players arrested in 1884 for playing baseball on Sunday, in the first on-field Sunday baseball arrests in a major league game. (National Baseball Hall of Fame Library, Cooperstown, N.Y.)

By losing the legal battle, Columbus was forced to cancel the scheduled Sunday games for July 6, 13, and 20. As the Columbus management had forecast, the canceled Sunday games during July did cripple the club's finances. While the club did eventually regain the ability to play on Sunday in September, it was far too late for the three Sunday games late in the season to matter. The team declared bankruptcy after the season ended, even though it had finished in second place behind the Metropolitan club.

The Association retracted to eight teams for the 1885 season, jettisoning the Indianapolis and Columbus clubs that had played Sunday home games as well as the Toledo and Washington clubs. Only one of the four new clubs in 1884 remained in the Association the following season—Brooklyn—which proceeded to maneuver to bring Sunday baseball to the eastern portion of the country.

Chapter 4

ST. LOUIS AND BROOKLYN EXULTED IN IT

After his team's experience with Sunday baseball arrests in Columbus, Brooklyn club president Charlie Byrne voiced some displeasure with the Sunday scheduling at the December 1884 annual meeting of the Association.

Byrne argued that "the current system was unfair because the schedule was drawn up so that western clubs could play at home on Sunday, while eastern clubs, for the most part based in sectors where Sunday baseball was illegal, often had to sit for days at a time in western cities, piling up road expenses in wait for a Sunday date."[1]

The other owners voted down Byrne's proposal to give the visiting team 25 percent of a gate, preferring to stay with the flat $65 guarantee. Byrne then proposed to double the guarantee for Sunday games. When this proposal also was voted down, Byrne decided to attack the issue head on by playing Sunday baseball on his home turf. This would not be an easy task in Brooklyn, known as the City of Churches, which had strong feelings about proper activities on the Lord's Day.

"Unfortunately there is a prejudice throughout the city to the proposed scheme of playing Sunday games at Coney Island," *Sporting Life* reported. "[Byrne] will certainly find it an uphill piece of business."[2]

Byrne expected to play Sunday games at a new park to be built at Coney Island, a significant exception to the Sunday piety practiced by the majority of Brooklyn residents. "Brooklyn's Coney Island grounds will be between the new and old iron piers and just in the rear of the Sea Beach hotel. The railroad will haul in soil, then it will be sodded, and stands and fencing built."[3]

Coney Island was located in the southern part of Kings County, several miles removed from the city of Brooklyn, lying on a stretch of land set off from the rest of the county. Coney Island was also already becoming a haven for Sunday pleasure seekers, some of whom Byrne hoped to attract to his Brooklyn team's games. Coney Island, however, was gaining an unsavory reputation for gambling and other sordid activities. Some commentators defended the Sunday baseball idea by contrasting it to activities already going on at Coney Island.

> It seems to me that it would be more within the bounds of consistency to first put a stop to the Sunday evils of gambling, dance halls, pool selling, and other violations of State laws on Sunday at Coney Island before troubling what is comparatively a venial offense. Stop Sunday ball playing if it be the desire of the community at large, but before that is done put a stop to the vile inequities referred to, which disgrace every day at Coney Island, not to mention Sunday.[4]

The 1885 Association schedule listed a dozen Sunday home games for Brooklyn, the first to be held on May 31.

Byrne seemed to be winning the battle when a court ruled that Sunday baseball was not a violation of the law "unless the playing is engaged in at such localities and is marked by such conduct as leads to a violation of the Sabbath repose of the community in which the offense is committed."[5]

When amateurs tested the law at the Sea Beach hotel grounds in late April, however, they were arrested. Even though a judge discharged the players on the grounds that they had disturbed no one, the actions were enough for Brooklyn to discard its plan to play Sunday baseball in 1885.[6]

Another new baseball grounds in 1885, though, held promise for Byrne's hopes to have his Brooklyn team to play home games on Sunday.

On Sunday, April 5, nearly 3,000 persons attended the opening of the ballpark at Ridgewood, Long Island, where the Atlantic Club of Brooklyn played an exhibition game with the Ridgewood Club. Prospects for continued Sunday use appeared good as "there was no interference with the game by the police and the managers said that the people would have no cause for complaint."[7]

Byrne successfully arranged to lease the park for the 1886 season and Sunday baseball at the major league level made its debut on the East Coast on April 25, 1886.

Well, sort of. In what was supposed to be the first Sunday championship game at Ridgewood, the April 25 game turned into an exhibition game and not a championship game when Baltimore manager Billy Barnie "declined to play it as such." Brooklyn defeated Baltimore 11–1 and waited a week to play its first official Sunday game.[8]

4. St. Louis and Brooklyn Exulted in It

Sunday games were often rescheduled from other weekday games on the Association schedule, as was the April 25 game, in order to get in as many Sunday games as possible. For instance, the original 1886 Association schedule didn't have a Sunday home game listed for Brooklyn until June 6. Schedules were often shifted during this era of major league baseball, often causing confusion and sometimes initiating disputes.

"The first championship game in the East, and over 7,000 people attended," *Sporting Life* reported on the May 2 game at Ridgewood. "The spectators encroached on the playing lines to such an extent that it was impossible for the outfielders to do their work and accounts for the heavy batting by both teams." The game ended in a 19–19 tie, when in the eighth inning, the entire supply of six new balls was exhausted due to the number of lost balls among the spectators.[9]

The ball grounds at Ridgewood were actually part of the larger Grauer's Ridgewood Park, where city residents flocked from New York on Sunday to enjoy outdoor activities and get away from the urban area. Many picnics and celebrations were held at Grauer's resort, like the annual picnic of the German lodges of the Order of Red Men on July 18, which attracted 20,000 people. With such large crowds seeking recreation every Sunday in then-rural Queens, there was a ready supply of spectators to take in the Association games played on the ball grounds by Charlie Byrne's Brooklyn team.

Ridgewood Park was located in Queens County, just over the border from Kings County in which the city of Brooklyn was located. In 1886, this was a rural area of Long Island comprised of small villages, one of which was Ridgewood, that was not all that easy nor pleasurable to reach. One writer described two ways to get to Ridgewood. The first was to "get on a horse car and when I was nearly starved to death to get off, and after walking several miles across the country, I would hear some yells. Follow the yells as the crow flies and I would soon be at Ridgewood Park." The other route was "getting a hack and riding over the cobble stones that pave the streets one will pass over on the way to Ridgewood," which the writer called a "gastronomic event" with his "insides shaken into a condensed vacuum after that ride."[10]

Kings Country at this time was also comprised of mostly rural area, as the city of Brooklyn then consisted of just the territory near where the Brooklyn Bridge connected Long Island to lower Manhattan Island. Ridgewood was five miles to the east of Brooklyn in 1886, as Williamsburg, Flatbush, and Bushwick were then independent entities within Kings County. Brooklyn would annex these towns in the next several years, before Brooklyn itself was annexed by New York in 1898. While on today's map, Ridgewood is right on the Brooklyn border, in 1886 the two places were not remotely adjacent to each other.[11]

Sunday-only ball grounds were notorious for being cramped in size and flimsy in quality. There was a special ground rule at Ridgewood in 1886 that any ball hitting the right field fence was a two-base hit. On July 25, Brooklyn defeated Allegheny 6–3 as eight of Brooklyn's 13 hits were of the "hit-fence" two-base variety, while only one of the Pittsburgh club's 10 hits was so poked. "To win at Ridgewood, batsmen should go in for high balls to right field, as they yield two baggers, when at Washington Park the same hits would yield catches five times out of six," the *Brooklyn Daily Eagle* remarked. Brooklyn broke a 3–3 tie in the seventh inning when "fence hits by Swartwood and Phillips and a splendid grounder to left field by Smith" gave the home club the lead.[12]

Sunday baseball drew large crowds to Ridgewood to see the Brooklyn club play. The 14 games at Ridgewood in 1886 averaged about 4,000 spectators apiece, which was nearly double the average crowd at Washington Park for weekday games. Put another way, the Ridgewood games were responsible for one-third of Brooklyn's total attendance in 1886, although the Ridgewood games represented just one-fifth of the club's home gates.

Because of the crowds, there was extreme sensitivity to proper decorum at the Sunday games, to try to appease the Sabbatarians seeking to shut down Sunday baseball and other Sunday activities. Newspapers often went to great lengths to convey the Sabbath-acceptable behavior of the numerous spectators at Sunday games. For instance, the *Brooklyn Daily Eagle* once described a Ridgewood crowd as "an exceptionally respectable and intelligent gathering of our best patrons of the game."[13]

Crowds, though, weren't always so prim and quiet, since the Sunday games did appeal to working people on their day off not just business owners and those of greater monetary means. The throng at the August 22 game between Brooklyn and the neighboring Metropolitan club from Manhattan was described as a "decidedly rough assemblage" that was "so imbued with Sullivanism that they did not know how to give a visiting team fair play." This crowd was characterized as "a regular East Brooklyn Sunday gang, mixing for once in these games at Ridgewood."[14]

Raucous crowds like those on August 22 aroused Sabbatarians to stop Sunday baseball at Ridgewood Park, as it disturbed their peace on the Lord's Day. On September 5, Sabbatarians managed to close all the Sunday ballparks in Queens County. "There was much rejoicing among the ball players on their arrival at the Ridgewood Park grounds, [as] they heard of the embargo that Judge McKenna and the Sheriff of Queens County had laid upon further Sunday ball playing in their district. [The action] meant a day off to go to picnics and enjoy schooners and libitum to the majority of ball tossers." Of all the ballparks, though, Grauer's Ridgewood Park remained open "by some kind of maneuvering."[15]

4. St. Louis and Brooklyn Exulted in It

The Brooklyn-Athletic game was played until the sixth inning, when "the sheriff of Queens County, accompanied by a dozen or more deputies, marched upon the diamond and ordered the players to desist." The sheriff did his work "in a very quiet and orderly manner, and the seven thousand people dispersed at once without a sign of disorder or lawlessness." Although Brooklyn was ahead 11–3, at the time, there was some question whether Brooklyn had won the game, "since the rules provide only for prevention by rain or darkness." Stoppage of a Sunday game by Sabbatarian action was viewed as an involuntary, permissible ending point, with Brooklyn awarded the victory.[16]

It was only a temporary disruption in Sunday play, and games at Ridgewood proceeded forward without interference on September 12 and 19.

While Sunday baseball was able to infiltrate the east in Brooklyn in 1886, there was another Sabbatarian victory in the west when Cincinnati stopped playing home games on Sunday.

New Cincinnati owner John Hauck, unlike his predecessors, was opposed to Sunday games despite their popularity within the city, and he eliminated Sunday games from the club's 1886 schedule. While Hauck's decision was certainly popular with the Cincinnati Law and Order Society, it may also have been somewhat prompted by the 1885 legal decisions handed down 250 miles to the north in Cleveland, where the team in the Western League had tested the Sunday laws.

In April 1885, Cleveland catcher Fleet Walker had been arrested for playing in the team's April 19 Sunday game on the charge of violating the city ordinance against playing games on the Sabbath. It seems Walker was singled out for arrest not because he was black, but simply because he was the team's catcher. Pitchers and catchers were routinely the ones arrested in these Sabbatarian actions. The team hired lawyers to defend Walker, who had played at the major league level with Toledo the previous season.

On May 3, Walker was found not guilty, as "the judge held that the code specifically banned only marbles and quoits. Whether baseball was another 'game or sport' as outlined in the code was a matter for legislative, not judicial reckoning."[17]

The victory for Sunday baseball was short lived. Later in May authorities arrested Cleveland's other catcher, Joe Sommers, for playing a Sunday game. Sommers was convicted under a state statute, rather than the city ordinance, which put a halt to Sunday games in Cleveland (and a halt to that Cleveland baseball team, as it soon dropped out of the league). The Sabbatarians had successfully used an Ohio law to halt working class people from attending baseball games, since Sunday was the only day they could attend games because of the typical six-day workweek.

"If the working classes became a regular core of fans," one writer remarked, "not only would Cleveland's pietistic Sabbatarians be genuinely offended, baseball as a privilege of the respectable classes would be negated as well."[18]

Although Cincinnati had no home games scheduled for Sunday in 1886, that didn't mean the team was passing up revenue from Sunday games. During its home stand in May, Cincinnati found a way to squeeze in two Sunday games. On May 2, Cincinnati traveled to nearby Louisville, just 100 miles away, to play on Sunday during its lull in the May 1–5 series with Louisville in Cincinnati.

Two weeks later, Cincinnati traveled to St. Louis after the Browns finished its series in Cincinnati to play the Browns at Sportsman's Park on Sunday, May 16. Both teams headed east thereafter, Cincinnati to Baltimore and St. Louis to Brooklyn. But the Sunday game on May 16 was lucrative enough to make both teams travel out of their way to squeeze it in.

This was the beginning of the one-game road trip, a concept made famous in the coming years by numerous teams that were prohibited from playing Sunday baseball on their home grounds. The schedules were rigorous, demanding the teams play Saturday afternoon, travel Saturday night, play Sunday afternoon, travel Sunday night, and perhaps even play Monday afternoon. Teams would go to tremendous extremes to get in a Sunday baseball game where legal so they could garner the visitor's share of the gate receipts from the usually larger crowds on the Lord's Day.

When Cincinnati played poorly in the first half of the season, however, Hauck reversed his decision to stop Sunday baseball in order to put the club financials back in the black. When Sunday games were reinstated with a game on July 4, the largest crowd of the year—and one of the rowdiest—showed up.

"The crowd was very noisy and disorderly, particularly in the Cincinnati half of the eighth inning when the crowd began to throw huge cannon fire crackers into the diamond while players were on bases," the *Cincinnati Enquirer* reported. Umpire Kelly stopped the game and pointed out throwers in the pavilion and instructed police to eject them, but "the crowd wouldn't have it, however, and the police were unable to do their duty."[19]

Cincinnati's opponent for the July 4 game, the Athletic club of Philadelphia, had brought only a skeleton crew to the park, convinced that game would be canceled by actions of the Law and Order League. When the game was to be played, the Athletic club had to recruit a player from among the 6,500 spectators in the stands to pitch against Cincinnati. Ed Clark pitched decently, yielding 10 hits, but the weak Athletic lineup behind

4. St. Louis and Brooklyn Exulted in It   57

him caused the Philadelphia club to lose 8–0. Clark pitched only two more innings in the major leagues, five years later with Columbus in 1891.

The following Sunday a riot ensued at the Cincinnati grounds during the July 11 game with Brooklyn, as "the game was marked by disgraceful conduct on the part of the spectators."[20]

The disagreement was captured in great detail in the next day's issue of the *Cincinnati Enquirer* in an article entitled "Base-Ball Riot" with the sub-head "Sensational Scenes at a Sunday Game." It all started in the sixth inning with two outs, two men on base, and Brooklyn's Adonis Terry at bat. Terry beat out an infield hit to shortstop and two men scored on the play, as the crowd jeered its disapproval of umpire Bradley's call.

"A man named Moran, who keeps a stand in Sixth-street Market, and who was put out of the grounds early in the game, threw a beer glass at Bradley, hitting him on the leg. His brother followed with another," the *Cincinnati Enquirer* related the early antics. "A young fellow named Clark, of Covington, jumped up and got back at the Morans for throwing the glasses. The Morans immediately set upon Clark and proceeded to do him up. Frank Bell, formerly a catcher of the Brooklyns, went to the rescue of Clark."[21]

"The fight was waxing hot when Bob Clark, in full uniform, jumped into the pavilion, bat in hand, to assist his brother, who was being whipped," the *Brooklyn Daily Eagle* described the ensuing action. "Then followed a pitched battle of the friends of the contestants. Bell's friends rushed to his rescue and the friends of Clark took a hand in the melee, which lasted fully fifteen minutes, during which the police seemed utterly paralyzed."[22]

"While this was going on, the crowd on the bleaching boards gave their attention to Umpire Bradley. They began to throw beer glasses by the dozen at him," the *Cincinnati Enquirer* reported. "The spectators in the pavilion joined those on the bleaching boards in hurling glasses at the umpire. One of these, thrown with a great deal of force, hit him on the leg."[23]

"Several thousand people jumped the stands into the field to mob Bradley," the *Sporting Life* reported. Bradley was hustled off the field by police "to save his life." Order was finally restored and Bradley "came out of hiding" and umpired the rest of the game "under protection of the authorities."[24]

Brooklyn won the "battle" 11–7, but only after the players took up bats to protect themselves from the raucous Cincinnati crowd.

"A blow was given to the Sunday games in Cincinnati by the behavior of the betting hoodlums, who gathered in force on the Cincinnati grounds yesterday and brutally attacked the umpire and even threatened the visiting players," the *Brooklyn Daily Eagle* commented. "The moment such rows mark Sunday ball playing the community will rise up against the playing of the game, even in the west."[25]

These outbursts served to further the Association's bad image for Sunday play, as critics contended that Sunday attendance by working-class people was the reason for the unruly spectators. They thus equated Sunday games with fostering an unsafe environment for spectators, obviously comparing the situation with the more pristine, non–Sunday-playing National League.

As the Association became more dependent on Sunday baseball for the profitability of its member clubs, and its image began to tarnish due to unruly crowds at the Sabbath games, the Allegheny club from the Pittsburgh area defected to the National League after the 1886 season.

Allegheny's departure from the Association was one of the early blows to Sunday baseball. This occurred not so much from the club's play on the Lord's Day, since the team only played Sunday games on the road, but from creating a chink in the strength of the Association that Sunday baseball was so instrumental in developing.

A disagreement between Allegheny and Baltimore over the right to purchase a St. Louis player led to a quarrel between St. Louis owner Von der Ahe and Association president McKnight. Eventually, both the Allegheny club and McKnight left the Association, the former voluntarily after overtures from the League, while the latter was ousted involuntarily. Leadership in the Association was weak thereafter, and not even Sunday baseball could maintain its strength.

Allegheny-cum-Pittsburgh has been in the National League ever since its five-year run in the Association ended in 1886.

Another event after the 1886 season gave Sabbatarians renewed hope in their quest to eradicate Sunday baseball.

The St. Louis Maroons, the former Union team that had moved into the League after the Union Association folded after the 1884 season, were banished from the League following the 1886 season due to persistent petitioning to play Sunday baseball. Because of the success of the Browns in the Association, winning consecutive pennants in 1885 and 1886, the crosstown Maroons needed Sunday play to make a profit.

After the 1885 season, the Maroons and Browns did play two exhibition games on the Sunday lulls in the post-season series between the champions of the Association and the League, the Browns and Chicago. In its four years of "world series" play between 1885 and 1888, St. Louis played no Sunday contests with the League opposition. Instead, the Browns filled Sundays with exhibition games.

4. St. Louis and Brooklyn Exulted in It

On Sunday, October 18, 1885, the Browns defeated the Maroons 5–2 at Sportsman's Park before 10,000 spectators. Technically, the Maroons hadn't violated the League prohibition against playing on Sunday, since on Saturday "the Maroons disbanded as a League team and reorganized as an independent nine to play the Browns to exempt themselves from the League rules against Sunday games."[26]

Another 10,000 witnessed the Sunday game between the two teams on October 25, this time at the League team's home Union Park Grounds. The Browns won 6–0 as the Maroons could only venture four hits off the Browns.

The following spring the Maroons and Browns played three more Sunday games in their pre-season exhibition series on March 28, April 4, and April 11.

This relatively blatant disregard by the Maroons for the League gospel against Sunday baseball was too much for League officials. After a second lackluster season in the League after burning up the Union Association competition, the League moved to boot out the Maroons.

With the 1886 ouster of the St. Louis Maroons from the League for its Sunday-playing habits, the Sabbatarian movement in 1887 took aim at the pinnacle of Sunday baseball—and the unquestioned leader in Association play—the St. Louis Browns.

St. Louis, one of the two initiators of Sunday home games at the major league level in 1882, consistently drew large throngs to its Sunday games. In 1885, before the team's string of Association championships increased its stature, there was some minor Sabbatarian resistance in the city where the Continental Sabbath was a tradition. "According to a clerical report, intended to show that piety was waning, a Sunday survey tallied only 10,000 churchgoers, while on the same day, 20,000 crowded the ball parks, another 20,000 gathered at the beer gardens, and 5,000 assembled to hear two lectures by Colonel Bob Ingersoll, the great agnostic."[27]

By 1887, the team had won consecutive Association pennants in 1885 and 1886. The Browns had also captured the 1886 post-season "world series" championship at the expense of the League's best, the Chicago White Stockings. The Browns were in first place again in the summer of 1887, when Sabbatarians were able to take a different approach to their vigilance over stopping professional baseball play on the Lord's Day.

Earlier in 1887, the state legislature had modified the state's Sunday law, which went into effect on July 1, potentially impacting both the sale of liquor and baseball games on the Sabbath.

"If this reaches base ball, it will stop the running of street cars, shut up livery stables, and in fact will stop all character of amusements, entertainment and work now done on the Sabbath," one commentator noted. "It is safe to say this Hoosier hay seed law will never interfere with Sunday games in St. Louis. It was passed by a lot of country fakirs, who imagine they know something of city legislation, what the needs are for a metropolis."[28]

In June, though, Judge Noonan interpreted the state's law forbidding labor on Sunday to apply to baseball. But then in early July, Judge Noonan determined that beer and wine were "food," a necessity, so that waiters and others connected with its sale were performing necessary labor under the Sunday law. Whisky, however, was not "food" and therefore its sale was prohibited on Sunday.

The scheduled St. Louis game with Baltimore on Sunday, July 10, was in distinct jeopardy. While it was permissible to sell beer and wine on Sunday, it was seemingly not okay to play baseball on Sunday. The Sunday baseball issue was headed for a showdown.

"The question comes up as to whether a game of base ball is not as great a work of necessity as the running of a street car and whether a singer in a church choir is not just as amenable to the law as the opera singer in a [beer] garden," prosecuting attorney Claiborne said regarding the July 10 game at Sportsman's Park.[29]

If the baseball game was to be played, police chief Huebler was going to follow the orders of the Police Board issued on July 8. "We shall arrest Mr. Von der Ahe if he attempts to play a game. If the players then go on the field and attempt to resume their playing then we will arrest them just as we arrest barkeepers who try to run the saloon after the proprietor has been taken in."[30]

"President Von der Ahe of the St. Louis Browns clings to his determination to play the game with the Baltimores to-morrow afternoon at Sportsman's Park, or at least to attempt to play it," the *St. Louis Post-Dispatch* reported in its Saturday afternoon edition. "If he is not allowed and is arrested, which he will undoubtedly be according to Chief Huebler's statement, he will be in a position to test the question and obtain a decision as to the validity of the Sunday law with regard to base ball."[31]

Although understanding that the game was in doubt, 8,000 people did show up at Sportsman's Park on July 10 to see if the game would be stopped. The club gave patrons "sun checks," which were good for admission to any future game, if the game was halted.

With 25 mounted policemen on the grounds when the game started at 3:30, Sergeant Phillip Florrich promptly arrested Von der Ahe from his grandstand box, took him by carriage to the local police station, and booked him for breaking the Sunday law. Far from being unruly, the crowd at Sportsman's Park was good-natured about the arrest and simply yelled, "Play ball!"

4. St. Louis and Brooklyn Exulted in It 61

Von der Ahe had no problem posting the $100 bond for his release until the trial to be held that Friday, July 15, before Judge Noonan.

J. G. Lodge, one of Von der Ahe's attorneys, laid out his defense to newspapermen on the morning of July 11, saying that recreation was not prohibited under the Sunday law. "Recreation is a necessity," Lodge explained. "When this law was passed Missouri was not much of a manufacturing State. Her condition of life and her needs have changed. We will let the court interpret what is necessary. Perhaps it will hold that amusement is."[32]

At the trial on July 15, Sergeant Florrich, the arresting officer, provided more help to the defense than to the prosecution. Upon cross-examination by Von der Ahe's attorneys, Florrich said that during his 12 years being stationed as a policeman in the district near Sportsman's Park, "The conduct of the game and those who attended was always very orderly. This same excellent order was observable last Sunday when the arrests were made. People were as orderly there as at a theater." Florrich added he "had never known of a Sunday game of ball being interfered with before" and "had stopped the game last Sunday because of the order of this superiors and not because it was disorderly."[33]

Attorneys for Von der Ahe had lined up an impressive array of witnesses in his defense. Three property owners near Sportsman's Park said the ball games were not a nuisance. Charles Turner, who had helped build the original Grand Avenue Park 18 years earlier, testified that he "did not consider the game labor and it was not so regarded generally." When asked on cross-examination by prosecuting attorney Claiborne "if the game of baseball was not harder than driving a team of horses along a shady road," Turner remarked that "it required more exercise, but that it was not so irksome."[34]

To further counter the "labor" aspect of baseball, Congressman John O'Neill spoke on Von der Ahe's behalf and delivered an eloquent speech from the witness stand extolling the benefits of baseball as recreation for the workingman.

O'Neill "was a great witness and his testimony was a eulogy of the national game as the most entertaining and exhilarating sport one could witness or enjoy on earth," the *St. Louis Globe-Democrat* observed. "Ministers of the gospel had expressed themselves to him as being in favor of Sunday base-ball. Ladies visited the games ... the only noise was the cheers provoked by the enthusiasm over the brilliant plays."[35]

"During the present season, he had seen an aggregate of 50,000 or 60,000 people at the games and had not seen one drunken man nor one row," the *St. Louis Post-Dispatch* reported O'Neill's testimony. "Witness said he regarded the game as the most entertaining and exhilarating sport any person could witness." Lodge, Von der Ahe's attorney, said that O'Neill's statement was submitted as "the opinion of an expert, and not as a crank," to the roar of laughter in the courtroom and cries of order from the judge.[36]

In closing statements, prosecutor Claiborne tried to counter the impact of O'Neill's comments by emphasizing that "the players were servants of the defendant, his employees, and worked on that day for pay and not for recreation." Claiborne then helped sink his own case by saying, "The recreation was for the spectators, but the players labored and in doing so violated the law."[37]

Defense attorney Lodge rebutted Claiborne by saying, "The character of the labor in the [law] was manual labor and not the recreation kind used in any exercise or sport." Lodge went on to use an example. "A lecturer or speaker would have to think, read, perhaps study, and do the hardest kind of mental work on Sunday, but the law didn't prohibit that. That was not the kind of labor meant. The law was to protect the laborer, the servant, the craftsman from the imposition of a master."[38]

Judge Noonan seemed to be swayed by Lodge and O'Neill and changed his previous opinion:

> Our Supreme Court in 1876 decided that hunting game on Sunday was not work or labor within the statute. Since that case was decided, our Legislature has made hunting game a violation of the Sunday law. But they have not prohibited, either expressly or by construction, base ball carried on decently, orderly and quietly on Sunday. I might say in addition to this that the game was a reasonable sport and use of nature's powers, and while the evidence showed that money was taken and money paid to the players, it in my mind is not within the meaning of this statute any more than the paying of any piano player or singer that might come into the home of a citizen on Sunday to contribute to his entertainment. I therefore find the defendant, under the laws and evidence, not guilty, and discharge him.[39]

Noonan's verdict not only permitted Sunday baseball in St. Louis but also set the standard for its prohibition to be the state legislature's creation of a law making Sunday baseball illegal in Missouri. Given the public's love of Sunday baseball in the city of St. Louis, this was an inordinately high hurdle for Sunday-baseball opponents to overcome.

Although Sabbatarian groups in Missouri would mount future challenges to Sunday baseball, the 1887 decision in *State vs. Chris Von der Ahe* was never in serious jeopardy of being overturned.

With Sunday baseball firmly affixed in St. Louis, to be a foundation for major league baseball, other cities were now more energized to try to play Sunday baseball.

St. Louis Post-Dispatch headline in 1887 after St. Louis Browns owner Chris Von der Ahe was declared not guilty in his trial for staging a Sunday baseball game.

Following the Von der Ahe decision, Cleveland was the first major league team to mount an assault on the Sunday baseball prohibitions of its city.

Frank Robison, owner of the Cleveland club, was also a streetcar magnate. He was just as interested in filling streetcars as he was in filling seats at Association Park where his baseball team played. Sunday games were a way to do both, possibly at greater levels than during the workweek.

While the Ohio law that had thwarted Sunday games in Cleveland in 1885 was still in effect, Robison convinced the Cleveland Common Council to change its "marbles and quoits" ordinance to explicitly permit Sunday baseball, apparently hoping to overpower the state law. The Council passed such an ordinance to become effective July 29. Because the Cleveland club was then engaged in a road trip, Sunday games at Association Park would commence when the club returned to Cleveland, with the first Sunday game planned for August 21.

Obtaining the ability to play Sunday baseball in Cleveland was far more difficult than its geographic location would otherwise indicate, being plainly on the western side of the Appalachian Mountains and situated several hundreds of miles from the eastern seaboard. Cleveland was much closer in religious conviction to eastern cities such as Boston and Brooklyn, however, than it was to cities closer in proximity such as Cincinnati and Louisville.

The area around Cleveland was originally part of Connecticut, in what was called the Connecticut Western Reserve. In 1786, Congress had granted Connecticut land in northern Ohio in exchange for Connecticut ceding other land claims. Connecticut then sold the Ohio land to settlers to raise money for public education in Connecticut.

New England settlers to the Connecticut Western Reserve in the early 19th century brought with them the protestant religions of their Puritan forebears. "No other five thousand square miles of territory in the United States, lying in a body outside of New England, ever had, to begin with, so pure a New England population," one historian wrote.[40]

Congregationalists and Presbyterians dominated these early settlers, members of religious sects that had formal beliefs in the Sunday day of rest principle. Their ancestors formed the backbone of the Law and Order beliefs in Cleveland regarding Sunday baseball.

"When Sunday games come, I anticipate a nasty fight on the club by the Law and Order crowd," *Sporting Life* proclaimed. The weekly publication then mocked the Law and Order stance by remarking that the reason was "many of the masculine members of which play poker too late on Sunday morning to get up in time to see the Sunday afternoon games."[41]

To test the waters with Sunday baseball, Robison scheduled an amateur game at Association Park for Sunday, August 7, with the Graphics team from Cleveland taking on a team from nearby Akron.

The Law and Order League, however, was furious at the brazen attempt to play Sunday baseball, "notifying the Cleveland club that the Akron-Graphics game last Sunday would not be tolerated" and that they would block the August 21 game with the Metropolitan club.[42]

Robison scrambled to find an alternate site for the August 21 game that now seemed impossible to hold at Association Park. He settled on the Cedar Avenue Driving Park.

Baseball clubs sometimes used the local race track courses as baseball grounds, due to their expanse of grass within an enclosed area, existing seating (although limited in size), and name recognition as a destination. With limited area within the track's infield to set up a diamond, these factors didn't always translate into optimal playing conditions.

On a rainy August 21, the Metropolitans defeated Cleveland 7–5 at Cedar Avenue Driving Park, as the crowd of 2,500 was "a very respectable one and there was no unnecessary noise during the game." Many spectators came in horse-drawn carriages, which were "parked on the track beyond the outfielders" and apparently in play. In the sixth inning, Ed McKean "hit a ball over the carriages for three bases," while in the seventh inning Charlie Reipschlager hit a "drive over the carriages for two bases."[43]

Moving the game from Association Park to the Cedar Avenue Driving Park didn't allow the Cleveland club to escape prosecution. Second baseman John "Cub" Stricker, the team captain, was arrested after the game for playing baseball on Sunday and tried in police court on Thursday, August 25.

Prosecutor Estep simply contended that the July 29 city ordinance was illegal and invalid under the state statute prohibiting Sunday baseball. Stricker's attorney, Judge John Hutchins, argued eloquently otherwise, perhaps hoping to duplicate the results of Congressman O'Neill in the Von der Ahe trial six weeks earlier. Hutchins waxed on about the Romans practicing healthful games, eventually connecting to baseball and the changing Sabbath habits, as well as the need to provide amusements to young men to keep them from the saloons.

"Last Sunday, the Cleveland base ball association threw open its gates to the public that a game of base ball might be witnessed by scores of people who were anxious to see it," Hutchins said. "Our public libraries are open now [on Sunday] and hundreds enjoy themselves there. The parks are open, the street cars run, the German play houses

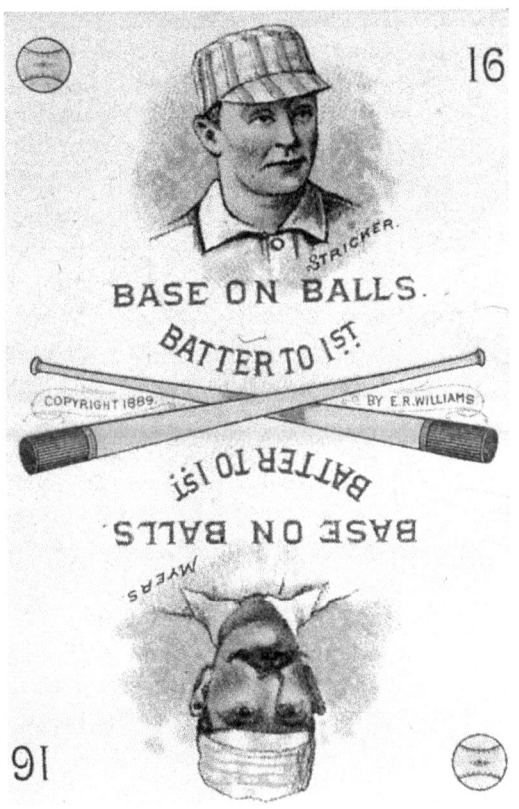

Cub Stricker, depicted here on a card from an 1889 baseball card game, was arrested in 1887 after the first attempt to play Sunday baseball at the major league level in the Cleveland area. (Transcendental Graphics, Boulder, Colorado)

were thrown open, and not long ago the Cyclorama threw open its doors on Sunday. These are all healthful and innocent avenues for the people to pass in and occupy their time."[44]

"The city council ... knew it was better for the workingmen to go to the ball grounds and see a quiet game than to frequent saloons," Hutchins expounded on Stricker's behalf. "The saloonkeepers all along the line to the ball grounds were among the chief ones who objected to the playing of ball on Sunday. Why? Because the game interfered with their profits. They were against it because men left their places and went to the ball grounds. The church and the saloons are against the playing of ball on Sunday. They are against it, but vary widely in their reasons. One works for the Lord; the other for the devil. The two elements occupy the same bed, as it were, against this playing of ball on Sunday."[45]

Judge Coates rejected the remarks of Hutchins and found Stricker guilty, imposing a fine of $10 and costs.

With Sunday baseball firmly affixed in the western cities of the Association, with the exception of Cleveland, Sunday baseball took steps forward in 1887 to establish a firmer position in the east.

Ridgewood Park was upgraded for the 1887 season, with a "new free stand" installed to handle larger crowds, which averaged about 6,500 per game that season, a significant increase over Sunday crowds in 1886. Sabbatarians managed to stop the April 17 game with the Metropolitans, as "a sudden moral streak fell upon the authorities," disappointing 8,000 people who had journeyed to Ridgewood to see the game.[46]

Sunday baseball returned the following Sunday, April 24, as nearly 10,000 saw Brooklyn defeat Baltimore 12–8. Crowds remained large after the team returned in June from a western road trip, as about 9,000 witnessed both the June 12 game with Cincinnati and the June 19 game with the Metropolitans. Crowds such as these boosted the stature of Brooklyn within the Association and rivaled that of St. Louis, then the king of Sunday baseball.

Although the June 19 game with the Metropolitans at Ridgewood attracted the largest crowd of the season for Brooklyn, the Metropolitan club had become the decided second choice of baseball spectators in Manhattan behind the League's New York Giants. John Day, who once owned both teams, left the Metropolitan team languishing when he shuttled its best players to the Giants after the 1884 season.

In its final days as a franchise, the Metropolitan club experimented with Sunday play across the Hudson River at the Monitor Grounds in Weehawken, New Jersey. These contests set the stage for Weehawken to eventually become a haven for Sunday baseball play for New York–based teams as well as other clubs in town as visiting teams.

On Sunday, September 4, Metropolitan scheduled a championship game with St. Louis at Weehawken. More than 6,000 people showed up to see the champion Browns squad at a facility that accommodated just 2,000. The overflow crowd lent new fervor to the bad reputation of Sunday baseball spectators, who were being stereotyped as thugs that couldn't control their bad behavior. Unruly Sunday crowds continued to undermine the Association to the benefit of the League.

Police had the overflow crowd line the field, forming a human fence, but "when the game opened the mob had invaded the playing ground, and neither first or third base could be seen from the grand stand." After an inning of this close proximity between players and spectators, umpire Ferguson "said that no base-ball could be played with such surroundings" and stopped the game.[47]

As the "lawless crowd of roughs" made a raid on the box office for a return of their money, "the St. Louis players got in their carriages to leave for New York, but they soon discovered their mistake," the *Brooklyn Daily Eagle* reported. "The crowd simply unhitched the horses and started to upset the carriages, players and all." When Von der Ahe promised that the St. Louis team would resume play, the crowd backed off.[48]

When Ferguson refused to restart the game after the disturbance, a substitute umpire was procured and another five innings were played as an exhibition game. St. Louis outscored Metropolitan 16–6, but "it was a miserable game, no batter being allowed more than a single base on any hit that went into the crowd."[49]

The Metropolitans tried Sunday baseball again the following Sunday, September 11, playing Louisville in half of a doubleheader. St. Louis was supposed to play the Cuban Giants in the other game, but "to the disgust of the crowd, however, Von der Ahe telegraphed that his team could not leave Philadelphia and over 8,000 of a pretty rough gathering were disappointed." Only about a thousand people stayed to watch the Louisville game.[50]

"There was a good force of police on hand at Weehawken yesterday and the crowd ... was held in check," the *New York Times* blandly reported the 10–6 Louisville victory. "In consequence, the game was played without any disruption."[51]

Sunday games at Weehawken were a disappointment all around for the Metropolitan club and resulted in a somewhat ignoble end to the dying franchise. Brooklyn bought out the Metropolitan club following the 1887 season. Since the Ridgewood facility for Sunday games worked well for Charlie Byrne and the Brooklyn club, and there were so many crowd control problems with the two Sunday games in New Jersey, Sunday games at the major league level in Weehawken wouldn't reappear for several years.

Sunday baseball got a huge boost from several actions voted on by the Association owners for the 1888 season.

Owners invited Kansas City into the Association to replace the defunct Metropolitan club, adding a fifth Sunday-playing city to the circuit to augment Brooklyn, Cincinnati, Louisville, and St. Louis. While crowds were never that large in Kansas City, its desire and ability to play Sunday baseball ensured that eastern teams could play every Sunday on their road swings through the west. With Cleveland as the fourth team on the western road trip, playing every Sunday was never assured because of its continuing inability to play Sunday home games. The Stricker decision in 1887 only solidified that concern.

Kansas City played its first Sunday home game on April 22, with Cincinnati winning 10–8 before 4,000 people in an error-filled contest. Cincinnati won despite making 14 errors, while Kansas City committed 9 errors.

Sunday games were obviously becoming a key to attracting a large seasonal attendance and thus directly correlated to an Association club being a profitable venture. St. Louis and Brooklyn were having the most success both at the gate and on the field. St. Louis had won three consecutive pennants and Brooklyn now attracted the most attendance, with St. Louis close behind. Sunday baseball largely drove both successes, as the two teams between them were responsible for 40 percent of the 1.3 million people who attended Association games in 1887 and nearly 50 percent of the 950,000 in attendance during 1888.

To assuage the other clubs not legally able to play at home on Sunday, and keep the Association alive, Brooklyn owner Charlie Byrne proposed once more to up the ante for the share of the gate that went to the visiting team. Byrne proposed that the visitor's share be the greater of 30 percent of the gate or the current $65 guarantee, with double the guarantee on Sunday to $130. This time, owners agreed with the proposal.[52]

Of course, Byrne wasn't being solely magnanimous with his fellow owners. The new visitor's share wasn't all that generous, since the Association had adopted the League standard of a 50-cent admission rate, hoping to capitalize on its success to date. Byrne also received 19 Sunday playing dates for Brooklyn on the 1888 schedule as the only Sunday-playing club in the east (clubs in the west had 12 or 13 Sunday games).

Sunday ball was played every Sunday at Ridgewood Park except when Brooklyn was traveling in the west. This included the first ten Sundays on the 1888 schedule, April 22 through June 24. When Brooklyn played road games in the east, the club arranged for its own one-game road trips back to Brooklyn to play Sunday games at Ridgewood Park.

4. St. Louis and Brooklyn Exulted in It 69

For the May 13 game at Ridgewood with the Athletics, the two teams trained north from Philadelphia where they had played a four-game series. After the Sunday game, Brooklyn then headed west to Cleveland and the Athletic club south to Baltimore. To cap the Sunday streak on June 24 after an extended home stand (including a record crowd over 10,500 on June 3 for the St. Louis game), Brooklyn came in from Philadelphia to play Baltimore on Sunday before heading west for Louisville after the game.

This renewed emphasis on Sunday baseball spurred creative thought on the part of Association club owners that were drawing smaller crowds than the league's elite teams.

First, some games were transferred to sites where attendance would likely be greater than at the scheduled home team's grounds (particularly on a Sunday date). This approach gave the "home" team greater revenue from the 30 percent visitor's share than it would get with 70 percent of the home team share after making good on the $65 guarantee.

At least 17 games were transferred to Cincinnati for this reason. During the 1886–1888 period, Cincinnati played more Sunday games than any other day of the week, despite not playing on Sunday for the first half of 1886. Cincinnati played 41 games on Sunday in that three-year stretch, with Saturday the next most popular at 39, followed by Wednesday at 35 (Monday was the least popular, at 17). The average attendance on Sunday was more than double that of any other weekday. Sunday games averaged 4,075 while the Saturday average was 1,843 people.[53]

Second, owners located in non–Sunday-playing cities exercised additional creativity to devise ways to play Sunday baseball. For instance, the Athletic club of Philadelphia looked across the Delaware River, saw Gloucester, New Jersey, at the other end of the ferry that crossed the river and built ball grounds in another state to stage Sunday games.

Gloucester was a popular beach resort and horse-racing venue. Adding baseball grounds would capitalize on a popular area for Sunday excursions, including existing transportation arrangements, just as the Brooklyn club had done by using the grounds at the popular Ridgewood destination.

"New grounds in Gloucester are located within a short distance of the ferry, directly in back of Thompson's Hotel," *Sporting Life* noted that May. "The ground is 400 by 600 feet. It is enclosed by a high board fence, and open seats to accommodate 3,500 people have been erected. A new grandstand, capable of seating 3,500 people, is to be built at once, and the accommodations are to be first class in every respect."[54]

On May 16, the Gloucester City Council passed a resolution to permit ball playing on Sunday. The Athletic club then scheduled an exhibition game with Baltimore for the following Sunday, May 20. The game was wildly more popular than anyone could have imagined beforehand.

"Whatever may be said of the morality of Sunday ball playing, there is no question of the popularity of the innovation in this city if the enormous attendance at Gloucester last Sunday is any indication," *Sporting Life* remarked on the first Philadelphia-area major league baseball game on Sunday.[55]

A crowd mobbed the undermanned ferry house on the South Street wharf on the Philadelphia side of the Delaware River, eventually crashing it down, while others "hung on the edges of the boats and lined the beach from early in the day until the last boat started for Philadelphia." By 3:00, about 10,000 people were in the ball grounds, as people jumped fences and even burrowed through the soft sand under the fence to gain entrance to the ball grounds.[56]

The game lasted only one inning, though. The Athletics scored one run in the top of the first inning, after Tom Poorman "was sent to first on balls," Harry Stovey made a hit ("the seas of humanity sent up an unearthly yell"), and Mike Sullivan made another hit to score Poorman. After the first three Baltimore batters were retired, "the crowd broke onto the field and covered the diamond." When the crowd refused to move back and allow the game to proceed, the spectators in the reserved seats (who paid an extra 10 cents for a cushion) "threw their cushions down on the yelling mob below." The cushions were thrown back at the reserved seating area and a "cushion battle" ensued for the next 15 minutes, as all hope of completing the game ended at that point.[57]

Crowds were a bit more reticent for the next two Sunday exhibition games, as the pure novelty of Sunday baseball wore off. Even with an exhibition format on May 27, the game attracted 5,000 patrons to see Athletic pitcher Ed Seward throw a five-hitter to shutout Kansas City 9–0.

Two weeks later, on Sunday, June 10, the Athletics played their "first championship game at Gloucester," defeating Baltimore 11–4 before a crowd of 3,000. The grandstand at the Gloucester grounds was finally completed, with 4,000 open seats in place. "All the spectators were accommodated with seats, but none of them were shaded," the *Philadelphia Inquirer* remarked about a ball ground built on a beach. "The sun boiled down in torrid rays and its reflection on the new boards and sandy soil made the temperature inside the grounds almost unbearable."[58]

As the Athletics departed for a western road trip, the club thought it had played its first Sunday game that counted in the Association standings. They were wrong. Association president Wheeler Wyckoff disallowed the results of the June 10 game at Gloucester, contending that the game hadn't been properly transferred from its previously scheduled day to the Sunday date.

The first Gloucester game officially in the Association record books was played on August 5, when Seward threw another shutout against Kansas City, this time yielding just four hits, in a 6–0 Athletic victory before 4,250. Denny Lyons hit two home runs to lead the Athletic batting attack.

With Philadelphia having successfully navigated the Sunday baseball waters by playing on a Sunday-only grounds in a different state, Frank Robison set out to find another way to play Sunday baseball in Cleveland as a way to boost the flagging attendance at his club's games. Attendance averaged just 700 a game at the end of a 24-game home stand in June.

"The Sunday game idea is not flourishing to any great extent," *The Sporting News* wrote in June, as the 1887 Stricker decision made it futile to try to play Sunday baseball within Cleveland proper. "The suburban ground scheme is drifting along and bids fair to be dually abandoned and it now looks as if Cleveland wouldn't have any Sunday games this season."[59]

Robison hit upon the idea of avoiding any Sabbatarian interference from the Cleveland religious faithful by playing on a Sunday-only grounds far outside the city limits, not just a slight way beyond the city limits as the Sunday-only grounds in Philadelphia and Brooklyn were. It was a risky idea, though, as it would be a difficult journey for city residents to reach such an isolated ball grounds in those days predating the automobile. Railroad connections would be vitally important.

In need of averting financial plight with his baseball club, Robison convinced the local railway line—the New York, Pennsylvania, and Ohio—and an amusement park operator to erect a ball ground. The site was 20 miles south of Cleveland at Geauga Lake, a popular resort for Sunday excursions that were just becoming fashionable as amusements began to legitimately encroach upon a day once reserved for devotion to church services.

Six games were slated to be played at Geauga Lake—two each in July, August, and September—by the Cleveland club, which had won just one-third of its 60 games played to that point and was in seventh place. To allay any possible Sabbatarian concerns about Sunday baseball at the Geauga Lake grounds, Robison put the word out to the newspapers that the games there weren't meant to appeal to pious, church-going Cleveland citizens.

"Great Sunday crowds are drawn at the expense of steady weekday attendance," *Sporting Life* wrote, espousing a principle that would appeal to Sunday baseball opponents. "The Cleveland club's new Sunday grounds will not come so broadly into the latter trouble. They are so located as to draw on Sunday from territory to which weekday games are closed."[60]

Cleveland opened the Geauga Lake Sunday schedule on July 22, defeating Baltimore 6–2 before 4,000 spectators, double the seating capacity at the grounds. Despite the line about attracting spectators from non–Cleveland areas, the team did count on customers taking the train from Cleveland to Geauga Lake.

Train problems, however, beset the operation. Four trains were scheduled to leave the NYP&O depot to reach the game before its 3:00 start— at 9:30, 10:40, 12:45, and 1:15. Tickets cost 75 cents and included fare both ways and admission to the game. The 1:15 train didn't arrive at the grounds until 3:30, so its fares didn't see two innings of the game. Even worse, the return trip "took ninety minutes to come from the lake to Cleveland, as the train stopped at every crossing and for every freight train."[61]

On the following Sunday, July 29, "railroad accommodations were much improved" with train service leaving Cleveland at earlier times. St. Louis defeated Cleveland 7–4 before 3,500 spectators in the second Sunday game at Geauga Lake. The July 29 game was the last at the resort site, though, as the difficult access to the Geauga Lake grounds made the Sunday proposition less viable than originally thought.[62]

Even as the Geauga Lake grounds were being built, "an athletic park, with a good ball field, is being established at Newburgh, four miles from the center of town. It is not unlikely that the Sunday games of 1889 will be played upon it. Newburgh is a liberal quarter and more easily reached than Geauga Lake." The ball grounds at Beyerle's Park in Newburgh opened on July 15, with a Sunday game between the Graphics and Malleables.[63]

By August, Robison was angling to sell Cleveland players and the franchise altogether, and he canceled the scheduled two Sunday games that month. "We cannot hold together on a twenty-five cent tariff," Robison said regarding the Association's recent move to abandon the 50 cent standard in favor of its previous quarter-ball policy. "We are now over $16,000 in debt besides our $10,000 capital and we do not propose to go any deeper. This is a good fifty cent ball town and a League club would draw better here."[64]

With the hassle to get to Geauga Lake, and the revenue from games there not overwhelming, Robison tried Sunday games in September at the Newburgh location. On September 2, Cleveland trounced Louisville 11–1 at Beyerle's Park. But the facilities there posed just as many problems as had those at Geauga Lake.

"The crowd was 2,500 strong and the arrangements bad," the *Cleveland Plain Dealer* reported. The spectators spilled onto the field and the Louisville players protested long and hard in the third inning until the crowd was cleared from the field and ground rules established to offset the playing interference. "If games are to go on at Beyerle's Park, there must be a dozen policemen on the ground and barriers erected to keep the crowd on foul ground." The grounds were also "rather rough and full of large pebbles, making infield stops very uncertain."[65]

Cleveland defeated Kansas City 7–5 in an exhibition game on September 9 at Beyerle's Park. Robison had wanted to play Cincinnati on September 9 to attract a large crowd to see the in-state rivalry, but Kansas City nixed that idea. "Kansas City acted badly," the *Cleveland Plain Dealer* wrote. "They pleaded a previous contract and prevented Cincinnati from staying over [from Saturday] and then refused to play a championship game."[66]

Whether Robison really was losing money, or just courting the National League for a better opportunity, September 9 was the last game before the club called it quits on Sunday baseball—and the American Association—when Robison made good on his semi-veiled threat. Cleveland bolted the Association to join the National League for the 1889 season by taking over the Detroit franchise.

September 1888 was a height of Sunday baseball expansion at the major league level, as seven of the eight teams in the American Association were able to schedule home games on the Lord's Day. Baltimore was the lone exception to Sunday baseball play. It would be more than 20 years, in 1911, before seven major league teams could once again schedule Sunday games on their home grounds on a regular basis.

During the 1889 season, Sabbatarian groups began to gain an upper hand in the battle being waged with major league baseball owners over the propriety of professional baseball on the Lord's Day. Of particular help to the Sabbatarian effort was the Sunday rest-day bill introduced in the U.S. Senate in 1888 by New Hampshire Senator Henry Blair, who was chairman of the Senate Committee on Education and Labor.[67]

Through the combined efforts of labor unions and Sabbatarian groups, a petition campaign for a national Sunday day of rest swept across the country, producing more than 14 million signatures. "By expressing their conviction that a day of rest was a citizen's right, Sabbatarians were able to enlist the support of various labor organizations across the country," McCrossen wrote in her book, *Holy Day, Holiday*. "Together they entered campaigns against Sunday labor in steel and chemical manufacture, gas companies, breweries, bakeries and barber shops, gaining the trust of working people. Sympathy and support for these efforts were abundant; numerous editorials, didactic stories, and forums decried Sunday labor in workshops and on the railroad."[68]

The Sunday rest-day bill appeared to have a good chance to become the law of the land. If so, Sunday baseball would become illegal everywhere, not just in the east and parts of the midwest, since "Blair's Sunday rest law aimed to prohibit most of the recreations and activities that characterized working people's Sundays."[69]

It was too soon for Sunday baseball to take hold with America. The concept was still seen as radical by much of the eastern section of the country. Immigrants were becoming more populous in the nation by the 1880s, but they had not yet obtained any significant political power. Sunday baseball would need the credibility of play in the larger cities of the National League and a nudge by the progressive movement before the entire country would be ready to embrace it.

But first, the baseball owners needed to wrest control of the direction of Sunday baseball from the Sabbatarians who advocated the Sunday rest-day bill.

Chapter 5

SABBATARIANS HATED IT

Seven of the eight Association teams scheduled Sunday home games for the 1889 season. To replace the Cleveland club that defected to the League, the Association signed up another Ohio team that could play Sunday baseball—Columbus—to maintain its strong presence on the diamond for Sabbath games.

While a similar number of teams had played Sunday baseball in the latter stages of the 1888 season, there was a distinct difference in the nature of Sunday ball in 1889. On the upswing throughout the Association's first seven years, Sunday baseball began to experience definite cracks in its foundation during the 1889 season.

To many Sabbatarian groups, "exorcising the demon of Sunday baseball seemed a clear and absolute necessity" at this time when a National Sunday Law that would mandate a day of rest for the entire nation was under consideration in the U.S. Senate. "The nation stood at a moral crossroads, they argued," George Gipe wrote in a 1974 *Sports Illustrated* article. "If America did not draw the line at Sunday baseball, the country's future would be downhill all the way, a la Rome and numerous other hedonistic societies."[1]

The cracks were not confined only to the east either, as would be expected given the region's historical attitude toward the piety of Sunday, but were also more noticeable in the west. As the 1889 season progressed, cracks in the mantle of Sunday baseball cropped up in Brooklyn and Cincinnati, two outposts that were essential to continued Association prosperity.

In Brooklyn, the good reputation that Sunday baseball had achieved over the previous three seasons at Ridgewood Park began to tarnish in 1889.

When an unruly crowd at the May 5 game overran the field, the umpire awarded the game to the Athletic club by forfeit, 9–0. With a huge crowd of 12,614 on hand at Ridgewood Park, many people had encircled the field. In the bottom of the sixth inning with Athletic ahead 5–1 after just scoring four runs in the top part of the inning, it seems that Athletic outfielders Curt Welch and Harry Stovey were looking to lock in the victory right then and there. Welch and Stovey told the crowd that it could move in closer.

When umpire Holland instructed Brooklyn president Charlie Byrne to move the crowd back, but Byrne couldn't entice the crowd to move, the Athletics exercised their right to leave the field. Holland first declared the game a draw (not being totally familiar with the rules), but the Association later changed the decision (correctly) to be a forfeit.

Byrne claimed unsuccessfully that it was an "orderly crowd provoked into action," and then later pressed to have Welch removed from the team for "conduct unbecoming a ballplayer."[2]

Another forfeiture at the September 8 game, this time the 9–0 victory awarded to Brooklyn due to the failure of the St. Louis club to show up at the grounds, may have been the last straw for Brooklyn opponents of Sunday baseball.

"Between 15,000 and 20,000 people went to the Ridgewood Park, Long Island, to witness this game," the *Sporting Life* correspondent reported. "The crowd had been admitted to the grounds free, [with] admission to the grand stand only being charged. To amuse the crowd, an exhibition game was arranged."[3]

The St. Louis refusal to even show up at Ridgewood Park for the September 8 Sunday match stemmed from the infamous "candlelight game" the day before.

With St. Louis ahead 4–2, manager Comiskey withdrew his team from the field claiming it was too dark to continue play. Umpire Goldsmith, however, disagreed with Comiskey's opinion on the level of light at Washington Park and decided that the game should continue. When St. Louis refused to take the field again, Goldsmith forfeited the game to Brooklyn.

What may have prompted Goldsmith to ignore the looming darkness, though, was the ostentatious display by the St. Louis team of its opinion about the sufficiency of daylight to continue the game. "At the end of the eighth [inning], the St. Louis players on the bench, reinforced by two or three of their followers, took out a few tallow candles and lit them," the *Brooklyn Daily Eagle* reported. "They evidently thought that they had the game well in hand and were holding a wake over the Brooklyn corpse."[4]

St. Louis was liable for a $1,500 fine for its no-show appearance, but that was of small consolation to Byrne, whose Brooklyn club lost a $3,000 payday due to the non-appearance. To substitute for the aborted Sunday game on September 8, Brooklyn split up the team into two squads for an exhibition game. The Foutz's Nine defeated the O'Brien's Nine 7–5 in a five-inning match. Manager Billy McGunnigle filled in at shortstop for the O'Brien's Nine, collecting three hits.[5]

Von der Ahe had his reasons for the St. Louis no-show. "If, with their police arrangements at Washington Park on Saturday, they could not protect us, how would they do it at Ridgewood without police?" Von der Ahe inquired of the newspapers. "I was stoned at Ridgewood last year and I don't want any more of it. My players told me last night that they wouldn't go to Ridgewood for $1,000 each. They were afraid of their lives."[6]

Although Brooklyn was on its way to winning the Association pennant in 1889, sentiment was brewing to stop Sunday baseball at Ridgewood. Less than a week after the shenanigans with the St. Louis games, a grand jury was being empanelled to look into the Sunday issue.

"It is hardly probable that base ball on Sunday will be tolerated at Ridgewood another season," the *Brooklyn Daily Eagle* reported in a September article "The End of Ridgewood" about the likely grand jury in Queens County to investigate the Sunday parks. "And with the abatement of ball playing will go under the parks where music is played and dancing and beer drinking are the chief pleasures. Some of these latter places would shame the worst evils of the Bowery."[7]

A. A. Robbins, president of the Kings County Sabbath Observance Society, announced that he'd present witnesses to testify that the Ridgewood Amusement Company "maintains a public nuisance by inducing illegal assemblages and holding forbidden sports on Sunday." About 25,000 people went to Ridgewood every Sunday by horse-car routes or elevated railroad.

"I do not see why we should allow Brooklyn and New York people to do things at Ridgewood that wouldn't be tolerated in either city," one grand juror told the *Brooklyn Daily Eagle*. "Why don't they play ball at Washington Park or the Polo Grounds? I tell you the Grand Jury means business."[8]

The Ridgewood Amusement Company was eventually found guilty of violating Sunday laws and fined $500, "which effectively stopped commercial Sunday baseball in the metropolitan area" of New York.[9]

Brooklyn played its last regular season Sunday game at Ridgewood on October 6, 1889, defeating the Athletic club 9–0 before a small gathering of 2,488 as "none but the enthusiastic class of patrons known as cranks went out to Ridgewood." Each team collected only four hits, but Athletic pitcher Sadie McMahon issued 14 bases on balls to give Brooklyn an edge.[10]

In between games of the post-season series with the League champion New York Giants, Brooklyn played an exhibition game on Sunday, October 20. Brooklyn defeated Baltimore 6–2 before 3,000 at Ridgewood, rallying for four runs in the ninth inning to win. This was Brooklyn's last Sunday game at Ridgewood, as the planned October 27 game was rained out.[11]

Matters in Cincinnati took a more ominous turn on the Sunday baseball issue, for a city whose citizens generally advocated the Continental Sabbath.

Cincinnati management had tried to appease the local Sabbatarians for the past several years, in 1886 even declining to schedule Sunday home games prior to the July 4 holiday. With rumors circulating for weeks that both Cincinnati and Brooklyn would abandon the Association and defect to the League for the 1890 season, the Cincinnati Law and Order Society charged forward to take action in August.

The last Sunday home game for Cincinnati in the Association was played on August 11, as 8,000 "orderly spectators" viewed a 4–3 defeat at the hands of Baltimore. "Block-headed base-running, stupid fielding, combined with the element of hard luck, was all that kept the Reds [in fifth place] from clinching a good hold on a place right up on the heels of Baltimore [in third place]."[12]

To appease the Law and Order Society, Cincinnati management looked to move its Sunday games elsewhere. Not only did the ball grounds need to be in a "Sunday friendly" area, but the grounds needed to be served by adequate transportation so that spectators could get to the game.

The club initially settled on Ludlow, Kentucky, located across the Ohio River from Cincinnati, where ferry service could bring patrons to the Sunday games. After the club signed an option to use Ludlow Base-Ball Park for Sunday games the rest of the 1889 season, and rescheduled the August 18 game with Columbus to Ludlow, local authorities in Kentucky stepped in to prevent the game.[13]

Next on the list of possible Sunday sites was Hamilton, Ohio, located 25 miles north of Cincinnati, where the local minor league team in the Tri-State League did play Sunday games outside the city limits. With train service available to Hamilton, the Cincinnati club arranged for the August 25 game with Brooklyn to be played there. The club had also arranged with the local authorities to play the game unimpeded—or so they thought.

Before the game, managers and players of both teams "were taken and arraigned before a white whiskered, red nosed country squire, who informed them that they were under arrest for violating the state law that forbids the playing of ball on Sunday," the *Brooklyn Daily Eagle* reported. "That was all of the legal interference [supposed to occur] at that time."[14]

About 5,000 people crowded into the Hamilton ball grounds, where many had to stand around the perimeter of the field to watch the game. In the fourth inning of a 2–2 tie game, with Joe Visner on first base and

Brooklyn's star pitcher Bob Caruthers at bat, several police officers led by Chief Lindsey walked onto the grounds.

"When the squad of bluecoats marched through the park gate they were vigorously cheered by the spectators, most of them laboring under the impression that the minions of the law had come to preserve order and to put the crowd back," the *Cincinnati Enquirer* related the incident. "As the errand of the police became apparent, howls and groans rent the air."[15]

The police had come to arrest the players in the game, not to move the standing-room crowd farther from the diamond. In the confusion, spectators swarmed onto the field, allowing several players to escape the grasp of police. Several Cincinnati players ran to the train depot to get out of town. Brooklyn's Bob Ferguson quickly blended into the crowd to escape detection, as he "pulled off his gray cap, stacked his time worn straw upon his head and sauntered off to view the scenery from the beautiful hills far away."[16]

Police managed to capture Cincinnati players John Reilly, Hick Carpenter, Elmer Smith, and Kid Baldwin, along with several Brooklyn players. The players were taken in a covered wagon to Mayor Dick's office, who "evidently expected the 'pinch' to occur, for he was at his desk, something unusual for a municipal officer on a Sunday."[17]

Cincinnati had managed to pacify the Law and Order Society of its own city, but was done in by the Law and Order League of Hamilton, which made the complaint that precipitated the arrests.

President Stern of the Cincinnati club disregarded his lawyer's advice to fight the arrests in court and instead asked the mayor to set a suitable fine that Stern could pay for all 18 players in the game, not just those players the police were able to chase down.

"The mayor at first thought $13 per person would about fix the offense, but afterward reduced it to $5 plus costs, or $8.30 per man," the *Cincinnati Enquirer* reported. "Stern offered to give his check for the entire amount, but this was not acceptable. He therefore returned to the hotel and a few moments later counted out $149.40 into the mayor's hand, payment in full for both the Cincinnati and Brooklyn players."[18]

After the incident concluded, Stern told the newspapers, "Had I known that we were to be arrested, I would not have played here and would have telegraphed to stop the excursion. I was given to understand that there would be no interference of any kind."[19]

One of the Cincinnati players arrested was John Reilly, a Cincinnati native who had a successful baseball career with his hometown teams. Reilly initially starred for several independent teams in Cincinnati before playing nine years with the Cincinnati team in the Association, beginning in

1883 and continuing through 1891 when the team had joined the National League.

Reilly posted a .289 career batting average while holding down the first base position for Cincinnati, including five seasons that were above .300. In 1884, after being arrested for playing Sunday baseball in Indianapolis, Reilly had his best year, batting .339 with 152 hits, both good for second best in the Association behind Dave Orr.

"Reilly was an intelligent and self-disciplined man who took good care of himself and was devoted to his team," David Bell wrote about Reilly in *Baseball's First Stars*. "His intensity put him at odds sometimes with less stable and team-oriented players. Fred Lewis, a brilliant outfielder who was drowning his career in a sea of alcohol, reportedly ended his brief career with the Reds in 1886 by punching Reilly in the face."[20]

Reilly worked as an artist at Strobridge Lithographing in the off-season

John Reilly was one of the Cincinnati ball players that police managed to nab during arrests at an 1889 Sunday baseball game played in Hamilton, Ohio. (Transcendental Graphics, Boulder, Colorado)

and after his playing days were over, probably earning more as an artist than as a ballplayer.

Cincinnati was headed off for a September road trip, but Stern was forced to cancel the team's last two Sunday baseball games scheduled for October 6 and 13.

Despite the indignity of Stern's check being refused by the local mayor, the Hamilton Sunday incident seemed to be a win-win situation. The Law and Order Society could claim a victory for the Sabbatarian cause, while Cincinnati management solidified its argument for why the team needed to leave the Association and join the League.

"Since our Sunday games were stopped, we lost $15,000," Stern stated after the 1889 season concluded. "We would have made [it] up during the week days at fifty cents had we been in the League."[21]

With Brooklyn and Cincinnati both seemingly unable to schedule Sunday baseball games for the 1890 season, the two clubs bolted the Association to join the National League once the 1889 season had concluded.

Brooklyn and Cincinnati weren't the only teams to abandon the Association for the 1890 season, Baltimore and Kansas City did as well, but to join minor leagues. It seems odd today that a major league team would choose to downsize its ambitions by joining a less prestigious minor league, but such moves made financial sense in 1890 as three major leagues vied for the economic dollar of baseball patrons that year.

Discontent among the players for the reserve clause led to the formation of the Players League in 1890, a third major league to compete with the National League and the American Association. While there were enough players to stock 24 major league teams, there were not nearly enough interested spectators to make that many teams profitable.

In addition to Sunday baseball obstacles and the rise of the Players League, another contributing factor to Brooklyn and Cincinnati leaving the Association was the dominance of Association play by the St. Louis Browns and the insufferable attitude of its owner, Chris Von der Ahe. St. Louis may have reaped the largest financial rewards from Sunday baseball, and dodged the potential shutdown of its Sunday baseball moneymaker in Von der Ahe's 1887 Sunday baseball trial, but the success of the St. Louis Browns ultimately led to the demise of the Association. The rise of the Players League simply escalated the Association's death.

The Association was the only one of the three major leagues in 1890 to play Sunday baseball. Unlike the Union Association that had played Sunday baseball in 1884 in its attempt to secure a sustainable position as a major league, the Players League in 1890 did not play baseball on the Lord's Day (although it did permit on-premise beer sales). Many of the players that defected to the Players League were National League veterans and had become accustomed to the League's policy that disdained Sunday play.

As the commercial nature of Sunday baseball was more widely recognized, local Sabbatarian organizations had taken this opening to relegate the Sunday game to "play" by amateurs, as courts began to rule consistently that the professional game on the Sabbath was "work" and thus violated state laws prohibiting work on Sunday.

With Brooklyn and Cincinnati leaving the Association for the League, St. Louis became the primary proponent for Sunday baseball in the Association. St. Louis, therefore, became a lighting rod for Sunday baseball opponents to attack, as Sunday-playing Louisville and Columbus drew much smaller Sunday crowds in their less-populated cities.

League owners no doubt fueled the ire for Von der Ahe among other Association owners to help bring about the collapse of the Association. League owners may have also abetted the Sabbatarian causes to defeat Sunday baseball, which would have been a sure-fire method to bring the Association to its knees.

The success of Sunday baseball in the Association during the 1882–1889 period, unfortunately, helped to befall the Association. The more the Association tried to use Sunday baseball as the tool to heal its financial woes in 1890 and 1891, the more the Sabbatarians were victorious.

With Baltimore now departed from the circuit—the last of the Association clubs that didn't play Sunday home games—the Association adopted a policy for the 1890 season to require all clubs to play Sunday home games. This was a requirement for the four new clubs joining the Association that season.

Toledo, Rochester, and Syracuse all moved up from the International Association to join the Association, with the fourth new club another Brooklyn team to replace the pennant-winning, top-drawing Brooklyn club that had defected to the League. With the Athletic club expected to be in a precarious position in Philadelphia battling competitors from both the National League and Players League, the Association moved to establish a new club in Brooklyn to serve as the eastern flagship club.

This all-inclusive Sunday baseball policy would be a challenging task for the Association. All four new teams were in states that had laws restricting Sunday activities, which had been recently applied to stop Sunday baseball. But the Association had little choice but to go with smaller cities, since the Players League had spotted teams in most of the major cities, making it financial suicide for the Association to attempt to place a third entry in such locales.

When the Association schedule was released on March 14 at its league meeting at the Leland Hotel in Syracuse all teams were slated to play Sunday baseball except the Athletic club of Philadelphia. There was hope that further Sunday games in Gloucester, New Jersey, could be arranged, but some New Jersey courts had ruled that baseball could not be legally played on Sunday, jeopardizing the Athletic games at the Sunday haven in Gloucester.[22]

5. Sabbatarians Hated It

Following the 1889 Sabbatarian success in squelching Sunday baseball in Brooklyn and Cincinnati, the Association's 1890 push for Sunday baseball did little to enhance its acceptance and most likely set back the Sunday baseball movement for several years.

Toledo experimented with Sunday baseball in an April 13 exhibition game with Akron. Toledo handily defeated the cross-state visitors 13–0, and then began its off-field battle with the local constabulary. When its case for playing baseball on Sunday was called in court the following Thursday, though, the judge postponed it until May 2.

"On that date, it may be postponed because public sentiment here is very favorable to Sunday base ball and if the right course is pursued, there will probably be no more trouble," the Toledo correspondent to *Sporting Life* wrote. He added that the club was taking every precaution to have orderly games, emphasizing its liquor policy as the club "would not permit the sale of any conversation water on the grounds."[23]

The clergy helped Toledo in its quest to play Sunday baseball, however, rather than oppose it as many men of the cloth did in those years to support Sabbatarian efforts.

On Sunday, April 27, Father Quigley of St. Francis de Sales Church said from the pulpit that "everybody needed harmless Sunday recreation, that it was good for the soul and good for the body." Father Quigley said that he "did not consider Sunday base ball sinful." He didn't want members to neglect their church duties, "but saw no harm in the boys going to a ball game after they had attended church."[24]

Toledo had no further trouble with its Sunday baseball play for the 1890 season. The club played its first Sunday home game on May 4, defeating Columbus 11–3 in chilly weather as a crowd of 7,000 people shivered through the game.

While Toledo experienced little resistance to Sunday baseball during the 1890 season, the same could not be said of either the new Syracuse or Rochester franchises.

Each team used Sunday-only grounds. Rochester played its Sunday games at Windsor Beach, located about 10 miles north of Rochester on the shores of Lake Ontario in the town of Irondequoit. Syracuse played its Sunday games at Three Rivers, located about 15 miles northwest of Syracuse on a rail route to the confluence of the Oswego and Oneida Rivers.

Neither Syracuse nor Rochester got off to an auspicious start with Sunday baseball, as both their initial Sunday games scheduled for May 4 were canceled due to bad weather.

"A dense fog hung over the Windsor beach ball grounds yesterday, an icy Canadian wind blew across the diamond and a drizzling, misty rain fell at intervals during the day," the *Rochester Herald* reported of the aborted May 4 Sunday contest, where players had donned heavy winter overcoats. "But in spite of all these drawbacks, nearly 500 of the most rabid ball cranks went down to the lakeside to see the game between the Rochesters and the Athletics should they be so foolhardy as to play."[25]

Balky spring weather in upstate New York made Sunday baseball a perilous undertaking, even before the Sabbatarians got involved.

Of its scheduled 13 Sunday games, Rochester was slated to play six straight Sunday home games from May 4 through June 8. The club managed to get in just four of those games, however, as the other two were cancelled by the elements.

Sunday baseball made its debut on May 11, when 5,500 people went to Windsor Beach to watch Rochester defeat Syracuse 10–1. Rochester native Will Calihan pitched Rochester to victory, yielding just seven hits to Syracuse, while Ted Scheffler had three hits for the home team.

While Windsor Beach was far from the majority of inhabitants of the city of Rochester, reducing the risk of opposition to Sunday play, its proximity to Lake Ontario hindered its ability to be a first-class ball ground. The lakeside grounds had a difficult time absorbing the wet weather, which had a negative effect on playing conditions for the Sunday games.

"The grounds were in very bad condition. Whenever the ball [was] struck in the outfield it stopped dead still, not rolling an inch," the *Rochester Herald* described the field conditions on May 11. "Occasionally, a fielder would run into a small lake in the outfield and the water would splash into the air, showering him generously."[26]

Despite the poor field conditions, spectators still flocked to the Sunday games at Windsor Beach. A crowd of 5,500 attended the inaugural Sunday game on May 11, and crowds of 3,000 to 4,000 attended the next three Sunday games. Rochester, however, proceeded to lose all three contests.

At Syracuse, before the 1890 season even began, the people of Phoenix in Oswego County, near the Three Rivers ball grounds, met in a church and raised $1,500 to engage a lawyer to talk to the district attorney and the sheriff's office to prevent the Sunday games. There was also talk that the Rome, Watertown, and Ogdensburg Railroad might not run Sunday excursion trains to Three Rivers, which would have ended Sunday baseball for Syracuse, since there was "no way to get to Three Rivers except for driving 12 miles." In 1890, that was a significant distance by horse-drawn wagon.[27]

After the postponement of the May 4 game, the first Sunday game at Three Rivers was played on May 18 when Syracuse defeated St. Louis 11–9 before about 3,000 spectators. The same wet weather that hampered the

Windsor Beach grounds for Rochester also inflicted Syracuse at Three Rivers. At the May 18 game, the infield conditions were so poor that the game was played on a makeshift diamond marked off in the outfield.[28]

The following Sunday still found "the grounds in wretched condition" at Three Rivers, as Syracuse lost to Louisville 14–12 on May 25. Syracuse banged out 20 hits but also made seven errors in the field. Worst still, "at the conclusion of the game, part of the grand stand fell in with a crash and fifty persons went down with it." No one was seriously injured in the collapse of the apparently poorly constructed seating area, a notorious aspect of Sunday-only ball grounds, although "a number were taken out from under timbers."[29]

Rochester hadn't tried to play its game with Toledo scheduled for that day at Windsor Beach, due to the poor weather. Owners, like those at Syracuse, often went forward with Sunday games in bad weather to capture the gate receipts from whatever crowd would attend the game, since that level of spectators would likely exceed the volume expected from a rescheduled contest during the normal work week.

Rooters in Rochester and Syracuse loved Sunday baseball, despite the lousy weather conditions and spotty won-loss record by the home teams in the Sunday games. Following the apparent success of being able to play Sunday baseball in upstate New York, several teams in the minor league Atlantic League decided to schedule Sunday contests.

This was too much for the Sabbatarians. The Irondequoit Law and Order Society took action with the June 1 game at Windsor Beach between Louisville and Rochester, issuing a legal complaint about the Sunday game that resulted in indictments against both clubs following the game.[30]

The legal complaint didn't stop Rochester from playing the Athletic club the following Sunday, June 8, as 3,000 people went to Windsor Beach to watch the Philadelphia visitors defeat Rochester 3–1. Once again, the Law and Order Society issued a complaint and a grand jury eventually indicted the players on both teams on the charge of Sabbath-breaking.[31]

Both incidents didn't deter Rochester; in fact, they seemed to spur the team on.

"If this little trip to Irondequoit had anything to do with the playing of the Rochester boys at Culver Park yesterday afternoon, the management should hire special policemen by the season to arrest the club just before every game," the *Rochester Herald* commented on the team's 9–3 victory the following day on June 9. "An adult sized injection of Brown-Sequard's elixir could not have put more life into the home team."[32]

At the next game at Windsor Beach on Sunday, June 22, while both Rochester and the opposing Brooklyn team expected the game to be stopped, the game went on unimpeded by Sabbatarian action. Rochester might have wished the game had been stopped, as Brooklyn defeated Rochester 18–7 for one of its only 26 victories that season. Brooklyn reached Rochester pitchers for 16 hits and capitalized on seven Rochester errors.

Since legal complaints had not swayed the Rochester management to stop playing Sunday games at Windsor Beach, the Irondequoit Law and Order Society decided to take a more drastic action. With Rochester leaving for a long road trip to play the western cities in the Association, the Law and Order Society wanted to send a message for the team to contemplate during the four-week lull in Sunday baseball in upstate New York. Led by Herbert Agate, the group persuaded Justice of the Peace Coy of Irondequoit to issue warrants for the arrest of the Rochester players at a June 23 exhibition game in Elmira.[33]

"The opponents of Sunday ball playing have been more than usually active and aggressive this season," *Sporting Life* commented in an article entitled "Sabbatarians Work" that summer. "Probably because the area of Sunday playing territory is widening the high pressure speed at which professional base ball is being conducted, making such remunerative games absolutely necessary to the clubs which had hitherto abstained from playing on the first day of the week, at home, at least."[34]

In the Atlantic Association, with Newark and Jersey City already playing Sunday baseball, American Association expatriot Baltimore experimented with Sunday baseball in Brooklyn, Maryland, which was located a few miles south of Baltimore in Anne Arundel County.

Some 10,000 spectators filled the wooden bleachers at Samuel Acorn's resort in Brooklyn on June 8. About 8,000 paid to see Washington defeat Baltimore 5–4 in ten innings, with the rest climbing over the fence and mixing with the overflow crowd in the outfield before being caught. There was no interference at the June 8 game "since the son of the proprietor [of the grounds] is a deputy sheriff."[35]

With local Sabbatarians aghast that a baseball game would be played on the Sabbath, they demanded that James Armiger, the sheriff of Anne Arundel County, take action. At the June 15 game, Armiger watched the game and then arrested Baltimore's Billy Barnie afterward for having performed "bodily labor on the Lord's Day," a violation of Maryland law. Barnie paid the $5 fine, but vowed to continue Sunday games.

"Until now we have been a decent city," Reverend A. C. Dixon of Baltimore exclaimed. "No base-ball team has dared to desecrate our Sabbath and thus debase our youth. But today one of our large railroad corporations has advertised excursions to the base-ball ground. Shame on the corporation and shame on the public sentiment that will allow it!"[36]

Washington, itself an expatriot of the National League, played the first Sunday game in the D.C. area on June 15 when 2,000 people witnessed a game at Driving Park in Alexandria, Virginia. Washington defeated Wilmington 23–14 in an Atlantic Association game played on a hastily laid out diamond on the infield of the race track.[37]

"The infield abounded in little hillocks that rendered judgment of a ground hit extremely difficult," the *Washington Post* described the playing conditions. "...Daisies grew so deep that the ball was lost once on a fly hit to center field." In the seventh inning with three men on base, Williams of Wilmington hit a ball out to Bader, which passed through his legs and was swallowed up by the high grass as "everyone on base trotted home while a large contingent of the home nine was searching for the lost ball."[38]

Both Baltimore and Washington played again on June 22, but the Sunday baseball experiments were quickly abandoned following the games on June 29. At Brooklyn, Maryland, Sheriff Armiger arrested Barnie and catcher Tate in the second inning of the game with Hartford. At Alexandria, Virginia, Sheriff Beach arrested Washington club secretary Burket also in the second inning. After the game ended, Burket's lawyer demanded an immediate trial before whatever justice was available on the grounds, which happened to be a "colored" justice of the peace, "Squire" Drummond. After much squabbling between the sheriff and his posse of men, the "trial" proceeded forward. Burket pleaded guilty and Justice Drummond fined Burket $2 for each man plus costs, which added up to $47.60. Burket quickly paid the fine and he and his lawyer high-tailed it out of the Alexandria grounds before the sheriff could think twice about the suitability of the justice and the fine meted out in the stands of the ball grounds.[39]

Sunday baseball in the Atlantic Association suffered more when games in Newark were discontinued after residents of East Orange, New Jersey, complained and plans for Wilmington to play at Atlantic City were scuttled.[40]

As the Sabbatarians were succeeding in stopping Sunday baseball on the East Coast, the Rochester correspondent to *Sporting Life* laid out the rationale for why Sunday baseball was good and should be continued in upstate New York:

> We cannot see the consistency of these people in trying to stop ball playing and allow Sunday liquor selling, music, dancing, and other sports to have full swing. The ball grounds [at Windsor Beach] are situated remote to any dwellings and the games there have been attended by a quiet, orderly class of people; mostly clerks and mechanics who cannot afford to lose the time to go to the games during the week and the same time gives them an opportunity to enjoy the pure air of the lake, which gives them health and strength for their work.[41]

Those arguments failed to register with Herbert Agate, Justice Coy, and members of the Law and Order Society of Irondequoit. Spurred on by the success of Sabbatarian groups in Baltimore, Washington, and other East Coast cities, the Irondequoit Law and Society seemed intent on shutting down Sunday baseball for good in the Rochester area.

When Rochester returned from its road trip in mid-July, the club proceeded forward with its next scheduled Sunday game at Windsor Beach on July 20 against Columbus. In the third inning of the July 20 game, Justice Coy accompanied by several constables and members of the Law and Order Society marched onto the diamond in single file and ordered the players to stop the game.

As the local newspaper related the next day, "The good people of the town of Irondequoit gave another manifestation that those were no idle threats which they had made that there would be trouble if the Rochester base ball association should continue to play Sunday ball games at Windsor Beach."[42]

They may have underestimated the intensity of the club's followers, especially since they lacked a warrant to arrest the players and thus had trespassed onto private property.

"As the players came in ... spectators began to pour out upon the diamond and shout derisively at the officers," the *Rochester Herald* described the scene. "Here and there a cushion seat went flying through the air and the crowd surged thicker and thicker about the Irondequoit people and called the players to continue the game."[43]

"It looked for a few moments that there would be a row," when Rochester manager Pat Powers stepped in and using his verbal abilities "persuaded the farmers to leave the diamond." Powers assured the Law and Order people that if they'd let the game continue, then the players would report the next day to any place that Justice Coy desired.[44]

"Coy looked at the crowd gathered around him and, deeming discretion the better part of valor, accepted the terms and departed," the *Rochester Herald* reported, adding that Coy ordered Powers to have the players at the office of W. Martin Jones at 9:00 Monday morning.[45]

Rochester management pulled a fast one on the Irondequoit intruders, though. After the game (which Rochester won 8–3), Powers arranged for the players of both teams to be arrested on the complaint of an Irondequoit resident who was not a Law and Order man, and taken before Justice Baird, another Irondequoit justice.[46]

Justice Baird freed them on bond Sunday afternoon in Irondequoit and arraigned the players Monday morning at the Forest House in Rochester, in time for the players to get to the afternoon game at Culver Field.

As the players were warming up at Culver Field and the spectators assembling in the stands, Coy, Agate, and a constable from Irondequoit all appeared at the park looking for Powers. They had warrants for the arrest of Rochester players Bill Greenwood, Harry Lyons, and Ledell Titcomb as well as subpoenas for Powers and umpire Curry. "Powers produced a paper signed by Justice Baird and stating that both clubs had been arrested and bound over by him for the next Grand Jury on the charge of playing ball on Sunday July 20," the *Rochester Democrat and Chronicle* reported. "Justice Coy refused to look at this paper and demanded, by virtue of his subpoenas, that the persons mentioned go at once to Irondequoit. Powers refused and the game was played."[47]

If Coy and Agate were displeased that Powers had hoodwinked them in the selection of a justice of the peace to hear the case, they were no doubt furious that Powers had ignored their legal instruments. On Tuesday, Agate obtained a warrant for the arrest of General Brinker, president of the Rochester ball club, and Edward Bohackek, secretary of the club. Both men were arrested that evening and went to Justice Coy's residence where they gave bond.[48]

The tactics employed by Powers had enabled the July 20 game to be completed. But when he subverted the Law and Order Society afterward, the July 20 game turned out to be the last Sunday home game for the Rochester club in the Association.

"It becomes not a question of playing ball on Sunday but of the defiance of the officers of the law," an irate Agate wrote in a letter published later that week in the *Rochester Democrat and Chronicle*. "Such open defiance of the law if made in a Southern or Western community would be looked upon as outrageous. It seems almost incredible that, in the Empire State, in the county of Monroe, a body of men dare publicly avow their intention not only to violate the law, but also to resist the lawful authorities should any attempt be made to arrest them."[49]

Sheriff Hodgson announced that he would have 20 men on hand at the scheduled July 27 game with Louisville to enforce the Sunday law. "I anticipate and hope that there will be no attempt to play ball at Windsor Beach next Sunday," Hodgson declared. "In view of all that has transpired, the base ball association could, I think, now announce its abandonment of the plan of playing Sunday games with good grace." A Rochester club official responded to Hodgson's statement by saying, "If the club is prevented from playing, then the sheriff must close the museums, switch-back railways, and other places of entertainment at Ontario Beach. Those forms of amusement are certainly as great a violation of the law as is ball playing."[50]

All attempts at compromise with the Irondequoit Law and Order Society failed and the July 27 game was canceled, along with the remainder of the Sunday schedule at Windsor Beach. "In deference to public opinion and to a rigid construction of the law, the Rochesters wish to state that they have decided to abandon their Sunday games at Windsor Beach," manager Powers said in a statement. "We now accept the situation and hope that all lovers of the sport will patronize the games at Culver Park more liberally than in the past."[51]

"Sunday ball playing in Rochester is a thing of the past," the *Rochester Democrat and Chronicle* wrote. "The Irondequoit people have won the fight and the Rochester club has submitted to the inevitable."[52]

The abandonment of Sunday games led the Irondequoit Law and Order Society to drop its legal suits against the Rochester management. But as one wag noted, "This action, of course, does not affect the cases against the players, now before the court."[53]

Powers tried once more to have the Rochester club play Sunday baseball. Efforts were made to try to play the August 3 game at McPherson's Point at Conesus Lake before rescheduling it to the Players League grounds in Buffalo. About 2,500 people had gathered on the grounds to see the Rochester-St. Louis game, when police captain Kaiser rode into the grounds on horseback and told the people to disperse and he would not allow a professional game to be played on the grounds.[54]

Powers had just made his initial mark on Sunday baseball with the Rochester team in 1890. Later, Powers would lead the charge for the Eastern League, which eventually transformed into the International League, to play Sunday baseball in the late 1890s and early 1900s. Actions by Powers in the Federal League in 1915 would also be instrumental in accelerating Sunday baseball at the major league level in New York.

Over in Syracuse, the sheriff of Oswego County stopped the July 27 game at Three Rivers Point to seemingly end Sunday baseball in that Association city as well. The Syracuse club, however, like Rochester, also rescheduled its August 3 game. Syracuse switched the game to Iron Pier on the shores of Onondaga Lake, just a few miles from the center of the city and, unlike Three Rivers, within the city limits.

Both the Syracuse and Louisville teams had been notified by the police authorities not to play the game at Iron Pier. Louisville, a bastion of Sunday baseball for many years, was probably amused by all the goings-on in upstate New York over the Sunday issue. Since Louisville's Sunday game scheduled the previous week at Rochester had been canceled, the team left Syracuse on an early train Sunday to go back to Louisville. Curry, the umpire scheduled for the game, had also left the city. The Syracuse team, though, was in uniform on the Iron Pier field at 3:30 ready to go. The club rustled up a substitute umpire, Lee Norton, who, after pitcher John Keefe delivered one toss to catcher Grant Briggs, declared the game forfeited to Syracuse by a 9–0 score.[55]

Louisville obviously cried foul at the ruling, believing the game being declared illegal should be enough to justify its no-show appearance. The directors of the Association felt otherwise, and upheld the ruling at an August 13 meeting.

Such was life in the topsy-turvy world of Sunday baseball skewed by Sabbatarian actions.

The final new club in the Association for the 1890 season was the replacement Brooklyn team, which couldn't duplicate the former club's success. The old Brooklyn club was still around, now in the National League, and still playing its regular games at Washington Park, while there was a third major league team competing for Brooklyn spectators in the Players League.

Brooklyn's new Association club was thus forced to play all its home games at outlying Ridgewood Park, which not only cut down substantially on the attendance during the week, but also undermined the park's "special" atmosphere for Sunday games. For the clincher, the new Brooklyn club was awful on the field (26–73 record before folding) while the old club now in the National League enjoyed its second consecutive pennant-winning season and the Players League entry in Brooklyn finished in second place.

Sabbatarians could have moved in to quash Sunday baseball in Brooklyn in 1890, but Sunday baseball died a natural death when the new Brooklyn club in the Association, dubbed Kennedy's Kid after its youthful 22-year-old manager and its inexperienced lot of players, disbanded that summer.

On May 18, the first Sunday of the Association season, only 4,000 showed up at Ridgewood Park to watch Brooklyn defeat Syracuse 9–8. This was a noticeable reduction, as the old Brooklyn team had averaged 7,000 to its Sunday games the year before. The following week on Sunday, May 25, just 500 showed up for the morning game of a doubleheader against Columbus and only 3,000 were on hand for the afternoon game.[56]

With meager crowds during the other six days of the week, the Brooklyn club was facing big financial losses when in June it decided to break its lease with the Ridgewood Exposition Company, which operated Ridgewood Park. The club decided to book some games at the Polo Grounds in Manhattan, where it might attract a larger crowd than it could in the far-removed grounds in Queens.

Ridgewood Exposition Company didn't take kindly to this action and banned Brooklyn from playing its Sunday games there following the June 8 game, a 9–5 win over Syracuse before 2,000 spectators. Following Sunday games in Philadelphia and Rochester, and a long western road trip, Brooklyn then took to the Long Island Grounds in Maspeth to play Sunday games.

At the first game in Maspeth on July 27, only 1,000 people showed up. In another of the odd occurrences at Sunday games in the Association, Brooklyn wound up losing the game to Columbus in a forfeit.

Brooklyn was ahead 13–8 in the eighth inning when Columbus batter John Sneed fouled off a pitch over the stands. Umpire Peoples then called for a new ball, but there were no new balls left to put into play. In a déjà vu moment—Brooklyn had experienced this situation before in its first-ever Sunday game in 1886 when the club depleted its ball supply—the nearly bankrupt 1890 Brooklyn club had run out of baseballs and was forced to forfeit the July 27 game.

What made the situation "ludicrous in the extreme," according to the *Brooklyn Daily Eagle*, was that one of the lost balls had been thrown onto the diamond from the grandstand and picked up by the umpire. Captain Jim McTamany of the Columbus team "very emphatically said he would not play unless a new ball was forthcoming." So with old ball in hand, umpire Peoples awarded Columbus a forfeit.[57]

"There is no rule by which Peoples could do any such high-handed act as this," the *New York Times* indicated, adding that the Columbus club had apparently gotten Peoples appointed as an umpire and "he felt duty bound to favor them."[58]

After the second Sunday game at the Long Island Grounds on August 3, a 9–2 Toledo victory over Brooklyn, the club disbanded. The Baltimore team in the Atlantic Association, which had been in the American Association less than a year earlier, took Brooklyn's place on the schedule and finished out the season. After Baltimore's failed attempt that season to play Sunday baseball in Brooklyn, Maryland, outside of Baltimore, the club was perhaps willing to entertain any scheme to help it remain financially afloat. Taking over the schedule of another Brooklyn entity, this time one from Brooklyn, New York, seemed like an idea as good as any other.

Sunday baseball was an unmitigated disaster among eastern cities in 1890. The concept was quashed in New York at Brooklyn, Rochester, and Syracuse. It was also abandoned in Philadelphia, where the Athletic club was pushed into the financial abyss due to stiff competition from the Players League team.

The Athletics "got into such financial straights that they were compelled to release their high-priced men and finished out the season with a pick-up team that hardly won a game," the *Reach Guide* explained. The last major league game at Gloucester, New Jersey, was a five-inning affair on Sunday, October 12, when Syracuse routed a makeshift Athletic team 12–2.[59]

The Philadelphia squad consisted only of three "regular" players, all who had just joined the team in September—George Carman, Andy Knox, and Joe Daly. A fourth regular was pitcher Ed O'Neil, who was pressed into service in the field, while George Crawford played in his fifth, and final, major league game in a one-week span. For the other four players—Hampton Sweigert, Bob Stafford, John McBride, and John Sterling—the October 12 game was their one and only major league appearance.

Syracuse rapped 16 hits off pitcher Sterling, before he could retire 15 batters in five innings. "The visitors took kindly to the curves of Sterling, a young man of Camden, who was arrayed in a black cloth suit, with low cut vest and white stand-up collar," the *Philadelphia Inquirer* described the Athletic newcomer, who apparently pitched in street clothes rather than in a baseball uniform. "Before they had finished with him, the Jerseyman's spirits were as wilted as his collar."[60]

It was another ignoble finale for Sunday baseball in the Association.

The setbacks in Sunday baseball definitely imperiled the viability of the Association for the 1891 season. Rochester, Syracuse, and Toledo were let go for the 1891 season. In their stead were teams from Boston (the champions of the Players League), Washington, and Cincinnati. The Philadelphia club from the Players League was also signed on to substitute for the disbanded Athletic club that had played nine years in the Association.

Three holdover clubs continued to play Sunday baseball—St. Louis, Louisville, and Columbus—but of the new outfits, only Cincinnati gave Sunday baseball a whirl. Given the legal status of Sunday baseball when the previous Cincinnati club had left the Association following the 1889 season, playing Sundays in Cincinnati was a proposition fraught with peril.

The Cincinnati club played its games five miles to the east of the National League grounds in an outlying area called Pendleton. East End Park in Pendleton was located on a stretch of land hemmed in by the Ohio River on one side and a beer garden on the other. The grounds may have been fine for a Sunday-only venue, but the remoteness from downtown Cincinnati constrained attendance during the other six days of the week.

What propped up attendance was the hiring of Mike Kelly, of "Slide, Kelly, Slide" fame, as manager. Kelly had propelled the Boston team in the Players League to a pennant the preceding season. The Cincinnati team became known as Kelly's Killers, although they vanquished the opposing team less than half the time (a 43–57 record during its brief stay in the

Association). The team also enjoyed a Sunday game of a different sort with the local police.

Cincinnati's first Sunday game at East End Park was played on April 26 before 7,000 spectators. The 12–6 Cincinnati victory over Louisville was unimpeded by police action. Following the game, both teams were arrested for violation of the Sunday law.

"All the players that took part in the Louisville-Cincinnati game yesterday were arrested at the close of the contest," the *Cincinnati Enquirer* noted in an incidental manner in its baseball notes column. "They walked down to the station-house at the close of the game and gave bond for their appearance in the Police Court. President Ronan went on their bond."[61]

Kelly's Killers began a cat-and-mouse game with the cops over Sunday baseball.

"Each Sunday they would play, and each Sunday evening, would find themselves in the local lockup, paying a fine, or spending the night in jail," Kelly biographer Marty Appel wrote in *Slide, Kelly, Slide*. "They would repeat the practice each Sunday the team was at home. It became a joke to them."[62]

Cincinnati mayor John Mosby was outraged that the team attempted to play Sunday baseball and demanded that Cincinnati management cancel the next scheduled Sunday game on May 3 versus St. Louis. Mosby had been elected in 1889 on the platform of enforcing the Sunday laws and had been successful in shutting down Sunday ball two years earlier to cause the Association team to defect to the National League.

Although Cincinnati considered switching the game to St. Louis, where the teams would have no problem getting the game in, the May 3 game was played at Pendleton. Extra street cars and ferry boats were on hand to handle the crowd to see Cincinnati defeat St. Louis 3–2, as Ed "Cannonball" Crane outdueled Jack Stivetts. Players of both teams dutifully reported to the police station after the game was concluded.[63]

Kelly was subjected to a jury trial for each of these Sunday baseball offenses, and each time the jury acquitted him. The Sabbatarians might have suspended their efforts at trying to stop Sunday baseball at East End Park had the Cincinnati club not tried to escalate the number of Sunday games there.[64]

Taking the jury acquittals as a sign that Sunday baseball was unstoppable, Cincinnati management convinced Philadelphia management to switch the scheduled June 5 game on a Friday in Philadelphia to a Sunday game in Cincinnati on May 24. With a chance for attendance to top 10,000 for the Sunday game, Philadelphia's visitor's share of the gate in Cincinnati would no doubt greatly exceed its home share of a Friday game in

Philadelphia. After Cincinnati and Philadelphia played an afternoon game in Philadelphia on Saturday, May 23, the two teams boarded a special train on the Baltimore and Ohio Railroad that left Philadelphia at 6:00. The players traveled all night and into Sunday morning, arriving in Cincinnati around 1:00 for the game two hours later that afternoon.[65]

The promotion machine was in full blast for the May 24 game. An ad in the *Cincinnati Enquirer* for a 20-minute boat trip on The Missouri to the game down the Ohio River blared, "Base-Ball! The Association Flyer! King Kel's Special! Ten-Mile Ride on the River for 15 Cents."[66]

Mayor Mosby had sent word to Cincinnati management that the game with the Athletics "would be prevented by police and by arresting of players on the field, if necessary." There was some speculation that the game would be transferred across the Ohio River to Covington, Kentucky, to avoid a police action. But full of confidence that its position on Sunday baseball would be vindicated, Cincinnati didn't capitulate.[67]

When the club went forward with the game at Pendleton, Mosby followed through with his threat and police stopped the May 24 game in the top half of the first inning. Both teams were arrested and the players were held for $300 bail each, a staggering sum for that time period. Otto Betz, a club official, signed the bail bonds aggregating $5,400 for the 18 players in the game and the players were released.[68]

The aborted May 24 game was played the next day on Monday. It was small consolation for the overnight trip made for the love for Sunday baseball and its financial rewards, which had gone unrequited for all the trouble both teams went through to travel to Cincinnati in the first place.

As Cincinnati awaited the outcome of the latest Sunday baseball arrests at the court trials scheduled for June 3, the May 31 Sunday game with Baltimore was canceled. Cincinnati management claimed it lost $4,000 by Mayor Mosby stopping the last two Sunday games.[69]

At the June 3 court session, the prosecution, rather than put the popular Mike Kelly on trial once again and risk an almost certain acquittal, decided to present its case against Cincinnati pitcher Willie Mains.

The first witness for the prosecution was Lieutenant Gill, who told about the arrest and what he saw. On cross-examination, though, Gill said he saw no ball game. The next witness, Chief Deitsch, also told of the arrest, but when asked what he considered baseball, Deitsch said nine innings. Prosecutor Hertenstein had several spats with Judge Gregg, and he objected often during the trial to the questions posed by Mains' attorneys Hart and Pugh, who vigorously established a case "to show that Mains had not played ball as there was no game."[70]

At 7:00 that night, the case went to the jury and, as *Sporting Life* observed, "from that hour to 12:30 they wrestled with the national game and its propriety as a Sunday entertainment."

On the first jury ballot, five jurors voted guilty and seven voted not guilty. One person switched his vote to not guilty on the second ballot, making it 8–4 for acquittal, but the other four jurors maintained their guilty votes for the next four ballots. Finally, on the seventh ballot, three people switched to not guilty to make the vote 11–1 for acquittal. That last guilty vote, however, was steadfast, as through six more ballots, the count remained 11–1 for acquittal.

The holdout to convict Mains was A. E. Higbee, a juror chosen by Judge Gregg. When originally questioned as to his fitness to be a juror, Higbee, a life insurance salesman, said that he "devoted himself to religion more than base ball on Sunday." After the thirteenth ballot in the jury room, the jury asked to see Gregg, and Higbee asked the judge to repeat his charge to the jury. Judge Gregg told Higbee that it was his duty "to find the defendant guilty if the evidence showed that base ball had been played on Sunday." The judge added, "The question of innings [played] is not a question of law."

Nothing changed on the fourteenth ballot. On the fifteenth ballot, Higbee changed his vote and the jury rendered a verdict of not guilty.

Willie Mains had an abbreviated major league baseball record, pitching just one complete season (1891 with Cincinnati) and portions of two others, to post a 16–17 record. Mains, though, had a very impressive minor league career, pitching 19 seasons from 1887 to 1906 to become "the first minor league hurler to win 300 games," compiling a 318–183 lifetime minor league mark.[71]

The lanky, over six-foot tall, "quaint character" from Maine won 32 games for St. Paul in the Western Association in 1889, the year his visage appeared on a tobacco card in the Old Judge series. In his only full season in the major leagues, Mains posted a 12–14 record in 1891 for the Cincinnati club in the Association. He then embarked on a lengthy minor league career mostly in the New England League and the New York State League (where he averaged 20 wins a season from 1899 to 1905).

Mains operated a bat factory in his native Maine following his playing days.

Jubilation over the Sunday baseball victory in Cincinnati was short-lived. After three jury acquittals, the prosecutor still refused to concede the issue. On Sunday, June 7, Cincinnati played Washington at East End Park and won handily 13–1. Following the game, police arrested the players once again and the legal battle continued.

This time, the prosecutor was determined to pull out all stops and

5. Sabbatarians Hated It

called for separate jury trials for all 18 players on the two teams. Surprisingly the attorney for the Washington club pleaded the players guilty and the judge assessed a fine equal to court costs. This action mildly undercut the prosecutor, who was rebuffed by the judge on June 12 when he placed all the Cincinnati players on open docket, except for Kelly, who was to face his third trial by jury.[72]

Since the Sunday baseball issue defied resolution in Cincinnati, at a special meeting the Association decided to seek another playing grounds for the Cincinnati club that was more accessible to spectators for weekday games. They also advocated the team playing its Sunday games across the river in Covington, Kentucky, to avoid future skirmishes with Mayor Mosby and the police.

On Sunday, June 14, Cincinnati played Columbus at Pendleton and "after the game, the players were, as usual, arrested and released on bail." It was the last time that players were arrested on the field in Cincinnati for an alleged violation of the Sunday law. Kelly was acquitted in his third trial, even with a Baptist preacher on the jury. The clergyman held out for two hours with the lone vote for guilty, but eventually changed his mind and voted not guilty.[73]

The Cincinnati club had beaten the legal system four times on the Sunday baseball issue. Even packing the jury with a minister for Kelly's third trial could not gain the prosecution a guilty verdict. The prosecution finally gave up "as the public prosecutor will waste no more time on such cases,

Willie Mains was acquitted by a Cincinnati jury in his 1891 Sunday baseball trial, after a lone holdout juror changed his vote on the fifteenth ballot. (National Baseball Hall of Fame Library, Cooperstown

no matter what the law may be, because due to public sentiment, it is impossible to secure a conviction."[74]

For the remainder of the 1891 season, Sunday baseball in Cincinnati went on unimpeded by the police.

Sunday baseball by 1891 was becoming firmly imbedded in the fabric of baseball leagues across most of the country, not just in the American Association.

All minor leagues in the National Agreement, except the New England League, played Sunday baseball to one degree or another. It was not unusual for amateur games in Chicago and New York to be played for gate receipts, while similar amateurs in Cleveland and Pittsburgh played for the joy of the game on the Lord's Day. Sunday baseball, though, had yet to infiltrate Boston and Philadelphia among the nation's big cities.

Of particular concern to the Sabbatarians, Sunday baseball had become an essential ingredient in the financial equation of baseball.

"Under the present high pressure and extravagant methods of conducting base ball, such games have become practically indispensable to all leagues and clubs except the National League," *Sporting Life* expounded in its article "Sunday Playing," subtitled "Necessity of Sunday Games," on the front page of a June 1891 issue. "Even some of the clubs of that organization would find Sunday games in the West a great relief from financial worriment."[75]

The weekly sporting publication opined that professional baseball at the nationwide level couldn't exist without Sunday baseball.

> A good deal of contumely has been heaped upon the American Association by League writers and partisans for the playing of Sunday games. These writers in their diatribes, however, either ignorantly or designedly shut their eyes and ears persistently to the fact that the Association really is not after all so much to blame for Sunday playing as it cannot be denied that its Western patrons absolutely demand such games and would not patronize any club that doesn't cater to them in this particular. For this reason, the Association could not exist without Sunday games, inasmuch, without considering the question of profit and loss, without Sunday games the Association could not maintain a Western circuit and would quickly degenerate into a mere regional league."[76]

In support of the premise that Sunday baseball was a necessary financial ingredient in major league baseball, the Boston club of the Association played Sunday games on the road in 1891.

This was a new milestone in the progress of Sunday baseball in the Puritan bastion of Boston. The Association team played on Sundays in the middle of the 1891 schedule, unlike the Boston Unions in 1884 that waited until their home schedule had finished before embarking on Sunday games on the road. Boston won the Association pennant in 1891 and didn't seem to suffer for patronage at the gate for its home games at the Congress Street Grounds.

Boston opened its Sunday road season with an 8–5 victory in Columbus on May 31, the day after the Decoration Day holiday. The following Sunday, June 7, in St. Louis, 17,439 spectators jammed into Sportsman's Park to see the two league leaders battle for first place. The St. Louis attendance was the third largest in Association history and the largest Sunday attendance (as well as non-holiday) the circuit would ever achieve.

Boston defeated St. Louis 6–3 on the strength of back-to-back home runs by Duke Farrell and Morgan Murphy, as the visitor's share of those two gates certainly went a long way to support Boston's baseball operations.

The Association also announced in 1891 a concerted effort for its four eastern clubs, which couldn't legally play Sunday home games, to play Sunday exhibition games at grounds outside each city. Such games would not only expand the reach of Sunday baseball in the east but also add to the financial coffers of each team.

Philadelphia was to use the grounds in Gloucester, New Jersey, that the Athletic club has used for three years to play Sunday home games. Baltimore was to try playing in Anne Arundel County again, and Washington would experiment again at the Alexandria Driving Grounds in Virginia. Boston would travel 40 miles south to Rocky Point, Rhode Island, to use the grounds that the Providence team of the Eastern League was just beginning to make famous for Sunday baseball games.

Cincinnati had won in the courts, but then eventually lost on the playing fields. The team folded in August that year, as the Association began to crumble.

Milwaukee replaced Cincinnati for the remainder of its schedule and played four Sunday games at the tail end of the 1891 season.

Looking to maximize attendance in its few home dates, Milwaukee played one of the earliest single-admission Sunday doubleheaders in the major leagues on September 13. In front of a crowd of 10,000 people, Milwaukee split the two games with the Athletics, losing the first game 8–7 but winning the second game 7–3. League-leading Boston came to Milwaukee the following week and played a Sunday game on September 20, which drew 12,000 spectators.

As cold weather set in during early autumn, Milwaukee drew just 400 people on October 4 in the last Sunday game to be played in the history of the major league American Association.

"It would have been difficult to have picked out a more miserable day for the closing of the baseball season that was yesterday," the *Milwaukee Sentinel* reported on Milwaukee's 8–4 victory over Columbus. "The rain of the night previous had left the grounds in a condition of muddiness rivaling the bogs of the Dismal Swamp and it was almost worth a man's life to attempt to run between the bases." For example, in the first inning, George Shoch hit the ball to right field and "ploughed through the mud to second base." When Bob Pettit hit the ball to center, "the ball got stuck in the mud and while Easton was excavating it, Shoch scored." Fans had been promised two games as a farewell performance, but in the wintry weather "spectators were amply satisfied with one game, as they would have frozen to death sitting through another one."[77]

With the American Association at death's door by the end of the 1891 season, the future of Sunday baseball at the major league level was, at best, precarious and, more likely, on the verge of eradication. The big reason Sunday baseball remained afloat and not destined to a bleak future was the defeat of the Sabbatarians in their campaign for a national Sunday rest-day law. Proposed by the Blair bill in 1888, the Sunday rest-day law never materialized.

"Sabbatarians failed to abolish Sunday labor because they had much broader goals than simply protecting working people's right to a day of rest. They wanted to define rest itself," McCrossen wrote in *Holy Day, Holiday*. The Blair bill sought not only to restrict labor on Sunday but also to restrict recreational activities on that day as well.[78]

The real agenda of the Sabbatarians came to light in 1891, before the Blair bill came to a vote in the U.S. Senate, when Massachusetts Senator Henry Dawes introduced a bill to prohibit "the opening of any exhibition or exposition on Sunday where appropriations of the United States are expended." The Dawes bill was aimed at the Columbian Exposition, or World's Fair, which was slated to run in Chicago during 1893.[79]

There was a groundswell of popular opinion that the World's Fair ought to open on Sunday, in direct opposition to the Sabbatarian belief that it should be closed that day. The Dawes bill "destroyed whatever momentum the Sunday rest-day law might have had." Citizen petitions supporting the opening of the World's Fair on Sunday poured into the Senate, while those seeking the Sunday rest law plummeted dramatically. The battle about opening the Columbian Exposition on Sunday greatly overshadowed the debate on the Sunday rest-day bill, and "made it clear that defining rest would lead to the disintegration of the consensus in favor of Sunday as the day of rest." The alliance between Sabbatarians and those committed to worker's rights "fell apart, in large part because of the multivalence of the term 'rest'."[80]

The Sabbatarians had a brief three-year stretch from 1889 to 1891 in which they controlled the direction of Sunday baseball in the major leagues. With the demise of the national Sunday rest-day bill, though, the baseball owners would regain the upper hand on Sunday baseball.

Chapter 6

NATIONAL LEAGUE EMBRACED IT

Ironically, the National League—a staunch opponent of Sunday baseball for so many years—salvaged Sunday baseball from its impending demise as part of the merger negotiations with the American Association in the fall of 1891.

Following the merger talks that concluded at a joint League-Association owners meeting on December 18 in Indianapolis, four Association teams were absorbed into the National League to form a new 12-team league. Variations on the Association's three primary principles were also adopted for the 1892 season:

(1) Admission for 25 cents was okay, but 50 cents was preferred,
(2) Clubs could decide for themselves whether to sell alcoholic beverages in their home parks, and
(3) Sunday baseball could be played in all cities where allowed, although no club could be compelled to play on Sunday.

"Thus it was that three of the Association's founding principles came to be a universally accepted part of the framework of our national pastime in 1892 and remain so today," Nemec wrote in *The Beer and Whisky League* about the Association's legacy to major league baseball.[1]

Why did the League accede to incorporating Association principles such as Sunday baseball, when the League held the upper hand in the negotiations with the Association? The League seemingly could have quelled the Sunday baseball issue and it wouldn't have arisen at the major league level until several years later.

Money was likely a compelling reason. The skirmish with the Players League had sapped the finances of League clubs and owners were anxious to begin operating in the black again. First, the League owners needed to eliminate the rest of the competition, namely the Association, at whatever cost. Second, they needed a plan to recover past losses.

Of the eight Association clubs, the League bought out the remnants of the Boston, Philadelphia, Columbus (actually Chicago, which was slated to replace it), and Milwaukee clubs. Since the St. Louis, Louisville, Washington, and Baltimore clubs represented new markets and extensions of League territory, these four clubs were offered League membership.

Sunday baseball still thrived in St. Louis and Louisville. League owners recognized that playing Sunday baseball on the road could be beneficial to offsetting the red ink from the Players League war, which was now exacerbated by the six-figure buyout needed to make the remaining Association franchises disappear. Playing Sunday baseball on the road, far from their home grounds where customers might be sensitive to such games, was an economic measure to help League clubs return to profitability.

There was also the Von der Ahe factor. Appeasing the St. Louis owner (some would say buying him off) was critical to effecting the Association merger. If Von der Ahe believed the deal was good, he still held enough sway with the other Association owners to convince them to go along with it. Allowing Von der Ahe to continue to play Sunday baseball in St. Louis was a necessary evil for the League owners in order to accomplish their loftier goals.

To be sure, Sunday baseball was just one measure, a limited one as seen by the League owners, to help them return to prosperity. Institution of a salary cap to keep expenses down was another owner tactic to improve the financial picture. Others were designed to improve spectator interest and increase demand for tickets, such as playing half seasons in 1892 to spur more interest in second-half games (an idea that lasted just one year) and creating more batting action in 1893 by lengthening the pitching distance several feet (a permanent idea).

Owners may have seen Sunday baseball as a temporary measure for the League. They may have even imagined jettisoning the two Sunday-playing franchises in St. Louis and Louisville once they'd served their purpose in restoring financial sanity to the other League clubs. This was, in fact, a half-truth, taking eight years, when perhaps the owners had contemplated three or four years.

Sunday baseball was, however, becoming more palatable to the League in general, a decided change from the League's previous hostility to Sunday baseball.

Half of the League's eight teams in 1891 were former Association franchises. Three of the four—Brooklyn, Cincinnati, and Cleveland—had all played Sunday baseball at one time both at home and on the road. They clearly understood the economic impact of Sunday baseball. The fourth club, Pittsburgh, certainly knew the pleasure of a visitor's share of a Sunday road gate from its five years in the Association.

Another reason was widespread adoption of Sunday baseball in the minor leagues, as the concept extended well beyond just the cities in the Association. A larger and larger share of American baseball spectators began to see Sunday baseball as a normal occurrence, not something abnormal that happened just in the western parts of the country.

Lastly, the Sabbatarian luster was dimming, as the national Sunday rest-day bill had died in Congress. The Sunday baseball opponents were still a force to be reckoned with, to be sure, but it was a declining force.

Albert Spalding, owner of the Chicago franchise and former cohort of William Hulbert who had first initiated the Sunday baseball prohibition, was still a leading opponent of Sunday baseball in the League. While baseball historians have often painted Spalding as a died-in-the-wool Sabbatarian, calling the Chicago club a "citadel of Sunday piety," Spalding was more of a shrewd businessman than proselytizing Sunday crusader.[2]

Early in the League's formative years, Spalding acquired contracts to be the exclusive provider of baseballs to the League and to publish the League's annual guide. With these lucrative deals, Spalding had no incentive to rock the boat on the Sunday baseball issue with either Hulbert, his boss, or with the other League owners after Hulbert's death in 1882. The market for Spalding's sporting goods business was then also predominately upper- and middle-class customers, providing further disincentive to advocate Sunday play.

Spalding's published Sunday baseball comments usually were clothed around the patronage concern, not the Sunday aspect, such as these comments he made in 1885:

> I have no doubt but that we could fill every seat in our grounds were we to play scheduled games here Sunday. The theatres, billiard halls, saloons, and all other resorts for amusement and recreation are kept open on Sunday and seem to be well patronized. But I do not believe that the club would be better off financially in the end. I am sure we should not stand so high in the estimation of the better class of citizens. I do not believe they would endorse Sunday games and as theirs is the kind of patronage I want, in the interests of and for the general good of the game in Chicago, I do not propose to disregard their sentiments on the subject.[3]

Spalding later remarked, "The League's rule of business always has been to prohibit the playing of Sunday games ... the Association rule is to admit of Sunday games ... there can be no compromise on this plain distinction. Clubs must cater either for grand stand occupants or those of the bleaching boards and the latter plan requires the 25 cent admission fees, Sunday games and a license to sell liquor on the premises."[4]

Once the League merged with the Association in 1891, Spalding softened his position on Sunday baseball to accept its use where legal. But Chicago never played a Sunday game while Spalding was team president. Only when Jim Hart took over as president for the 1893 season did Chicago play on Sundays.

So while the League adopted a Sunday baseball measure for the first time for the 1892 season, its permeation through the League, while not at a glacial pace, was rather sluggish due to Spalding's continued involvement in League affairs.

Despite the literal trials and tribulations that the 1889 and 1891 Cincinnati entries in the Association went through to play Sunday baseball, the League's Cincinnati club sought to play Sunday baseball at League Park during the 1892 season. Cincinnati thus joined newcomers St. Louis and Louisville as a third city to play Sunday baseball on its home grounds in the National League's inaugural season of Sunday baseball.

Rather than contend with the uncertainty of police action stopping its games, Cincinnati management agreed to pay the stipulated fine for each Sunday game at League Park. In essence, the fine for violating the state statute was treated as a cost of doing business. Cincinnati carried on this practice until 1897, when the local district attorney finally relented on the enforcement of the statute, following the Sunday baseball developments upstate in Cleveland that year.[5]

Only three of the remaining nine clubs in the 12-team League were willing to play Sunday baseball on the road—Baltimore, Washington, and Cleveland. Neither Brooklyn nor Pittsburgh, both members of the Association in the near past, was willing to play Sundays on the road in 1892. League stalwarts Boston, Chicago, New York, and Philadelphia also would not take the plunge for Sunday road play in 1892.

Initial indications prior to the merger announcement were that four existing League clubs would play Sunday baseball in 1892. In the end, though, only two clubs did, splitting the League evenly between the six clubs that would play Sunday baseball on the road and the six clubs that continued to abstain from it.

The first Sunday game in National League history was played on April 17, 1892, at Sportsman's Park in St. Louis. Cincinnati defeated St. Louis 5–1 before a crowd of 10,000.

On the following Sunday, April 24, the two teams switched venues as

6. National League Embraced It

16,968 jammed into Cincinnati's League Park to see the Reds defeat the Browns again, this time by a 10–2 score.

Eastern teams began their Sunday road debuts on May 1, when Washington visited St. Louis (and lost 6–4) and Baltimore played at Louisville (and lost 11–2).

The first League vestiges of the one-game Sunday series, which would become a staple of major league scheduling for the next four decades, occurred on May 8. The one-game Sunday series, a single game inserted into the schedule on Sunday as a side trip between games in other cities, was often terribly inconvenient for the players, but was financially worthwhile for the owners. Teams would travel overnight on Saturday following their games that afternoon, play the Sunday game, then depart Sunday evening for the destination of their Monday afternoon games.

On Sunday, May 8, the League played three Sunday games, the maximum possible in 1892 based on three cities that had opted to play Sunday home games. Since the visiting teams in the Saturday, May 7, games at Cincinnati, Louisville, and St. Louis all were of the non–Sunday-playing persuasion—Boston, Brooklyn, and Philadelphia—three teams needed to shuttle into town for the Sunday games.

For two teams, the trip for the Sunday game was not overly burdensome. Washington left Pittsburgh on Saturday for its game in Louisville on Sunday, a 350-mile trip. Baltimore departed from its home city for a game in Cincinnati, a 500-mile trip. Both teams would at least stay in those cities following the Sunday game to play further games there.

For the third team, Cleveland, it was an arduous journey for a Sunday game in the League's first one-game Sunday series.

Cleveland had also played in Baltimore on Saturday but needed to get to St. Louis for its Sunday game, an excursion of more than 800 miles. Cleveland then needed to travel home to Cleveland for a game on Monday with Boston.

After losing the Saturday game 4–3 to Baltimore, the Cleveland club took a train from Baltimore to Toledo, then caught a connecting train to St. Louis. The club arrived at 1:00 P.M. for that afternoon's game with the Browns. First-year pitcher George Cuppy seemed no worse for the wear from the train trip, as he yielded just two hits to the Browns in Cleveland's 10–2 victory before 5,300 onlookers. Cuppy and his compatriots then jumped on a 6:00 train that night to go back home to Cleveland.[6]

A Boston newspaper didn't think much of Cleveland's Herculean effort to get in a Sunday game, a trip that had been paid for by St. Louis owner Von der Ahe. The paper's attitude was not surprising since it was illegal for anyone in Boston to play any type of game on Sunday.

The *Boston Herald* commented that Cleveland would be "so fatigued from their long and hurried ride that they will be easy victims for the Bostons." The Boston team had arrived in Cleveland on Sunday morning from its game in Cincinnati the previous day "and will have ample rest" before Monday's game.[7]

"Nine weary, bedraggled, dust-stained men arrived in the city at 2:00 this afternoon, snatched a sandwich, a bottle of lake water, rubbed the soot marks off their faces, and then went out to League Park to play a game of ball," the *Boston Post* described the Cleveland team that day. "While the wheels rumbled and rolled and the cars shook [Cleveland's train from St. Louis], the Bostons were sleeping the sleep of the brave Bean Eater in the more or less downy beds of a local tavern."[8]

The rest did Boston little good, as the team bowed to Cleveland 5–3 on Monday as Cy Young outdueled John Clarkson in a matchup of two future Hall of Fame pitchers that only 2,100 witnessed.

Chicago became the first of the four League purebreds to break ranks on the Sunday baseball issue, after Spalding sold the club following the 1892 season to focus on his sporting goods business. New owner Jim Hart had a vastly different stance toward Sunday baseball than did Spalding.

When asked if Sunday games would be played in Chicago, Hart replied, "Well, it looks that way. The old stockholders who objected to Sunday games having retired there seems to be no reason why we should not play on that day. I shall urge the new board to adopt a more liberal policy and I have every reason to believe that the vote will be in favor of open Sundays."[9]

On April 30, 1893, Chicago became the first "home-grown" National League team, one without any roots in the American Association, to play an official game on Sunday when it defeated Cincinnati 7–1 at League Park in Cincinnati.

Chicago also became the first League purebred to play Sunday baseball at its home grounds. Hart had to build a new park for the Sunday games, though, erecting the West Side Grounds at Lincoln and Polk Streets.

Hart needed a new facility for Sunday games because the team's lease on South Side Park prohibited Sunday amusements. Hart also couldn't go back to the old West Side Park, where the team had played before 1892, since the Columbian Exposition had expropriated the park to use as part of the World's Fair to honor the 500th anniversary of the arrival of Christopher Columbus on North American shores.[10]

The Columbian Exposition was a perfect vehicle to help Hart to interject professional Sunday baseball into Chicago. There was a brewing battle in 1892 between Chicago Sabbatarian groups and operators of the

Columbian Exposition. At issue was the proposed opening of the Exposition on Sundays.

"Should Congress persist in holding the World's Fair management to the narrow minded policy with regard to the Sunday question, it will be positively necessary that as many harmless places of amusement as possible be open on Sundays to visitors who will be in the city," Hart remarked. "And base ball is the king of American outdoor amusement."[11]

Conversely, if the Sunday advocates for the Exposition were successful, Hart would also have a ready opening to consider Sunday baseball in the Windy City.

Hart went ahead and began construction of the West Side Grounds for Sunday baseball. Hart originally intended the new park to be just for Sunday games, with the team continuing to play its games the other six days of the week at South Side Park.

The Columbian Exposition, where the Ferris Wheel ride made its debut, opened its gates for patrons to visit the fair on May 1, 1893. The Exposition was closed on Sunday, May 7, but opened for visitors to walk through beginning May 14.

Also on May 14, the first Sunday game in Chicago was played at West Side Grounds as 13,500 spectators crammed into the new park, the largest crowd ever to attend a ball game in Chicago at that time. It appeared the game would be a blowout for Chicago. Chicago led 11–2 when Cincinnati came to bat in the bottom of the seventh inning (Chicago, the home team, had elected to bat first as the rules permitted at the time). However, Cincinnati scored 11 runs in the next three innings, including four in the bottom of the ninth, for a 13–12 victory.

The May 14, 1893, inaugural Sunday game in Chicago went on without Sabbatarian interference, after the lack of success in stopping the Columbian Exposition from opening on Sundays. That didn't mean that Hart's club was home free on the Sunday issue. The Sabbatarians merely delayed action until the Exposition completed its run.

Since Chicago, the once-staunch opponent of Sunday baseball among League clubs, had embraced the Sunday baseball concept, on the following Sunday, May 21, the New York and Brooklyn clubs played an exhibition game at Eastern Park in Brooklyn to benefit Darby O'Brien, a former Brooklyn player who was dying. About 10,000 people witnessed the benefit game, which Brooklyn won 13–7. Before the game, a favorable editorial had appeared in the *Brooklyn Daily Eagle*:

> Sunday amusements of any kind require the attention of none who is opposed to them, but they can certainly draw the attendance of others in

favor of them in such a way that the latter will in no manner impale the privileges or rights of strict Sabbatarians.[12]

This was one of the first indications that Sunday baseball was beginning to be accepted in the eastern strongholds of the Sabbatarians. *Sporting Life* remarked, "Most people in mature life can remember—not so long ago, either—when such teaching and such treatment of Sunday laws would have filled most of the old Sabbatarians with well displayed horror."[13]

With no apparent major repercussions to home attendance from the Sunday benefit game, Brooklyn began to play Sunday baseball on the road six weeks later. One aspect of the May 21 exhibition, however, did provide fodder to Sabbatarians. The incident, along with several other Sunday-related incidents over the next few years, gave rise to the assertion that there were real-life examples where the Lord looked unfavorably upon Sunday baseball.

Bill Collins, who played in just four major league games in his career, was the New York catcher in the Darby O'Brien benefit game. Unfortunately, Collins died two weeks later on June 8 of a severe cold, apparently contracted at Eastern Park during the benefit game.[14]

Some Sabbatarians viewed Sunday-related deaths, train wrecks, and ballpark fires as indications of the Lord's displeasure with Sunday baseball. "There are those who see in the lynchings and the disorders of the land a withdrawal of God's favors for our desecration of the day of rest," one Brooklyn minister said from the church pulpit.[15]

Brooklyn went forward with its foray into Sunday baseball on the road with its July 9 game at Louisville. The *Brooklyn Daily Eagle* was rather nonchalant about reporting the local team's inaugural Sunday game in the National League, mentioning nary a word about that aspect in its article about the 19–8 Louisville victory. Only a sub-headline "Brooklyn Loses a Sunday Game at Louisville" remarked about the Sabbath aspect.[16]

The Brooklyn-Louisville game on July 9 was the first Sunday game at the new Eclipse Park. It was also the last Sunday home game played by Louisville for the 1893 season.

Louisville had, until that point in time, a relatively quiet history with Sunday baseball activities over the 11 years that pro baseball had been played on Sunday in Louisville since 1882. That was at the old Eclipse Park, though, which was situated within the city limits of Louisville before it burned down in late September 1892.

A new Eclipse Park was built for the 1893 season right across 28th Street from the old park, which technically put the new park about a hundred yards outside the Louisville city limits into the town of Parkland. It's a matter of conjecture whether the good citizens of Parkland were really concerned "that base ball on Sunday was not really the proper thing" or that they had spotted a new revenue source for the town treasury.[17]

Since the new ballpark was so close to the old one, it does seem somewhat spurious that an orderly Sabbath was the primary concern of the Parklanders. And since the Louisville club had just shelled out a few dollars to build the new park, it would be easy to believe that the club could be persuaded to part with a portion of its Sunday revenue in order to obtain a return on its investment in the park.

The Parkland Town Council overplayed its hand, though. The Council passed an ordinance prohibiting Sunday baseball with a heavy fine that would have made Sunday games uneconomical for the ball club. The baseball team took its case to the Louisville politicians for relief. The Louisville City Council's answer was to extend the city limits and annex the portion of Parkland where the new Eclipse Park was located.[18]

This annexation allowed the July 9 game to be played. "The people of Parkland may visit their next door neighbors this afternoon and witness a base-ball game and drink beer to their hearts' content," the *Louisville Courier-Journal* wrote. "This is something they could not do last Sunday, for then the ball park was in Parkland, but still they don't appreciate the privilege."[19]

Parkland officials decried the annexation as an illegal land taking and appealed the action. While the appeal worked its way through the court system, however, Louisville was precluded from playing any of its scheduled Sunday games in the new Eclipse Park.

In October, the court rebuffed the apparently greedy Parkland opportunists. Judge Edwards of the Chancery Division of the Circuit Court ruled that "the base ball park had been annexed to Louisville in a perfectly legal manner and the town of Parkland was permanently enjoined from interfering with Mr. Ruckstahl in permitting Sunday games."[20]

"Had the Parkland citizens acted with any degree of sense, they could have gone on forever collecting taxes and a reasonable fine for Sunday games," *Sporting Life* remarked, since Louisville, like Cincinnati, was willing to pay a small fine as a cost of doing business on Sunday. "Now, the Parklanders hear the howls of the cranks on the Sabbath, but do not hear the merry clink in their pockets of Mr. Ruckstuhl's dollars."[21]

The upholding of the land annexation came too late in the 1893 season for Louisville to play any more Sunday games. Chicago, however, was able to accommodate the rescheduling of several of Louisville's aborted Sunday dates, since the new West Side Grounds were just sitting there idle on Sundays while the Chicago club was on the road. The added revenue would help Hart to more quickly recoup his investment in the ballpark.

This quest for additional lucrative Sunday gates, in the wake of Louisville's suspension of Sunday games pending the legal outcome of the annexation issue, led to further expansion of the one-game Sunday series concept. Since the Sunday games were not part of the original schedule, though, teams often took extreme measures to get in the Sunday games at Chicago.

While things went fine with the July 30 rescheduled game, the same could not be said for the game the following Sunday, August 6, at Chicago.

In order to get in the Sunday game, both Chicago and Louisville needed to train to Chicago from their games in Cleveland and Louisville, respectively. After Saturday's game in Cleveland, the Chicago team boarded the westbound New York & Chicago Limited passenger train. The team did not reach Chicago on time because the train ran off its rails in Lindsey, Ohio, outside of the city of Fremont about thirty miles southeast of Toledo and crashed into a stationary freight train.

"No. 9 passenger train, west bound, due here at 9:50 Saturday evening, met with a terrible accident at Lindsey, in which three lives were lost and nine persons were injured, two of them probably fatally," the *Fremont Daily News* reported. "The accident happened at 10:20 P.M.; the train being about ten minutes late in leaving Fremont, and running at a high rate of speed when the accident occurred. Just before Lindsey is reached there is a heavy grade and the train went thundering through the little village at about 45 or 50 miles per hour."[22]

Two Chicago ball players, outfielder Jimmy Ryan and catcher Malachi Kittridge, were seriously injured in the train wreck. Both players insisted on proceeding on their journey to Chicago after initial treatment on the scene by Doctors Woland and Stierwait of Lindsey. Their train arrived at the Van Buren Street depot in Chicago at 9:00 Sunday morning, two hours behind schedule.

"Jimmy Ryan was carried from the train on a stretcher and taken in a carriage to Mercy Hospital," the *Chicago Tribune* reported. "His right leg is badly lacerated and his head cut and bruised, causing intense suffering." Kittridge carried his right arm in a sling. Three other players were also hurt in the wreck—Cap Anson (bruised head), Willie McGill (head and arm bruises), and Walt Wilmot (bruises)—and had their heads in bandages. "The wounds of the injured men had only been roughly dressed on board the train and their bloody clothes and disfigured features were a sad sight for the many friends and relatives who had gathered to meet them."[23]

Upon his arrival at Mercy Hospital, Ryan "had the wounds on his legs reopened and sewed up a second time. A gash on his right leg seven inches long and two inches wide was inflicted." Coming out from under the influence of ether after the surgery on his leg, Ryan said, "I cannot remember any of the circumstances I passed through except that I heard a loud report and the next thing I remember I was standing on the roof of a freight car that lay on a side track. I spent the rest of the night in perfect torture."

Kittridge, who was less injured, was able to provide a more complete account of the accident.

> I had gone into my berth. The forward end of the car was demolished, and the remainder was pushed on top of the engine of the freight train and turned over to one side. My coat was hanging on a hook on the side of the berth, and I held myself up with this with one hand, while I broke the window with the other, cutting great gashes in my hand and arm, and in crawling through the window I cut my body badly in several places. As I came through the sleeping-car window I saw just below me the legs of the engineer and head brakeman projecting from a heavy set of trucks. They were already dead. Arriving on the outside I went over the roofs of the broken cars to the freight car roof, where Ryan was, his eyes blinded by the blood that was running down his face. Ryan had the presence of mind enough to tell the sleeping car porter, who was there also, that his friend West was down below, pointing to a pile of debris.

In Saturday's 8–4 loss at Cleveland, Ryan had played well with two hits in five at bats, and he almost had more as "twice Ryan was put out on flys that Burkett [the left fielder] nearly fell in getting." Ryan couldn't play in the Sunday game that the No. 9 train was transporting the team to from Cleveland, so George Decker assumed Ryan's spot in the Chicago outfield. Decker went four for five in Sunday's 12–7 victory over Louisville, before the team hopped onto the train again to go to Pittsburgh for a game on Monday.

The *Chicago Tribune* had noted that Ryan would be able to play again in two to three weeks, but Ryan's injuries kept him on the sideline for the remainder of the 1893 season. Kittridge returned to action one week later on August 16.

Jimmy Ryan was an icon in Chicago, playing 14 years with the Chicago National League team from 1886 to 1900. The left-handed outfielder's tenure with the League team in Chicago was interrupted only by the one year Ryan played for the Chicago team in the Players League in 1890. Ryan compiled a .309 career batting average, which ranks just outside the top 100 all-time. His 451 doubles, 157 triples, and 1,642 runs scored all rank among the top 75 all-time.

Following the 1893 train accident on the way to a Sunday game in Chicago, Ryan rebounded in 1894 with a great season, batting .361 in the second year of higher overall batting averages due to the lengthened pitching

OLD JUDGE CIGARETTES Goodwin & Co., New York.

Jimmy Ryan was seriously injured in a train wreck outside Fremont, Ohio, in 1893 as the Chicago ball club was traveling to play a one-game Sunday series in Chicago the following day. (National Baseball Hall of Fame Library, Cooperstown, N.Y.)

distance in 1893. Ryan's best season was 1888 when he led the National League with 182 hits and finished second in batting with a .332 average, behind teammate and player-manager Cap Anson.

Ryan "was not one of Anson's favorites." Anson thought Ryan lacked hustle and even alleged that Ryan conspired with club management to remove Anson as manager after the 1897 season. When new manager Tom Burns named Ryan as captain in 1898, the team refused to play and Burns was forced to capitulate.[24]

The escapades with one-game Sunday series were just one manifestation of the gymnastics that teams would go through to play Sunday baseball in 1893 to earn the larger gate receipts typical of those playing dates.

Eastern owners had criticized travel schedules earlier in 1893 surrounding the two Sunday games on June 18, St. Louis at Chicago and Louisville at Cincinnati. All four teams involved in those two games had finished up series with eastern teams on Friday and used that Saturday as a travel day to reach their destinations for the Sunday games. Eastern teams regarded Saturday as the best playing date, without the ability to play Sunday baseball, and some owners were upset that the scheduling seemed to deprive them of needed Saturday revenue in favor of Sunday baseball in the west.[25]

Sunday games in 1893 were so successful financially for the Chicago club that Hart decided to play all the team's home games in 1894 at the West Side Grounds and forsake playing at South Side Park.

With the heightened commercialization of Sunday baseball in Chicago, the International Sunday Observance League, led by the Rev. W. W. Clark, went to court in 1894 to stop the games at West Side Grounds. The group opposed the Sunday games because "the games were a public nuisance that had caused a sharp decline in property values and encouraged the establishment of several disorderly saloons in the vicinity of the ball park."[26]

On August 5, a near tragedy occurred at the Sunday game in Chicago. "Fire and panic drove 5,000 people in a wild stampede through a high and strong barbed wire fence at West Side Ball Park yesterday afternoon. Not less than 500 men and boys were torn and lacerated by the sharp barbs," the *Chicago Tribune* reported about the fence erected to keep the sometime raucous spectators from going on the playing field. "Men began to clamber up these wires like rats in a cage and drop over into the field below. Men and boys fought and clawed at each other to get a chance at the rasping barrier. Men came popping out through the wires, their faces and hands torn and bloody, their clothes in rags, wild with fright. The wires were strung with hair and strips of skin and flesh."[27]

Chicago players, led by Wilmot, Ryan, and Decker, used bats to try to bring down the barrier so spectators could escape the fire. Finally, the staples holding the wires to the wooden posts let go and the fence came down to let the other spectators onto the field.

Chicago defeated Cincinnati 8–1 in the fire-shortened, six-inning game.

Rather than feel sympathy for the trapped spectators at the West Side Grounds, the Sabbatarians used the fire incident as an opportunity to stop Sunday baseball there. Five days later, on Friday August 10, the Chicago club was slapped with an injunction not to play Sunday at West Side Grounds. Judge Horton dissolved the injunction on August 11, permitting the August 12 Sunday game to go on as scheduled (which Chicago won 16–5 over Cleveland).[28]

Hart was "indignant at the devices resorted to by the Sabbatarians to bring about their ends." In an interview in *Sporting Life*, Hart had some harsh words for those trying to stop Sunday baseball in Chicago.

> Their strongest capital is falsehood. They cannot confine themselves to the truth. The affidavit was a tissue of hearsay gush, without any evidence in fact. I do not claim that the patrons of the game are not at some stages of the game noisy, but there have been no drunken men on the grounds. A bold attempt was made to injure our business. I like fair play, but will not stand underhand methods such as have been resorted to in the present case.[29]

On August 30, another fire broke out at the West Side Grounds, destroying the reconstruction of the stands from the August 5 fire. Since the Chicago team was on an eastern road trip at the time, the fire was "believed to be the work of an incendiary." Hart later was quoted as saying he was "not sure of the incendiary's motive," but he may well have thought that those who didn't approve of Sunday baseball might have taken their cause too far.[30]

Undaunted by the legal setback, the Sabbatarians in 1895 instigated a test case for the courts to determine the legality of Sunday baseball in Chicago. On June 23, police arrested the Chicago players in the third inning before 10,000 spectators at West Side Grounds in a pre-planned police action.

Umpire Galvin before the game had announced to the crowd, "The game will be delayed for five minutes after the third inning." After the Colts were retired for a third time by Cleveland, "Capt. Anson called them to him and all trotted off to the club-house to be arrested and released on bail. The crowd waited patiently, and in less than five minutes play was resumed."[31]

Secured earlier in the day from Justice Cleveland of Norwood Park, the warrants were served on the Chicago team after Reverend Clark had witnessed the game being played from his perch on the roof of a house overlooking the ballpark. As fast as the players could sign their names to bail bonds in the clubhouse, they were released. After taking the field again, Chicago defeated Cleveland 13–4.

The Chicago players were initially found guilty in September and fined $4 apiece. On appeal, the decision was reversed in January 1896. Only one player, Walt Wilmot, was put on trial, with the expectation that if he were found not guilty, Judge Freeman would apply that decision to the cases of the remaining players.

At the January 13 trial, the prosecution, under the advisory of the International Sunday Observance League, attempted to show that noise and the character of the crowd at the Sunday games disrupted the peace of neighbors to the West Side Grounds. The prosecution's case was disrupted when it was revealed that one of its witnesses, Edward Thompson of 789 West Taylor Street, "had sold seats on his rear shed to persons wishing to view the ball game in progress on the eventful Sunday." Thompson claimed that the case was about "the peace and quiet of the West Side Sabbath," not whether he "had accumulated any wealth in this connection."[32]

Wilmot was found not guilty, and Sunday baseball was legitimatized in Chicago. There was some noise in future years about legal action on Sunday baseball, but no further decisions changed the January 1896 ruling. As late as 1919, former Cubs owner Charles Murphy remarked casually about the lack of enforcement of an Illinois law on Sunday baseball.

"We have in Illinois an archaic statute forbidding baseball on Sunday—and have had for many years—but it is played by municipal tolerance," Murphy wrote. "Public sentiment is for it and no man holding elective office, who would oppose Sunday baseball, could be re-elected. When I was president of the Cubs, I was never arrested for violation of that archaic law, because it is looked upon as a dead letter. The Chicago people realize that Sunday baseball is a great moral agent and that it lessens crime."[33]

With Sunday baseball firmly established in Chicago, other National League teams located farther east could now more confidently proceed forward to try to win approval for Sunday games.

Chapter 7

CLEVELAND ATTEMPTED IT

With all the legal maneuvering in Chicago having arrived at a favorable conclusion for Sunday baseball for the League owners in 1896, Cleveland owner and streetcar magnate Frank Robison began to contemplate playing Sunday baseball at League Park within the Cleveland city limits.

Robison hoped attendance at Sunday games would prop up sagging attendance. Despite two second-place finishes in 1894 and 1895, which resulted in appearances in the Temple Cup series each year, the team did not draw well in Cleveland.

While Sunday baseball at the professional level in Cleveland hadn't been tested since its legal setbacks in the 1880s, amateur baseball on Sunday did thrive in Cleveland in the early 1890s. In the summer of 1895, one commentator believed that 50 to 60 amateur games of baseball were played each Sunday in the city of Cleveland and he pleaded for consistency between the amateur and the professional game.

> They were played in the back yards, open spaces, at street intersections, on the river bed, at the east end and the west end, and all around. Any objection? Not a bit. They were scrappy games. There were shouting and confusion. There were some knock-downs and drag-outs. Not a protest. But a League game in an enclosure, with no rioting, no confusion, is different. It's base ball you have to pay for.[1]

Not only did the Cleveland populace not want Robison's team to play Sunday games at home, but its citizens also were reputedly so averse to the team playing Sunday games on the road that they declined to patronize the Cleveland home games.

"If these people who have stayed away from our home games because of the fact that we played Sunday ball will come out and make this good, we will be happy and will play no more Sunday games," Robison said that winter, calling the city's bluff by announcing no Sunday road games will be played in 1896. "I don't believe fifty people in the city of Cleveland stay away from games because we play in cities like Chicago, Cincinnati, and St. Louis on Sunday. I hope I am in error. I hope the people of Cleveland will appreciate our sacrifice and patronize our splendid club."[2]

Additionally, many newspapermen blamed Cleveland's fall from first place in July 1895 on the team's numerous losses in Sunday games on the road.

Indeed, Cleveland did drop four consecutive Sunday games in July, games that had been scheduled as one-game series in Chicago, Louisville, and Cincinnati. Not only were the defeats demoralizing, but the additional train travel contributed to the fatigue of the team as it played its weekday games. The Sunday scheduling could have partially accounted for Cleveland finishing in second place in 1895, rather than in first place.

While Cleveland's 5–9 record on Sundays in 1895 was certainly a contributing factor in failing to finish in first place, a bigger element was the reluctance of the team's star pitcher to appear in Sunday games. Cy Young, who had compiled a superlative 35–10 record for Cleveland in 1895, was not the starting pitcher in any of Cleveland's 14 Sunday games that year.

Young was one of the few players who held strong Sabbatarian beliefs, and as a premier pitcher he could command a clause in his contract that prohibited him from participating in Sunday games. In the heat of the 1895 pennant race, though, Young relented on his contract stipulation and told Cleveland manager Patsy Tebeau that he'd pitch on Sunday if the team needed him.

On September 15, with less than three weeks left in the 1895 season, Young appeared in his only Sunday game of the year, in a relief role in the second game of a doubleheader against a hapless St. Louis team. Cleveland had crushed St. Louis 19–9 in the opening game of the doubleheader, but starting pitcher Phil Knell had pitched ineffectively in the second game and the Spiders were losing as darkness loomed.

With no other rested pitchers available, Young consented to pitch relief that Sunday afternoon. Young wasn't overly sharp, but he didn't need to be against the next-to-last-place St. Louis team. Cleveland rallied and won 8–5 in seven innings.

The relief appearance became one of Young's favorite anecdotes later in life, according to biographer Reed Browning in his book *Cy Young: A Baseball Life*. "The Bible stated that rescuing your neighbor's ass from the pit on the Sabbath was not a sin," Young would begin his retelling to a group of observers. "Well, boys, I'll be durned if I know any bigger ass than Tebeau anywhere, and he certainly was in an awful hole. So I helped him out."[3]

The National League schedule for the 1896 season did not call for Cleveland to play any Sunday games in either of its two scheduled trips to Cincinnati, Louisville, Chicago, or St. Louis. That no-Sunday policy, though, lasted just half a season.

Even with the new half-holiday law in effect for the first time in 1896, allowing workers the chance to attend Saturday afternoon games, there was no appreciable overall increase in attendance at League Park in the early part of the season. During an 18-game home stand in May, Cleveland drew crowds of just 600–800 people to its home games even as the team played well enough to capture first place in the League standings by mid–June.

Statue of Cy Young on the campus of Northeastern University in Boston, Massachusetts. Young had fewer Sunday baseball problems in Puritanical Boston, where the concept was forbidden, than when he pitched in Cleveland. (Author's collection)

"The Goody-Goods who were so shocked at the idea of Sunday games told Mr. Robison his attendance was hurt from 2,000 to 2,500 a day because of the club's wickedness. One or two local papers joined in the demand and said fully 2,000 people were kept at home by reason of this," *Sporting Life* related. "As everyone who knew anything at all knew full well the 'holler' against Sunday games was made by a few extremists, who never saw a base ball game in their life."[4]

On the club's eastern road trip, "Robison says his club will resume Sunday ball playing on the next trip through the west," adding that the lack of Sunday games had cost him $10,000. Interestingly, the 1896 schedule contained an open date for each Sunday in July at one of the four western cities, perhaps designed to accommodate a potential reversal in Robison's Sunday policy.[5]

Cleveland played its first Sunday game of the 1896 season on July 12, a 5–2 victory for the Spiders over the Colts in Chicago. On Sunday, July 19, Cleveland played a doubleheader at Louisville where Cy Young, who had previously held strong Sunday beliefs, pitched the second game for a 7–0 victory. Young scattered nine hits and struck out seven, as Jesse Burkett whacked five hits in five at bats. Cleveland fell out of first place in Cincinnati, losing the July 26 Sunday game 10–1. The club finished in second place for the 1896 season and lost the Temple Cup post-season series to first-place Baltimore in four straight games.

In Cincinnati on July 19, 1896, a new National League attendance mark was set when 24,900 ventured into League Park to see the game with Baltimore. The game between the first and second place teams eclipsed the previous high of 24,000 that had witnessed a Decoration Day holiday game in New York in 1894.

For the first time in the five-year history of Sunday play in the National League, a Sunday game had established a National League attendance record, since all previous League highs had been established on holidays. Clearly, Sunday baseball was on an upswing.

"Such an assemblage of people has never before witnessed a ball game ... a new record for the entire league was established by yesterday's unprecedented turn out," the *Cincinnati Enquirer* puffed, although the Reds lost the game 14–6. "It was people everywhere you looked. Only a limited part of the lot was left for the ball game ... baseball rooters were perched on the top of fences and on every pinnacle or projection from which they could command a view of the game."[6]

Sunday baseball seemed to be the one possible panacea to cure Robison's financial ills with the Cleveland team. After the attendance debacle following the policy of no Sunday road games in 1896, Robison moved forward for his team to play home games on Sunday during the 1897 season, despite the unfavorable past history that Robison had with Sunday baseball in Cleveland. Robison also quickly let the newspapers know that if he wasn't able to play Sunday ball in Cleveland, he'd move the team elsewhere.

"President Robison decided to play Sunday games and after negotiating for grounds in the suburbs with unsatisfactory results, announced that they would be played on the Lexington Avenue grounds [at League Park]," *The Sporting News* reported in March 1897. "Robison announced that if Sunday games were prohibited he would transfer the club to another city."[7]

The possibility that the Cleveland team might transfer to St. Louis was raised that winter. "St. Louis is the third best base ball city in the Union [second only to New York and Philadelphia] yet possesses the weakest team in the League. Cleveland is the poorest in patronage of the League cities, but has one of the strongest teams to represent it," *The Sporting News* analyzed the situation. "The Cleveland team in St. Louis would be a 'gold mine' to its owners. The St. Louis team in Cleveland could draw scarcely worse than Tebeau's great team has been doing. It would be a wise business transaction for the St. Louis and Cleveland clubs to pool and transfer teams. Such a consummation is not at all improbable."[8]

Robison's quest to play Sunday baseball in Cleveland proper was not without resistance. Immediately after Robison's announcement that he intended to play on Sunday, both the Congregationalist and the Presbyterian ministers adopted a formal protest against the action.

Not only were religious leaders against Robison's plan to play Sunday baseball, but Cleveland mayor Robert McKisson was also. The Cleveland city ordinance permitting Sunday baseball to be played within an enclosed area within city limits conflicted with Ohio state law. While that law was seldom enforced anywhere in Ohio but in Cleveland, McKisson intended to enforce the state law and continue to forbid Sunday baseball.

In April, as preparations were made for the first professional Sunday game in Cleveland since 1887 to be held on May 16, Robison said he expected that he, not any players, would be arrested after the first Sunday game. He also "didn't think a jury could be found in Cuyahoga County to convict either him or the players." Robison had also apparently demurred on the subject of selling or moving the team. "There was some talk of transferring the Cleveland club, but I desire to try on Sunday ball before taking any further steps," Robison explained.[9]

As the date for the first Sunday game on May 16 came closer, the Sabbatarian groups revved up their rhetoric.

> Inasmuch as the Honorable Robert McKisson, mayor of the city of Cleveland, has publicly declared that he will enforce the law of the state in regard to the playing of base ball in this city on Sunday and will do all in his power to prevent Sunday games ... we recommend the actions of the mayor to all law-abiding citizens of this city and suggest that in some way they assure the mayor of their support in his efforts to uphold the laws of this commonwealth.[10]

There was another unsuspected ally of the clergy in this Sabbatarian movement, though—the Liquor League. The unlikely duo of church and booze, "necessity makes strange bed fellows" the *Cleveland Plain Dealer* once remarked, teamed up to quash Sunday baseball in Cleveland.[11]

7. Cleveland Attempted It

In a *Sporting Life* article entitled "The Conflicting Elements Opposed to Sunday Baseball" with the sub-headline "The Church Finds an Ally in the Saloon in the Coming Local War on the Working Man's Only Innocent Sunday Amusement," a spokesman for the saloonkeepers said:

> Sunday ball games will simply empty the downtown saloons of the city on that day. Men and boys, instead of lingering in barrooms, visiting, playing cards or shaking [dice] for drinks will go to the games and spend the 75 cents or a dollar each, they otherwise leave with us. If Sunday games are played, we will lose three-fourths of this patronage. We can afford to unite and expend $5,000 or $10,000 if necessary to defeat the project to play Sunday games in this city.[12]

"It is a notorious fact that Sunday in Cleveland is the most fruitful day for the saloon keepers of any in the week," *Sporting Life* concluded in the article. "The crowd of rum-soaked unfortunates in the police court every Monday morning is sufficient proof of this fact."[13]

To maintain political control, Mayor McKisson may have been as motivated to appease the liquor interests in his attempt to shut down Sunday baseball as he was to keep the religious interests content.

On May 16, a huge crowd tried to enter League Park for the first Sunday game in Cleveland in a decade. Since the game was heavily advertised, easily 10,000 people passed through the turnstiles to enter the park. After the gates were closed at 2:30 for the 3:00 game, there were reportedly more people outside the gates trying to get in than there were in the grounds. Cash checks were issued with each ticket, as the club expected the game to be stopped.

Both teams were retired in the first inning of the game without a score. But when Cleveland went to bat in the top of the second inning, police captain English and owner Robison approached umpire Tim Hurst and informed him that the game was to be halted. English then arrested the nine players in the game from each team and took them to the central police station four miles from the park. After the arrests, Robison turned to the huge crowd and said, "The authorities have stopped the game and it cannot continue. We do not want the slightest disorder or trouble of any kind on the grounds. I am sorry the game has been stopped, but we will fight the case in the courts and hope to soon give you Sunday ball in Cleveland."[14]

"Sunday baseball in Cleveland was not a roaring success yesterday, and the long fight on the subject was ended, for the time being, by the arrests of the players of the Cleveland and Washington teams after one inning had been played," the *Cleveland Plain Dealer* reported. "The game was stopped according to program and that means a victory against Sunday ball—but for whom is the victory? It was not the Clevelands nor yet the Washingtons, it may have been the city Ministers' Union, but there are strong indications that it was the Liquor League."[15]

There was a festive atmosphere in the arrest process after the players arrived by carriage at the police station. The players were ushered into the turnkey's room and "then the stately Lieut. Herman Felhaber, with a new filled fountain pen in his hand, marched to the registration window, laid violent hands upon the blotter, and called: 'Step up, gentlemen, and get your tickets. You will have a full half hour before the main circus in the large tent commences.' [He then] booked Umpire Hurst." Burkett was the first ball player to be booked and was "to all outward appearances, far from unhappy. He smiled and talked pleasantly with the lieutenant, and seemed to relish the entire proceeding as an 18-karat joke." After the players were booked, they went to the turnkey's desk, where Clerk Honecker had them sign their bail bonds ($100 each, paid for by Robison) and they were released.[16]

Of all 18 arrested players, Jack Powell would obtain immortality in legal circles for having played one inning for Cleveland on May 16, 1897. "Arrangement has been made with the authorities whereby only one man will of necessity appear. This one will be Powell, who was put in the game yesterday and assigned to first base," the *Cleveland Plain Dealer* reported. "It will be a test case. Powell will know a whole lot about the baseball law when it is finished." Powell, a pitcher in his first year in the major leagues, played one inning at first base while Zeke Wilson took the mound that day.[17]

Powell sat through a trial in the police court that week and a jury found him guilty of violating Section 7032a of the Ohio statutes, which provided that:

> Whoever on the first day of the week, commonly called Sunday, participates in or exhibits to the public, with or without charge for admittance, in any building, room, ground, garden or other place in this state ... any baseball playing, he or she shall, on complaint made within twenty days thereafter, be fined in any sum not exceeding $100, or be confined in the county jail not exceeding six months, or both, at the discretion of the court.[18]

With the Cleveland police court upholding the Ohio Sunday law, it was clear that Robison was going to have to find another legal avenue in order for his Cleveland Spiders to play baseball on Sunday. The jury verdict in the Powell trial caused Robison to cancel the Sunday, May 23, game slated to be played with Baltimore.

Robison enlisted the help of the law firm Solders, Hogsett & Tilden to appeal Powell's conviction on the ground that the Ohio Sunday law was unconstitutional. They argued that the Sunday law violated the Ohio constitution, specifically sections one and seven of its bill of rights, by infringing on Powell's personal individual liberty and by compelling a religious observance.[19]

Judge Walter Ong of the Common Pleas Court agreed with the constitutional arguments. On July 9, Judge Ong overturned Powell's conviction and declared the statute unconstitutional. The *Cleveland Plain Dealer* trumpeted the decision in the headline "Base Ball Playing Not a Crime."[20]

Ong decided that the validity of the statute rested on one of two predicates: "It must either be unlawful or an offense to play or exhibit baseball on Sunday because it is a Sunday, or it must rest upon the fact that it is an immoral game or exhibition falling clearly within the police power or regulation." Ong determined that the statute was enacted to "compel the observance of that day as a day of religious worship," not "as a day of rest," and that baseball was not immoral as the other games and actions cited in the statute.[21]

Jack Powell pitched 16 years in the major leagues from 1897 to 1912. The right-hander threw with a free and easy sidearm delivery, compiling a 245–254 won-loss record in 578 games and nearly 4400 innings pitched. His 254 career losses have the dubious distinction of ranking #8 all-time behind such greats as Cy Young, Nolan Ryan, and Walter Johnson.

Early in his career, Powell teamed with Young as the 1-2 combination of the pitching staff for the Cleveland and St. Louis teams of 1898–1900. In the year following his celebrated Sunday baseball court case, Powell won 23 games for Cleveland in 1898 and followed up with another 23 wins in 1899 when both he and Young were transferred to St. Louis, the other team owned by Frank Robison.

Powell took a liking to St.

Jack Powell was convicted of playing Sunday baseball for Cleveland in 1897 and appeals in his case, *State v. Powell*, went all the way to the Ohio Supreme Court, which upheld his original guilty verdict. (National Baseball Hall of Fame Library, Cooperstown, N.Y.)

Louis, pitching for the St. Louis club in the American League for nine years following his stint with the National League team in St. Louis. He even opened a saloon in St. Louis with his brother-in-law and former batterymate, Jack O'Connor.[22]

The prosecutor appealed Ong's ruling to the Ohio Supreme Court. But since that appeal would take some time, Robison was able to resume Sunday baseball games at League Park until the Powell case was finally resolved.

On July 11, Cleveland staged the first of six Sunday home games in 1897, played under the auspices of Judge Ong's ruling that the Sunday law was unconstitutional. Befitting the occasion, Powell—he of the legal case making its way to the Ohio Supreme Court—pitched for the Spiders on that first legally sanctioned Sunday game in Cleveland. Powell gave up 13 hits to the Washington batters on July 11, but yielded only four runs as Cleveland trounced Washington 15–4 on a rainy day before less than 1,000 spectators at League Park.

"John Powell, the player who was tried on the Sunday ball case, won as decisive a victory as he did in the courts and one which can never be reversed," the *Cleveland Plain Dealer* commented. "Rain fell at intervals in the first few innings, but the game was played just the same and the consummation of the victory for Sunday baseball accomplished." The article was headlined "Weather and Law: Sunday Baseball Has Proved Itself Victorious Over Both."[23]

The timing was perfect for the newfound ability to play on Sunday. The eastern teams were just making a western swing, and Cleveland could schedule the three Sunday-playing eastern teams for Sunday engagements at League Park.

Powell also won the following week's Sunday game on July 18, pitching more effectively against Brooklyn, yielding only five hits in an 8–1 rout by Cleveland. Baltimore defeated Cleveland 6–5 the following Sunday, though, to break the Sunday winning streak.

Robison was only able to schedule three more Sunday games the remainder of the season, all against western teams where they had openings. Powell won his third 1897 Sunday game on August 15, a 13–3 pasting of St. Louis as the Spiders supported Powell with 20 hits, including four by his catcher Chief Zimmer. St. Louis had a horrible team in 1897, finishing the season with a 29–102 record mired in last place with no other team remotely contesting it for the bottom spot.

A month later, on September 12, Cleveland pummeled St. Louis again on a Sunday, a 15–4 beating as the Spiders collected 22 hits. The Sunday season concluded at League Park on September 26, with a 4–3 loss to Louisville.

7. Cleveland Attempted It

Hedging his bet on the Ohio Supreme Court, Robison worked with a local legislator to sponsor the MacBroom bill in the Ohio General Assembly that would permit Sunday baseball if the court reversed Judge Ong in the Powell case.

Either way, Robison expected to play Sunday games in Cleveland in 1898 and had the 1898 National League schedule drawn up that way. With the proximity of Pittsburgh, just 150 miles to the east of Cleveland, as a natural rivalry to attract customers for Sunday games, Pittsburgh owners were enticed to start engaging in Sunday road games for the first time in 1898. The National League schedule paired up the two clubs for six Sunday games in Cleveland, four of the back-to-back, home-and-away variety on Saturday and Sunday to maximize interest.

Conservatives thwarted the Robison plans. On April 19, the Ohio Supreme Court issued its decision in *State v. Powell* to uphold the state law prohibiting baseball on Sunday. The timing couldn't have been worse, as that day was the eve of adjournment that year for the General Assembly of Ohio, making it impossible for a bill to be passed in 1898 to modify the supreme court decision.

The court ruled that the law "neither requires nor prohibits any religious observance, and does not therefore violate the right of conscience in matters of religion." The court went on to say that the legislature has the power "to adopt all such wholesome laws as may be necessary to promote the peace, health, and well-being of society. Laws fixing regularly recurring days of rest from all secular pursuits, such as our Sunday laws, are of this character, and do not violate the personal liberty of the individual."[24]

As it turned out, the Ohio Supreme Court decision changed the course of National League history in a significant way.

While Robison had lost a major battle, he didn't yet concede the war. He tried once again to get Mayor McKisson to support Sunday baseball, to join mayors in other larger Ohio cities—not just Cincinnati but also Columbus, Toledo, Dayton, and Canton—that gave their blessing to non-enforcement of the Sunday law based on perceived public sentiment on the issue.

One positive factor in Robison's favor, an outgrowth of the six 1897 Sunday games in Cleveland, was the city police force as a strong advocate of a non-interference policy for Sunday ball games. "On Sunday when ball games are played at League Park, [the police] have nothing to do as the down-town saloons are drained empty and there is no drunkenness and consequently no disorderly conduct in the city," one writer pointed out the positive social value of Sunday ball games.[25]

Mayor McKisson did not relent on Sunday baseball, though, and attendance at League Park immediately plummeted once the 1898 season began. Less than 1,000 people went to the opening day game.

Robison scrambled to retool the Sunday schedule for his Cleveland team. The canceled May 1 Sunday game with St. Louis was combined into a doubleheader on May 3 with the rained out May 2 contest. Even a doubleheader drew only a few hundred spectators. A big crowd that was anticipated for the first Pittsburgh Sunday match-up on May 8 could not be recovered.

The club also switched dates with Chicago for their mid–May series to move the May 15 Sunday game from Cleveland to Chicago. Cleveland defeated Chicago 5–2 at West Side Grounds. Cleveland was in second place after the victory with a 16–6 record, but home games at League Park were now sparsely attended.

Robison reverted to a plan that he had used 10 years earlier in 1888 when his American Association team played several games at an amusement area on Geauga Lake. One of the sites that Robison looked at in 1898 was the budding Cedar Point amusement park in Sandusky, Ohio, about 40 miles west of Cleveland. Robison eventually settled on the more nearby Euclid Beach Park, 10 miles to the east and, not coincidentally, right on a streetcar line owned by Robison.

At the time, Euclid Beach Park was in the town of Collinwood, outside the city limits of Cleveland. The amusement park had been in operation since 1895 and Robison expected that the forbearance of the Collinwood town fathers for Sunday crowds at the amusement park would spill over to baseball played there on Sunday.

The first Sunday game at Euclid Beach Park was scheduled for June 12 against Pittsburgh. Robison no doubt had high hopes of salvaging some of the financial rewards that had originally been expected from the six scheduled Sunday matches between Cleveland and Pittsburgh.

Not surprisingly, the Cleveland anti–Sunday-baseball groups tried to stop the game at Euclid Beach Park. "Judges Dissette, Dellenbaugh, and Logue stated Saturday that it is almost impossible to stop the game by means of injunction," the *Cleveland Plain Dealer* reported on the day of the game. "The only manner for the authorities of Collinwood to pursue in order to stop the playing of Sunday ball is to arrest the players engaged in the game." But Robison seemed to have the situation under control. "I have discussed the Sunday ball question with many property owners in Collinwood and have found none who anticipate any annoyance," Robison told the newspaper. "In fact, the grounds will be so far away from any residence that there will be no harm done to anyone."[26]

The June 12 game went on unimpeded by authorities or Sabbatarians, as "the Collinwood opposition to Sunday ball failed to oppose, although two or three leading spirits were known to be present." The rain storm that day, however, may have had more to do with the lack of a dispute over the game.[27]

Bad weather held attendance down to 6,000 and shortened the game. After five innings, the game was called, with Pittsburgh winning 3–1. Powell, who had lost the Sunday battle in court, also lost the Sunday battle on this field as well, taking the loss as the Cleveland pitcher that day.

Sunday baseball may have survived to go on at Euclid Beach Park except for a letter from Robison to the *Plain Dealer* sporting editor that was published in the June 18 issue of the newspaper. In the letter, Robison railed at several Collinwood citizens:

> In the *Cleveland Leader* of June 9, appears the following notice: "Collinwood does not propose to have the discarded filth of Cleveland dumped upon the village, Secretary Clarke of the Young Men's Christian Association said yesterday." Could a more terrible statement than this be made? At the game at Euclid Beach Park last Sunday, the Rev. Berry of Collinwood was, as I understand, an attendant. He saw within the grounds thousands of men, women, and children. I would like to ask him publicly if he saw one disorderly or one intoxicated person. The ministers who are fighting baseball on Sunday may find a better and more Christianlike work to do in many other ways.[28]

Robison might have survived those words, but several sentences later in the letter probably did him in with the Collinwood residents:

> It looks to me as though some of the ministers who were fighting the cause like to see their names appear in the newspapers and as some of them are tolerably good politicians, they may have the idea that newspaper notoriety may get them a better job at a higher salary.

The June 19 game proceeded without interference only until the eighth inning. After Pittsburgh pitcher Jim Gardner hit a batter to force in a run to put Cleveland ahead 4–3, Marshall Waite and Constable Mayo of Collinwood appeared on the field with warrants sworn out by Reverend George Berry to arrest the Cleveland players. Berry, a Congregational minister, was a holdover from New England values of the Puritan Congregational ways and had great influence in Collinwood matters. The game was stopped at that point, but the players were actually arrested after they changed out of their uniforms into street clothes.[29]

Not only was that the last pitch the 3,000 spectators would see that day, it was also the last gasp of Sunday baseball for the League team in Cleveland.

Robison attempted to go forward with the June 26 game with the New York Giants. Mayor L. A. Hall of Collinwood, however, paid a visit that day to Stanley Robison, Frank's brother and a vice president of the Cleveland team, and "informed him that they would be arrested if they began playing" that Sunday. Hall, not only the mayor but also the proprietor of a local dry goods establishment in Collinwood, "explained that warrants had been secured the same as last Sunday, but that they would be served as soon as playing began and not after the game as they were a week ago."[30]

L. A. Hall, the mayor of the village of Collinwood, also operated a "Groceries and Dry Goods" business at 180 Collamer Street on the main thoroughfare in the village. Hall's store was located at the corner of Collamer Street and Manchester Avenue, right across the street from the Town Hall on Collamer Street and just a short distance from the Congregational Church (where George Berry was pastor) at the corner of Manchester and Mars. According to Hall's ad in *The Official Directory of Collinwood for 1899*, the store carried "Fruits, Vegetables, Fancy Groceries, Teas, Coffees, Canned Goods, Butter, Eggs, and the Best grades of Flour at reasonable prices."[31]

Talk of transferring the Indians, as the newspapers occasionally referred to the team rather than the Spiders, intensified following the forced cancellation of the June 26 game. Robison must have been furious, for he decided to forego the remainder of the Cleveland home schedule—not just Sunday games, but *all* of its home games. Instead, the team became an orphan team, playing its remaining games on the road. Some "home" games were switched to Philadelphia and Chicago, but for the majority of the time the Cleveland Spiders were the visiting team.

Mayor L. A. Hall of Collinwood stopped the Cleveland ball club in the National League from playing further Sunday games in that suburban Cleveland location in 1898. (*The Official Directory of Collinwood for 1899*)

The wandering Cleveland team did return home for one brief three-game series at League Park with the New York Giants from August 24 to 26. The games in Cleveland were not for sentimental reasons, but rather to launch the team's experiment to play an entire three-game series at a neutral site location in Rochester, New York. The series with Brooklyn included a Sunday game on August 28, sandwiched in between games on Saturday and Monday.

"After Friday's game the Indians were hustled off to Rochester for this series of games, apparently a most foolish proceeding, as it meant a financial loss to both teams," *Sporting Life* commented on the situation. These games added to "the anger of the faithful whose temper has been sorely tried by the transfer of games with the evident object of retaliating on the patrons of this city."[32]

Robison evidently must have negotiated a good deal with Rochester officials to keep his costs down. He seems to have sold hope that really wasn't obtainable.

"Rochester will be treated to three games of National League base ball," the *Rochester Herald* reported. "It is given out that if the games are sufficiently well patronized, the Cleveland team will be transferring to this city and the remaining home games of this season's schedule be played here."[33]

The two games at Culver Field in Rochester, New York, on Saturday and Monday attracted a fair crowd as upstate New York was treated to major league baseball for the first time since 1890. Of greater historical significance, though, was the August 28 Sunday game at Ontario Beach in Charlotte, New York, which was about 10 miles north of Rochester right on Lake Ontario. This game was the first use of a neutral site to play a Sunday game in the major leagues.

While an outgrowth of Cleveland's orphan status in 1898, the use of the Ontario Beach Grounds for the August 28, 1898, game pioneered the neutral-site Sunday strategy—the use of a ball park not close in proximity to the regular home grounds and not used regularly by the team. This strategy differed from the use of Sunday-only grounds, which were typically owned or under lease, and games were regularly played there. Neutral-site games were sporadic and the grounds used for just one day.

Rochester teams played Sunday games in the late 1890s at Ontario Beach. The Rochester team in the Eastern League had experimented with playing Sunday games there in 1897, setting the stage for Robison to play a major league game there in 1898.

Brooklyn defeated Cleveland 7–5 in the Sunday game at Ontario Beach. Brooklyn was aided both by five Cleveland errors on the lakeside grounds and the recently mown outfield, where the clippings of the previously standing tall grass had been simply tossed against the fence.

After hitting a long fly to right field in the seventh inning, Brooklyn's Fielder Jones circled the bases for a home run when right fielder Jack O'Connor fell down and then couldn't locate the ball in the dried grass against the fence. Mike Griffin scored ahead of Jones on the play, as Brooklyn benefited from the groundskeeper's actions.

Brooklyn fared better in an earlier, similar play when Tebeau's "fly was knocked into this grass and [Jimmy] Sheckard had to grab a handful of grass to get the ball quickly. When he threw the ball, he also scattered what looked to be about a bale of hay in the air," the *Rochester Herald* reported.[34]

Only about 1,000 attended the Sunday game. "The Sunday habitues of Charlotte are not of the baseball-attending kind," the *Rochester Democrat* reported, "while the usual patrons apparently will not go there on Sunday, even to see a game."[35]

It seemed fitting that Jack Powell pitched this last Sunday "home game" for Cleveland, even if he took the loss in the game.

While Cleveland finished with a respectable 81–68 record for fifth place in 1898, the team disintegrated in 1899 into one of the worst teams that ever played in the National League, compiling a dismal 20–134 record for a .130 winning percentage.

Robison purchased the St. Louis franchise in March 1899, and as permitted under the rules at the time, owned both teams during the 1899 season. Robison transferred his best Cleveland players to the St. Louis team and moved many of the last-place St. Louis players to the Cleveland team, adding a further dose of indignity to what few Cleveland baseball followers were left in the city.

The August 28, 1898, neutral-site Sunday game in Rochester was one of five National League games played that Sunday, a new high for the league as games were also played in the four western cities—Cincinnati, Chicago, Louisville, and St. Louis. While there had been four Sunday-playing western cities in the league since 1893, what made the five-game Sunday schedule possible in 1898 was the addition of two more eastern teams willing to play Sunday games on the road—New York and Pittsburgh.

As the Social Gospel Movement began to sweep through the ranks of Christian churches during the 1890s, opposition to Sunday baseball was defused a bit. The more tolerant religious attitude combined with the impact of the nation's economic depression in the mid–1890s led both the Pittsburgh Pirates and the New York Giants to participate in Sunday road games beginning with the 1898 season.

Pittsburgh was slated to play the first four Sundays in 1898, starting

7. Cleveland Attempted It 131

the season with a western swing. On April 17, Pittsburgh played its first championship Sunday game at Louisville. Before more than 10,000 spectators, Pittsburgh won 5–4 as Jesse Tannehill pitched and batted the Pirates to victory, with a home run that brought home the winning run. "There was no standing room to be had in the bleachers or the grand stand, and the space between the ropes and the left field seats was not large enough to accommodate the people," the *Pittsburgh Post* reported of the city's "first Sunday game in years."[36]

Crowds were large as well at Pittsburgh's next two Sunday stops in St. Louis and Cincinnati, ensuring a good fiscal start for Pittsburgh, even though its fourth Sunday game, scheduled for May 8 in Cleveland, was canceled due to the Ohio Supreme Court decision a few weeks earlier.

Not all churchmen, of course, were happy with Pittsburgh's decision to play Sunday baseball after an 11-year abstinence from such play in its American Association days. Two years later in 1900, the Rev. George Hawes of the town of Braddock, just east of Pittsburgh, said that "the Lord had assumed the management of the Pittsburgh club and had crippled several of the players for their Sunday work." Hawes blamed Pittsburgh's playing woes on Sunday baseball and "expressed belief that Sunday playing left little hope for them."[37]

Hawes failed to explain the impact of Sunday baseball on several other National League clubs. "Mr. Hawes should inform an awestricken, but puzzled world why the Lord is punishing Boston, a non–Sunday-playing club, by depriving it of the pennant last year and keeping it at the tail end of the League procession so far this year," *Sporting Life* jokingly commented. "And why the Lord has never yet permitted that other consistent and strict non–Sunday-playing League club, Philadelphia, to come within hailing distance of the championship."[38]

Boston and Philadelphia were the last holdouts for Sunday baseball, continuing to defer from playing Sunday road games to appease the customers on their home grounds.

The New York Giants played the team's inaugural Sunday road game on May 22, 1898, before 12,000 spectators at Sportsman's Park in St. Louis. Amos Rusie pitched New York to a 10–5 victory.

Back east, the Giants also began to play Sunday exhibition games on Sunday in Fairway, New Jersey, about nine miles from New York City. Special excursion tickets were available on the Erie Railroad for New York patrons to see the Sunday games. Tickets were sold at a reduced price of 15 cents, less than half the regular fare of 40 cents.[39]

The New Jersey exhibitions were so successful the Giants played two championship games that September. On September 11, the Giants defeated

Washington 8–2 at the West New York Field Club grounds in Weehawken. As the game was a makeup of a postponed game earlier in the season, Washington took the train from Philadelphia on Saturday, while New York came from Boston. The grounds seated 5,000 and were "comfortably filled" when the game began at 3:00.

A week later, 4,000 attended the New York-Brooklyn game at Weehawken to see the Giants win 7–3.

In 1899, the Giants played four more games in Weehawken, before the Sunday games were discontinued after that season.

Sunday baseball reached its 19th-century zenith on April 30, 1899, in Chicago when 27,489 persons crowded into West Side Grounds to see Chicago defeat St. Louis 4–0.

"The huge bleachers were piled full of joyous but uncomfortable spectators and around the field crowding in almost to the diamond was a circular mass of people," the *Chicago Tribune* described the throng at the game. "At times the field crowd would stampede and, sweeping away all the police, would bear down upon the players as if to break up the game, while the masses in the stands would rise as one man and cheer while the police in cordons drove back the encroaching mob. Yet not once during the game did the umpire have to call a halt."[40]

Thirty-four balls were lost during the game, "most of them falling into the hands of greedy small boys. The skirmishes between the police and retreating youngsters who had stolen balls furnished amusement for those who could not break through the ring of men to see the game."[41]

On August 12, Eclipse Park in Louisville burned down two months before the end of the 1899 season. The Louisville team tried to continue games, using temporary stands for spectators, but attendance dwindled.

Louisville's last Sunday game at Eclipse Park was on August 27, a doubleheader with Baltimore. While the Orioles won the first game 7–3 behind the seven-hit pitching of Joe McGinnity, the second game ended in a 4–4 tie after eight innings and was marred by a bizarre "two balls in play" situation.

Gene DeMontreville had hit a line drive past Fred Clarke in the outfield (the live ball). As DeMontreville rounded second base and was heading to third base for a three-base hit, a second ball (the dead ball), one that had been fouled out of play into the spectators innings before, was thrown in the direction of Louisville third baseman Tommy Leach.

Since Leach was looking for a throw of the live ball, he missed the dead ball. DeMontreville, who was oblivious to there being two balls on the field, saw a ball go past Leach so he rounded third base to head for home plate to score. After the live ball was thrown to the catcher who put out DeMontreville, "a big row ensued and trouble seemed imminent" with the recalcitrant Orioles squad.

Clarke of the Colonels and Aleck Smith of the Orioles were ejected from the game by umpire O'Day. When O'Day called the game after eight innings due to darkness, an ironic ending as darkness dawned on major league Sunday baseball in Louisville, "he called for police protection until leaving the grounds."[42]

Following the series with Washington that concluded on Saturday, September 2, Louisville owner Barney Dreyfuss rescheduled the club's remaining 14 home games as Louisville converted into an orphan team for the final six weeks of the National League season. Things looked dreary for Louisville as "some people profess to believe that it is the last League game that Louisville patrons will ever see."[43]

The wandering Louisville team used Sundays at the other three Sunday-playing cities to play in several unusual doubleheaders. The twist to the doubleheaders was that one team played two games, with each game against a different opponent. Many of these late-season doubleheaders involved the two orphan League teams, Louisville and Cleveland.

On Sunday, September 3, Louisville played in Cincinnati. The Reds played two games that Sunday, losing to Louisville 7–6 in the first game and then defeating Cleveland 3–1 in the second game. The following Sunday, Louisville and Cincinnati played again, with Cincinnati winning both games this time, first defeating Cleveland and then downing Louisville.

After Louisville did an eastern swing, the club landed at St. Louis for a doubleheader on Sunday, September 24. Rather than the home team St. Louis playing two games that day, as Cincinnati had earlier in the month, Louisville the visiting team played both games of the doubleheader. Louisville won both games, defeating St. Louis 7–6 in the first game and in an essentially neutral-site game defeated Cleveland 5–1 in the second game.

Louisville played the final three Sundays at Chicago, though they only actually played two games. On October 1, the weather was bad so Louisville passed on playing the second game of the doubleheader with Chicago. Only 700 people came in the drizzle for the first game between Chicago and Cincinnati. The following Sunday, October 8, Chicago did get in two games: a 13–0 victory over the hapless Cleveland team in the morning and a 7–3 win over Louisville in the afternoon game.

On October 15, Louisville played its last National League game in the second game of the doubleheader at Chicago before 7,000 spectators. Louisville won 9–5 in an eight-inning game called by darkness, although Chicago, with nothing to gain, "played a dreadfully bad exhibition."[44]

Clearly, the 12-team National League was an unwieldy number of teams and spectator interest waned in many cities early in the season when it became apparent those teams had no chance to win the pennant. Adding further embarrassment, syndicate baseball had decimated the teams in Cleveland and Baltimore, while Louisville had become an orphan team late in the season. These three teams, along with Washington, were dropped from the National League after the 1899 season ended, cutting the league back to its eight-team structure prior to the merger with the American Association for the 1892 season. Basically, the League dropped the franchises representing the four teams taken in from the Association, as the Cleveland team was the remnants of the St. Louis franchise.

After winning a legal victory in Chicago in 1896, but losing one in Cleveland in 1898, Sunday baseball in the National League received a shot in the arm in 1900 when the Missouri Supreme Court declared that Sunday baseball in the home state of St. Louis was proper and legal.

"Base ball does not belong to the same class, kind, species, or genus as horse racing, cock-fighting, or card-playing. It is a game of chance only to the same extent that chance or luck may enter into anything man may do," the court ruled. "Until the lawmakers expressly provide for such sweeping change in the lives and customs and habits of our people, it is not proper for the courts by construction to impair their natural rights to enjoy sports or amusements that are neither immoral nor hurtful to the body or soul. We, therefore, conclude that there is no law in this State which prevents playing a game of base ball on Sunday."[45]

While the National League had created a solid triumvirate of Sunday-playing clubs in Chicago, Cincinnati, and St. Louis by 1900, it would be a new major league in 1901 that would propel further activity on the Sunday baseball front in the next decade.

Chapter 8

AMERICAN LEAGUE LIKED IT

When the American League moved up to major league status for the 1901 season, Sunday baseball achieved greater geographical breadth at the top level of the game to regain some territory that it had lost with the contraction of the National League after the 1899 season.

The elevation of the American League from minor to major league status increased the stature of Sunday baseball in several ways.

In the inaugural American League season, three teams played Sunday baseball at home—Chicago, Detroit, and Milwaukee. The addition of the latter two cities increased the number of major league cities that played Sunday baseball at home to five, augmenting Chicago, Cincinnati, and St. Louis in the National League.

All eight American League teams played Sunday baseball on the road, a scheduling structure that the Boston and Philadelphia clubs seemingly had little qualm to pursue. This contrasted sharply with the position of the National League clubs in Boston and Philadelphia, which still refused to play Sundays on the road.

Chicago became the capital of Sunday baseball in the major leagues. With teams in both the American and National Leagues ready, willing, and able to schedule games on the Lord's Day, the city of Chicago enjoyed professional baseball nearly every Sunday of the major league season.

The ascension of Chicago to Sunday baseball capital was a major driver for the further acceptance of Sunday baseball. While the transition of Sunday baseball leadership from St. Louis to Chicago had been percolating since the mid–1890s, Chicago began to assert its prominence when the club drew three crowds of more than 20,000 spectators to Sunday games in 1898 and 1899. The April 30, 1899, game was perhaps the turning point, as 27,489 persons squeezed into the West Side Grounds to see Chicago defeat St. Louis 4–0. The attendance established a new major league record at the time, topping the previous high-water mark by more than 2,000 persons.[1]

Chicago's role in Sunday baseball was critical to the development of the Sunday game in eastern cities. When St. Louis and Louisville had been the primary seats of Sunday baseball power in both the latter days of the American Association and in the post–1891 National League, opponents of Sunday baseball could easily disparage it as being liquor-sponsored, immigrant-focused, or anti-church. With the flagship of Sunday baseball now in Al Spalding's backyard in Chicago, the nation's second largest city at the turn of the century, attacking Sunday baseball involved different tactics.

Contributing to Chicago's ascent in Sunday baseball was the decline in influence of St. Louis, then the fourth largest city in the country. The National League club in St. Louis by 1901 had lost the aura of its championship teams during the Chris Von der Ahe era, and was now genealogically more of Cleveland origin under the ownership of Frank Robison than St. Louis bred. Louisville was no longer a factor, having been summarily dismissed from its National League membership after the 1899 season. Cincinnati, while drawing good Sunday crowds, was only the tenth largest city in the country and possessed just one major league team, limiting its Sunday baseball influence compared to that of Chicago.

Sunday baseball had been instrumental in the rise of the American League during its days as a minor league. Two years before its initial major league season, the American League had operated as the Western League, which then consisted of midwestern teams for the most part, with its easternmost outpost in Buffalo, New York.

In 1899, all eight teams began the season playing Sunday home games. Kansas City, Milwaukee, and Columbus/Grand Rapids did not have trouble with Sunday play, while the Minneapolis and St. Paul teams used Sunday-only ball grounds to circumvent strong local resistance to Sunday play. Attempts by Buffalo and Indianapolis to use their regular grounds for Sunday games were eventually stopped by authorities before the end of the 1899 season. Detroit used a Sunday-only grounds for its Sunday games but even then faced the frown of the local sheriff, and the club had to defend itself in court.

Detroit played its first Sunday home game on April 30, 1899, at a new ball grounds in the township of Ecorse, located six miles southwest of the city but reachable by streetcar from center city Detroit. Detroit defeated Columbus 6–4 before 3,500 spectators "on the new ball field in Ecorse, just west of River Rouge, and the interference that many expected failed to materialize, the two teams being permitted to play the full game."[2]

Sunday play continued uninterrupted until June, before crowds of 4,000–5,000 people, when Sheriff Duff Stewart of Wayne County took up the cudgel to try to stop Sunday baseball in Ecorse. Stewart arranged for a test case to see if a conviction was possible under the statute forbidding Sunday amusements.

At the June 11 game in Ecorse, Sheriff Stewart stopped the game in the seventh inning. "I'll have it to a vote of the crowd whether we stop the game now or wait until it is completed," Stewart announced to the crowd. "It is not our intention to interfere with the sport, but we want to test the law and find out whether Sunday baseball is legal." With Detroit leading Minneapolis by two runs, the crowd voted unanimously to continue the game. Minneapolis scored three runs in the eighth inning to take the lead, but a two-run homer by Stallings gave Detroit a 10–9 victory.[3]

Sheriff Stewart arrested the players of both the Detroit and Minneapolis teams after the game concluded. When the local justice of the peace discharged the case against the players, Stewart then pursued the Detroit club officials. Even that action was unsuccessful. On June 21, Justice Burke of Ecorse acquitted the Detroit club on the charge of playing Sunday baseball.[4]

A six-man jury found William Harris, of the Detroit club, not guilty in Justice Burke's court. William Corbett, attorney for Harris, "had a receipt from Treasurer Beaubleu of Ecorse for $22.50 which had been paid into the poor fund of the township." Prosecutor Fales claimed the donation from the Detroit baseball club was simply a subterfuge to influence public opinion and quoted law and court decisions on the subject of Sunday baseball, but he was "unable to answer Corbett's arguments to the satisfaction of the jury." So began the legacy in Detroit of charitable contributions to obtain permission to play Sunday baseball.[5]

With Sunday baseball now "approved" in Wayne County, Jim Burns bought the Detroit club in 1900. Burns built a new Sunday-only ball grounds in the township of Springwells, which was then just outside the Detroit city limits but, at about three miles out, closer to Detroit center city than the Ecorse grounds. Not surprisingly, the new owner named the facility Burns Park.[6]

Indianapolis helped christen the new Sunday-only grounds on May 6, 1900, with an 11–5 victory over Detroit. The overflow crowd at the game was described in the following *Detroit Free Press* account entitled "More Crowd Than Ball" with a sub-headline, "Swarmed All Over the Field of Burns Park Yesterday":

> Burns Park, as the new Sunday ball grounds in this city have been named, was formally opened yesterday afternoon with an alleged game of baseball between the Detroit and Indianapolis teams. The park is roomy and seating accommodations for fully 3,000 people had been provided, but they were entirely inadequate and long before the hour for commencing play

arrived the crowd had commenced to swarm over the field. Ticket selling conveniences were also lacking and the people soon tired of standing in a line over a block long, so the gate keepers were forced to take money while many men and boys clambered over the high fence. There was no police protection, and finding how easy it was to gain admission, the enthusiasts went so far as to tear boards off the fence in the outfield, the result being that while the paid attendance was in the neighborhood of 4,000, fully 5,500 people were on the grounds.[7]

The overflow crowds indicated how popular Sunday baseball was in Detroit, since Burns Park wasn't located in a highly desirable area. Most references to its location cite its proximity to the stockyards, which must have lent a certain undesired scent to the air at the ball grounds. One description called Burns Park "the Sunday grounds, which is a vast stretch of glittering sand. This sand reflects and intensifies the heat of the sun's rays. Despite this, 4,000 people took their lives in their hands and went out to see what proved to be a great struggle."[8]

When the Western League adopted the moniker American League for the 1900 season, seven of its eight teams played Sunday home games. Buffalo emulated Detroit by playing at a Sunday-only grounds in Schwab. Cleveland also joined the American League in 1900, after losing its franchise in the National League. After Frank Robison's hassles with Sunday baseball in 1897–98, though, the Cleveland club in the American League didn't attempt Sunday games at home.

While Sunday baseball helped to finance the league's ambitions to reach major league status, league president Ban Johnson needed to jettison most of the cities that played in the 1899 and 1900 seasons to inject eastern blood into the league in order to make a run at the National League monopoly. Only Detroit, Cleveland, and Milwaukee survived for the 1901 season. Chicago was added in the western segment of the league. Baltimore, Boston, Philadelphia, and Washington were picked up to form an eastern component.

Although Johnson hadn't formally attempted to play Sunday baseball in or near the cities that formed the eastern segment of the American League, Sunday baseball was rapidly gaining acceptance in second-tier cities on the East Coast. In the Eastern League, baseball was played on Sunday in Providence, Rochester, and Syracuse (and in Montreal, Canada). Other league teams played Sunday baseball on the road, including the New England cities of Hartford, Springfield, and Worcester.

As the acceptability of minor league baseball on Sunday crept closer to major urban areas, it seemed only a matter of time before professional Sunday baseball reached acceptability in the major cities of Boston, New York, and Philadelphia.

8. American League Liked It

Sunday baseball at the major league level debuted in the American League on April 28, 1901, with games at Chicago and Detroit.

Chicago hosted Cleveland at White Stocking Park before 15,000 spectators who saw Clark Griffith pitch a seven-hitter in a 13–1 Chicago victory.

Since management would customarily almost never turn away a paying customer, when all the spectators couldn't fit into the seating area the excess patrons were allowed to stand behind a rope in the outfield in front of the fence to watch the game. The crowd standing in the outfield in Chicago was so large that "it was only by the combined effort of a row of blue coats, using everything from persuasion to threats and clubs, that a space was cleared sufficiently large to permit any kind of ball playing, and at best it turned the game into something of a farce."[9]

When a ball was hit into the mass of people standing in the outfield, the usual rule at most ball grounds was for the hit to be a double. But the Chicago crowd was so large that at the April 28 game everything hit into the crowd was a ground-rule single (Chicago had 23 hits that Sunday, all singles). Outfielders even played shallow to throw batters out at first base.

In the other American League Sunday debut at Burns Park, Detroit staged a roaring comeback, scoring four runs in the ninth inning to defeat Milwaukee 12–11 before 9,500 enthusiasts who made the excursion to the outskirts of Detroit.

In its 13 Sunday games at Burns Park in 1901, the Detroit club posted a 9–4 record. Boston, Philadelphia, and Washington won their only games played at Burns Park that season, while Detroit feasted on Cleveland (three wins, one loss) as well as Baltimore, Chicago, and Milwaukee (two wins each).

Detroit won its first three Sunday games at Burns Park, from April 28 through May 12, as hordes of people flocked to see the team play on Sunday. Like many Sunday-only grounds, however, the park was makeshift in quality.

Cold weather on April 20 canceled an exhibition game scheduled with Grand Rapids, but high winds "played havoc with the grand stand at Burns Park and the roof was carried out onto the diamond." Then at the April 28 Sunday game, the roof over the refreshment stand collapsed. "Although no one was hurt, several of those who had taken seats on the roof were jarred a bit," the *Detroit Free Press* reported, "and some will have to buy new suits of clothes, being caught in the nails as they fell to the ground."[10]

Crowds at Burns Park were often rowdy and the seating area was too small to accommodate everyone that wished to see the games.

"The addition made to the Burns Park grandstand has been found totally inadequate for the crowds and carpenters started work yesterday to increase the capacity still more," *Sporting Life* reported of the effort to accommodate a larger number of spectators. "A bleacher 160 feet long is also being constructed down the right field foul line. The work will be pushed in an effort to have a seating capacity of 8,000. Pres. Burns is also making arrangements for special trains to run from populous suburban points to Burns Park."[11]

In its last game of the 1901 season at Burns Park, Detroit pummeled Cleveland 21–0 on September 15 before about 5,000 spectators. The game lasted just seven and a half innings, as the game was called to allow Cleveland enough time to catch its train out of town. Ed Siever pitched a five-hitter for Detroit, while 20-year-old Cleveland hurler Jack Bracken surrendered 23 hits. Every Detroit player had at least one hit, while first baseman Pop Dillon collected four hits for the Tigers and four other players had three hits apiece.

Milwaukee played its first official Sunday home game in the American League on May 5, 1901. The Brewers routed the Chicago White Stockings 21–7 before 8,000 spectators at the Lloyd Street Grounds. Milwaukee collected 25 hits off Chicago pitcher Roy Patterson, a Wisconsin native who pitched the entire game, including five hits apiece by Billy Gilbert and Bill Hallman.

Eastern teams made their Sunday debuts on May 26 when Philadelphia lost 6–5 at Milwaukee and Baltimore lost 5–0 at Chicago. Washington was slated to also make its Sunday debut on May 26, but its game was rained out in Detroit. Washington instead played its first Sunday game on June 2 at Chicago, defeating the White Stockings 7–5.

Boston's first Sunday road game, in Milwaukee, was also on June 2. Boston was the odd team out in the May 26 eastern team Sunday debuts, having played the series in Cleveland where Sunday baseball was still not permitted. Cleveland had to make due with three one-game road trips to play on Sunday in 1901, one trip each to the three Sunday-playing cities in the American League—Detroit (May 19), Milwaukee (July 7), and Chicago (August 11).

The Boston-Milwaukee game on June 2 highlighted both the perils of playing before overflow crowds at the Sunday games and the difficulties of traveling on the road with few extra players as reserves.

An overflow crowd packed the Lloyd Street Grounds on June 2, as 8,500 people sought to see the game. In the fifth inning, umpire Haskell ejected two Boston players for complaining about his call that Tommy Dowd had been put out in his steal attempt after he overslid second base. "Freeman shoved and pulled him about until ordered to the bench and out of the game," the *Milwaukee Sentinel* indicated. "Collins being similarly disciplined for wagging his tongue too freely."[12]

With third baseman Jimmy Collins (also the manager) and first baseman Buck Freeman out of the game, Collins needed to improvise with the few substitute players he had on hand. He installed pitcher Charlie Beville at first base, moved Dowd from left field to third base, and then inserted pitcher Nig Cuppy in left field.

With the makeshift lineup for Boston, Milwaukee hung tough in the game and trailed just 4–2 going into the ninth inning. Pitcher Bill Reidy had recorded two Boston outs, when the overflow Sunday crowd did in the Milwaukee club.

"Two were out when Beville pounded the ball into the left field. Under ordinary circumstances Hallman would have got it, making the third out, but the ball got in the crowd and Beville scored two bases," the *Boston Globe* reported on the beginning of a two-out, nine-run Boston rally. "Then Parent came to bat and hit the ball over the left field fence and the slaughter was on. As others came to bat, they found Reidy with an ease that surprised him."[13]

Boston went on to win 13–2, as the Milwaukee standing-room crowd yielded several more ground-rule doubles in the ninth inning. Beville had two doubles in that ninth inning, which turned out to be the only hits of his short major league career. The various baseball encyclopedias obscure Beville's accomplishment on June 2. Since he was primarily a pitcher, Beville is listed in the pitching section of encyclopedias, which contain mostly pitching statistics with simply an abbreviated summary of his batting statistics.

Beville might have recorded a .000 career batting average had Collins and Freeman not been ejected from that game, and had not so many people come out to the Lloyd Street Grounds to see that Sunday game. His ninth-inning fly ball probably should have been an easy out for left fielder Bill Hallman to end the game. But other circumstances intervened, and Beville collected two doubles in the same inning to become one of several players that hold that major league record.

Milwaukee played just one season in the American League, finishing in last place with a 48–89 record, as Johnson decided the league would be better served with a franchise in St. Louis. Always known as a good Sunday-playing city, St. Louis looked to benefit the American League since the National League entrant was relatively weak. St. Louis became a two-team city in 1902, with Sunday baseball debuting there in the American League on April 27, 1902, when the newly recreated Browns lost 6–1 to Detroit.

Despite the city's short stays in the major leagues before 1953, Milwaukee did help to further advance the Sunday baseball cause. The 1884 replacement team in the Union Association perpetuated Sunday baseball to the bitter end of that lone major league season. The 1891 American Association team that transferred from Cincinnati also contributed to Sunday baseball becoming a fixture in the National League the following season, although Milwaukee didn't.

Ban Johnson not only installed a team in St. Louis where Sunday baseball was popular, but he also tried to maximize Sunday play in the west with a foursome of Sunday-playing clubs to increase the American League's competitive edge over the National League.

The fourth city was Cleveland, with its decidedly checkered history of playing Sunday baseball due to the Sabbatarian influence in the city. Cleveland had tried four alternative sites for Sunday baseball in the last 15 years (five sites if the 1898 game in Rochester, New York, is included) when the city had teams in the American Association and the National League. In 1897, Cleveland also had a brief run of Sunday games at League Park in between court appeals for Sunday baseball arrests.

For 1902, arrangements were made for Cleveland to play Sunday games in Newburgh, the second time around for major league Sunday games in that Cleveland suburb, having hosted several games there in 1888. The 1902 American League schedule was released with Cleveland having a full slate of Sunday home games, the first one slated for May 11.

Sunday baseball in Cleveland had never been easy, and memories of the 1898 Ohio Supreme Court ruling upholding the illegality of Sunday baseball hadn't faded much in four years time.

To fight the latest 1902 insurgence of Sunday baseball, Cleveland ministers induced several citizens of Newburgh to seek a court injunction to prevent the Sunday games. The case was heard on May 10. When there was no immediate decision by Judge Babcock, Sheriff Barry announced his intent to stop the game "by force if it were attempted." The May 11 game with St. Louis was canceled.[14]

When the court ruled in favor of the Sabbatarians, Cleveland transferred the May 18 Sunday game with Detroit, which was slated to be played in Newburgh, to Burns Park outside Detroit.

It was a setback not only for Cleveland, but more broadly for the American League (and Ban Johnson) in its continuing battle with the National League. The ability for all American League teams to play every Sunday when east visited west, and half the remaining time, would be an important financial ingredient in winning the war with the National League. With Philadelphia and Boston in the National League as the last holdouts to refrain from playing Sundays on the road, Sunday baseball was a powerful weapon for the American League.

8. American League Liked It

The latest inability to play Sunday baseball in Cleveland could well have helped Cleveland secure the services of Nap Lajoie, when the Pennsylvania Supreme Court ruled that he had illegally jumped his Philadelphia National League contract to play with the Philadelphia Athletics in the American League. Lajoie, the 1901 American League batting champion, couldn't play within the state of Pennsylvania (except for the Phillies), so Ban Johnson needed to arrange for Lajoie to play somewhere else in the American League. On May 23, word leaked that Lajoie would be transferred to Cleveland, which would boost weekday attendance at League Park to partially compensate for the lack of Sunday play.

Cleveland did try a novel solution to its Sunday home game dilemma by playing several games in 1902 at neutral sites within a 100–200 mile radius of Cleveland. The club played five neutral-site Sunday games during the 1902 season—two at Fort Wayne, Indiana, and three within Ohio at Canton, Columbus, and Dayton.

On June 8, Cleveland played its first neutral-site game at Fairview Park in Dayton, losing to Baltimore 6–2 before 4,876 onlookers. The remaining six American League teams played in Chicago, Detroit, and St. Louis that day, marking the first time that the entire American League had played on a Sunday, providing at least some measure of Sunday supremacy, and its financial rewards, over the National League.

The biggest Sunday crowd for Cleveland in 1902 came at Mahaffey Park in Canton, 40 miles from Cleveland, where 6,000 spectators packed into a facility designed for 2,000. "The manager of the park had not stretched any ropes to keep the crowd back and as a result they crowded close up to the base line and surrounded the outfielders, as well as the catcher and the umpire," the *Cleveland Plain Dealer* reported. "Several times the game had to be stopped as [umpire] O'Laughlin could not see first base." Boston defeated Cleveland 5–2, in part because "Jimmy Collins' men seemed to be better able to poke the ball into the crowd [for a ground-rule double] than were the Clevelands." Boston had six doubles while Cleveland tallied four.[15]

Cleveland didn't do particularly well on the field at the neutral-site games, losing four of the five games in 1902, and the club looked to downsize its neutral-site Sunday games in 1903 for several other reasons as well.

Because of the small-sized minor league parks, the games didn't draw unusually well at the gate, with the top crowd at 6,000 for the June 15 game in Canton, Ohio. Transportation costs from Cleveland to the neutral site ate up a good chunk of the gate, and the team didn't totally escape Sunday troubles at the neutral sites as local ministers' associations did try to stop the games. The minor league parks were crude imitations of major league ones, both of quality and size, resulting in collapsed stands and injured spectators.

While the neutral-site games were surely popular with the spectators in outlying areas from Cleveland, the games were hardly popular with the other American League teams. Games were often farcical on the small fields, resulting in an unusual number of ground-rule doubles due to the overflow spectators encircling the outfield.

With just two Sunday games scheduled in 1903 at neutral sites, Cleveland looked to garner Sunday baseball revenue by playing four one-game Sunday series in close-by Detroit. The trip to Detroit was just a boat ride away across Lake Erie and was nearer to Cleveland than either the Dayton or Fort Wayne neutral sites used in 1902.

The only problem was that Detroit, with a full slate of Sunday games on the 1903 American League schedule, was having difficulty arranging to continue play at its Sunday-only grounds at Burns Park.

In 1902, after owner Jim Burns sold the Detroit club to Sam Angus, Detroit had played another 10 games at West End Park (the former Burns Park), concluding with the September 7 game in which Detroit defeated Baltimore 11–6 before a sparse crowd of 1,787. Angus announced in early 1903 that Detroit wouldn't play any more Sunday games there.

"Angus was personally responsible for the abandonment of Sunday ball in Detroit, believing that the financial returns were not sufficient to make the Sabbath day game of great importance, while Sunday ball in his opinion detracts from the tone of the sport," *Sporting Life* reported the public reason for the stoppage of Sunday games.[16]

The real reason seems to be that the Detroit ball club's accountant, Frank Navin, also worked nights in a gambling establishment. Navin had a conflict with the well-connected Frank Croul, who had placed a $500 bet with Navin on a horse race at three-to-one odds. Croul's pick won the race, but Navin reputedly welched on the bet by claiming that Croul had placed it too late. According to a Navin biographer, "Croul was a politically prominent figure, and knowing that Sunday baseball would be a financial windfall for Navin, he used his influence to prohibit it."[17]

Although Angus had asked Johnson not to schedule any Sunday games in Detroit for the 1903 season, the American League schedule called for 10 games in Detroit that season, putting Angus in a difficult situation. At first, he mentioned "the poor grounds at West End Park" and that "several of the teams kicked against playing on the bad diamond."[18]

Angus then trotted out the age-old Sunday excuse that Sabbatarians had caused the stoppage, saying that the Sabbath Observance League had served notice that the Sunday games must not be played in Wayne County.

8. American League Liked It

When the Toledo, Ohio, club declined to let Detroit use its field for Sunday games, the April 26 game with Cleveland was canceled.[19]

Detroit adopted the neutral-site model used by Cleveland in 1902, and played three such games in 1903. Detroit's first neutral-site game was played at Grand Rapids on May 24, where Detroit edged Washington 5–4 before 6,000 spectators crammed into the tiny Grand Rapids field. Not only were "the outfielders browsing on an elevated and sloping plane," but there was also an unusual feature in the outfield:

> In right field there is an immense tree that cast a grateful shade on Messrs. Holmes and Lush and that would have figured largely in the game had its presence been known of in time for a little batting practice. Every man who went to bat had his eye on that tree, knowing that a fly of any kind into its branches was good for a two-base hit. There were some good shots, but generally the approach was foozled.[20]

Detroit finally gained permission to play at Toledo, where it hosted two more neutral-site games. But attendance couldn't compensate for the trips, even when Toledo native George Mullin pitched for Detroit at its last neutral-site game in Toledo.

Cleveland played three neutral-site Sunday games in 1903, the two originally scheduled games plus a third one that was rescheduled from the four ill-fated Detroit Sunday games (in which Cleveland defeated Detroit 6–2 at Canton on May 10). The last neutral-site game was on June 21 in Canton, where Boston defeated Cleveland 12–7 in a slugging match at Mahaffey Park. Boston, the eventual pennant winner that year in the American League, collected 16 hits off Cleveland pitchers Ed Walker and Gus Dorner, including five by Buck Freeman (home run, triple, and three singles). Cleveland had 11 hits.

The neutral-site strategy wasn't successful for either Cleveland or Detroit, and both teams abandoned the idea after the 1903 season. Neutral-site games made a brief reappearance in 1905, when Detroit scheduled a two-game, Saturday-Sunday series in Columbus, Ohio, against the champions from the previous two years, the Boston Americans.

Without the neutral-site Sunday games for Cleveland or Detroit, the American League was left with just two Sunday-playing cities (Chicago and St. Louis) until the two cities could work out agreeable arrangements to host Sunday games.

At Cleveland's May 17, 1903, game in Columbus, another Sunday baseball phenomenon was illustrated when New York Highlander outfielder Dave Fultz was not in the lineup that day. Fultz was one of several players that, due to religious convictions, refused to play on Sunday and "according to a clause in his contract, it is said he is not compelled to play in games on Sunday."[21]

Chicago outfielder Billy Sunday "was said to have been the first baseball player to refuse to play on Sundays," according to biographer Wendy Knickerbocker in her book *Sunday at the Ballpark: Billy Sunday's Professional Baseball Career, 1883–1890*. "After he took up Christian service, Sunday undoubtedly would have refused to play on the Sabbath, but the issue was moot. In the 1880s, the National League did not schedule baseball games on Sundays."[22]

While Billy Sunday, a.k.a Reverend William Sunday, did eventually speak out against playing on the Sabbath, the irony of a man with the surname Sunday refusing to play on the day named Sunday is not supported by fact. Like many baseball anecdotes, it makes a great story, but simply is not true.

Paul Radford, who played with the 1888 Brooklyn team in the American Association, was one of the first ball players to abstain from playing on Sundays. Radford, a regular outfielder for Brooklyn in its games on Monday through Saturday, did not participate in the team's games played on Sunday.

Branch Rickey has received perhaps the most publicity surrounding his decision as a player not to play in Sunday games, stemming from his fame as a general manager following his playing days. Rickey's decision to sit out games on the Lord's Day became legendary in the 1930s during his reign as general manager of the St. Louis Cardinals, including one 1935 headline entitled "Rickey Fired Because He Refuses to Play on Sunday."[23]

Rickey was just a backup catcher with the Cincinnati Reds in September 1904 when he told Cincinnati manager Joe Kelley that he wouldn't appear at the ballpark for Cincinnati's Sunday games, adding that he "considered his abstinence a moral act in consonance with his family's faith." Cincinnati sold Rickey's contract—he had never appeared in a game with the Reds—to the Chicago White Sox, which then sold it to the St. Louis Browns. Since the Browns needed a catcher, the Browns agreed to a clause in Rickey's contract that he was not obligated to play on Sundays.[24]

"I try to be both a consistent ballplayer and a consistent Christian," Rickey once explained to a reporter how religion mixed with professional baseball. "Sunday to me has always been a day apart. I can't help it. It was bred in me. You might almost call it a prejudice. So I won't play Sunday ball. Instead, I go to church. I see no reason why a man can't play professional ball week days and be a consistent Christian all week long."[25]

After just a few years as a catcher, Rickey found that he was a better administrator than a ball player. As a general manager, though, some accused Rickey of hypocrisy, saying, "He may not be at the game [on Sunday], but he's always at the cash box on Monday to count the gate receipts."²⁶

Christy Mathewson was perhaps the most renowned player to refrain from playing on Sunday. "Personally, it always has been a little against my grain to play Sunday baseball, and in the past I never did so," Mathewson told the *New York Times* in 1920 after his playing days were over. Mathewson had promised his parents that he would never pitch on Sunday and "he never violated that promise," according to biographer Ray Robinson in his book *Matty*.²⁷

An August 16, 1908, doubleheader in St. Louis, during the heat of a three-way pennant race among New York, Chicago, and Pittsburgh, cast a light on Matty's scruples about Sunday baseball. The Giants lost both games of the doubleheader, with Joe McGinnity and Red Ames taking the losses in close 6–5 and 3–2 games. Mathewson at the time had defeated St. Louis in 22 consecutive games dating back to mid–1904, and likely would have been an easy winner in one of the two games. Mathewson was said to have later told manager John McGraw that if the doubleheaders started to pile up, he'd be willing to start in a Sunday game, thus "in the name of team spirit, he was willing to abrogate his long-held principles."²⁸

The Giants lost the pennant by one game to the Chicago Cubs that season. Fred Merkle is remembered as the "goat" of the 1908 Giants, though, for failing to touch second base after the game-winning hit in the September 23 game against Chicago. Long forgotten is the doubleheader loss in St. Louis where Sunday baseball principles precluded Mathewson from pitching. The Giants did win the pennant the next three years, as Mathewson made sure by pitching on Mondays and Saturdays that his Sunday principles didn't interfere with his duty to the New York Giants.

Mathewson changed his viewpoint over the years after he became the manager of the Cincinnati Reds.

> Is Sunday ball good or bad for the community? It seems to me that this is the most important point to be settled. If playing games on Sunday makes for orderliness and keeps young men out of harm during the day of rest who otherwise would be getting into trouble or taking their pleasure in less wholesome manner, it seems to me there can be no evil in it. [I am told] in communities where Sunday baseball has been played, the police blotters show a marked decrease in the number of arrests for disorderliness or petty crimes on the Sabbath. If this is true, I cannot help feeling that Sunday baseball must be an influence for good, and without being a philosopher, it doesn't seem as though a man whose acts are influencing the community for good can be accused of sin or irreverence while performing these acts.²⁹

As the acceptability of Sunday baseball spread throughout the country, fewer players declined to play Sunday baseball. Also, in 1903, the last holdouts among major league teams to play Sunday baseball on the road shed their Sunday baseball resistance.

Boston and Philadelphia in the National League were the last Sunday baseball holdouts, which among other things alleviated the scheduling challenges for the National League when the eastern teams conducted their western road trips. When Boston and Philadelphia played in western cities, the National League needed to work around their unwillingness to play on Sunday in the three Sunday-playing National League cities.

For instance, in 1902, on Saturday, August 23, Boston played at Chicago and Philadelphia at Cincinnati. To get in Sunday games in both Chicago and Cincinnati, the National League had Pittsburgh and Brooklyn, which had been playing in Pittsburgh, travel to Cincinnati and Chicago, respectively, for a one-game Sunday series on August 24. Both teams returned to Pittsburgh for games on Monday, August 25, with Boston and Philadelphia resuming their series in Chicago and Cincinnati, respectively.

When Boston or Philadelphia was in St. Louis, an arduous one-day trip from Pittsburgh, the National League would start new series on a Sunday. For example, in 1902, on Saturday, May 10, Philadelphia played at St. Louis and Boston was at Cincinnati. For the Sunday, May 11, games, New York and Brooklyn started new series in St. Louis and Chicago, respectively, while Pittsburgh traveled to Cincinnati for a one-game series. Boston and Philadelphia then started new series on Monday, May 12, in Pittsburgh and Cincinnati, respectively.

The war between the American and National Leagues had been a costly one, as teams fought in the courts over player contracts and battled over spectator patronage in the dual-team cities of Boston, Chicago, Philadelphia, and St. Louis. The popularity of the sport was rising quickly, though, and with it attendance figures. Revenues from Sunday baseball were needed to respond to both factors,

Philadelphia and Boston in the National League were especially hurt financially by the new American League competition. After resisting for 11 years, both clubs succumbed in 1903 to the temptation of Sunday baseball games on the road for the financial gain to offset declining gate receipts at the home grounds.

The Americans outdrew the Nationals from the outset in Boston, attracting twice as many patrons to the Huntington Avenue Grounds in 1901 as passed through the turnstiles at the South End Grounds. For the Boston entry in the National League, it was the lowest level of attendance since 1892 and nearly a 25 percent drop from the previous year's draw.

Things got worse for the Nationals in 1902 as the popularity of the Americans escalated. The Huntington Avenue Grounds attracted 348,500 customers while attendance at the neighboring South End Grounds was barely one-third that at 116,900, the team's lowest level since 1885.

In order to generate more revenue to pay the bills, the team dropped its Sabbath discipline to gain a share of the lucrative Sunday gates by playing Sunday baseball on the road hundreds of miles away from Boston and far removed from the Massachusetts blue laws. The only public awareness of the team's Sunday play was Monday newspaper accounts and perhaps a brief mention in the agate type in the Sunday newspaper about that day's game.

Boston first experimented with exhibition games in Hoboken, New Jersey, and Syracuse, New York, on May 10 and May 31, respectively. With no apparent customer backlash, the Boston Nationals then proceeded to play regular season Sunday games, beginning in St. Louis on June 14. "Boston took part in its first Sunday game here this afternoon," the *Boston Post* reported from St. Louis on the 5–1 victory by the Boston Nationals.[30]

Philadelphia, under new ownership in 1903 after A. J. Reach sold the club in March, commenced Sunday play on the road a week before Boston, with a 3–1 win in Cincinnati on June 7. "Manager Zimmer fears some of his players will object to playing the first Sunday game for which a Quaker City National League team was ever scheduled," the *Philadelphia Inquirer* reported in its article "Phillies to Play First Sunday Game" on the day of the game in Cincinnati. "There were mutterings today, but no decided objections."[31]

The revenue quest even led Boston to play a Sunday "home" game that September at Rocky Point Park outside Providence, Rhode Island. Rocky Point was accustomed to Sunday baseball, serving as a Sunday haven for the local Providence minor league team for many years.

To make-up rainouts earlier in the year, Boston and Philadelphia were slated to play three doubleheaders on Saturday, September 5; Monday, September 7 (Labor Day); and Tuesday, September 8; before Boston headed off on a road trip for the remainder of the year. Rain ended the first game on Saturday in a 6–6 tie after just six innings, and the precipitation canceled the second game.

With no other chance to play the Phillies in a game at the South End Grounds, Boston and Philadelphia agreed to play on Sunday at Rocky Point. On September 6, Boston defeated Philadelphia 3–2 before 6,500 spectators in Rhode Island as Vic Willis hurled Boston to victory. Willis yielded just six hits to Philadelphia batters while Duff Cooley collected three hits to lead the Boston offense.[32]

In the Labor Day editions of Boston newspapers, the Rocky Point game received minimal coverage, likely because the game was between sixth- and seventh-place teams while the Boston Americans were then en route to the American League pennant. Or perhaps the low-key coverage was meant to allay the concerns of advocates of the Sunday blue laws.

Whatever the reason, Boston did not play another Sunday home game until 1929, after the law preventing Sunday baseball was finally repealed.

Another catalyst to the Sunday baseball development among eastern teams was the dropping of the Baltimore franchise in favor of a team in New York City for the 1903 season. The arrival of an American League club in Manhattan brought increased intra-city competition to New York. The Highlanders, as the team was known before changing its name to the Yankees, challenged the monopoly that the Giants had on the island and the Brooklyn hold on its spectator base, to the extent that the team could draw customers across the Brooklyn Bridge from the other borough.

Sabbatarian concerns were still paramount in Massachusetts, New York, and Pennsylvania and continued to forestall regular Sunday games in Boston, New York, Brooklyn, Philadelphia, and Pittsburgh. That didn't mean, however, that those teams couldn't find a nearby location to schedule exhibition games where the locals weren't as sensitive to Sabbath field contests.

The area of New Jersey across the Hudson River from Manhattan became a Sunday playing haven for not only the three New York teams but also teams from both leagues that were making stopovers in New York and Boston.

Hoboken was a particularly popular site at the turn of the century. For instance, the Boston Americans defeated the Hoboken team 7–4 at St. George's Cricket Grounds on July 13, 1902, and the New York Giants defeated Hoboken 5–2 on May 17, 1903.

On Sunday, October 4, 1903, while the Boston Americans and Pittsburgh Pirates were traveling from Boston to Pittsburgh following the third game of the world's championship series being conducted between the two clubs, several other major league clubs were engaged in Sunday exhibition games.

The two Chicago teams played each other in a city series, as the two St. Louis teams did likewise, while Cleveland played at Cincinnati. In the New York City area, Brooklyn played that day in Bayonne, New Jersey, losing 1–0 to the Bayside A.C., while the Giants broke new ground in Sunday baseball with an exhibition game in Manhattan.

More than 7,000 persons crowded into Olympia Field, located at 135th Street and Lenox Avenue in Manhattan, to see the New York Giants play the semi-pro Murray Hill Base Ball Association and become the "first major league nine to play Sunday on Manhattan Island." The spectator overflow was so huge that it ringed the outfield to such a depth that "no hit was worth more than a single with so many people standing on the field." The Giants won the exhibition game 4–1, as manager John McGraw himself played left field and reached Murray Hill pitcher Deegan for one hit.[33]

The Giants also won what would be the first round in an initial three-year battle over the right to play Sunday baseball at the major league level in New York City.

In order to avert a violation of New York law, the Giants perpetrated the same ruse that many semi-pro teams in New York often used to circumvent the law on charging admission for a baseball game played on Sunday. Rather than buy a ticket to the game, patrons were asked to purchase a scorecard for the inflated price of 25 cents before entering the park for the baseball game (scorecards usually cost 5 cents at the time).

The October 4 game at Olympia Field was played without interruption by the authorities, as the Giants successfully pushed the envelope on major league teams playing Sunday baseball in the city.

A few weeks later, George McClellan, the Tammany Hall candidate, was elected mayor of New York City. His election virtually ensured a temperate attitude toward issues impacting working-class New Yorkers. The McClellan mayoral victory began the wheels turning in the minds of the owners of the three New York major league teams to concoct a way to stage Sunday baseball on an ongoing basis during the regular baseball season.

Chapter 9

BROOKLYN USED SUBTERFUGE TO DO IT

Soon after New Year's Day in 1904, the New York Highlanders announced that the team would play Sunday games during the 1904 baseball season at Ridgewood Park in Queens.

Fifteen years earlier, the Brooklyn team in the American Association had successfully used Queens-based Ridgewood Park as an artifice around Sabbatarian concerns over Sunday baseball at Washington Park in the heart of Brooklyn. The Highlanders were seeking to score a coup over both Sunday baseball and their National League neighbors across the Brooklyn Bridge from Manhattan.

Charlie Ebbets immediately cried foul and sought relief from the National Commission that the Highlanders' proposed use of Ridgewood Park was an infringement on Brooklyn's territorial rights. The Commission upheld Ebbets' argument and told the New York club to forget about using Ridgewood Park for Sunday games.

The Highlanders went forward with the Sunday plan anyway, playing as the New York Americans. On April 10, the team played its first Sunday game at Ridgewood Park, defeating a team of semi-pros representing the Ridgewood Park Exposition Company 14–2. The match seemed a financial success, as it was played before a crowd of 10,000 as the second part of a doubleheader. In the opening game, the Ridgewood team defeated the Philadelphia Giants, a team of Negro players, by a 6–3 score.

Ebbets objected once again to the Highlanders' play at Ridgewood, since the owners of the New York American League Club claimed, somewhat correctly, "that the decision of the National Commission ordering them not to play at Ridgewood Park referred to championship and not to exhibition games."[1]

Once the Highlanders cast the opening salvo on April 10, the Sunday baseball issue quickly picked up steam. If Ebbets hadn't been contemplating a strategy for his Brooklyn team to play Sunday baseball in 1904, the Highlanders' action certainly advanced his thought process. Brooklyn management immediately announced that the Superbas would play a National League championship game at Washington Park the following Sunday, April 17.

"A professional club went to Ridgewood last Sunday and played a game and we feel justified in doing the same," Ebbets said. "Ridgewood Park is partly in Brooklyn and partly in Queens and wholly in Greater New York. There is ball playing all over the borough every Sunday as well and we see no reason therefore why Washington Park should be out of it."[2]

Ebbets tried to line up the New York Giants, the team's cross-town rivals, to play on the 17th. The Giants, however, opted to stay with their scheduled game with the Newark, New Jersey, minor league team that day, possibly believing authorities would stop the Brooklyn game and they'd come away empty handed financially. Boston, which only two years earlier had steadfastly refused to play Sunday games, signed on as the Brooklyn opponent for the first official major league game played in New York City.

Police Commissioner William McAdoo issued the tough-sounding statement that he had "instructed Brooklyn police to see that the law is not violated" at the April 17 game. His words, though, were relatively hollow, since the New York courts differed materially regarding what kind of baseball on Sunday actually constituted a violation of the law. Judges in Manhattan took a harsher view of Sunday games than those in Brooklyn, the latter who invariably discharged Sunday baseball cases unless an admission was charged. Even then, Judge William Gaynor had recently discharged a young boy who was arrested for playing baseball where an admission was charged.[3]

Brooklyn management was quite upfront in acknowledging that the team would seek to escape a legal violation by not charging admission but rather by charging inflated prices for scorecards.

"Patrons were admitted to the grounds free, but once inside they were held up by men selling score cards, and they were made to purchase these at the regular admission prices prevailing on week days (75 cents for grandstand, field seats 50 cents, bleachers 25 cents)," the *Brooklyn Daily Eagle* explained. "Those who refused to pay for score cards were not permitted to go any further. There were probably not more than a dozen of them all told." This was not a new artifice to elude the law prohibiting admission fees for baseball on Sunday. "The law says nothing about selling score cards, a fact of which half a dozen amateur teams throughout the borough have been taking advantage for the past couple of years."[4]

A crowd of 12,000 witnessed the 9–1 Brooklyn victory over Boston on April 17, as no effort was made to stop the game at Washington Park. Police, however, did arrest two ticket sellers at the Ridgewood Park game between the New York Americans and the Brooklyn Field Club, won by New York 17–4 before 6,000 spectators. Over in Newark, the Giants won 3–1 before 10,000 "enthusiastic rooters."

Including the two exhibition games played by the two New York teams, the *New York Times* expounded in a headline the next day that "Nearly 100,000 Persons Saw Seven Major League Games" on April 17. Sunday baseball was clearly accepted by the general public.

The two games in Chicago that day drew one-third of the overall total, as 17,000 attended the Cleveland-Chicago game at South Side Park while 16,849 were reported to be at the Cincinnati-Chicago game at the West Side Grounds. The day's largest attendance was in St. Louis, where 23,250 went to see the Pittsburgh game there at Robison Field. Only 3,000 were at the other game in St. Louis between the Browns and the Tigers at Sportsman's Park.

While Charlie Ebbets was basking in the glow of the apparent successful breakthrough of Sunday baseball in Brooklyn, his cross-town rivals were angling for similar treatment in Manhattan. John Brush, owner of the Giants, announced that he favored Sunday baseball, and the New York Americans "expressed belief that playing on the Sabbath at American League Park would not be objectionable to the owners of the grounds, notwithstanding a clause in the lease that prohibits it."[5]

Police commissioner McAdoo, though, was catching some heat for permitting the game in Brooklyn to go on unimpeded. McAdoo told reporters in regard to the Brooklyn game "that Capt. White had reported to him that there was no violation of the law." When McAdoo was asked whether the charging of 50 cents for a program, when usually bought for five cents, was not a subterfuge, McAdoo's reply "was that he hadn't looked into the matter." The commissioner also had no comment on the game at Ridgewood Park that day.[6]

On Friday, April 22, two days before the next Sunday game in Brooklyn, McAdoo met with James N. King, president of the Kings County Sunday Observance Association, and representatives of the New York Sabbath Committee, after they had met with the mayor. McAdoo told reporters in the morning, "My position in this baseball matter is taken now, and it will not be changed by anything that the [Sunday Observance] committee may say."[7]

McAdoo had issued a pronouncement that day that he would allow Sunday games in isolated neighborhoods but would not permit ball games at either of the league grounds in Manhattan.

9. Brooklyn Used Subterfuge to Do It

"I personally visited both of the parks [Ridgewood and Washington]. They are almost isolated from any residences, being most surrounded by factories and large vacant spaces," McAdoo commented. "During the three Sundays that baseball was played in Queens and Brooklyn, not one single complaint was received in this office from any one residing in the neighborhood of these parks."[8]

Sunday games in Manhattan were a different situation. "The neighborhoods are thickly populated and the traffic arrangements for handling large crowds on Sunday afternoons might possibly create confusion and annoyance," McAdoo said. "I would therefore be opposed to allowing a match game of baseball to be played Sunday at either of these parks."

While the words of the Sunday Observance Association at the Friday meeting may not have moved McAdoo on the subject of Sunday baseball, it appears the words of the mayor did sway the police commissioner. By Sunday, McAdoo had changed his position on Sunday baseball and ordered the arrests of three players and three program sellers at Washington Park on April 24 to test the law.

At the beginning of the Brooklyn-Philadelphia game, police arrested two Brooklyn players—starting pitcher Ed Poole and catcher Fred Jacklitsch—and one Philadelphia player, the first batter to the plate, Frank Roth. The charge was violating section 265 of the penal code, which prohibited racing, gaming, or other sports on the first day of the week. The players changed in the clubhouse and were taken to the 46th precinct station house at 6th Avenue and Bergen Street where they were released upon posting of bonds. The three program sellers, arrested for allegedly violating Section 267 of the penal code that prohibited sale or offers of sale on the Sabbath, were William Brown of Hempstead, Oscar Oberg of Brooklyn, and William Mullin of Brooklyn.[9]

None of the three arrested players appeared in the box score for the April 24 game in which Brooklyn defeated Philadelphia 8–6 before 13,000 spectators. Grant Thatcher replaced Poole as pitcher and Lew Ritter was the new catcher. Thirty-seven-year-old Hugh Duffy had been scheduled to be Philadelphia's first batter, but Roth volunteered to have the test arrest made on him rather than Duffy.

Washington Park wasn't the only place arrests were made for Sunday baseball on April 24. Five people were arrested at Ridgewood Park after the first game of the doubleheader there—the Ridgewood manager, two players, and two ticket sellers. The *New York Times* reported that city magistrate Connerton paroled them and he then "hurried to the ball park to witness the second game between Stamford (Connecticut) and the Ridgewoods."[10]

In Bayonne, New Jersey, where the Philadelphia Athletics were playing an exhibition game with Jersey City, in the third inning police arrested two Jersey City players—pitcher Eason and catcher Vandagrift—and the team's president Howard Griffith. Philadelphia went on to win 7–2. Games in Hoboken played by the New York Giants and in Newark played by the Boston Americans went on uninterrupted by authorities.

McAdoo had received protests not only from the Sunday Observance Association but also from the Law Enforcement Society of Brooklyn and the South Brooklyn Ministers Association. Clergymen also publicly denounced McAdoo at church services that Sunday.

At the First Presbyterian Church Reverend William Hubbell condemned Sunday baseball. "There is no prosperity for virtue if we lose our Sabbath day. If we take away our Sunday and its religious character, we are gone as a people in receipt of God's favors," Hubbell said. "There are those who see in the lynchings and the disorders of the land a withdrawal of God's favors for our desecration of the day of rest."[11]

On April 27, Brooklyn president Charles Ebbets announced that there would be no more Sunday playing at Washington Park until the cases then pending were resolved. With the hearing scheduled for May 3, the May 1 game at Washington Park was canceled.

McAdoo kept the Sunday baseball issue in the news, though, speaking at a benefit for St. Leonard's Academy on Sunday night. His comments appeared in the *New York Times* the next day under the headline, "McAdoo Upholds Sunday Ball."

"I believe that the city boy has as much right to get away from the crowded tenement districts on Sunday and enjoy himself under the blue sky and in the open air as has the country boy," McAdoo told the audience. "If he chooses to find his enjoyment in watching a ball game, I do not think that the people of the State have any right to pass laws instructing me to throw him in a dungeon for doing so. And yet there are zealous reformers who tell me that I should arrest and jail those who go to Sunday ball games and that if I refuse to do so, I should be thrown into jail myself."[12]

With Brooklyn off on a three-week road trip, Justice Gaynor ruled on May 3 in favor of Sunday baseball at Washington Park.

"Justice Gaynor practically reaffirms the decision rendered by Justice Barnard about ten years ago that baseball itself is not contrary to law, either on week days or on Sundays," Brooklyn district attorney John Clarke said. "If a baseball game disturbs the peace and the rest of the community, it is then contrary to law and should be prohibited by the police."[13]

Clarke appealed the Gaynor decision since the case didn't touch the legality of selling admission tickets. Clarke arranged for another test case of the Sunday baseball issue at the next Brooklyn Sunday home game on May 29.

With the New York Giants as opposition on May 29, Washington Park attracted 15,000 spectators to view the game between the intra-city rivals, won by New York 7–3. No arrests were made at the game, but the police took notes and names and addresses to submit evidence to Clarke's office, including the fact that Ed Poole also pitched this Sunday game for Brooklyn with Lew Ritter as catcher.

Giants team president Brush attended the May 29 game and commented to the press, "There will be no Sunday baseball at the Polo Grounds until it is well settled that it is not unlawful."[14]

While Sunday baseball was popular with many Brooklyn residents, the team wasn't playing very well in 1904. Attendance at the Sunday games at Washington Park to see the sixth-place Superbas began to decline following the huge throng at the May 29 game. Crowds the next two Sundays were 8,000 and 6,000 to witness two exciting 4–3 games. Even a rematch with the Giants on June 19 attracted only 6,000, as the Giants pasted the Superbas 11–0.

Despite his liberal inclinations, Justice Gaynor ruled against Sunday baseball the second time around. On June 18, Gaynor denied a motion to dismiss the complaint that arose from the May 29 game at Washington Park.

"In the case of Rath and others which were recently before me on the writ of habeas corpus, the complaint was simply that the defendants played a game of baseball on Sunday. The complaint presented nothing but the case of ordinary private games of baseball on Sunday ... which are not prohibited by the statute," Gaynor wrote in his opinion in the case of *People v. Poole*. "The present case is different. The complaint is of a public game of baseball, i.e., of a game to which the public were invited, and to which an admission fee was charged. Is such a game prohibited by the statute? I think it is."[15]

Ed Poole pitched just 80 major league games, compiling an unremarkable 34–34 record from 1900 to 1904 pitching for Pittsburgh, Cincinnati, and Brooklyn. Two Sunday games that Poole pitched for Brooklyn in 1904, though, propelled Poole into an obscure spot in baseball history as the defendant in *People v. Poole*. The legal case became an oft-cited precedent in the two-decade-long battle to legalize Sunday baseball in New York.

Justice Gaynor, who would go on to greater fame as mayor of New York from 1910 to 1913, was a staunch supporter of a liberal Sunday.

"I believe myself in the observance of the Sabbath," Gaynor said while campaigning for mayor in 1909. "But if we go to church Sunday morning, or do something good, can't we go to Coney Island or Rockaway? Can't our children go on a merry-go-round there without being hounded by a police commissioner or a mayor?"[16]

With his liberal stance on Sunday activities, Gaynor was supportive of Sunday baseball. But as lawyer and judge, he backed the law. Gaynor straddled the two often divergent camps by explaining the whys of the existing law—as in his 1904 opinion in *People v. Poole*—and building a foundation for correcting the law if one disagreed with its execution.

Back in 1894, Gaynor gained acclaim by complaining to the police about the arrest of nine South Brooklyn boys for playing ball in Prospect Park on Sunday. Their bats and balls had been confiscated and they were locked up until midnight before they could be released on bail.

"The police assumed to imprison these boys at will and even to confiscate their property," Gaynor wrote in a long letter to Brooklyn police commissioner Welles. "But they had not committed a criminal offense. They had not begun to play ball, and if they had, it was not a public but a private game, which is no more a criminal offense on Sunday than on a weekday, unless it attracted a noisy throng and disturbed the peace."[17]

In August, Brooklyn police announced that they "would not interfere with boys who play ball in isolated places in the new wards, provided they play the game orderly and do not create any disturbances."[18]

The important legal principles that Gaynor hammered at time and time again on the Sunday baseball issue were the public nature of professional baseball and the disturbance of the peace factor.

While mayor in 1913, Gaynor lashed out at police commissioner Waldo about Sunday baseball. It seems a mounted police officer went onto a ball field on a Sunday and straddled home plate with his horse in order to stop a baseball game.

"It seems that the inspector and captains over in Queens borough assume to close up ball games on Sunday. Is it possible that you and I are not understood by these leatherheads about this matter yet?" Gaynor wrote the commissioner. "I know of no reason why [Sunday ball games] should be interfered with so long as they do not set up public games and charge admission therefore. *That is the law.* I do not wish to have a recurrence of scenes like this. If the inspector and captains who are doing this are doing it on the theory that boys and men can not play ball on Sunday, I want them removed at once from the borough and put in some place where they can do no harm."[19]

As Ebbets appealed the second Gaynor ruling, Brooklyn tried one more attempt at Sunday baseball in 1904. Only 1,000 people went to Washington Park on June 26 to watch the Brooklyn-Pittsburgh game, an 8–2 whipping by the Superbas.

There was some confusion between the umpire and the police over exactly when the arrests at the game were to be made. Umpire Johnstone announced to the crowd that the Brooklyn battery would be Garvin and Ritter, when Oscar Jones was on the mound and Fred Jacklitsch was behind the plate at catcher. Then after Jones proceeded to pitch the first ball to batter Phil Geier, everyone looked over at Captain White in the stands expecting him to get up and arrest Jones and Jacklitsch. White just sat there. Jones tossed a second pitch and still no movement from White. Finally, after Jones tossed five balls, White went onto the field to arrest the Brooklyn players.

Arrests for Sunday baseball were becoming old hat in Brooklyn. The hearing on the June 26 arrests "lacked the spirit characteristic of the crusade when it was begun a few weeks ago," the *Brooklyn Daily Eagle* reported, "neither the ball playing fraternity nor the church people being so largely represented as they were when the proceedings were more of a novelty than they were today."[20]

The New York Highlanders tried to take advantage of Brooklyn's Sunday baseball difficulties by scheduling its own Sunday game to be played at Wiedenmeyer's Park in Newark, New Jersey, on July 17. A crowd of 6,700 watched the Highlanders defeat Detroit 3–1, as player-manager Clark Griffith hurled a three-hitter against the Tigers.

The Highlanders' Sunday baseball home debut did not go unnoticed by local Newark Sabbatarians, though. Although Judge Tighe dismissed the complaints against the ball players the next day, New York did not schedule any more regular Sunday contests in Newark—or anywhere else in the New York City area. The July 17 game was the American League team's first and only attempt at playing a regular season game on Sunday for more than a dozen years.

After canceling the remainder of the Sunday schedule in 1904 following the June 26 arrests, Charlie Ebbets received a reprieve on the Sunday baseball issue in September when Poole and the other Brooklyn players were acquitted in the appeal.

Brooklyn resumed Sunday play at the beginning of the 1905 season, with no efforts by the police or the Sabbath Observance Association to stop it. Since the court had not stopped the purchase of a scorecard at a marked-up price in lieu of an admission ticket, Brooklyn continued the practice to circumvent the perceived illegalities associated with explicit Sunday admission charges.

The first Sunday game at Washington Park in 1905, a 4–0 Brooklyn win over Boston before 11,642 spectators, was on April 23. About two dozen police officers were sprinkled around the park at entrance gates. They simply took names of players, program sellers, and witnesses but arrested no one.

On April 30, close to 30,000 people jammed into Washington Park to see the Brooklyn-New York game, and the Giants defeated the Superbas 5–3. Spectators stood 20 to 30 deep in the outfield to see the National League champions play the home team that day, as others claimed whatever vantage point they could gain in the aisles, on railings, or on back fences.

Brooklyn played the following three Sundays as well, but just like in 1904, attendance began to drop off as the Brooklyn team failed to win a majority of its games. By the fifth-straight Sunday game on May 21, Brooklyn was in seventh place in the National League with a 13–21 record, and only about 5,000 attended the Brooklyn-Chicago game that day.

Police commissioner McAdoo began to feel the pressure again from community groups to stop the Sunday games, as the King County Sunday Observance Association renewed its efforts to stop Sunday baseball.

McAdoo caved into the political pressure to stop Sunday baseball by ordering the stoppage of such games where programs were sold that entitled the holder to admission to the grounds. "McAdoo holds that the selling of a programme is a mere subterfuge and that there shall be no further evasion of the law until the matter is fully settled by the courts," the *New York Times* reported.[21]

The police action came at a particularly vulnerable time for Brooklyn, financially, as the team was forced to cancel its lucrative Sunday match with the Giants slated for May 28. Washington Park wasn't singled out, though, as Sunday games were halted at Equitable Park and Olympia Field in the Bronx and even a game at the Catholic Protectionary Grounds.

On Monday, May 29, McAdoo clarified the rules for allowable Sunday games, since some of the games stopped the previous day should have been allowed to proceed since strictly amateur players were involved in them. Sunday games were not permissible where (1) admission was charged, (2) scorecards were sold, (3) the games were advertised, or (4) the games were an annoyance to the neighborhood.[22]

With Sunday baseball no longer financially feasible for Brooklyn, Ebbets halted the games for the remainder of the 1905 season.

Brooklyn tried a new technique to play Sunday baseball for the 1906 season. Instead of the program ruse that the courts now recognized as a sham, the team instituted a voluntary contribution box system for patrons to drop "donations" before entering the gates at Washington Park. The first "contribution box" game at Washington Park was on Sunday, April 15.

The expectation was that most, if not all, people would drop money in the box in order to see a game on Sunday. This system wasn't foolproof, as more than a few people deposited "counterfeit coins, metal advertisements, foreign money, and pennies wrapped up in silver foil."[23]

Two weeks later on April 29, the New York Highlanders played the first Sunday game at American League Park. The mayor had approved the exhibition game with Philadelphia, because proceeds were to aid people impacted by the San Francisco earthquake. The April 29 game attracted 14,000 persons, and New York won 11–8. Total receipts of $5,602.25 were turned over to the Red Cross.[24]

Brooklyn played three Sunday games funded by the contribution box system without challenge before an incident at the fourth such game on June 3 aroused attention.

At the June 3 game with Boston, people entered through the pavilion and bleacher gates at Washington Park and then climbed over fences to enter the grandstand. The *Brooklyn Daily Eagle* reported that "there was a mighty hustling of them and crowding of them out until [deputy commissioner] O'Keefe took a hand and said that as no person had a right to charge admission on Sunday, they must not be interfered with."[25]

Charlie Ebbets maintained that he was "within the law when he reserves the right to determine who shall occupy his grandstand." Ebbets said that at the June 10 game the invaders would find the way barred by high board fences that they couldn't scale.[26]

That the contribution boxes weren't exactly "voluntary" was the problem the police had with the system. Ebbets, and other ball-field managers, tried to exact the appropriate amount in coin from patrons entering through certain gates that led to particular parts of the seating area. Change was provided at the gate so that everyone could contribute a definite sum.

On Friday, June 8, new police commissioner Bingham stopped the contribution box practice by announcing that police would stop all Sunday games where any money was received for admission. "It was entirely wrong to accept money by any subterfuge for attendance at any baseball game on the Sabbath, and even contribution boxes and voluntary contributions will not be allowed" Bingham said, calling the practice an evasion of the law.[27]

Faced with the new police rules governing Sunday baseball, Brooklyn was forced to cancel the Sunday, June 10, game with Chicago. Ebbets tried to keep the Sunday baseball issue alive by playing the game with free admission, but Chicago passed on the chance, even when Ebbets offered to pay Chicago a flat $500 out of the club's own pocket. Chicago preferred to play the game on Wednesday, June 13, for its share of regular admissions.[28]

So the "No Game To-day" sign hung out front at Washington Park on June 10, even as 1,200 persons gathered anyway hoping to see a game or a clash with police.

There was one variation attempted that Sunday to evade Bingham's new Sunday baseball order. At a game at 49th Street and Second Avenue, police allowed Manhattan Beach to play Bay Ridge when no contribution boxes or other signs of money being taken in were seen. As the game ended, though, and the crowd was leaving, contribution boxes were set up at convenient places on the grounds. Police then arrested the two team managers, who claimed "that as the boxes were not set up until after the game had ended, the spectators were not contributing to see the game played. The police refused to look at it in that way."[29]

"We are not through with Sunday ball yet by any means," Ebbets told the newspaper reporters. He tried one more attempt at Sunday baseball on June 17, knowing that the game would be stopped, but it was a last gasp try to get a court to rule that contribution boxes didn't violate the law. Cincinnati shutout Brooklyn 3–0 as 10,000 spectators dropped donations into contribution boxes.

Volunteers were solicited from both teams to be arrested at the beginning of the June 17 game. "Mal Eason of the Brooklyns and Chic Fraser of the Reds displayed marked bravery (published by special request of the press agent) in stepping forward and volunteering to become martyrs," the *Brooklyn Daily Eagle* remarked in jest.[30]

The Cincinnati team had a little fun with picking which player would be the first batter and therefore subjected to arrest. Manager Ned Hanlon had originally picked Charlie Chech, a little-used pitcher, to be the first batter. Chech, though, pleaded off on the assignment. Hanlon then offered $25 to any Cincinnati player to substitute. Fraser, a regular pitcher, volunteered to become an "arrestee for hire."[31]

"Fraser displayed the proper diffidence at the crucial moment. It was seen that he faltered somewhat in his farcical attempt to avoid hitting the two balls pitched by Eason and the act was somewhat strained because of the delay on the part of Captain Baldwin and his plain clothes men in responding to their cues," the *Brooklyn Daily Eagle* continued its humorous report on the arrests. "However, the police finally entered L.C. upon the stage—beg pardon, diamond—as the chief villains. They were properly hissed at by the assembled populace, showing that their parts were in capable hands."[32]

Police arrested 37 players and managers at various baseball fields in New York on June 17, many of them semi-pro games. The arrests were all catalogued in a police-blotter article the following day in the *Brooklyn Daily Eagle*, including "Charles C. Fraser, 31 years old, of Edison Park, Ill." and "Malcolm N. Eason, 26 years old, of 321 Quincy Street."

The efforts of Fraser and Eason to volunteer for arrest went for naught. When the court inevitably ruled against the Brooklyn club in July, Ebbets was forced to take the legislative route to seek redress on the legality of Sunday baseball. That approach would take much longer than expected. The June 17, 1906, Sunday game was the last one that Ebbets' team played in the borough for another ten years.

With Brooklyn's three-year experiment having concluded in 1906 by the shutting of the gates at Washington Park on the Lord's Day, major league baseball reached a new ebb in Sunday baseball sites after five years of competition between the American and National Leagues.

Sunday baseball was safely ensconced in Chicago and St. Louis for each city's two teams. But after that, only Cincinnati was playing Sunday baseball on its home grounds. Sunday baseball in the American League had contracted to just two of eight sites following the failure of the neutral-site strategy in Cleveland and Detroit. In the National League, the scope of Sunday baseball was little better, with just three of eight clubs hosting Sunday games. The good news was that all 16 teams were playing Sunday baseball on the road.

The 1906 pennant races gave a renewed shot in the arm to Sunday baseball proponents. The champions of both leagues resided in Chicago. The Cubs strung together an incredible 116 wins during the 154-game season while the White Sox nosed out the New York Highlanders in a tight race in the American League.

Chicago was truly the capital of Sunday baseball now. Major league baseball was played in Chicago every Sunday in 1905 and all but one Sunday in 1906 (the May 27 scheduled game with the Cubs was rained out) as the two teams coordinated their schedules such that one team was always at home while the other was on the road. There were also a dozen times that both teams were in town on Sunday. In all, the Cubs and the White Sox played 32 Sunday home dates in 1906.

Attendance skyrocketed in Chicago. The Cubs, with 15 Sunday dates, set a new high for National League attendance in 1906 with 654,000 spectators, which equaled one-ninth of the total attendance for all 16 major league teams. The Cubs won the National League pennant in four of the five years from 1906 to 1910, which also helped attract more people to its Sunday games.

In 1906, for the first time, there was a possibility that a World Series game could be played on Sunday. The World Series was gaining national attention now and a Series game on Sunday would greatly enhance the nation's perspective on the Sunday baseball concept.

There was no set schedule for the World Series in 1906, as the National Commission established it each year. For 1906, the first six games alternated between each team's home park, with the location of a seventh game to be determined following the sixth game if no team had won the Series by then.

When the 1906 World Series began on Tuesday, October 9, the Cubs were expected to trounce their cross-town rivals. The White Sox, however, stifled the powerful Cubs team, which was anchored by the famous Tinkers to Evers to Chance infield. The White Sox defeated the Cubs four games to two, gaining the championship with an 8–3 victory in the concluding sixth game played on Sunday, October 14, at the White Sox's home grounds, South Side Park.

The official attendance for the sixth game was 19,249, more than 4,000 less than the attendance of 23,257 announced for the fifth game at the Cubs' West Side Grounds. Attendance was down because the Sunday game had gotten the better of some Chicago residents.

"While the official attendance was given at 19,249, there must have been 23,000 persons there," *Sporting Life* commented. "Every usher and every policeman was working the golden graft. Coppers tore boards off fences and let fans through for a dollar or two a head and the ushers slipped hundreds through the side gate."[33]

While major league baseball on Sunday was limited to just three western cities at the beginning of the 1907 season, this didn't mean the clubs remained idol on Sundays while in the East. Hoboken, New Jersey, was a popular site for both New York teams as well as visiting teams passing through. Amusement parks in Rocky Point, Rhode Island, and Bridgeport, Connecticut, also saw a flurry of Sunday baseball action at this time.

The Providence team in the Eastern League, one of the few professional teams in New England to play home games on Sunday, played Sunday games at Rocky Point. There was a more relaxed attitude toward Sabbath activities in Rhode Island, since the state's first white settler, Roger Williams, had been banished from the Puritan colony in Massachusetts for his liberal views.

"The New England descendants of the Puritans looked down upon the little state of Rhode Island as a sort of annex to Satan's hideout, because the lax officials of that state made it possible for the baseball fans of Providence and vicinity to revel in professional games on Sundays by traveling on crowded excursion boats down the river to an isolated resort call Rocky Point," one commentator described the Sunday baseball haven. "And the Providence team was considered a desirable member of its league because of this ability to gather in the Sunday shekels even under that kind of a handicap."[34]

Eastern League president Pat Powers was said to have "a very nice thing of it in the Sunday games" at Rocky Point, which was "a nice sail of say three-quarters of an hour" from Providence down Narragansett Bay. Besides its unique status as a Sunday playing haven near Boston, reaching the ball grounds also then required a boat, a mode of transportation that was an unusual requirement to get to a baseball game.[35]

The Boston Nationals were a natural Sunday opponent for Providence at Rocky Point, and other National League teams often stopped in as well. For instance, in 1906 Providence entertained the Pittsburgh club on August 12 and then Boston the following Sunday, August 19.

Providence would often go to great lengths to play a Sunday game at Rocky Point. In order to play the World Series champion Chicago Cubs on Sunday, August 25, 1907, in between the Cubs' Saturday and Monday games in Boston, Providence traveled all the way from its Saturday game in Rochester, New York, and then returned to Buffalo, New York, for a Monday game. Bill Mack pitched a three-hitter for Providence to blank the Cubs 3–0 in the exhibition game.[36]

Sometimes a good outing in a Sunday exhibition game with a big league team led to bigger and better things for a player. The Cubs were so impressed with the opposing Providence pitcher that the club purchased his contract during the 1908 season. Mack, though, lasted just two games and six innings in his short stint in the major leagues with the Cubs. The prohibition against Sunday games in Boston, New York, and Philadelphia gave many young players like Mack a shot at testing their talents against the best in baseball. Once Sunday baseball became universally accepted, these opportunities for minor leagues became much rarer.

These Sunday exhibition games also gave the League players a chance to relax at the expense of their employers. "After the defeat, they had a plunge in the ocean and then sat down to a special shore dinner," the *Chicago Tribune* related. "The players returned full of beautiful scenery, salt water, clams, and lobsters and no one remembered how the game came out, except acting manager Sheckard."[37]

In truth, the Cubs may have been a bit rattled from their Sunday exhibition game experience the previous week in Bridgeport, Connecticut. On August 18, the Cubs were scheduled to play the Bridgeport team of the Connecticut League at Steeplechase Park, which was considered Connecticut's Coney Island. About 20 minutes before the game was to start, however, a fire broke out under the bleachers at the old bicycle racing park (that had been turned into a ball grounds).

"During the course of the conflagration, against which there was no adequate protection, eight thousand persons gathered in the stadium to watch a baseball game were thrown into panic, many being trampled upon when the mad rush for the exits came," the *Bridgeport Post* reported of the fire that threatened to burn the entire amusement resort and harm 20,000 people.[38]

The Chicago players temporarily turned into fire fighters. "Players worked like mad tearing down the wire screen and low fence in front of the stand, then helped out the frightened women and frantic men over the railing," the *Chicago Tribune* reported on the incident. "Cubs players helped 1,000 rooters, many of them women, risking serious injury to prevent a panic and the possible loss of life."[39]

In all the commotion about the fire, people from the other part of the island amusement park had wandered over to see what was happening. Since no rain checks had been issued to ball-grounds patrons, everyone was let into the game that wished to see it (about 10,000 people). This caused a swelling of people around the edges of the infield about 20 deep, as well as ringing the outfield, which constricted the amount of playing area available.

"A five-inning game was played, while flames crackled in the ruins on one side and a crowd of several thousand cheered on the other," the *Bridgeport Post* remarked. Chicago defeated the Bridgeport Orators 3–1 in the shortened game, behind the pitching of Chick Fraser and "his wet curve" (spitball), before escaping with their lives from the exhibition game.[40]

Fraser added fire fighter to his Sunday baseball resume in addition to his previous role as "arrestee for hire" in the last Brooklyn Sunday game in 1906 while then a member of the Cincinnati team.

Chick Fraser pitched 13 major league seasons from 1896 to 1908, accumulating a 176–214 won-loss record with seven teams. Fraser was a 20-game

Chick Fraser volunteered to be arrested for a Sunday baseball violation in Brooklyn in 1906. Fraser also helped to save spectators from a fire at a 1907 Sunday exhibition game in Bridgeport, Connecticut. (National Baseball Hall of Fame Library, Cooperstown, N.Y.)

winner with both the Philadelphia teams tallying 21 wins for the Phillies in 1899 and 22 wins for the Athletics in 1901.

While Nap Lajoie was the celebrated contract jumper from the Phillies to the Athletics for the inaugural American League season in 1901, Fraser was also involved in those lawsuits. In April 1902 when the Pennsylvania Supreme Court reversed the decision that had allowed Lajoie, Fraser, and several others to play in the American League, Fraser returned to the Phillies. He was never again as effective a pitcher, however, losing 20 games in each of three consecutive seasons from 1904 to 1906 while playing for three different teams.

One great post–1901 moment came on September 18, 1903, when Fraser pitched a no-hitter against the Chicago Cubs. Certainly less remembered are Fraser's exploits as a designated Sunday baseball arrestee, when he volunteered to be the first Cincinnati batter in a 1906 game in Brooklyn, and as an impromptu fireman for the Cubs in a 1907 Sunday exhibition game in Bridgeport, Connecticut.

With the Detroit Tigers hot on the trail of the team's first American League pennant in 1907, the team took the opportunity to push a little harder for Sunday baseball at Bennett Park. Part of the motivation was to not miss out on a potential Sunday home game in the World Series if the team did finish in first place.

Ever since Detroit and Cleveland abandoned the neutral-site strategy for Sunday games after the 1903 season, the two teams engaged in scheduling gymnastics to get in as many Sunday road games as possible. The one-game Sunday road trip had become a staple of both teams by 1906. The American League schedule maker tried to tack the one-game Sunday road trip onto a home series with the same team, or insert the Sunday game into the midst of a series, to level the playing field for the Sunday game as both teams would be traveling at the same time.

For instance, on Sunday, July 1, Detroit played at St. Louis while Cleveland was at Chicago. Over the previous three days, June 28–30, St. Louis had played at Detroit and Chicago at Cleveland. Similarly, the Sunday, September 2, games of Detroit at St. Louis and Cleveland at Chicago were one-day excursions in the middle of series back in Detroit and Cleveland from August 31 to September 4. To be sure, there were also "conventional" one-game Sunday road trips on September 16 and October 7 (last day of the season) where Detroit played at Chicago and Cleveland was at St. Louis.

With the Tigers in first place in early August and on its way to its first American League pennant, Detroit owner Bill Yawkey (who had bought the team from Angus) seized the opportunity in the moment of public glory to test the waters for Sunday baseball at Bennett Park. The club announced it would play a Sunday game on August 18 against Boston, on the tail end of its series ending on Saturday, August 17.

"The adjoining property owners are all friends of the club, the police commissioner has pledged himself not to interfere, the sheriff is Jimmie Burns, a former owner of the club and a good sport, while the prosecuting attorney and the mayor have made no objections," the press expounded on the favorable prospects. "Sunday theatres are allowed in Detroit and the club has a strong talking point." Seating was added in the outfield to accommodate the expected influx of fans for Sunday baseball and "in case of a world championship series."[41]

New York actually wound up as the visiting team for the August 18 game, as the team was coming to town for a series originally slated to begin on Monday, August 19. Detroit defeated New York 13–6 before 10,000 people, the second largest crowd of the year at Bennett Park.

"We have conducted one game for the purpose of learning definitely whether or not the public wishes the Sunday game," Frank Navin said after the game. "A glance at the gathering in the stand of itself is sufficient to show that Sunday ball draws a representative crowd." The Detroit club gave $200 of the Sunday receipts to charity, $100 to the Protestant Orphan Asylum, and $100 to the Roman Catholic Orphan Asylum, with the gifts to continue with each Sunday game.[42]

Boston did play the following Sunday in Detroit, playing an impromptu one-game series on August 25 between games at Cleveland. Two Sunday home games were all Detroit could squeeze in during 1907, as the club played its remaining schedule on the road.

"After lobbying with legislatures, circulating petitions, taking an active hand in local politics, and conducting an agitation of every sort calculated to secure permission of a formal character for the staging of base ball games at Bennett Park on Sunday, the Detroit club just went ahead the other day and played," *Sporting Life* summarized the Sunday strategy for its readers. "No protest of a coherent character was made. They played again. Nobody had a word to say. As a result, it seems that Sunday baseball is pretty firmly established in Detroit." Not everyone was pleased with the change in Sunday scheduling, though. "The move will be an unwelcome one to the players of the visiting clubs who have come to regard Sundays in Detroit as sure signs of fishing trips."[43]

Ban Johnson seemed to engineer the inauguration of Sunday baseball at Bennett Park. The *Detroit Free Press* reported that Johnson left the city on August 14 and "it is understood that the Sunday ball proposition was acted on favorably while he was here."[44]

Jimmie Burns, the former owner, as Wayne County sheriff was probably helpful, although Frank Croul, whom Navin had allegedly jilted in a wager, was still prominent in politics (and would soon become the police commissioner). The charitable contributions no doubt came out of the negotiations with Johnson, perhaps suggested by Burns from a reminiscence about how Sunday baseball became accepted at the old Ecorse grounds in 1899.[45]

Detroit won the American League pennant in 1907 on the strength of league-leading hitter Ty Cobb and the strong arm of Wild Bill Donovan, who posted a 25–4 record. The way the World Series was scheduled in 1907, Detroit didn't get a Sunday date. The first two games were in Chicago, the next three in Detroit (Thursday through Saturday), and the sixth game scheduled for Sunday, October 13, in Chicago, if necessary. The sixth game wasn't necessary as Chicago swept Detroit four games to none, with a tie in the second game.

Detroit won the pennant again in each of the next two years, but alas received no Sunday date in the World Series either year. The second game in 1908 was played on Sunday, October 11, in Chicago. There was no Sunday game in the 1909 Series with Pittsburgh. If Detroit had clinched the American League pennant early enough, the third game of the 1909 World Series would have been played in Detroit on Sunday, October 10. The tight pennant race with Philadelphia, however, forced the National Commission to set aside that Sunday as an open date in case Philadelphia, with its strict Sunday laws prohibiting baseball, won the pennant.

Perhaps another reason Detroit wanted to play Sunday baseball at Bennett Park was that Yawkey wanted to sell out, and the ability to schedule Sunday baseball would increase the value of the franchise (by 50 percent according to some estimates). Yawkey transferred half the team to Navin at the end of 1907 and sold the remainder (retaining a one-quarter interest).

Sunday baseball, and the resulting revenue from its attendance, enabled Navin to tear down the wooden Bennett Park and construct a steel and concrete structure in 1912, named appropriately enough as Navin Field. This same structure would eventually become Tiger Stadium.

Cleveland continued to wallow in a Sunday baseball malaise. Following the success of Detroit in cracking the Sunday baseball prohibition in that city, Cleveland president John Kilfoyl said the team wasn't interested in the subject of Sunday baseball anymore.

"There was a time when we felt that there was a popular demand for Sunday games in Cleveland and we made an effort along that line, but learned that we were mistaken," Kilfoyl said. "Since we gave up the idea of playing Sunday baseball, our weekday business has been so good that we have lost interest in this question."[46]

Cleveland management seemed to cling to the hope that Sunday baseball was not necessary and could be ably substituted financially by a half-holiday available to workers on Saturday, a story line contained in the 1909 Zane Grey novel *The Shortstop*. Before becoming a writer, Grey had played minor league baseball in the late 1890s and evidently incorporated some of his Sunday baseball exposure into this book.

Chase Alloway, an 18-year-old baseball player for a fictional team based in Findlay, Ohio, in the Tri-State League, agonized over trying to balance his religious convictions with his desire to play baseball for a living. When he discovered new faces in the Sunday crowd—"men and boys who worked every hour of daylight six days in the week"—he decided Sunday baseball could be a good deed. Alloway also discovered opposition from non-religious elements. "I find road houses and dance halls bitterly opposed to Sunday ball. Their Sunday business was ruined," Alloway said in the novel. "I had seen some of these places when in full blast on a busy Sunday. The beer ran in streams and the air reeked."[47]

Alloway was arrested for playing Sunday baseball on a complaint sworn out by Reverend Marsden. In an interesting morality tradeoff, Judge Duff decreed, for the good of the community of Findlay, that he would compel employers to give employees a half-holiday on Saturdays so that there would be no need for Sunday baseball. The Judge, as well as author Grey, failed to mention that debauchery in the roadhouses and dance halls was still permissible on Sunday, while baseball games were forbidden.

Grey's plot line was remarkably similar to real-life events in Cleveland. A half-holiday law was implemented in 1896 but failed to deter then-owner Frank Robison from trying to play Sunday baseball. Liquor interests had also teamed up with Sabbatarian groups to stop Robison's efforts in 1897–98.

Tom Johnson, mayor of Cleveland from 1901 to 1909, was known as a progressive mayor that fought for municipal reform and improved facilities to help the city's lower-income residents. While Johnson fought for a reduction to a three-cent fare for streetcars and urged municipal ownership of public utilities, his reforms did not include Sunday baseball. Johnson "was against Sunday base ball and will not permit the Cleveland Club to play such games at home," *Sporting Life* indicated early in Johnson's mayoral administration.[48]

Following the aborted 1902 attempt to play Sunday games in suburban Newburgh, no owner of the Cleveland ball club attempted Sunday baseball during Johnson's tenure as mayor. Once Johnson finally lost re-election and Herman Baehr became mayor in 1909, serious movement on Sunday baseball in Cleveland began anew. When Johnson died in April 1911, his influence that had impeded Sunday baseball passed as well.

While Cincinnati and a host of Ohio cities closed their eyes to Sunday baseball's technical violation of the Ohio law, the 1898 Ohio Supreme Court ruling in *State v. Powell* continued to hinder the playing of professional baseball in Cleveland on Sunday. Major renovations to expand League Park in 1910, though, created a greater urgency to overturn Cleveland's decade-long abstention from Sunday baseball participation. Getting the Ohio legislature to pass a law permitting Sunday baseball was the only certain way to defuse *State v. Powell*.

The Ohio legislature had debated Sunday baseball bills for a decade and had not been able to reach an accord among legislators. Finally, the local-option concept was introduced. Rather than create a law with blanket approval across the state, a local-option law permitted each city and town to decide for itself whether the law would apply to its citizens. Local option enabled the Ohio legislators to arrive at a consensus for a Sunday baseball law.

Another turning point in the Ohio legislative efforts for Sunday baseball occurred in February 1911 when the supreme court in neighboring, conservative Indiana declared constitutional that state's 1909 law permitting Sunday baseball. Indiana's narrow 3–2 decision created the opportunity for more Ohio legislators to support a similar measure.

"The decision of the Supreme Court of Indiana ... is the most direct and important judicial declaration on the subject of Sunday ball yet made," *Sporting Life* declared in an editorial. The Indiana law prohibited people to labor or follow their usual avocation on Sunday, with certain exceptions. One exception was playing baseball between the hours of 1:00 and 6:00 in the afternoon if not less than 1000 feet from any church or hospital.[49]

"The general movement for games on Sunday is a tribute to the advance of the game—an advance to the point where no one can find words to speak in criticism of the national pastime as now conducted," *Sporting Life* editorialized in 1911. "The standard of the game was never higher ... the last argument against base ball has faded and the sport stands today as good for body and soul on Sunday as it is on Monday or any other day of the week."[50]

On February 28, 1911, the Ohio House of Representatives passed the Greeves bill, a local-option Sunday baseball bill, by a vote of 61–46. The bill negated the existing statute that prohibited Sunday baseball and transferred to municipal councils the power to regulate the playing of sports on Sunday.

During the House debate on the bill, two ministers who were also elected Representatives had an interesting exchange. When Reverend H. L. Guard of Urbana objected to the "commercializing of the Lord's Day,"

Reverend J. H. Lorenz from Springfield interrupted Guard by asking, "What do you mean when you say commercializing the Sabbath? Don't you get paid for preaching on the Sabbath and isn't that commercializing the day?" The bill's sponsor Representative Joseph Greeves countered the remarks of Reverend Guard by saying the bill "was not a step toward irrelevance or paganism, but was making legal what was already a common practice."[51]

Representative H. Fellinger of Cleveland said the character of the population in Ohio had changed in the 50 years since the statute was enacted, as the vast majority then lived in rural sections while now they were in the cities. "Base ball is now being played in every large city of the state by professionals save in Cleveland," Fellinger said. "But there they had four hundred clubs, many of them representing churches, which played on Sunday afternoon. This bill will simply legalize what is now a general and inoffensive practice."[52]

The bill was passed by the Ohio Senate and then went on to the governor for his signature. Before he'd sign the bill, Governor Judson Harmon held hearings.

Leading the opposition to the Greeves bill was Reverend Gregg, head of the Civic Reform League of Cleveland. "Should the bill be signed, there will be a terrific fight in the Cleveland City Council to keep out Sunday base ball," Gregg offered before the governor's hearing.[53]

While Harmon in the past had indicated support for the Sunday baseball bill, apparently the hearings dissuaded him from a formal approval, as the bill became law without his signature. "The Greeves bill, providing for Sunday base ball in cities with the consent of the city council, became a law Saturday midnight through the failure of Gov. Harmon to exercise the veto power," *The Sporting News* communicated.[54]

The first legal Sunday game in Cleveland was played on May 14, as Cleveland resoundingly defeated New York 14–3 before a crowd of 15,585. George Stovall, the Cleveland first baseman, went four for five that day, while pitcher Spec Harkness not only pitched effectively but also went three for five at the plate.

"Sunday ball is a success," Mayor Baehr remarked. "Cleveland people have shown themselves capable of acting with decorum at a ball game. It was a splendidly well behaved one. I congratulate the Cleveland fans for their conduct today."[55]

Since the American League schedule had naturally been drawn up reflecting no Sunday dates in Cleveland, the Indians scrambled to reconfigure its schedule to move games to Sundays.

Cleveland had been the king of the one-game Sunday road trip for the past seven years since 1904, enriching the coffers of St. Louis and

Chicago (and Detroit since 1908), with between three to six Sunday games fitted in between home games at League Park. Cleveland now became a Sunday haven for eastern clubs.

Late in 1911, Philadelphia made its first one-game Sunday road trip to Cleveland. On September 24, Philadelphia defeated Cleveland 5–3 after making the trip following its Saturday game at Shibe Park, while Cleveland came in from Washington to play its first one-game Sunday home series. In 1912, Washington made a one-game Sunday journey to play in Cleveland on May 12 and Philadelphia likewise on July 14.

Washington and Philadelphia joined Pittsburgh as Sunday hoppers in the major leagues. Over the previous 12 years, Pittsburgh had made frequent journeys to both Cincinnati and Chicago to play Sunday games during its home stands in western Pennsylvania. For instance, in 1911, Pittsburgh played six one-game Sunday series, four in Cincinnati and two in Chicago.

With Sunday baseball gaining momentum with approvals in Detroit and Cleveland, it seemed as though it would be just a short time before Sunday baseball would be legalized in New York.

Chapter 10

NEW YORK WANTED IT

After Charlie Ebbets failed in his three-year quest to obtain court approval for Sunday baseball, New York proponents of Sunday baseball were forced to return to the state legislature in 1907 to find a sanction for playing the game on the Lord's Day.

Getting the New York legislature to pass a law permitting Sunday baseball, though, was a very challenging prospect for Sunday baseball proponents. Such bills had been proposed every year since the Sullivan bill had first been introduced on this issue in 1897, but none was able to survive the political process to become law.

Republicans not only controlled both branches of the New York legislature, the Assembly and the Senate, but the manner in which legislative districts were created also virtually assured continued Republican dominance over Democratic interests.

The Republican control of the Assembly arose "courtesy of an antiquated system that gave upstate areas, lavish in space but sparse in citizenry, the majority of districts," as historian Robert Slayton wrote in *Empire Statesman: The Rise and Redemption of Al Smith*. "In time this produced an anti–New York City bloc, as voters elected a group of patricians terrified of the urban, immigrant, industrial proletariat of the nation's largest metropolis."[1]

After the 1892 Lexow Commission, which was investigating corruption in New York City, determined that the police and vice lords were consorting together through the efforts of Tammany Hall political bosses, a new system of legislative apportionment was created. The new system stripped the cities of as many districts as possible, "denying representation to new generations of urban immigrants." For example, the new apportionment scheme provided that "no two counties divided by a river could command more than half the seats in the legislature, even if their population justified it." As historian Slayton wryly observed, "Strangely, only New

York and Kings counties, otherwise known as Manhattan and Brooklyn, fit this description."[2]

Although New York City had a majority of the state's residents, the new legislative apportionment allowed the city's residents only 67 of the 150 seats in the Assembly and 25 of the 56 seats in the Senate. Between 1904–1910, when Sunday baseball was a burning issue in New York, the Republicans commanded no fewer than 94 seats, or 62 percent, of the Assembly.

Prospects for passage of a Sunday baseball bill, therefore, started out with a bleak outlook due to Republican opposition to such activities.

Amateurs and semi-professional teams played baseball on Sunday in many parts of New York state in the late 19th century, but under inconsistent application of the state law that prohibited public sports on Sunday.

In the 1890s, baseball on Sunday was played mostly in rural areas, outside of the vastly more populated city centers. At that time, rural villages still dominated the landscape only five miles outside of the city. Unlike the city where formal police departments and judges in courtrooms enforced the law, in rural areas county sheriffs and justices of the peace maintained order on a less rigid basis.

Also in the early 1890s, New York City had not taken on the territorial scope that it has now. Manhattan was New York City at the time, while Brooklyn was an independent city (and of much smaller area than the borough is today). The Bronx was a collection of small independent villages as was Queens County where Flushing was an independent entity. Much of Kings County outside Brooklyn proper was also comprised of small villages such Flatbush and Gravesend, which gradually were annexed by Brooklyn in the mid–1890s. By 1898, Manhattan, Brooklyn, Bronx, Queens, and Staten Island were all consolidated to create Greater New York, now known as New York City.

Law enforcement in rural towns such as those in Queens and Kings counties was at the whim of the constable and justice of the peace. These village officials often ignored state laws that their town's citizens didn't approve of, and on the flip side could enforce local ordinances that ran afoul of a state law that the citizens felt was unjustified. Wealthy and influential citizens, particularly a local manufacturer whose business drove the village economy, could also tilt law enforcement their way in these rural outposts. Money was known to change hands occasionally from proprietors of parks to those charged with enforcing the law.

It was not surprising that some villages outside Manhattan enjoyed the economic stimulus injected by Sunday visitors, while other villages loathed the noisy Sunday crowds. This led to differing opinions by the various jurisdictions involved in allegations of Sunday law violations.

For instance, in 1886 William Monteverde was convicted and fined $250 for "keeping a nuisance" at Grand Street Park in Maspeth, where as many as three thousand people attended baseball games on Sunday. In neighboring Long Island City, though, Sunday recreation flourished as Mayor Gleason instructed his constabulary not to interfere with activities at the People's Recreation Grounds. Justices had also been more forgiving in Long Island City. Two years earlier in 1884, Justice Delahanty ruled that a Sunday baseball participant named Patrick Ryan was innocent of the charges due to a technicality.[3]

Even when justices ruled Sunday baseball illegal, the citizens often acted to signal their disagreement with the verdict.

In 1891, players of the local Domestics team were arrested in Far Rockaway, Long Island, for playing baseball on Sunday, although they had played such games for years on the grounds in the center of the village. At the trial held on September 2 in the village hall, citizens packed the hall and yelled at the complainant, Henry Schrymser.

After Justice Seaman convicted the players and fined them five dollars each, the "spectators hissed and hooted at Schrymser, who beat a hasty retreat. The crowd outside [the hall] hustled him and pelted him with rotten eggs and other objectionable missiles until he jumped into his carriage and drove away from their reach." The convicted players were cheered as they exited the hall.[4]

Rather than contend with the vagaries of the judicial landscape on Long Island, and as well as the relative difficulty for patrons to get to the isolated ball grounds in Queens, the New York City professional teams began to play Sunday games in New Jersey. The New York Giants especially, given the proximity of New Jersey to Manhattan, took this avenue for Sunday play.

Following the consolidation of Greater New York in 1898, New Jersey became the preferred outlet for Sunday baseball, since the villages in Long Island were now under the jurisdiction of Greater New York, which enforced the Manhattan interpretation of the Sunday laws—that is, a rigid construction. Sunday baseball in Manhattan had consistently been ruled illegal before the consolidation, as early as 1885, and there were few places to play anyway on the island. It was illegal to play ball in Central Park, an activity that was prohibited there until 1920.[5]

The New York Sabbath Committee also wielded great influence on Manhattan. This interdenominational group, established in 1857, "entered almost every battle over leisure activities that reconfigured American culture—

saloons, excursions, newspapers, museums, baseball, motion pictures, radio, and dancing highlight the list." The New York Sabbath Committee, along with numerous other Sabbatarian organizations that formed in the last quarter of the 19th century, "was intent on keeping rest and leisure in separate spheres."[6]

Sabbatarians desired to maintain an American Sabbath in the nation's largest city to set an example for their colleagues elsewhere. "If they could defeat the 'un-Godly' in this stronghold [of immigrant population], then the devout were confident of triumph in other cities."[7]

While urban New York City experienced resistance to Sunday baseball, many other cities within New York State with minor league baseball teams had capitulated on the concept. Sunday baseball success came first in the minor leagues, as it did across much of the country. Only one-third of residents in the cities that made up major league baseball could see baseball on Sunday in 1911, while the majority of citizens in minor league cities could. This was especially the case at the highest level of the minors (Class A at the time), particularly in the midwest and western regions.

"In the five great leagues of the Class A division, three—the American Association, the Pacific Coast League, and the Western League—are unanimously in favor of Sunday baseball, while the Southern Association and the Eastern League are divided among themselves," F. C. Lane wrote in a Sunday baseball analysis in *Baseball Magazine* in 1911. Three of eight cities in the Southern Association hosted Sunday baseball (Memphis, New Orleans, and Mobile).[8]

Four of eight teams in the Eastern League, where Pat Powers was president and had pushed hard for Sunday baseball in the east, hosted Sunday baseball (Providence, Jersey City, Newark, and Montreal). While Buffalo and Rochester in the Eastern League did not host Sunday baseball, several smaller New York cities with teams in the Class B New York State League did host Sunday baseball. These Sunday-playing cities included Albany (the state capital), Elmira, Utica, and Syracuse.

"Sunday baseball is necessary to the success of many minor league organizations," Lane wrote. "The whole existence of the minor league structure is threatened and the surest way of turning ruinous deficits into profits lies in the profits of Sunday baseball. The very existence of many minor league organizations seems to depend on the inauguration of a system of Sunday games, when the largest crowds may be expected and the greatest financial returns obtained."[9]

Baseball Magazine, the first national monthly periodical dedicated to baseball, elevated the Sunday baseball issue through articles written by prominent men of the time.

The Greatest Problem in the National Game

The Critical Situation in Sunday Baseball

By F. C. Lane

*The following article presents a graphic picture of the present situation in Sunday baseball. The subject is one of much deeper importance than is commonly supposed, and its final settlement strikes deep at the root of all future prosperity in the National game. Because we believe that such a movement is necessary for the largest measure of success in organized baseball, and because we believe, further, that it answers the needs and merits the support of the great majority throughout the United States, the Baseball Magazine wishes to make clear its firm stand in favor of Sunday baseball.

Baseball Magazine was an ardent supporter of Sunday baseball, as indicated in this 1911 headline from one of its articles, and helped to advance the Sunday baseball cause in New York.

"In Chicago, Cincinnati and St. Louis they play Sunday baseball," William Kirk wrote in "Shall We Have Sunday Baseball?" published by *Baseball Magazine* in 1908. "Chicago, Cincinnati and St. Louis are not disorderly cities. The percentage of crime in those centers is not so great as in some of our eastern towns, where Sunday baseball is not even a possibility at the present time." Kirk went to conclude, "The world is growing more liberal with the passing years, and possibly within the next decade we shall look with tolerance on Sunday baseball in every corner of the country."[10]

In its early days, *Baseball Magazine* invited divergent opinion on the issue of Sunday baseball, particularly from ministers.

"I am against Sabbath desecration under all circumstances," the Rev. Billy Sunday, the former ball player turned evangelist, wrote in response to the Kirk article. "The first day of the week is holy and such blatant sport as baseball pollutes its sanctity. Baseball is a great game and too much cannot be said in its favor, but ... when it usurps the day of the Lord it has overstepped itself and must be curbed. One day a week is not too much to give up to higher things. This giving up cannot be done on baseball bleachers on a Sunday afternoon."[11]

Rabbi Charles Fleischer had a different perspective than the Rev. Sunday. "I believe in one day's rest in seven and preferably on Sunday, the day enshrined in the reverent affection of the vast majority of Americans,"

Fleischer wrote. "But a day's rest is not idle dilly-dallying in one's room or on one's veranda, but active participation in something healthful and helpful." Fleischer concluded, "Give them the sunshine, and their pleasure of pleasures by throwing aside Colonial narrowness and by making antiquated the law against Sunday baseball."[12]

Baseball Magazine was an unabashed supporter of Sunday baseball. The magazine's printing of numerous Sunday baseball–related articles helped to bring about change in the eastern part of the country, albeit slowly.

In New York, Sunday baseball at the professional level had already infiltrated the state through cities in the Class B New York State League. Having it reach the major population centers of the state, however, proved to be a more difficult challenge.

On April 15, 1907, the Codes Committee of the New York Assembly held a hearing on the Mooney bill to permit Sunday baseball. Speakers at the hearing clearly demonstrated the two sides of the Sunday baseball issue.

Several clergymen spoke against the Mooney bill, enunciating that the Sunday laws were necessary to protect public morals, safeguard the beliefs of religious citizens, and defend the population's enjoyment of the day of rest.

Proponents of the bill pointed out that Sunday baseball provided a positive experience for youth through a healthful and moral activity. Assemblyman Alfred E. Smith, then an unknown and relatively inexperienced politician, pointed out the flaw in the Sabbatarian argument. "We tolerate such places as Coney Island and Rockaway Beach, but when it comes to allowing an innocent game of baseball on Sunday, then there is a howl," Smith told the committee. "We are willing to allow the youths to go where there are evil influences, but keep from them things which cannot possibly harm. Then why not allow Sunday baseball?"[13]

Al Smith, the Fulton Fish Market employee turned Democratic legislator, would ultimately serve four terms as governor of New York, run for president in 1928, and sign the eventual Sunday baseball bill that became law in New York. But all those accomplishments were more than a dozen years away in 1907, when the Republican-dominated Assembly quashed the Mooney bill.

Sunday baseball bills found new life in 1910 when a scandal swept Republican legislative circles. Several leading Republicans were found to have illegally taken public funds to speculate in the stock market, particularly payments from bridge companies to influence legislation. Suddenly, Republicans were more amenable to Sunday baseball.

In an April 26 debate on the McGrath bill to permit Sunday baseball,

Speaker of the Assembly James W. Wadsworth Jr., a Republican, took the unusual action of surrendering the gavel to the Democratic Minority Leader to make a speech from the floor during the two-hour acrimonious debate.

"Our Sunday laws as they are discriminate against the poor and are in favor of the rich," Wadsworth said. "We don't hear the churches complain of the rich man who attends divine services in the forenoon and plays golf or tennis all afternoon at the country club. But against this bill they raise vehement protest. It is injustice of this kind that moves me to vote for this bill."[14]

Wadsworth then uttered a line that would be used many times over, in several variations, by future legislators debating Sunday baseball bills.

"I would rather have a boy of mine on the bleachers shouting himself hoarse or scampering around a baseball field trying to stretch a three-bagger into a home run than trying to buy an illegal drink at the corner saloon," Wadsworth offered. "He would be a healthier boy and he would grow up to be a better Christian citizen."[15]

Following Wadsworth's stirring words, the Assembly passed the McGrath bill by a 77–67 vote. With a progressive Republican governor in office, Charles Evans Hughes, Sunday baseball proponents had hope for the law's passage. Those hopes were dashed when the Senate refused to pass a similar bill, however, and the legal status of Sunday baseball remained unchanged.

Democrats swept into power after the 1910 fall elections in the wake of the Republican scandal. Voters elected the state's first Democratic governor in 17 years (John Dix) and Democrats won enough seats to control both the Assembly and the Senate. Things looked auspicious for passage of a Sunday baseball bill in New York.

On March 14, 1911, though, the McGrath bill was defeated in the Assembly by a vote of 65–73 in what the *New York Times* described as "a bitter debate." Rather than appeal to religious grounds, Reverend Julius Lincoln, who also was the Assemblyman from the First District of Chatauqua County, appealed to a more Democratic concern. Reverend Lincoln declared that "with Sunday thrown open to sports and week day amusements, the movement to make the half holiday on Saturday more general would suffer."[16]

Apparently, Lincoln's speech persuaded some Democrats, now in the majority in the Assembly, to favor a five-and-a-half day workweek over Sunday baseball.

In the Senate on March 23, the Codes Committee approved the Sullivan bill, which provided for both amateurs and professionals to play Sunday baseball, although the mention of an admission fee was absent from the bill.[17]

Sentiment for Sunday baseball among Democrats was derailed, however, when 146 people died in a factory fire at the Triangle Shirtwaist Company on March 25. This catastrophe caused a realignment of the Democratic political agenda and lowered the priority of Sunday baseball.

Democrats were now able to enact numerous labor laws concerning health and fire protection to protect factory workers, due to the Triangle Shirtwaist fire. Laws were passed to have all doors open outwards, to prohibit locked doors during working hours, and for sprinkler systems to be installed in factories. So many people died in the fire because doors at the factory opened inwards and several were locked (ostensibly to prevent employee theft).

Progress was made on the Sunday baseball front on July 12 when the Assembly by a narrow margin passed the Bush bill 85–83. Borrowing a concept from the successful Ohio Sunday baseball legislation, the Bush bill introduced a key component to the eventual passage of a Sunday baseball law in New York—the local option provision. Under the Bush bill, five percent of voters in a city, town, or village were needed to call for a vote on Sunday baseball and a majority was needed to decide the question.[18]

The Sunday baseball law passed in Ohio that May contained a local option provision, which helped to appease the Sabbatarian interests in that Sunday baseball matter. In New York, though, Sabbatarian groups only worked harder.

The New York Civic League launched campaigns to persuade citizens to stop the roll back of Sunday law provisions. Reverend Miller of the League boasted that his group had helped to defeat the McGrath bill in 1911 by arousing public sentiment on the matter through over 100,000 letters, telegrams, and circulars.[19]

The New York Sabbath Committee produced numerous publications and circulars on the Sunday baseball issue hoping to sway public opinion to retain the Sunday laws. On the cover of one issue of the *Bulletin of the New York Sabbath Committee* was a drawing entitled "The Break in the Levee: Are You Helping to Widen the Breach?" The drawing showed workers with picks making a hole in a levee labeled "Sabbath Observance" under the direction of a man holding a sign labeled "Sunday Base Ball" so that water labeled "Irreligion" flowed through it to envelope a church near the levee.[20]

The open political window for Sunday baseball, partially shut by the Triangle Shirtwaist fire in 1911, was abruptly closed two years later in 1913 when scandal rocked the Democratic Party. Governor William Sulzer, who had succeeded Dix, was impeached on October 17, 1913, and removed from office, ending the realistic possibility that any Democratic legislation, not just Sunday baseball, could be effectuated. World War I then broke out several months later in 1914, putting a further damper on progressive legislation.

During the 1907–1914 period, Sunday baseball was played by professional teams in New York City only for two charity events.

On Sunday, July 4, 1909, a benefit game for newsboys was held at Brooklyn's Washington Park. Brooklyn defeated the New York Americans 7–3 with 10,000 newsboys in attendance.

On April 21, 1912, a benefit game for survivors of the Titanic ship disaster was held at the Polo Grounds. The game raised $9,425 as 14,083 spectators donated the usual price of a ticket to purchase a program. This was the first Sunday game ever played at the Polo Grounds.

In 1913 and 1914, the McMahon and DuBois bills continued the Sunday baseball legislative battle in the Assembly. But what really set in motion the legalization of Sunday ball in New York were two wars. One was of international scope and fought by soldiers with real guns in Europe. The other was domestic in nature and fought by baseball players with bats on American ball fields and by lawyers wielding pens in American courtrooms.

The 1914 launch of the Federal League, a third major league that competed with the American and National Leagues for two years until its demise following the 1915 season, significantly impacted the Sunday baseball legalization movement in New York.

Brooklyn had a franchise in the Federal League both seasons. To compete against the well-entrenched National League club now playing out of Ebbets Field, the BrookFeds (also known as the Tip Tops) adopted the policy that it would not play any Sunday games on the road. The club hoped to attract customers within the City of Churches that would patronize its games due to this lofty philosophy toward Sunday baseball, as opposed to the National League team's more liberal attitude of playing Sunday baseball on the road.

"President R. B. Ward of the Brooklyn Tip Tops came out yesterday emphatically against his team playing Sunday base ball," *Sporting Life* reported. "He pointed out it was not for the benefit of the present generation, but for the future base ball followers that he is insisting upon a strict observance of the Sabbath."[21]

"The Sabbath is a day of rest and ought to be so regarded," Ward said. "I wouldn't care to work on Sunday and I don't feel that I should force my men to do it when it may be avoided. There is really no need for playing Sunday ball. The players like to observe the days of rest just as anyone else. They are not machines."[22]

The failure of the Brooklyn Federal League team to sufficiently leverage this Sunday baseball policy by attracting huge home crowds did not assist Sunday baseball opponents at all in their continued quest to stop the New York Assembly from approving a Sunday baseball bill.

Even more compelling to Sunday baseball proponents in New York was the creation of the Newark, New Jersey, franchise for the 1915 Federal League season. Just 15 miles from the Polo Grounds on Manhattan Island, Newark played Sunday baseball at the major league level, which put additional pressure on New York legislators to finally legalize Sunday baseball games with paid admissions.

At its winter meetings in 1915, the Federal League set its sights to realign into the lucrative territory of metropolitan New York City to help stabilize the league financially. No one could be found, though, who wanted to take on competition in Manhattan with the powerful New York Giants, especially with secondary competition from the then lower profile New York club in the American League.

Pat Powers, the former Eastern League president who had nurtured that league into the powerful International League, was willing to launch a Federal League team in Newark, across the Hudson River from New York City. Powers had turned the Eastern League into a premium minor league partially through his Sunday baseball advocacy, which created the financial underpinning for profitable operation. Powers had gotten his feet wet in the Sunday baseball issue during his days as manager of the Rochester club in the American Association in 1890 when he was embroiled with the efforts of the Irondequoit Law and Order Society to stop Sunday baseball play at the Windsor Beach grounds.

With the backing of oil millionaire Harry Sinclair, Powers brought Sunday baseball on a legal basis at the major league level to within a short train ride from New York City. It was the farthest east that continuous Sunday baseball had been in 25 years, since Brooklyn last played Sunday games at Ridgewood Park in Queens during 1889 in its final year in the American Association.

After an aborted effort to transfer the Kansas City franchise to Newark (the Kansas City owners balked at the action and wished to retain the club), the Federal League orchestrated the move of the 1914 pennant winning, but deeply indebted, Indianapolis club to Newark. The new team was christened the Newark Peppers and consisted of most of the former HooFeds, except 1914 batting champion Bennie Kauff who went from the Hoosiers to Brooklyn.

Powers and his backers built a new stadium to seat 21,000 a short way from downtown Newark, across the Passaic River in adjoining Harrison.

A strong team, new stadium, proximity to millions of potential customers in the New York City area, and the ability to play Sunday baseball should have been enough to sustain the Newark club to rescue the financially strapped Federal League. But it wasn't enough.

On opening day April 16, 1915, nearly 30,000 people tried to jam into Harrison Park, only to see the Peppers lose 6–2 to Baltimore.

Despite an overweighted Sunday schedule, with 17 dates during the 26-week season, Newark couldn't leverage the New York City element.

Because Brooklyn still wouldn't play Sunday baseball on the road in 1915, Newark missed out on at least three potential big gates at Harrison Park (the number of road trips each team made to the other seven cities in the league). This was partially made up through half of the home-and-away holiday doubleheaders the Peppers played with the Tip Tops on Decoration Day, July 4th, and Labor Day. But Newark lost the opportunity to schedule isolated Sunday games with neighboring Brooklyn, while also playing other teams in the holiday doubleheaders.

League schedulers did accommodate Newark by slating Sunday dates consisting of one-game series to optimize the chance for financial success. Baltimore trained into Newark four times for one-game stands, and Buffalo did likewise twice. Usually, both Newark and the visiting team would train in for the game to alleviate the advantage that Newark might have from the added rest of a home game the preceding Saturday.

For instance, Newark played at Buffalo on May 14 and 15, then both teams trained to Newark to play Sunday, May 16, before both teams headed west—Buffalo to St. Louis and Newark to Pittsburgh. Even more train-intensive was the Baltimore-Newark game on Sunday, August 29, in Newark, that was sandwiched in between games between the same two teams in Baltimore on August 28 and 30.

Harrison Park was located between Second and Third Streets in Harrison, "a short distance from the Fourth Street Station of the Pennsylvania Railroad and the Harrison Station of the Manhattan line."[23]

The park was also billed as "being closer to midtown Manhattan than any other existing major league facility." Running time on the Pennsylvania Railroad from Penn Station in New York to the station near Harrison Park was said to be 14 minutes, shorter than the ride on the subway or elevated train to either the Polo Grounds or Ebbets Field.[24]

Despite the train connections, it was still a less-than-easy task for many spectators to reach Harrison Park, since most New Yorkers didn't live within short proximity of Penn Station. Harrison Park had what one scribe could best describe as "fairly convenient public transportation for Manhattanites."[25]

The perceived difficulty of getting to Harrison Park seemed to undermine Newark's chance to take serious advantage of the Sunday baseball opportunity. In July, the team convinced the local trolley company to lay a line over the Jackson Street Bridge to within one block of the park to provide a more convenient way for Newark fans to get to the games.[26]

Spectators didn't flock to Sunday games. To attract more spectators, the Peppers began to play doubleheaders on Sunday as early as June 13, nine in all, concluding with a season-ending twosome on October 3.

While the Peppers were trying to draw Sunday crowds, legal fees associated with the Federal League's anti-trust lawsuit against the National and American Leagues, along with other legal actions against individual teams, were pushing clubs to the brink of bankruptcy. The Federal League settled the lawsuits in December 1915 and went out of existence.

As part of the legal settlement, the ballparks owned by the Federal League teams become property of Organized Baseball. Today, the most famous remnant of the Federal League is Weeghman Park, which eventually became Wrigley Field after the Chicago National League club began to play its home games there in 1916.

While Harrison Field in Newark lay idle in 1916, it would soon play another role in the legislative fray over Sunday baseball in New York.

In New York, the McElroy bill was the first legislative response to major league baseball being played on Sunday in Newark. On March 17, 1915, the Codes Committee of the Assembly debated the McElroy bill, where Assemblyman Martin McCue of the 16th New York district called Sunday baseball opponents "involuntary agents of the devil."

"I'd sooner have my son in the bleachers Sunday afternoon screeching his lungs out while a player tries to stretch a three-bagger into a home run than have him in a basement on Second Avenue shooting craps," McCue declared, as he borrowed from Speaker Wadsworth's remarks of five years earlier on the subject. "I think if I watch the Giants perform on a bright Sunday afternoon, I am keeping the day holy as the Master intended it should be kept holy."[27]

Reverend W. P. Swartz of the New York Sabbath Committee thought the bill set bad precedent. Other representatives from Sabbatarian groups opposed the measure as fostering business interests on Sunday.

"Not one of you preachers here would dare get up in a New York City pulpit and advocate stopping Sunday excursion boats from running out of New York City. For those boats to run, capital must be invested and someone makes a profit," McCue, a former prize fighter, poked at the Sabbatarians with words. "And I have seen you preachers take a ride of a Sunday afternoon on a trolley car for the pleasure of it. Don't you think someone made a profit out of the nickel you paid?"[28]

The McElroy bill, like all its predecessors, failed to be enacted into law.

As the war in Europe reached its third anniversary during 1917, the United States entered the armed conflict that April. With this heightened public awareness of the war, the National Commission that governed major league baseball suggested that eastern teams play Sunday games in order to contribute the proceeds to war-related causes.

It sounded like an admirable aim. But as one wag put it, "It is just possible that in staging Sunday games for a patriotic purpose, the Commission had in mind conditioning public opinion in the East to demand Sunday ball as a regular diet in the future."[29]

New York mayor John Mitchel gave his approval to the idea in May and a new test was conducted of the state's Sunday laws forbidding baseball. There was no explicit admission charge to see the 1917 Sunday baseball games in New York. People could ostensibly see the games for free. Spectators, though, did pay to hear a patriotic concert that preceded each game. Tickets to the sacred concert in Brooklyn on July 1 had "free exhibition game" imprinted on the backside and ticket holders were directed to keep their seats after the concert. After the sacred concert was over, gates were opened to let in others without paying anything to see the baseball game.[30]

The Yankees hosted the first benefit game in 1917 on June 17 at the Polo Grounds. The St. Louis Browns defeated the Yankees 2–1, as nearly 25,000 people watched a patriotic concert and military drills prior to the game to raise money for the First Reserve Engineers Regiment of New York. Harry Ellis sang George Cohan's new song "Over There." Receipts for the game were over $10,000 to aid the families of the military unit expected to soon go overseas.

"It was something of a novelty, this playing of a championship game in New York on Sunday," the *New York Times* remarked of the game. "The crowd was on its Sunday behavior, for a more orderly gathering would be hard to find."[31]

The second benefit game was held on July 1 at Ebbets Field in Brooklyn, in what one newspaper called the "first regularly scheduled National League Sunday baseball game played in the borough across the bridge in many, many years." The 12,000 enthusiasts in the park saw a sacred concert and patriotic demonstration for the benefit of the Militia of Mercy, followed by an exciting baseball game in which the Dodgers beat the Phillies by a 3–2 score.[32]

Behind 2–1 in the bottom of the ninth, Brooklyn rallied to score two runs after a disputed play to overtake the Phillies. Umpire Bill Klem had ruled Casey Stengel out on an interference call and disallowed a Brooklyn run on the play. The controversial call was all but forgotten by Dodgers fans when Mike Mowrey doubled home two Brooklyn runners off relief pitcher Eppa Rixey to end the game in a Brooklyn victory.

Another controversial call after the game wouldn't be so short lived, though. Following the July 1 Sunday game, Dodgers president Charlie Ebbets and manager Wilbert Robinson were arrested for violating the Sunday law.

King County sheriff Riegelmann didn't make arrests at the game itself since he was unsure if a violation of the law had occurred as well as his "fear of starting a fuss, or possibly, a riot." Riegelmann had a concern about the procedures used to admit spectators to the "free" baseball game. As soon as the sacred concert was over, the gates were opened so that anyone could come in free—but only for 15 minutes. Then all the gates were closed except for one. Only people with concert tickets were admitted through that one open gate, and people without concert tickets were told to go around to the bleachers. After the sheriff's staff objected to this procedure, all the gates were opened.[33]

At the arraignment in Flatbush Police Court on July 6, Ebbets explained that all admission money was paid by patrons to hear the concert and that he stopped selling tickets when the concert ended and then admitted people free. Ebbets also said that the $5,321.73 proceeds were turned over to the Militia of Mercy, which represented all receipts less about $500 for ushers, program boys, and other workers.

Ebbets' words rang hollow to Magistrate Alexander Geisman, who asked him, "Do you take the position Mr. Ebbets that the sacred concert and the baseball game were as different as night is from day?" Ebbets replied, "That is it, exactly."[34]

Unbeknownst to Ebbets, the sheriff had arranged a plan to obtain evidence to the contrary. After the sacred concert ended, two deputy sheriffs in plain clothes left their seats reserved for the concert. As the baseball game was beginning, another deputy sheriff sat down in one of the vacated seats.

"An usher, he testified, told him to get out," the *Brooklyn Daily Eagle* reported. "He refused, calling attention to the fact that the baseball game was free. The usher called a special policeman and the latter pushed the sheriff out of the seat, according to the testimony."[35]

Ebbets was highly indignant at what he called a "frame-up," also saying the closing of the gates at the beginning of the baseball game was "done by mistake."

Magistrate Geisman was not swayed. "In my opinion, there is still prima facie evidence that there was a public exhibition of a game as a public sport on the Sabbath and evidence of disturbance of the peace and repose of the community," Geisman said. "I shall issue a warrant and require these men to answer," as he held Ebbets and Robinson over for trial in the Court of Special Sessions.[36]

These Sunday baseball arrests were the first steps toward the realistic passage of a Sunday baseball law in New York. The issue received substantial favorable coverage in the press, which began to sway politicians in Albany.

Although Ebbets pursued a number of legal maneuvers to try to extricate him and Robinson from the matter, the trial began on August 28 and Ebbets was forced to cancel further benefit games planned for September 2 and 9. Ultimately, both were found guilty on September 24, as a three-judge panel ruled that the charitable use of the profits didn't absolve them from a violation of the law.

"What was done with the money received from the guests is of no consequence in determining the question involved in this issue," Justice Clarence Edwards wrote in the court's opinion. "The thing forbidden is public sport and it is no less public and no less sport because the money received was devoted to patriotic purposes instead of to the emolument of those conducting the enterprise."[37]

"The decision seems to establish that as long as there is a law against Sunday sporting events there will be no Sunday baseball," the *Brooklyn Daily Eagle* commented on the decision in an article entitled "Ebbets and Robbie Found Guilty in Sunday Ball Case."[38]

Ebbets wrote an impassioned commentary on the situation in an article for *Baseball Magazine* entitled "A Defense of Sunday Baseball: Why I Believe Major League Baseball on Sunday Ought to be Permitted in the Eastern Cities."

"What was my surprise on the day following [the game] to be presented with a summons to appear in court and answer a charge of law-breaking," Ebbets wrote. "The instigators of this summons were the Law and Order Society with headquarters in Albany. Evidently they thought the peace of the nation was being disturbed by holding a ball game at the Brooklyn park."[39]

"It seems to me that the day is at hand when the public should decide if they wish to be bound by ancient legislation that was written in another age of the world, for another generation, under other than modern conditions," Ebbets went on. "Neither do I believe that the subject is a matter of interest to any persons in Albany, or elsewhere in the state. It is purely a local matter for the People of Brooklyn to decide for themselves or at least it should be such. What happens at Ebbets Field on a Sunday can certainly not be called a nuisance at Schnectady or Buffalo."

Ebbets concluded by saying, "Now I have no wish to pose as law

10. New York Wanted It

breaker. True the law which was invoked against our proposed Sunday game seems to me to be without logic and I am sure it is rankly discriminatory in its results. But if it be the avowed wish of the majority of Brooklyn people to prohibit Sunday baseball, I will bow gracefully to the verdict. Such, however, is not the case so far as I have been able to observe."

What really pushed the Sunday baseball issue to the public forefront was the third benefit game in New York hosted by the Giants. Originally scheduled for July 15 with the Chicago Cubs, that game was rained out and rescheduled for August 19. The rainout gave the wartime charities a chance to lobby Albany, specifically Governor Charles Whitman. Headed by James Campbell of the Militia of Mercy, representatives of wartime charities met with Whitman on July 30 and urged him to modify the Sunday law regarding baseball with admission fees. Whitman, however, was noncommittal.[40]

Festivities before the August 19 game at the Polo Grounds were under the auspices of the Friendly Sons of St. Patrick to benefit the families of the "Fighting 69th" regiment of the New York National Guard. The Giants lost to the Reds that day 5–0, as three men in the Giant lineup that day had other matters on their mind that day. George Burns, David Robertson, and Fred Anderson had all been ordered by their draft boards to appear on Monday for examination.

As the Fighting 69th paraded down Fifth Avenue on Monday in the first leg of its journey to France, one other New York Giant was being ordered to report somewhere. Magistrate Frothingham in the Washington Heights Court had issued a summons for Giants manager John McGraw to appear in court on August 21 along with Cincinnati Reds manager Christy Mathewson. The charge was violation of the Sunday laws.

While Ebbets had to undergo an actual trial in Brooklyn for his alleged Sunday misdeeds in hosting a benefit game, Magistrate Francis McQuade discharged McGraw and Mathewson for a similar action. McQuade "not only exonerated McGraw and Mathewson of any guilt in playing on Sunday, but commended the managers for lending their services to such a patriotic cause."[41]

While the Sabbatarians might have survived the publicity favoring Sunday baseball that arose from the Ebbets trial in Brooklyn, the arrest of Mathewson—a former star pitcher for the Giants, hero to many New Yorkers, and avowed abstainer from playing baseball on Sunday when he was a player—was an action way over the top.

"It is my opinion that there was no infraction of any statute. Playing ball on the first day of the week, when not amounting to any serious interruption of the repose and religious liberty of the community, is not a violation of this section [of the law]," Magistrate McQuade commented upon the release of McGraw and Mathewson. "There is not a scintilla of evidence of any one in the vicinity being disturbed. Instead of McGraw and Mathewson being summoned here to answer a charge of this kind, the public owes to each of them a vote of the highest commendation for lending their services gratis to this patriotic cause."[42]

The New York newspapers rode herd on the Sunday baseball issue now, so much so that it became an issue in the off-year elections that November. And it appeared very likely that a Sunday baseball bill would be passed in 1918.

A broad coalition had been formed to back the Sunday baseball bill. Baseball owners were joined not only by the majority of statewide newspapers but also organized labor, progressives, veterans' organizations, and women's groups. Baseball also teamed up with the movie industry, which was seeking the same ability to conduct its activities on Sunday. With the end of the war in sight, the reversal in attitude of women's groups to favor entertainment for returning soldiers over the traditional Sabbath helped to sway some Republicans to back the Sunday baseball bill.

The laws prohibiting Sunday baseball were prime fodder for newspaper cartoonists, as seen in this 1917 New York *Evening World* cartoon.

In March 1918, the Lawson bill was reported favorably out of the Codes Committee in the Senate. The Lawson bill provided for professional baseball after 2:00 in the afternoon with an admission charge on a local option basis. More formally, the bill—"An Act to Amend the Penal Law in Relation to Granting to Local Authorities the Power to Regulate Sports on Sunday"—would amend Section 2145 of the penal law to add the following language:

> It shall not be unlawful to play baseball games on the first day of the week after two o'clock in the afternoon and to witness which an admission fee may or may not be charged, in a city, town or village, if an ordinance shall not have been adopted by the common council or other legislative governing body of the city, town or village prohibiting such games on such day and after such hour.[43]

A 72-page missive on the merits of Sunday baseball was distributed to all members of the Senate and the Assembly, along with Governor Whitman. The booklet entitled "Letters, Comments and Editorials Endorsing Sunday Baseball" included letters from religious leaders citing the worthiness of Sunday baseball and letters from mayors across the nation attesting to the fact that Sunday baseball was not detrimental to the moral good and welfare of the community. The compendium also contained 40 pages of newspaper editorials, such as this excerpt from a New York *Evening World* editorial in 1917:

> Gov. Whitman can do some real good for the State of New York, if he wishes to, by having the "Sunday Law" repealed. Whether intentionally or not, the "Sunday Law" is directed against the interests of one class of people—those who WORK. A man who works six days a week needs recreation on his one day of rest. He might go fishing, but the "Sunday Law" forbids. He might play ball or compete in athletic sports, or go see a baseball game or a running race. The "Sunday Law" won't let him. He can't go during the week. His work won't let him. Any loafer can go on a week-day afternoon. The workingman can't. The "Sunday Law" flatly prohibits his enjoying the needed recreation on the one day he can call his own. *The "Sunday Law" should be repealed. It is a relic of the dark ages.*[44]

On April 4, the Senate voted 26–20 to approve the Lawson bill. "The bill now goes to the Assembly," the *New York Times* reported, "where it is expected to pass, although there will be a hard fight." Politics took over, however, as the Assembly Rules Committee decided on April 12 without a formal vote, not to report the Lawson bill. "The action virtually means the death of the measure," the *Times* noted.[45]

Governor Whitman was facing a tough re-election campaign that fall and felt that he needed to cater to upstate conservatives in order to win. As historian Steven Riess noted of Whitman, "On his orders, the Assembly's speaker buried the Lawson bill in the Rules Committee, where it died."[46]

Not only did the Lawson bill die, but so did Whitman's political career. Al Smith, the Democrat, defeated Whitman for the governor's office that November and went on to serve four terms as governor of New York.

Whitman was never elected to public office again. After practicing law for six years following his 1918 defeat at the polls, Whitman sought election as the district attorney for New York County, a post he had held prior to being elected governor in 1914, but was defeated. After supporting Fiorello LaGaurdia for mayor in 1933, Whitman was appointed chairman of the Port of New York Authority (reappointed in 1942), his last public position.[47]

In the spring of 1918, Organized Baseball put pressure on Governor Whitman after the Lawson bill died by posturing to play Sunday games at Harrison Field in Newark. The National Commission advanced the argument that it needed to generate revenue from the vacant field that it owned now as part of the 1915 settlement with the Federal League. Left unsaid was that a little additional pressure on the politicians wouldn't hurt the cause of the Sunday baseball proponents in New York.

On May 2, just two weeks after the Lawson bill was stymied, it was announced that the Yankees would play the Red Sox on Sunday, May 5, at Harrison Field. No one it seems bothered to ask the Newark team in the International League for its blessing on the matter. The war had taken a huge toll on the minor leagues, and Newark saw this action as a decided blow to its chances of survival.

New York owner Jake Ruppert sided with the territorial rights of the Newark minor league team, so the National Commission canceled the game and substituted a Brooklyn-Philadelphia matchup instead. Brooklyn owner Charlie Ebbets also sided with Newark, and that game was abandoned as well. All three New York teams decided that playing Sundays in Newark was an overt trampling of Newark's territorial rights, so the Newark idea was discarded for the moment.[48]

The New York teams also engaged in several one-day Sunday road trips in 1918, a practice they rarely used in previous years. On July 14, the Yankees traveled to Cleveland and the Giants to Cincinnati to signal the strong desire to play Sunday baseball.

Later in July, the Newark idea resurfaced as a Sunday baseball possibility, this time with the minor league team's explicit approval. Newark would play an International League game in the first half of a doubleheader at Harrison Field to be followed by a National League game in the second half. The first game between the Giants and the Cubs, was to be on August 4, with a second one on August 11 between the Giants and the Superbas.

"If they prove successful, the Sunday games over there will be regular institutions in the future, unless a Sunday baseball law is passed by the New York legislature," the *Brooklyn Daily Eagle* reported.[49]

While the games never materialized, the publicity did help to advance the Sunday baseball cause with New York legislators.

Sunday baseball did become legal in Washington, D.C., in 1918 when the Board of Commissioners of the District of Columbia rescinded its prohibitory regulations on May 14. The Board cited as reasons for permitting Sunday baseball the large increase in the population of the district since the war started and the need to provide recreation and amusement to this larger population.

"Soldiers in and around Washington will benefit by the new regulations," the *Washington Post* noted. "Two thousand of them will be admitted free every Sunday and arrangements are being made to set aside a certain space for them which will enable them to see the games without even paying a war tax."[50]

The Senators ball club rushed to put together plans for a game the following Sunday, May 19. At the time, scheduling convention for eastern teams was for a series between teams to end on Saturday, use Sunday as a travel day, and begin the next series on Monday. Since all American League teams were playing in the east on Saturday, May 18, there were no Sunday games scheduled.

Cleveland was asked to inaugurate the first Sunday game in Washington, as a return favor for the all the one-game road trips the Senators made to Cleveland for Sunday games since 1911 when Sunday games were legalized there.

Instead of taking the train to Boston for its series with Red Sox beginning Monday, the Indians trained south from Philadelphia to Washington first to play the Senators in the inaugural Sunday game at American League Park. As 15,000 spectators looked on, Washington squeaked out a 1–0 victory in 12 innings as Doc Ayers pitched a seven-hit shutout and scored the winning run for the Senators.

While newly elected New York governor Al Smith didn't bring a Democratic legislature with him, the end of the war in November 1918 and the passage of Prohibition to take effect in 1920 helped to make Sunday baseball in New York a legal reality in the spring of 1919.

Senator James Walker, a future mayor of New York City, was selected to introduce the Sunday baseball bill in the Senate in early 1919, with the same provisions as the Lawson bill introduced the previous year. It would be Walker, a Tammany Hall candidate with a future, who would reap the political rewards of the Sunday baseball law, not Lawson, who hailed from Brooklyn.

The Senate passed the Walker bill 29–22, as seven Republican senators broke ranks with their party's position and joined the Democrats in approving the bill. In the Assembly, the bill passed 82–60, as 30 of 94 Republicans joined with the Democrats to favor the bill (along with one member of the Socialist party). At the same time, the Thompson bill to permit Sunday movies was also passed, which Sunday baseball proponents used to help subdue the public announcement of Sunday baseball legality.

Governor Smith signed the Sunday baseball law on April 19, 1919.

"I realize that a very substantial portion of our people most conscientiously oppose permission to indulge in recreation or sports of any kind on Sunday," Smith said in a statement at the time of the signing. "I respect their opinions and I believe that in those opinions they are entirely conscientious." However, Smith went on to say, "I believe that before any class of our citizens should be given the right to impose their views upon this question, on which people so widely and conscientiously differ, upon those who disagree with them, they should, at least, represent the sentiment of the majority in their respective communities."[51]

The governor further declared that attending a baseball game on Sunday was a most harmless diversion. "It is in no sense deteriorating to the moral fiber of the witness," Smith said.

The Board of Alderman in New York City passed an ordinance on April 29 to permit Sunday baseball, as required by the new law. The vote was 64–0. Mayor John Hylan quickly signed the ordinance, and Sunday baseball at the major league level could finally be legally played in New York.

All three New York teams scrambled to reconfigure their schedules to play home games on Sunday, since the law was signed after the baseball season had already begun. Rather than advance Monday games to Sunday, a common practice over the years to get in Sunday games, the teams rescheduled games to be played later in the year to take advantage of the mid-summer weather and play seven games a week.

On May 4, 1919, the Giants and the Dodgers played the first legal major league Sunday games in New York, before the largest crowds ever to witness games in either ballpark (outside of a World Series game). At the Polo Grounds before 35,000, the Phillies defeated the Giants 4–3. At Ebbets Field before 22,000, Brooklyn defeated Boston 6–2.

"The two record crowds of yesterday formed the baseball public's verdict on a campaign for Sunday outdoor pastimes which has been going on for many years. Yesterday was the first time since Rip Van Winkle butted into the bowling party that folks have been able to see professional baseball without danger of being called before His Honor in the morning," the *New York Times* commented. "Those who have been skeptical about just how Sunday games would be received here were surprised that such a vast throng could come to the Polo Grounds on a Sunday afternoon, sit through two hours of baseball, and leave without any disorder or rowdyism."[52]

The fans in Brooklyn all seemed to get there just a few minutes before the game started. "When fans realize that Sunday baseball is really and truly an established institution and no longer subject to being raided and broken up just before the game begins, they will almost certainly buy reserved seats in advance, which will reduce the congestion at the ticket windows by several thousand," the *Brooklyn Daily Eagle* remarked.[53]

Sunday, May 4, 1919, was also the first time that all eight National League teams played on Sunday. In addition to the games in New York and Brooklyn, Chicago played before 18,000 in Cincinnati (losing 8–1) and Pittsburgh played in St. Louis (winning 3–1).

The following Sunday, the Yankees christened American League Sunday baseball in New York with a 0–0 tie with Washington on May 11. The game was stopped after 12 innings in the mistaken belief that Sunday games couldn't be played beyond 6:00, even though there was enough light to play longer. The law only provided that games couldn't start before 2:00 and made no provision for an ending time.

"It was the first Sunday contest on the home meadow of the Yankees and furnished a striking contrast to the Giants' opening tilt at the Polo Grounds last week when the McGraw clan played to a capacity throng," the *New York Times* remarked on the meager crowd of 3,000 that trekked to the Polo Grounds to see the game under cold and rainy conditions.[54]

Sunday baseball was played in at least one of the three New York City ballparks every Sunday in 1919 after the law's passage, except July 20 when rain canceled the Cincinnati-Brooklyn and White Sox-Yankees games that day.

Spectacular crowds for Sunday games in 1919 helped to push team attendance marks to new heights. The Giants outdrew the previous year by early June 1919 and welcomed 708,000 patrons by year-end. The Yankees established a new record attendance for the team, entertaining 619,000 persons in 1919, including 25,000 at the June 22 Sunday game with Boston to see the star Red Sox player Babe Ruth.

The Giants and Yankees were constrained from taking full advantage of Sunday games because they played in the same facility, the Polo Grounds. Games were held nearly every Sunday at the Polo Grounds, as the Giants and Yankees rotated their series so that one team would usually have the grounds on Sunday. This way, each team could squeeze in 12 or 13 Sunday games a season.

Unconstrained by a tenant, Brooklyn used Ebbets Field as often as it could for Sunday games. Brooklyn usually had an overweighted Sunday schedule compared with the Giants. For instance in 1920, Brooklyn played 20 Sunday games at Ebbets Field, compared to 13 for the Giants and 12 for the Yankees at the Polo Grounds. This was due to the availability of Ebbets Field and the league's desire to schedule Sunday games for Boston and Philadelphia. Both teams weren't yet legally allowed to play home games on Sunday, and thus they made frequent one-game road trips to Brooklyn to capture revenue from Sunday games.

With Sunday games helping the Yankees to break attendance records in 1919, owner Jake Ruppert made a purchase before the 1920 season that would forever change the landscape of major league baseball. Ruppert swung a deal with Red Sox owner Harry Frazee to purchase Babe Ruth for $100,000 cash and a $300,000 loan secured by a mortgage on Fenway Park. With the money Ruppert was sure to make from Sunday crowds coming to see the Babe, the purchase price was a steal.

History has focused on Frazee's desire to fund his theatrical productions as the reason for the sale of Ruth, which then resulted in the alleged Curse of the Bambino hampering future Red Sox teams from ever winning the World Series following its 1918 triumph. Long overlooked in this transaction is the revenue generation that a top draw like Ruth would have in a city that permitted Sunday baseball. With less than a year of Sunday games under his belt in 1919, Ruppert knew a winning idea when he saw it and was confident that Ruth would pack the Polo Grounds on Sundays in 1920.

Following the first two Sunday games in 1920, Ruppert was probably smiling at his good fortune in securing the services of the Babe. The first two Sunday games in 1920 both drew 25,000 people, on April 25 in a 2–1 loss to the Athletics and the following Sunday, May 2, in a 7–1 victory over the Red Sox when the Babe hit a home run.

The Giants, though, hated the attention lavished on Ruth. The Giants owned the Polo Grounds and had consented to rent space to the Yankees beginning with the 1913 season "since the tenant would provide a little revenue when the ballpark would otherwise be empty and there was, at the time, no risk of serious competition for fans or press attention." In 1920, that offer "suddenly needed to be reevaluated."[55]

Babe Ruth was the reason. After just two Sunday games in 1920, the Giants announced on May 14 that the Yankees would not be allowed to play at the Polo Grounds after its lease expired at the end of the 1920 season. The two teams soon patched up their differences for the short term, but the Yankees immediately laid plans to build a stadium of their own. Ruppert built not only his own ball grounds—Yankee Stadium—but one that could handle the largest crowds in the major leagues. Yankee Stadium could seat 60,000 paying customers.

In the first full season of Sunday games in New York in 1920, the Yankees counted an astonishing 1,289,000 in season attendance, the first team ever to have more than one million fans in attendance during a season. Ruth hit 54 home runs in 1920, setting a new major league record that shattered his old mark of 29 set just the year before in 1919 with the Red Sox.

All three New York teams established attendance records in 1920, as the Giants drew 929,000 and Brooklyn 808,000. But a new crowd favorite had been crowned. The Yankees drew more than a million fans in seven of the next eight years (all except 1925). Neither the Giants nor the Dodgers drew a million until 20 years later (Brooklyn in 1941, the Giants in 1945), even in the four consecutive years the Giants won the National League pennant from 1921 to 1924.

There were further signs that Sunday baseball was increasingly accepted across the nation. On July 25, 1920, all 16 major league teams played on Sunday for the first time. Then on October 9, 1921, Sunday games on the East Coast debuted in the World Series when the Giants defeated the Yankees 4–2 at the Polo Grounds in the fourth game of the 1921 World Series.[56]

Sunday baseball in New York was not all a bed of roses. Although drawing well in its pennant-winning year of 1920, Brooklyn remained a second fiddle in attendance to the Giants. Charlie Ebbets thus arranged for Sunday games at Ebbets Field whenever he could.

Ebbets tested the faith of the Brooklyn populace, however, in 1924 when he moved up the season's first home game at Ebbets Field from the Thursday, April 24, game with the Giants to a Sunday, April 20, game with the Phillies (in the midst of the Dodgers' road series in Philadelphia). What galled the Brooklyn citizens even more in 1924 was that April 20 was Easter Sunday. Ebbets had squarely pushed the envelope on Sunday baseball at any cost.

"The Brooklyn Robins stole in from Philadelphia yesterday and under cover of more or less secrecy played a scheduled championship game against the Phillies, postponing the ceremonies that go with the opening of the home schedule until the Giants journey across the bridge on Thursday," the *New York Times* reported of the Easter game. The Dodgers lost 4–1 in a rain-shortened six-inning game before a crowd of 22,000 at Ebbets Field.[57]

Yankee Stadium opened in 1923, and for the first time, Ruppert had control of his own revenues. On April 22, the first Sunday game at Yankee Stadium drew 65,000, and the team went to capture slightly more than one million fans in attendance. Washington defeated the Yankees 4–3 in the inaugural Sunday game at Yankee Stadium in front of the largest crowd by far to witness Sunday baseball in one place.

While many have referred to Yankee Stadium as "The House That Ruth Built," at least one author has suggested it could be called by a different appellation that is connected to Sunday baseball.

"Yankee attendance grew by two-thirds in 1920 and we may suppose that half the increase was because of Sunday baseball and half because of the excitement stirred by Ruth and company," Marshall Smelser wrote in his book *The Life That Ruth Built*. "Sunday baseball deserves part of the credit for the building of Yankee Stadium, though it may be going too far to call it The House That Sunday Baseball Built."[58]

Ruth himself stumped for Sunday baseball at times in the 1920s, indicating he was aware of how Sunday games impacted his fortunes.

While barnstorming in Scranton, Pennsylvania, after the 1923 World Series, Ruth made a plea for Sunday baseball at a meeting on October 25 of amateur baseball players. As the *New York Times* reported, "He said baseball on the Sabbath would keep young men away from crap games, card parties, and other forms of gambling." Ruth may have been speaking from direct experience from his Red Sox days when Sunday baseball was prohibited in Boston.[59]

With Sunday baseball firmly entrenched in New York City in the mid–1920s, there was little left but for the politicians to take credit for it to gain higher office.

When Gentleman Jimmy Walker ran for mayor of New York City in 1925, he used some of the political glory that he inherited from his friends in Tammany Hall with the passage of the Sunday baseball law in 1919. A very popular law with the many immigrants in the city, Walker whisked to victory under the slogan "Walker Gave Us Sunday Baseball." He even managed to get a plaque installed at the Polo Grounds, which was inscribed, "Friend and Fan, whose Sunday baseball law made it possible for millions of his fellow-citizens to enjoy the game."[60]

Walker, who did little to advance the Sunday baseball cause except to have his name embossed on the legislation, was able to parlay his political good fortune into a six-year stretch as New York mayor from 1926 to 1932. Walker's playboy image and lax work habits caught up with him, however, when a scandal forced him to resign his office in 1932.

Al Smith, the man who signed the Sunday baseball bill in 1919, did better than Walker. Smith served four terms as New York governor, the last three consecutively from 1923 to 1929. Smith also was the Democratic candidate for president of the United States in the 1928 election, although as an anti–Prohibition, avowed Catholic he was trounced by Republican Herbert Hoover. Smith, a hard worker, never tried to take political advantage of his role in the Sunday baseball law, though he didn't refuse the help of Babe Ruth to try to gain votes.

In one radio speech in late October, the Babe remarked, "I'm not in politics, I'm in baseball ... Governor Smith is the type of man who appeals not only to the baseball fan, but to all red-blooded lovers of American sport." Realizing that Smith had helped secure Sunday baseball in New York, and thinking it would help attract votes, Ruth then departed from the script and proceeded to give a five-minute lecture on why Sunday baseball was a great idea, to the consternation of Democratic Party officials.[61]

Sunday baseball reached a peak in New York during September 1928. With the Yankees battling the Athletics for first place as the season neared its end, the two teams were slated to play a doubleheader at Yankee Stadium on Sunday, September 9.

On September 6, the remaining reserved seats for the game went on sale. On a rainy day, 5,000 people waited in line to buy tickets. But not every one was rewarded for their effort, as reserved tickets were quickly sold out and tempers flared. "Yankee-Athletic Ticket Rush Brings Police to Quell Riot" was the *New York Times* headline of the article describing the disturbance.[62]

With the Athletics in first place by half a game on the morning of September 9, a crowd of 85,265 jammed into Yankee Stadium to watch the Yankees take both games of the doubleheader, 5–0 and 7–3. The crowd was the largest ever to watch a baseball game to that date. Reportedly, another 100,000 were turned away at the gates. It would be another 20 years before a larger crowd would attend a baseball game.

The Sunday doubleheader loss was disheartening for the Athletics and their fans, because it dashed the team's chances for the American League pennant. Perhaps it was even more disheartening due to the reminder that the gates were locked every Sunday at Shibe Park in Philadelphia, as it continued to be illegal to play professional baseball on Sunday in Pennsylvania.

Chapter 11

PHILADELPHIA EXPERIMENTED WITH IT

Quaker philosophy kept the three major league teams located in Pennsylvania on the Sunday baseball sidelines into the mid–1920s. A century-old Pennsylvania statute, the Sunday Act of 1794, prevented the Athletics, Phillies, and Pirates from engaging in baseball matches on the Lord's Day.

In 1926, seven years following the passage of Sunday baseball legislation in New York, there was still no progress in securing legal authority to conduct professional baseball on Sunday in Philadelphia and Pittsburgh. This never-on-Sunday attitude in Pennsylvania was now squarely opposite the norm among major league cities, as three-quarters of American League cities could now play Sunday baseball on their home grounds and five-eighths of the National League cities. Only the Boston, Massachusetts, teams now joined the three Pennsylvania teams in observing a day of rest within their home states on the Sunday baseball issue.

This is not to say that professional baseball was *never* played on Sunday within the Commonwealth of Pennsylvania. In 1926, minor league teams in Reading (International League), as well as Scranton, and Wilkes-Barre (NY-Penn League) played on Sunday, either under tacit approval of the local authorities or by simply paying the $4 fine stipulated as the penalty for breaching the 1794 law. Semi-pro teams survived in a "pass the hat" system of informal finances. It was only in the major urban areas of Philadelphia and Pittsburgh where strict enforcement of the 1794 law precluded baseball on Sunday.

The Pennsylvania blue laws were deeply ingrained in the fabric of the conservative Pennsylvanians who controlled the state's legislative Assembly. This conservatism stemmed from the beliefs of the Society of Friends, or Quakers as they're commonly called today, who were the first settlers in Pennsylvania.

11. Philadelphia Experimented with It

"The Sabbatarianism of William Penn's Colony was the result of a deep belief in the mystical and altruistic Quaker faith," John Lucas wrote in his 1971 article "The Unholy Experiment: Professional Baseball's Struggle Against Pennsylvania Sunday Blue Law 1926–1934" in *Pennsylvania History*. "The Inner Light ... this spirit of God within man is his hope of glory and is not dependent upon dogma nor even deep Bible study, but on the quality of the life he leads."[1]

As early as 1705, the Society of Friends influenced a Pennsylvania bill against "riotous Sports, Plays and Games," which was subsequently disallowed by the Queen of England in those days of colonial rule. The bill was probably aimed not so much at ball games but rather at horse racing, the most popular sport at the time among wealthy people and a source of immorality in gambling, and blood sports such as cock fighting.

By 1794, mounting diversions pursued on the Sabbath led the Pennsylvania legislature to pass "an Act for the prevention of vice and immorality, and of unlawful gaming, and to restrain disorderly sports and dissipation." The act stipulated:

> If any person shall do or perform, any worldly employment or business whatsoever on the Lord's day, commonly called Sunday, works of necessity and charity only excepted, or shall use or practice any unlawful game, hunting, shooting, sport or diversion whatsoever, on the same day, and be convicted thereof, every such person, so offending, shall for every such occurrence, forfeit and pay four dollars [or] suffer six days' imprisonment in the house of correction of the proper county.[2]

This law persisted through the 19th century and remained in place to thwart professional baseball in Pennsylvania throughout the first quarter of the 20th century.

Sunday baseball received a cool reception from clergymen and prominent laymen in Pennsylvania when the subject was broached. While World War I helped to advance Sunday baseball in the eastern cities of New York and Washington, a similar impact did not spill over to Philadelphia, even for proposed benefit games for the military.

"I am unalterably opposed to such a plan as the American League is said to be preparing," Mayor Thomas Smith said in May 1917 regarding Sunday baseball. "The exigencies of war do not demand a Sunday game with its proceeds to the Red Cross or the army. A Saturday game, with its proceeds so diverted, would be admirable."[3]

A proposal in 1918 to open up Shibe Park for use by soldiers and sailors to play baseball on Sunday was also scuttled after being proffered by the Philadelphia Athletics.

"I have the positive assurance of Mayor Smith in a letter written several months ago that he will not allow Sunday base ball in this city," said Reverend T. T. Mutchler of the Philadelphia Sabbath Association. "This offer of the ball parks by the owners for Sunday base ball I believe is an effort on their part to secure a semi-official sanction for Sunday games, which will open the wedge for further desecration of the Sabbath later on."[4]

Smith tried to balance the competing views. "I realize that my views will not meet with the approval of certain ministerial associations," Smith articulated. "But I think that we should all be patriotic enough to permit healthy entertainment for enlisted men, on Sunday, if it is conducted under proper conditions and safeguards." The Sabbatarians won the battle, though, as the only Sunday baseball played by servicemen in Philadelphia in 1918 was at the Philadelphia Navy Yard, where the municipal officials had no jurisdiction.[5]

The Athletics and Phillies waited out the Sunday baseball issue until the city decided whether it was legal for amateur teams to take up collections among the spectators at a Sunday game.

In 1920, police cracked down on Sunday baseball where collections were taken up, although team managers denied that collections were "authorized" by the teams. The city left the door ajar for Sunday baseball by amateur teams when police superintendent Mills stated his position that "if the managers can show a clean bill, and the games are conducted in an orderly manner and do not interfere with religious services or are not objected to by persons living near enough to be annoyed, they can go on."[6]

Police and amateur teams tussled over the Sunday baseball issue for the next several years, until newly elected mayor Freeland Kendrick issued a pronouncement in 1924 that permitted more widespread playing of Sunday baseball. "Hundreds of games were played and witnessed by thousands, without interference by police, except in a single instance when members of two teams were asked to shift their game from within two blocks of St. Barnabas' Catholic Church to a field more distant," the Philadelphia *Evening Bulletin* reported. "No complaints against the games were received by police and no incidents where 'donations' were collected from the spectators by the teams were reported."[7]

By 1926, with nearly two-thirds of major league teams able to play baseball on Sunday, and the mayor of Philadelphia ostensibly favoring Sunday baseball, the Philadelphia Athletics prepared to challenge the continued appropriateness of the 1794 statute prohibiting Sunday baseball at Shibe Park.

Like a number of major league teams in the previous 40 years, Philadelphia attempted to pursue the overturning of a Sunday statute through court interpretation rather than the legislature. While some teams had early success via this route, notably St. Louis in 1887 and Chicago in 1896, no team had been successful since 1900 to win a sanctioning of Sunday baseball through the courtroom rather than the legislative route.

Cleveland (1897) and Brooklyn (1904–1906) had been the last teams to mount significant courtroom challenges to try to secure Sunday baseball rights. Ultimately, both failed in their courtroom attempts, with Cleveland appealing unsuccessfully all the way to the Ohio Supreme Court. Both Cleveland and Brooklyn required years of legislative activity to prevail on the Sunday baseball issue.

Even with a significant advance of time and substantial changes in the nation's mores on Sunday recreation, Philadelphia would ultimately experience a similar journey as Cleveland and Brooklyn did on the Sunday baseball issue—first courtroom defeat, then an arduous legislative effort in victory.

The window of opportunity afforded New York and Washington in 1918–1919 to win Sunday baseball approvals was shuttered quickly by a conservative backlash in the 1920s.

On the one hand, society increasingly recognized the impact that industrialization had on its workers. Industry slowly moved to a five-day workweek and a new attitude toward the Sunday day of rest as recreation was more widely embraced on the principle of science rather religion.

On the other hand, the progressive movement petered out after 1920. At that time, the Republicans regained the White House and the Democrats lost national power in a massive negative reaction by voters to President Woodrow Wilson's backing of the League of Nations treaty.

"In repudiating Wilson, the treaty, the League, and the war itself, [voters] repudiated the progressive rhetoric and the progressive mode," historian Richard Hofstadter wrote of the changes that occurred in America due to the 1920 election in *The Age of Reform*. "Reaction went farther, it destroyed the popular impulse that had sustained progressive politics for well over a decade before 1914. The pressure for civic participation was followed by widespread apathy, the sense of responsibility was followed by widespread neglect, the call for sacrifice by hedonism."[8]

Sunday as a day of leisure, though, was beginning to be accepted as the norm in this dichotomy of society perspectives, as captured in the Heywood Broun 1920 essay "A Bolt From the Blue." Fundamentalist preacher John Stratton, after imploring Sabbatarians to hold their ground in opposition to Sunday baseball and failing to achieve success, journeyed to heaven on a hot Sunday in July to take his case directly to the Lord. Stratton asked the Lord to engulf the Polo Grounds in a tidal wave. Because it was the ninth inning, the score tied, two runners on base, and Babe Ruth at bat, the Lord replied to Stratton, "The time has not come," and waited till the end of the inning to grant Stratton's request.[9]

The day-of-leisure concept was not overpowering Pennsylvania, however. While Quakers had long since stopped dominating Pennsylvania politics in person, Quaker precepts did remain a strong foundation of the state's legal system.

Another factor was that neither Philadelphia nor Pittsburgh had as many immigrants as other major league cities to help propel the issue. Unlike Chicago, Detroit, and New York where foreign-born residents equaled 40 percent of the population in the late 19th century, the ratio in Pittsburgh never rose above 32 percent and in Philadelphia it topped out at 27 percent.[10]

The Athletics were forced to take the lead in fighting for Sunday baseball in Pennsylvania, because both the intra-city rival Phillies and the cross-state Pittsburgh Pirates took a passive stance on the issue.

The Phillies, along with Boston, were one of the last two National League teams to play a Sunday game on the road, not undertaking Lord's Day play until June 1903. Phillies' management deferred to the Athletics in the Philadelphia discussions on Sunday baseball.

Pittsburgh owner Barney Dreyfuss was publicly lukewarm on the Sunday baseball issue. Dreyfuss ostensibly supported the old Spalding contention that Sunday games simply detracted from attendance at games the other six days of the week, particularly Saturday. But Dreyfuss also had a good thing going with one-day Sunday road trips, which the Pittsburgh club had engaged in for the previous 20 years.

"It has been shrewdly pointed out that Barney is sitting pretty geographically," one commentator wrote. "Because his team can play no Sunday games at home, it is scheduled to play in Chicago or Cincinnati whenever possible on Sundays. And in return for not being able to get the big Sunday receipts at home, the Pittsburgh club is favored with all the holiday dates and as many Saturdays as possible without tangling the schedule."[11]

In the 1920s, Dreyfuss, along with presidents of several other major league teams and numerous amusement parks, did support the efforts of the Outdoor Recreation Bureau of the Anti Blue Law League of America. The Outdoor Recreation Bureau billed itself as "an organized, constantly functioning bureau for the prevention of further restrictions on outdoor Sunday recreation, BUT, an organization upholding a strictly American Sunday of three R's—Rest, Religion, Recreation." By defining its mission this way, the Outdoor Recreation Bureau could pursue its agenda without completely alienating people with Sabbatarian views.[12]

Especially in Pennsylvania, the Outdoor Recreation Bureau had its work cut out for it "in preserving Sunday recreation, particularly baseball and other sports and amusements on Sunday" as its staffers "have been kept so extremely busy with our work in the field combating the efforts of the Lord's Day Alliance to obtain Sunday closing legislation of a rigid nature."[13]

Because the Athletics were frequent visitors to Washington and New York to squeeze in Sunday games where possible in the midst of home stands at Shibe Park, the management of the Athletics saw firsthand how successful Sunday games were in the two eastern outposts where Sunday baseball had most recently been legalized. In 1925, Philadelphia played three Sunday games in Washington and two in Yankee Stadium. The club also conducted an overnight trip to Cleveland to play one game at League Park in Cleveland.

Those one-day, out-and-back trips from Philadelphia to Cleveland, which began back in 1911 when Sunday baseball was finally legalized in Cleveland, were energy zappers for the Athletics. These Cleveland excursions sometimes resulted in on-the-field oddities that would never have occurred otherwise.

For instance, after the Athletics lost 3–0 in the June 14 Sunday game in Cleveland in 1925, following a Saturday afternoon game in Philadelphia the day before, both teams trained back to Philadelphia for a game on the hot, muggy Monday afternoon of June 15. The listless Athletics spotted the Indians a 15–4 lead after seven innings, but then somehow gathered the energy to produce a 13-run rally in the bottom of the eighth inning to notch a 17–15 victory over the tuckered-out Indians.

Two considerations prodded the Athletics management into action to push the Sunday baseball issue in 1926.

First, the Athletics had expanded Shibe Park for the 1925 season by adding a second deck to accommodate more spectators. The Athletics had also shelled out some big money to sign two minor leaguers to improve the team—$100,000 for pitcher Lefty Grove and $50,000 for catcher Mickey Cochrane.

Together with two other raw talents at the time, Al Simmons and Jimmie Foxx, the four future Hall of Fame selections were the foundation that led the Athletics back to their previous glory days following seven consecutive years of last-place finishes from 1915 to 1921. The Athletics contended for first place for the first half of 1925 before falling back to a third-place finish and were expected to contend for the pennant again in 1926.

The Shibes, who owned the Athletics, needed revenue to pay back these expenditures (or more accurately the bank loans secured to finance these investments), and Sunday baseball was at the top of their list.

Second, the time seemed fortuitous in 1926 to pursue the legality of Sunday baseball. The Sesquicentennial Exposition was being held in Philadelphia that year to celebrate the 150th anniversary of the signing of the Declaration of Independence in 1776. The Sesquicentennial Exposition was to be open on Sundays, much to the dismay of Sabbatarian groups that believed the 1794 Sunday law should apply to the event, notwithstanding its national significance.

Much as Chicago had utilized the Columbian Exposition in 1893 as a wedge to legitimize Sunday baseball in the Windy City, the Athletics used the 1926 Sesquicentennial Exposition to capitalize on a world's fair to try to procure Sunday baseball in the City of Brotherly Love.

With Sabbatarian groups focused on preventing the Sunday opening of the Sesquicentennial Exposition, the Athletics hoped this distraction would be enough to engineer a legal okay for Sunday baseball on the coattails of the Exposition's Sunday-opening policy. Philadelphia mayor Freeland Kendrick, though, stepped in the way of the Athletics effort to obtain the right to play baseball on Sundays at Shibe Park.

Kendrick was mainly responsible for the Sesquicentennial Exposition being open on Sundays. The mayor fought hard for the Sunday opening and even defied a request from Pennsylvania governor Gifford Pinchot, just days before the first Sunday opening on July 4, to shut down the exposition on Sundays since only the city had the authority to do so, not the state.

Despite the rain storm on Sunday, July 4, which damaged several buildings at the exposition, an estimated 25,000 persons passed through the gates of the exposition that day. The exposition remained open through September, as the issue of its Sunday opening was debated in the court system.

It was at a July 23 hearing on an injunction to restrain the Sesquicentennial Exposition from opening on Sunday that the first word leaked of a plan to play a Sunday baseball game at Shibe Park in August.

At the July 23 hearing, testimony was provided in support of the exposition's opening that baseball was played on Sunday in many cities in Pennsylvania and that other amusements were permitted to run on Sunday without interference or at most with a small fine. John Shibe, vice president of the Athletics, said at the hearing, "Baseball should not be discriminated against."[14]

"Determined not to risk a situation that would result in the calling off of the game after the fans had gathered in Shibe Park," the Athletics sought to enlist Mayor Kendrick's endorsement of the proposed Sunday game. In early August, Charles Gartling, attorney for the Athletics, notified the mayor's office that on August 22 the club planned to play a baseball game on Sunday.[15]

While Kendrick may have favored Sunday openings for the Sesquicentennial Exposition, the mayor did not, however, favor opening Shibe Park for Sunday baseball. The plan for the Athletics to play on Sunday created a firestorm of opposition.

Mayor Kendrick seemed to be in an irreconcilable position. Remarked *The Sporting News*, "This excellent gentleman, who is for an open Sesquicentennial on Sunday and a closed baseball park on Sunday, immediately was in a position of doing one of the most difficult juggling acts ever seen outside of vaudeville."[16]

Kendrick denied the similarity of Sunday openings of the Sesquicentennial to the playing of Sunday baseball. "The former is educational, patriotic, and recreational in character," Kendrick said, adding, "and in my judgment does not conflict in any way with the laws of Pennsylvania covering Sunday observance."[17]

"Mr. Gartling did not vouchsafe any further information except to say he expected to confer with me next week," Kendrick was quoted in the August 5 Philadelphia *Evening Bulletin*. "I made it plain to him there will be no professional Sunday base ball until I have talked the matter over thoroughly with City Solicitor Gaffney," Kendrick announced. At the meeting, Kendrick said that he'd use the full power of his administration to prevent the Sunday baseball game, including the police. "I told Mr. Gartling and Mr. Shibe that I would send the police to the park immediately with orders to stop the game," Kendrick said. "I reiterated there would be no professional Sunday ball unless the courts decide otherwise."[18]

The Athletics countered Kendrick's statements by saying they'd play the August 22 game whether or not the mayor consented, since, as the ball club interpreted the law, police couldn't make arrests until the following day and couldn't interfere with the game unless there was a breach of peace. The Athletics went to court to secure an injunction to prevent the mayor and the police from interfering with the August 22 game.

"I have observed Sunday games in every city where the major leagues play Sunday baseball and I have yet to see a disturbance," Connie Mack told Judge Frank Smith at the injunction hearing on August 19 in Common Pleas Court. "A Sunday baseball crowd is a little bit different from a weekday gathering. The people dress a little bit differently and they also seem to have in mind that it is Sunday and do not reprove the players."[19]

John Shibe testified that the Athletics lost at least $20,000 a game by not being able to play on the Lord's Day. Police inspector William McFadden testified that while the cheering at Shibe Park could be heard three or four blocks away, he had never seen any disorder in his 16 years of service in or near the park.

"The action against organized baseball on Sunday is first up to the city authorities," said the Rev. William Forney, secretary of the Philadelphia Sabbath Association, which was also fighting the Sunday opening of the Sesquicentennial Exposition. "Our association will fight the playing of professional baseball on Sundays to the limit. Just what action and when it will be taken I am not prepared to say now."[20]

Judge Smith ruled on Saturday, August 21, that the Athletics could play the August 22 game free of police interference unless a breach of peace occurred or a nuisance was created. Smith was clear to point out that his decision provided no restraint on enforcing the 1794 Sunday law.

As one newspaper pointed out, however, "the weather forecast may be its own injunction" as rain was predicted for Sunday.[21]

"Philadelphia's first professional Sunday baseball was played yesterday afternoon on a rain-soaked field before 10,000 spectators who rode or walked to Shibe Park while heavy showers came from gray, low-lying clouds," the *Philadelphia Inquirer* described the city's first Sunday game.[22]

The Athletics defeated the Chicago White Sox 3–2 behind the pitching of Lefty Grove, who scattered eight hits and struck out seven batters as a light rain fell continually through the August 22 game. Tom Shibe later admitted that the game would have been postponed if it had been a weekday. But with the team determined to pursue the Sunday baseball issue, the game was played in the rain.

"There wasn't the remotest hint of disorder," said police inspector McFadden, who had been in charge of 75 patrolmen, sergeants, and lieutenants assigned to the game. "The noise was only a small fraction of what a crowd of the same size makes on a weekday."[23]

"I wish all those who oppose Sunday baseball could have been here today," said Mack. "They would see that we are not causing a lessening in church attendance."[24]

There was a certain uneasiness in the air around Shibe Park for Pennsylvania's first in-state major league game on Sunday. "A ball game on Sunday. Gee! Wonder if the cops'll come?" writer Cy Peterman recalled in a 1934 retrospective in the Philadelphia *Evening Bulletin*. "One heard it in the cars as they rolled up to Lehigh Avenue and as fans bought tickets with a surreptitious look over their shoulders. It was like going into a speakeasy," Peterman used a Depression-era analogy to describe people's attitudes.[25]

There were about half a dozen church observers in the grandstand at Shibe Park that rainy day, including ones from the Philadelphia Sabbath Association. The Rev. Forney watched from a window of a house on Twentieth

Street behind right field and "listened to occasional shouts that came when Robert Moses Grove struck out one of the White Sox in a tight emergency."[26]

No arrests were made and the game was allowed to proceed to its conclusion. The action continued in the legal arena, though. When the Athletics filed for a permanent injunction to prevent stoppage of Sunday games, the city took exception. Because the Athletics planned no more Sunday games for the 1926 season, the case was put off until the season concluded.

That timing wasn't good enough for Pennsylvania attorney general George Woodruff. On August 28, he instituted proceedings for the state in Dauphin County court, where the state capital of Harrisburg is located, against the Athletics for violating the 1794 Sunday law. Whereas the Athletics wanted to play on Sundays and simply pay the $4 fine stipulated in the 1794 law, the attorney general moved for a "quo warranto" penalty that would revoke the club's corporate charter for a willful violation of the 1794 law.

On September 11, the Athletics replied to the attorney general's filing by arguing that the 1794 law couldn't apply to baseball since the sport was unknown at the time the law was written. Additionally, the Athletics attacked the constitutionality of the 1794 law under the 14th Amendment.

After the case was argued in early October before a three-judge panel, a decision was rendered on October 28. As indicated in the front page headline the next day, "Athletics Ready to Appeal Ban on Sunday Baseball," it wasn't good news for the Athletics.[27]

The Dauphin County court ruled that Sunday baseball was illegal under the 1794 Sunday law because it was "a worldly employment or business" under that law. Judge William Hargest, who wrote the opinion, determined that the Athletics were "ousted from any right, privilege or authority to maintain or conduct upon its grounds in the city of Philadelphia any game of professional baseball on the Lord's Day, commonly called Sunday."

Judge Hargest also dismissed the contention of the Athletics that the law couldn't apply to sports that didn't exist when the statute was enacted.

"The contention that the proper construction of the act would not prohibit baseball because [it was] unknown at the time of its passage is unsound," Hargest wrote. "The act prohibits any unlawful game, hunting, shooting, sport or diversion whatever. Of course, this must be interpreted in a reasonable sense and not to apply to one who takes his family into the country on Sunday to enjoy the beauties of nature, even though that may be considered a diversion."

The Athletics vowed to appeal the decision. "We shall continue our fight for Sunday baseball through an appeal to the Supreme Court," club attorney Gartling announced after the ruling. "Our particular desire is to have the constitutionality of the law tested and a definite settlement of the issue of its applicability today to sports or other commercial operations which did not exist and were not dreamed of at the time the act was framed."

On April 12, the case was argued before the Pennsylvania Supreme Court. John Geyer, counsel for the Athletics, "declared the only obligation binding on the club for Sunday ball games was payment of the $4 fine plus costs, while an injunction restraining it from playing ball on Sunday was denial of its corporate rights." Deputy Attorney General John Jones "declared the issue to be decided was whether a corporation could be restrained from conspiring to commit a crime within the state and whether the Athletics, by virtue of their charter, had the implied right to do business on Sunday."[28]

On June 25, 1927, the Pennsylvania Supreme Court agreed with the

The Pennsylvania Supreme Court ruled in 1927 that Sunday baseball was illegal, as indicated by this *Philadelphia Inquirer* headline.

Attorney General and upheld the earlier court decision that Sunday baseball was illegal.

"Sunday Baseball Banned By Finding of the Supreme Court" blurted the headline in the *Philadelphia Inquirer*, delivering the bad news to baseball fans in a page 1 article. "Sunday professional baseball in Philadelphia was forbidden yesterday by the highest tribunal in Pennsylvania, the State Supreme Court. Under the ruling, which clinched the ban on Sunday pro ball here, both [the Athletics and Phillies] are prohibited from staging Sabbath contests here."[29]

In a unanimous 7–0 vote in *Commonwealth v. American Baseball Club of Philadelphia*, the Pennsylvania Supreme Court agreed with the lower court's ruling that baseball was worldly employment and thus the August 22, 1926 test game violated the 1794 act. The court was divided 5–2, however, regarding whether the revocation of the club's corporate charter was the appropriate penalty for continued violation of the act.

No one in baseball was terribly shocked that Sunday baseball in Pennsylvania was declared illegal, since the language of the 1794 act was quite clear regarding the performance of "any worldly employment or business whatsoever on the Lord's Day."

"We can not imagine in this sense anything more worldly or unreligious in the way of employment than the playing of professional baseball as it is played to-day," wrote Justice William Schaffer in the supreme court opinion. Schaffer cited a previous opinion that "very evidently, worldly is contrasted with religious and the worldly employments are prohibited for the sake of the religious ones." Further into the opinion, Schaffer wrote, "No one, we think, would contend that professional baseball partakes in any way of the nature of holiness."[30]

The court patently dismissed the argument of the Athletics that the act contained uncertainty because it predated the institution of baseball. "We can see no basis whatsoever for the argument that the act violates the 14th Amendment to the federal Constitution."

Where the disappointment among baseball people came was in the court's decision that quo warranto was the proper remedy under the law rather than the stipulated $4 fine.

"It would be an unthinkable proposition that the Commonwealth would create organizations to break its own laws," Schaffer wrote. "If the appellant's argument in this respect were to be upheld, then by the same token every merchandising corporation granted the privilege under its charter to sell its wares could open its doors for trade on Sunday."

Two members of the supreme court, including the chief justice, disagreed with the majority opinion regarding the quo warranto remedy.

"Vigorous dissent to this opinion was filed by Chief Justice Moschzisker and Justice Kephart. They held that the $4 fine or six days' imprisonment, if the defendant refused to pay the fine, which the act stipulated as the punishment, was the sole penalty which the State legally could inflict," the Literary Digest informed its readers in its article "Pennsylvania Bans Sunday Baseball as Unholy" a month following the court decision. "Under this minority interpretation, professional baseball could be played on Sunday, with the management submitting each Sunday to a fine of $4."[31]

"The penalty and also the appropriate remedy are provided in distinct and unmistakable terms by the Act of 1794 itself," Chief Justice Moschzisker wrote in his dissenting opinion. "Under well established rules of law, these provisions are exclusive, whether the offender be a corporation or otherwise. The fact that the defendant is a Pennsylvania corporation does not place it at the uncontrolled mercy of its creator."[32]

"If the law of the majority opinion is to be followed, the Attorney General ought to institute proceeding against all corporate violators of the Sunday law," wrote Justice Kephart in his dissenting opinion, "including railroad companies, trolley-car companies, all taxicab companies and motor-bus companies, all carriers whose passengers are not on their way to church or religious services, or travelers whom necessity compels to move, but are pleasure seekers or engaged in a business journey."[33]

The Athletics decided to appeal to the U.S. Supreme Court. "The decision of the State Supreme Court banning professional Sunday base ball in this city will be appealed to the United States Supreme Court, attorneys for the Athletics announced yesterday," the Philadelphia Evening Bulletin reported in early August.[34]

By October 15, though, the Athletics decided to abandon an appeal to the U.S. Supreme Court. "We feel it would be useless to carry an appeal to the United States Supreme Court and impossible to be successful in an appeal," attorney Gartling said of the club's final position in the matter.[35]

It was quite clear that Sunday baseball proponents would have to switch from a court-mandated solution to a legislative one. But that would be a difficult road to travel.

"If the advocates of a liberal Sunday shall now take this cause to the legislature and seek to change the law, no one can question their right," the Literary Digest remarked. "But they will have to meet a determined purpose, bred in the bone and sinew of Pennsylvania stock to keep Sunday a day apart from the other days of the week, holy and undisturbed for those who desire to worship. And a day of guaranteed rest for the millions of workers in the Commonwealth."[36]

One person who may not have been all that disappointed that Sunday games wouldn't be played at Shibe Park was Lefty Grove, the winning pitcher in the 1926 test game and a rising star for the Athletics. Grove sometimes pitched for semi-pro teams when the Athletics were idle, on Sundays or even weekdays, where he picked up extra cash to supplement his salary from the Athletics.

For example, on Friday, September 30, 1927, Grove pitched at the Worcester County Fair in Worcester, Massachusetts, for the East Douglas team. The opponent was the Holy Name team from Clinton, which had signed up Red Sox pitcher Danny MacFayden to take the mound for it. Minor league players stocked the rest of both teams. This wasn't a hush-hush event, as evidenced by the headline in the local paper the day of the game, "Lefty Grove Hurls at Fair Here Today."[37]

Millionaire manufacturer Walter Schuster ran the East Douglas team and reportedly paid Grove $500 plus $10 a strikeout to pitch the game. Grove struck out 18 of 28 batters in the 4–0 victory, at one point retiring nine straight batters on strikeouts, to collect a $680 payday before heading to Boston to rejoin the Athletics for the game with the Red Sox on Saturday.[38]

Grove nearly had a perfect game. The only hit he gave up was a bunt single to Dick Ryan in the first inning on a hit that the third baseman let go believing the ball would roll foul. Grove's catcher for the day, George Army, supplied most of the East Douglas firepower, as he had three of the team's eight hits including two RBI-singles.[39]

With Philadelphia stymied by the Pennsylvania Supreme Court in the Sunday baseball battle, the action shifted to Massachusetts where the Braves and Red Sox mounted a campaign in the 1920s to play baseball on Sundays.

Chapter 12

BOSTON FINALLY GOT IT

By 1929, ten years following the 1919 approval of the Sunday baseball law in New York, the Red Sox and the Braves finally were permitted to play Sunday baseball in Boston.

Passage of a Sunday baseball law in Massachusetts was an especially difficult endeavor because the state was settled by the Puritans, whose Yankee descendants were bastions of conservatism and steadfastly adhered to the Puritan principle of Sunday being a day for worship and a day of rest.

It was a long, torturous path of legislative initiatives, political wrangling, and public posturing to overturn a portion of the Puritan Sunday laws. Vestiges of Yankee mistrust of the immigrant groups that eventually outnumbered the Puritan descendants created enormous hurdles to legalization of Sunday baseball in the Commonwealth of Massachusetts.

And when it seemed that the first Sunday baseball game in Boston was just weeks away, politics managed to extend the process even further. A bribery scandal infiltrated a debate ostensibly between secular and religious interests, which exposed the darker commercial side to the Sunday baseball question, an aspect its opponents had warned Massachusetts citizens about for many years.

Massachusetts public officials charged with enforcing the Sunday blue laws, following their establishment in 1650 by the Puritans, took their responsibility seriously.

While Sunday baseball was commonly pursued in the 1880s by professional teams in the major league American Association, youngsters were still being arrested in Massachusetts for the simple act of playing a casual game of baseball on a Sunday. For instance, on Sunday, May 22, 1887, police arrested nine players on charges of playing ball on the Sabbath along with seven others for being present at the game played in South Boston.

"The commandment to keep holy the Sabbath seemed to have escaped the memory of a number of the residents of Crescent place yesterday," the

Boston Herald reported in an article entitled "Ball Tossers Arrested; South Boston Young Men Locked Up for Playing on Sunday." The article went on to say, "Their love of the national game so absorbed their attention that Sergeant Foster and Patrolman Wyman of the third police precinct managed to get into their midst before the players were aware of their approach."[1]

Justice was equally served in rural areas as it was in the cities. "Sunday officers Thompson and Collins arrested sixteen young men and boys at West Warren for playing base ball, after having warned them the week previous not to do so," the *Worcester Spy* reported of activities in the rural town of Warren in 1888. "They were brought before Trial Justice Tyler Monday morning and each fined $2.50 and costs."[2]

Even after the more respected National League adopted Sunday baseball in 1892 to extend the concept to teams located in eastern cities, if only for road games and for home games where legal, the Boston Nationals declined to play Sunday games as the visiting team for more than 10 years. The owners of the Nationals feared even this minor bending of the Puritan Sunday doctrine would alienate customers from attending home games at the South End Grounds. Boston did not play an official National League game on Sunday until the Nationals took the field in St. Louis on June 14, 1903. That was two years after the Boston Americans began Sunday play on the road in the American League.

Acceptance of Sunday baseball inexorably moved eastward from its everyday place in midwestern cities, if simply for amateur play while leaving the professionals on the sideline. But even prior to World War I, however, amateur play was prohibited by Massachusetts law.

One of the rare occurrences of legal Sunday baseball in Massachusetts was on land owned by the federal government, since federal law normally held in those jurisdictions.

In 1910, though, U.S. district attorney Asa French told soldiers at Fort Banks in Winthrop, a town next to East Boston, to cease playing baseball on Sunday, a practice that they had done for the previous three years. Opponents of Sunday baseball had discovered a loophole in federal law and acted upon it by having the pastor of the First Baptist Church of Winthrop make a complaint to the U.S. district attorney.[3]

French interpreted the law that where there is no punishment provided under U.S. law for an offense on government lands, the offender is liable under the laws of the state in which the lands are situated. Thus, Sunday baseball on federal land in Massachusetts was no longer permitted.

In New York, Sunday laws were generally applied to prohibit admissions for baseball games, not stop the games all together as was the case in

Massachusetts. This no-admissions approach appealed to supporters of the Sunday baseball rationale that youth should be permitted to exercise and others to enjoy the outdoors on the only day off in the then six-day workweek. But the arguments for exercise and good use of free time failed to gain acceptance in Massachusetts.

Joseph Lee, a social reformer, fought for Sunday sport in Boston. Lee founded the Massachusetts Civic League in 1897 as an organization for the careful study of Boston's social problems. He thought the Sabbath was the number one example of "legislation enjoining idleness and producing crime."

In 1899 the league's Committee on the Prevention of Juvenile Law-Breaking had determined that the crime rate for 10- to 15-year-old youths increased 119 percent in August while the crime rate for the city as a whole rose only 30 percent. The committee concluded these juveniles turned to crime for want of other activities. It also coincidentally reached the conclusion that the city's existing playgrounds were not used to nearly their full capacity, and the principal reason was lack of supervision (without a supervisor, bigger boys broke up constructive play by carrying off the balls and bats of the younger boys).

"What good were parks and playgrounds if they couldn't be used to full measure on the day with the greatest amount of free time?" Stephen Hardy wrote in his book *How Boston Played*. "Many people agreed with Lee and in 1911 there was a major campaign to change the [Sunday] law."[4]

Lee's efforts failed to secure changes to the Sunday laws that prohibited recreation, but he did raise consciousness in support of more supervised playgrounds. By 1913, Lee could point to 73 equipped and supervised playgrounds in Boston, though the playgrounds were little used on Sundays.

Proponents of Sunday baseball such as Joseph Lee had been trying to get the Sunday laws on sports changed in Massachusetts since the turn of the century. Every year their efforts in the legislature failed. Much as the composition of state's population had changed, reflecting the tide of immigrants that came to work in the state's textile and footwear industries, the political power was still dominated by the old-line Yankee descendants of the Puritans. And the Yankees didn't especially want Sunday sports.

At the dawn of World War I in April 1914, the Massachusetts House of Representatives once again disappointed advocates of Sunday baseball, voting 128–84 on a motion to kill a Sunday bill. "Sunday baseball was defeated in every form in which it was presented yesterday," the *Boston Globe* reported in an article entitled "House Frowns on Sunday Ball." As the members "did little all day but talk baseball and vote," Representative

Sawyer of Ware said in support of the bill, "Religious convictions should not be considered in the voting on the bill, but only the public welfare." But Representative Hawes of Medford responded, "If we are going to desecrate the Sabbath just for fun, let us have the Continental Sabbath and be done with it." [5]

World War I helped to move the battle along in Massachusetts, although not nearly as quickly as in New York where the war eased passage of an eventual Sunday baseball statute.

By the spring of 1918, Boston had witnessed a barrage of professional baseball success that had captivated the state's populace. The state's two professional teams had won their respective league titles in four of the previous six years. The Boston Red Sox, the old Boston Americans re-christened with a new name in 1907, had captured American League pennants in 1912, 1915, and 1916, while the Boston Braves, the old Nationals renamed in 1911, had won the National League pennant in 1914.

Even with such success at Fenway Park and Braves Field, Massachusetts legislators wouldn't budge on allowing a 12-year-old boy to play baseball for fun with his friends on a Sunday.

Influenced by the war being waged in Europe, the Massachusetts legislature did pass a bill in April 1918 to permit men in the army and navy to play baseball and football on Sunday. This law in essence brought the state back to its position on Sunday baseball that it had held in 1910 before the French decision stopped Sunday games at military bases. The games could not start before 1:00 in the afternoon in order to not disrupt church services, and no admission could be charged.[6]

Red Sox owner Harry Frazee, in what he must have felt was the spirit of the law, went ahead and scheduled a Red Cross benefit game for Sunday, May 26, moving up the Monday, May 27, game with the White Sox. Frazee believed playing the game on Sunday would raise $50,000 more for the Red Cross. The state police and the Boston Public Safety Committee gave the Red Sox licenses to play the game on Sunday.[7]

But spirit of the law didn't sway Boston police commissioner Stephen O'Meara, who voiced the opinion that the game would be in open violation of the Sunday law and, if played, would be the first legal test of the law. Frazee backed off and moved the game back to Monday.

The law to permit military games on Sunday was little progress in view of the passage of Sunday baseball laws in 1918 in Washington, D.C., and the following year in New York. Massachusetts appeared clearly behind the times with its Sunday baseball stance. "The relative speed with which the last resistance to Sunday baseball disappeared [following New York approval in 1919] was itself a sign of the iconoclastic spirit of the post-war era," historian Harold Seymour explained in his seminal work *Baseball: The Golden Age*.[8]

By the summer of 1919, Sunday baseball could be played in only six of the eight American League cities—all except Boston and Philadelphia. In the National League, Sunday baseball was legal in just five of the eight cities, the same two exceptions in the American League along with Pittsburgh.

"Does any sane man mean to tell me that the people of Chicago, St. Louis, and Cincinnati are any worse than those of ... Boston and Philadelphia because they sanction Sunday baseball?" Charles Murphy wrote in "The Pros and Cons of Sunday Baseball" in a 1919 issue of *Baseball Magazine*.[9]

"Is any moral question involved? No. I say the citizens of Chicago, St. Louis, and Cincinnati are simply a great many steps ahead of their eastern brethren in regard to the doctrine of human rights," Murphy continued. "No wonder there is a feeling of unrest among the workers of this country. The poor fellow who works hard all week to support his family is denied the most innocent forms of amusement on Sunday."

"One of the greatest curses of the age is the intolerance of the pulpit—in many places—and the desire to tell you and me what to do and what not to do," Murphy pointed a finger at the suspected culprit holding up Sunday baseball in Massachusetts and Pennsylvania, the only remaining states forestalling play of Sunday baseball on the home fields of all 16 major league teams.

There was a bit more progress in 1920 as the Massachusetts legislature finally consented to allow amateur play of Sunday sports. The use of the "local option" technique, which was included in both the 1911 Ohio and 1919 New York laws permitting Sunday baseball, was a key to the passage of the new Massachusetts law. A church proximity restriction, which was contained in the 1909 Indiana Sunday baseball law, also helped secure passage.

In March, the Committee on Legal Affairs reported favorably on a measure to provide for sports or games to take place on public playgrounds, parks, or other places designated by permit. The activities needed to take place between 2:00 and 6:00 in the afternoon, with no charge for admission, and with participants "that are not promised and do not receive, directly or indirectly, any pecuniary reward."[10]

Exceptions to the sports and games permitted on Sunday were horse races, automobile races, boxing matches, and hunting with firearms. Permitted sports and games could not take place within 1000 feet of a church. Perhaps most importantly, the law was subject to local option, that is, each community could decide for itself whether to allow the permitted sports and games on Sunday.

Massachusetts governor Calvin Coolidge, later that summer to become the vice presidential candidate for the Democratic Party, signed the amateur Sunday sports bill on April 2 following a short hearing on the bill in the state senate.

The bill's proponents ensured that religious backers of the bill attended the hearing. In answer to the charge that the law would be a step toward professional baseball on Sunday, Reverend E. D. Robinson of Holyoke declared that the amateur games on Sundays were part of the "fight against commercialism." Reverend Robinson then told the Senate hearing, "I'd like to know if it is holier to stand on the street corner Sunday afternoon, criticize the people who are passing and spit tobacco juice, than to take part in a good healthy game of baseball."[11]

Opposition also spoke at the hearing. "Reverend Martin Kneeland of the Lord's Day Alliance protested that Sunday baseball would lower the Sunday ideals of the community," the *Boston Globe* reported. Kneeland assailed the bill as passed by the legislature and declared it to be a "thoroughly bad measure."[12]

Local option and limiting the proximity of games to churches helped the measure finally break through the Puritan wall of Sunday sports prohibition. Mayor Andrew Peters of Boston eagerly signed the Sunday sports measure on April 9 after the Boston City Council accepted it. In 1920, baseball would finally be played on Sunday in Boston—by unpaid players at least.

The Boston City Council wouldn't be so quick to action in 1928, though, when the next Sunday sports measure came before the body.

If there was any doubt that amateur play of Sunday sports was as far as the Republican-controlled Massachusetts legislature wanted to go, the 1922 checkers bill was a telling sign of the difficulty in expanding the law's provisions. On February 3, 1922, the House of Representatives defeated a bill to legalize the playing of checkers and chess outdoors on Sunday.

A disabled man had recently been convicted and fined in Brockton for playing checkers on Sunday in a public park. The Massachusetts Checkers Association had sought to include checkers among the outdoor sports and games permitted between 2:00 and 6:00 on Sunday afternoons. The Massachusetts legislature didn't concur. "There's nothing in the law forbidding the games indoor on Sunday," one newspaper reported on the legislative action. "But they come under the ban of the old blue laws when played outdoors."[13]

New York lawyer Emil Fuchs purchased the Boston Braves in 1923. Since Fuchs had worked for the New York Giants and saw how successful

Sunday baseball was in New York, he went right to work trying to pass a similar bill in Massachusetts.

Rather than go the normal legislative route, which appeared to be a fruitless venture, Fuchs, a capable lawyer, sought another legal route. Amendments to the state constitution in 1918 permitted initiative petitions. With enough voter signatures on a petition, Fuchs could get a proposed law on the ballot for consideration by the voters even if the legislature disapproved of the matter.

In October 1923, C. Sinclair Weeks, treasurer of the Braves, filed a petition with the attorney general's office in just such an approach to start the ball rolling to put the matter of professional Sunday baseball to the voters. The petition was signed by 10 citizens, as required by law, including Charles Gorman, head of the athletic committee of the American Legion, and Thomas Bannon, head of the athletic committee at General Electric. Once the attorney general approved the petition as to form, 20,000 signatures would need to be filed; if the legislature failed to enact the bill, another 5,000 signatures would be needed to place the question on the state ballot.[14]

Having the Boston Braves lead the public charge for professional Sunday baseball would have smacked too much of commercialism and doomed the petition to failure. The proponents for the petition therefore enticed Fred Doe, an icon among local baseball followers for his work with young players and a long-time minor league player and manager in the New England League, to take up the banner for the professional Sunday baseball cause.

Doe symbolized the benefit that young people would get by attending professional and semi-pro baseball games on Sunday. The proponents also hoped that Doe's leadership would minimize the focus on the reality that the Braves and Red Sox might make a few dollars from expected large crowds at Sunday games. Doe helped to secure more than 26,000 signatures to support the initiative petition.

In February 1925, the Legislative Committee on Legal Affairs held hearings on the proposed initiative petition. Even though it had been nearly five years since the amateur Sunday sports bill had been passed by the Massachusetts legislature, its opponents hadn't forgotten how that bill came to be.

Horace Cole of the Massachusetts Civic League found himself now standing with the Lord's Day League. Cole said that he believed in Sunday sports as much as ever, "but there is a sharp distinction between legalizing amateur sports and encouraging our youth to sit on a board Sunday afternoon to watch hired players."[15]

"They said when they asked for Sunday baseball that it was sport for youth. We said then that it was purely a commercial proposition. It is and always has been," said ex–Representative G. W. Greenwood. "They ask that we do away with the Sabbath ordained by the Almighty God. We cannot do it."

Added the Rev. A. Z. Conrad, "I have been at hearings on amateur Sunday sports and heard these same men lift their hands and swear to Heaven they never would desecrate the Sabbath by charging admissions to a ball game. How they have the gall to come now and ask for admissions is beyond me."

The proponents were outgunned at the committee meeting as their arguments fell on deaf legislative ears.

"Forty-one thousand New Bedford mill workers who now never get a chance to see a Boston ball game without taking a day off can have such a chance on Sunday," argued ex-mayor Ashley of New Bedford.

"There is nothing new in commercializing Sunday," said ex-attorney general Herbert Parker, who said people will not tolerate the rigors of the New England Sabbath and that the concept of the Puritan Sabbath had passed. "The present law is based on subterfuge," Parker added, since money was being covertly paid to players for Sunday baseball.

When the House defeated the bill 152–51 and the Senate voted it down 25–7, Doe and his troops (including the Boston Braves management) charged on and looked toward the 1926 state election to get their initiative petition for professional Sunday baseball before the voters.

In early August, Doe filed 17,206 signatures, at least 7,500 not signers of the original petition—more than the 5,000 required—with the secretary of state to get the question on the November 1926 ballot. "The question of whether professional baseball games may be played on Sundays in Massachusetts will be on the ballot for approval or rejection by voters at the 1926 election," the *Boston Post* reported in an August article, "Sunday Ball on Ballot."[16]

A snag, however, derailed that plan.

The nearly 15 months until the next state election gave the Sunday baseball opponents ample time to continue their quest to defeat the initiative petition. Indeed, in February 1926, Samuel Mendum and several clergymen petitioned the secretary of state to refrain from placing the Sunday sports question on the November ballot, based on the constitutional grounds that the law related to religion, in essence an illegal mixing of church and state.[17]

The matter made its way all the way through the courts to the Massachusetts Supreme Judicial Court. Some of the petitions that voters signed, however, referenced "Sunday baseball," while other petitions referenced "Sunday sports," the latter being the language in the actual proposed law. The courts, therefore, considered that there were two separate petitions. Unfortunately, "as neither part had sufficient names alone to place it on the ballot, the Supreme Court following an appeal, decided that in the absence of the proper petition, it could not go on the ballot," *The Sporting News* reported on the incident.[18]

The opponents might have been better off allowing the issue to go forward that year. With Republicans sweeping the 1926 state elections, there was a very good chance that the referendum on Sunday sports would have been defeated and perhaps have quelled its proponents for a few more years.

As it turned out, the political climate in Massachusetts would change markedly two years later for the 1928 election, which enabled the passage of Sunday baseball at that time.

Unlike the Boston Braves that made frequent one-day Sunday trips to Brooklyn, and the Philadelphia and Pittsburgh teams that often journeyed on Sunday to Washington and Cincinnati, respectively, the Boston Red Sox did not have a convenient Sunday haven. After the June 22, 1919, game with the Yankees at the Polo Grounds, the Red Sox made infrequent one-day Sunday trips until 1926.

In 1926, the Braves even played an amateur team on a Sunday to generate revenue. On Sunday, May 9, in between games in Pittsburgh and Cincinnati (the Phillies played the Reds that Sunday), the Braves played the General Tire Company team in Akron, Ohio. Not surprisingly, the Braves stormed to a 19–6 victory over the industrial team.[19]

The Red Sox played a one-day Sunday series in Detroit the following Sunday, May 16. "Last evening at 7:35, the Red Sox had to board the Western Express and make a hurried one night's trip to Detroit where they play the Tigers this afternoon," *the Boston Post* reported. "This visit is for one game only as the Sox have to be back at Fenway Park tomorrow to meet the Browns. But it is a lot of traveling to do in less than 48 hours."[20]

It wasn't a picnic for the Tigers either, as Detroit shuttled in for the Sunday game at Navin Field in between its games in Philadelphia on Saturday and Monday. Detroit defeated Boston 6–5 in 11 innings, before a crowd of 25,000.

Sunday baseball proponents may have worked even harder after being outfoxed on a technicality with the initiative petition targeted for the 1926 state ballot. In March 1927, the professional Sunday sports bill was actually reported favorably out of the Legal Affairs Committee, by a sliver of a margin, eight votes to seven.

Proponents at the February 9 hearing emphasized the health of the youthful population who would benefit by attending games when they couldn't actually participate in them. They also strengthened their argument about under-the-table payments to players by showing that police were aware of the actions but did nothing to stop it. Thus if the law was to be broken time after time, legislation should be enacted.[21]

By now, seven years after the passage of the amateur Sunday sports bill, the opponents arguing that it was bad faith on the part of bill supporters to agitate further on the subject was becoming trite. But those arguments did help sway the House in general. The bill was defeated 129–98 a week later on March 16.

The change in the nation's attitude toward Sunday was becoming evident in Massachusetts. What was once firmly believed by most to be a "day of rest" was being transformed into a "day of leisure."

"Rep. Spear of Everett spoke for the opposition, asserting that those who were in favor of the bill were largely those who are financially interested in Sunday sports; those opposed believe in the Sabbath," the *Boston Herald* reported. "Rep. Kirkpatrick of Holyoke spoke for the bill, saying that those opposing it sit in their motor cars on Sunday [while driving them] and say that this bill is a violation of the Sabbath. Sunday is already desecrated and this bill will not add to the desecration" that movies and Vaudeville already had contributed to by being permitted on Sunday.[22]

The opponents were becoming more polarized, while the proponents were appealing to the concerns of the general population.

At the 1928 hearings on that year's Sunday baseball bill, the arguments got even testier. "Each side charged the other with bad faith," the *New York Times* reported from a more objective perch external to Boston. "The debate ranged over an immense field, bringing in Roger Williams, Salem witches, the French Revolution, Tex Richard [a boxing promoter], and Babe Ruth. It was a lively hearing."[23]

Proponents also lined up clergymen to speak on behalf of the bill to solidify their position. "I think Christ would be in favor of anything that would give the youth of the country honest recreation," Reverend Paul Sterling of Melrose said at the hearings. "If I can play golf on Sunday, if I can go to a movie theatre on Sunday, I don't see why I shouldn't be allowed to see a good game of baseball."[24]

Despite the growing wave of acceptance for the concept, the House once again voted down the measure. The 110–93 vote was improvement over the previous year's tally, though.[25]

Proponents had no trouble obtaining the required number of signatures to put the matter on the 1928 ballot as a voter referendum. Since it was a presidential election year, a large number of voters sympathetic to the cause of Sunday baseball were likely to vote. And this time, proponents ensured that the bureaucracy didn't do them in.

By the summer of 1928, organized baseball was in full bloom on Sundays in the Boston area, both from the perspective of amateur teams as well as the city's professional teams.

On Sunday, July 15, several neighborhood teams took the field on Boston playgrounds that Joseph Lee had worked so hard to obtain for the city's youth earlier in the century. For instance, Roxbury defeated Neponset 6–5 in a 10-inning game at the William Garvey Playground in the Neponset section of Boston. In what really was a semi-pro game in the Twilight League, South Boston defeated East Cambridge 5–3 at Thorndike Field in Cambridge. Since the Red Sox were in the midst of a home stand with the White Sox, on the idle Sunday the White Sox traveled to Tiverton, Rhode Island, to play an exhibition game with a Fall River team composed of Eastern League players and local semi-pros. The White Sox won 4–2 before returning to Boston to play the Red Sox on Monday.[26]

In August, with the Sunday sports initiative petition in the hands of Secretary of State Cook to verify its eligibility for the November ballot, organized opposition not surprisingly sprung up again. The Rev. Conrad, pastor of the Park Street Church and staunch opponent from the Lord's Day Alliance at the 1925 Sunday baseball hearings, formed a political organization called SOS Campaign Committee. The organization pledged "to work for the defeat of any initiative petition appearing on the ballot at the State election November 8 favoring commercialized or professional sports of any kind on the Lord's Day."[27]

The proponents countered by forming a branch of the Outdoor Recreation League, led by Claude Davidson, president of the New England League. Davidson had recently revived the venerable minor league, so his motivation was at least partially career survival, since the New England League desperately needed Sunday baseball to remain economically viable.

Conrad's group, however, could not repel the changing attitudes of the majority of the Massachusetts electorate.

The year 1928 turned out to be a defining year for Massachusetts, as the state "witnessed a striking transformation in the political status ... from a rock-bound Republican stronghold to a Democratic state," Joseph Huthmacher wrote in *Massachusetts People and Politics*.[28]

Sunday baseball was a huge beneficiary of that change in political mood.

Al Smith, governor of New York and Democratic Party candidate for president, was a big impetus behind the political transformation. Smith was also a Catholic, a fact that polarized opposition to him among the dry-Protestant-rural voters and generated huge support with the wet-Catholic-urban-immigrant affiliations.

While Smith lost the election in a landslide to Herbert Hoover, Smith did initiate a dramatic reversal in political power in Massachusetts. For the first time, a majority of the Massachusetts electorate voted for a Democratic candidate for president, as Smith carried the state by a slim margin. Republicans had badly misunderstood the voters in 1928.

"Because of the large scale unemployment in textile and shoes, the Massachusetts Republican party was in the difficult position of explaining why the Bay State was excluded from the apparent prosperity of the Coolidge era," historians Richard Brown and Jack Tager wrote of the times in *Massachusetts: A Concise History*.[29]

Between 1919 and 1929, Massachusetts lost more than 150,000 jobs in manufacturing, including 94,000 in the state's dominant industries of textiles and shoes, in an economy that was otherwise booming nationwide. In New Bedford, 82 percent of workers were in textiles; in Fall River the percentage was 78 percent and in Lawrence it was 76 percent. In Haverhill, 84 percent of workers were in boots and shoes, with 81 percent similarly situated in Brockton. "The prosperity of these communities was dependent on the growth of industries that were, owing to external low-wage competition, on the verge of a long-term slide into oblivion," Brown and Tager wrote.[30]

Republican support for Prohibition also "galled the French Canadians and Italians who usually voted Republican. That the national Republicans, supporting 'pure Americanism' were nativistic and anti–Catholic was enough to create a new coalition of Democrats in 1928."[31]

While Republicans couldn't stop the Sunday baseball initiative petition from making the ballot in 1928, they certainly didn't make passage easy.

In order for the referendum to pass, "yes" votes had to number at least 30 percent of the total vote cast. Republicans were hoping that many voters once choosing the candidates for offices would bypass the two questions at the end of the ballot, since the wording of the questions was extraordinarily complicated. The Sunday sports one was also very lengthy (a 243-word sentence, "probably the longest question, in a single sentence, ever appearing upon a ballot in this state" the *Boston Globe* reasoned the day before the election). Many voters did bypass the ballot questions, 21 percent of total ballots cast, but not enough to offset the overwhelming preference of voters that did vote one way or the other.

There was also that menacing line near the bottom of the question, if one did read that far, that reminded voters that the legislature had disapproved of the proposed law.

The Outdoor Recreation League organized efforts to counter these obstacles. As *The Sporting News* noted, "The state has been placarded and covered with letters and workers." Sample ballots were also a big item to avert the necessity of voters having to actually attempt to read the ballot question and just have them mark the "yes" box.[32]

Sunday sports were overwhelmingly approved by Massachusetts voters on November 6. The front pages of the newspapers two days later, though, spotlighted the sale of Rogers Hornsby from the Braves to the Chicago Cubs, along with his exorbitant $42,500 salary. Fuchs sold Hornsby's contract to Chicago for $200,000 plus five players. While the cash helped to solve some of the judge's financial concerns, none of the five players became standouts like Hornsby had been for the Braves.[33]

Question 2 on Sunday sports garnered 803,281 "yes" votes versus 467,550 "no" votes, for a resounding 63 percent of the tabulation of affirmative selections. There were 339,183 blanks among the 1,610,014 ballots cast, or 21 percent of the total vote. The "yes" vote nearly equaled a majority of all ballots—marked and blank—falling just shy at 49.9 percent.[34]

The state's largest county, Suffolk County, where Boston is located, voted 76 percent in the "yes" column to lead the way. Of the state's 14 counties, just three voted against the referendum—Duke, Barnstable, and Franklin—all rural and representing three of the four smallest voter populations in the state.

Urban areas such as Fall River, Lowell, and New Bedford all strongly voted in favor of Sunday sports. Many rural areas were not in favor, though, as well as some suburban Boston towns. Melrose, just north of Boston, was the largest place to vote against the referendum, with 6,212 "no" to 3,545 "yes."

Massachusetts thus joined 31 other states and the District of Columbia that permitted professional Sunday baseball.[35]

"Strict Sabbatarians may deplore the action of the voters in Massachusetts, approving by a decisive majority Sunday sports in the Bay State," the *Literary Digest* reported in its "Lifting the Ban on Sunday Sports" article in December 1928. "But, observes the neighboring *Providence Journal*, 'it reflects the prevalent modern sentiment on the question. From any unprejudiced point of view the move is evidence of no more than a reasonable liberality'."[36]

"The verdict of the Massachusetts voters in smashing Puritan intolerance and permitting baseball on Sunday isolates Pennsylvania as the only anti–Sunday baseball state in the two major leagues," *The Sporting News* reported. In an editorial, though, *The Sporting News* cautioned that Sunday baseball was not a certain ticket to financial success:

> There seems to be an impression that because Sunday baseball may be played in Boston, the Boston clubs of necessity will jump to affluence. To that we can hardly subscribe. Sunday baseball will not make a club in a major league successful—not one—if the owner of the club cannot put forth an attraction for Sunday spectators, and weekday spectators also. One is not likely to go unless there is a probability of seeing something which can offset a fine automobile ride, a trip to some beach, or a pleasant afternoon with a friend in the country. Sunday baseball is not an insurance of profit to any baseball club owner.[37]

Massachusetts voter approval, however, was just the first step toward having Sunday baseball in Boston. Because the law was "local option," the Braves and Red Sox needed to obtain approval from the Boston City Council before tickets could be printed for a Sunday game. While the count of Boston voters was substantially in favor of the Sunday sports initiative by more than three-to-one (172,800 to 54,418), those results did not mean, though, that the Boston City Council would necessarily be quick to act.

After the election results were certified by the state on December 6, the city council tabled an approval order for Sunday sports at its December 17 meeting, saying it wanted more time to study the bill.

"It was said that a large majority of the members of the Council are in favor of the bill," the *Boston Globe* reported of the city council meeting. "And there may actually be unanimous approval when the matter is brought to a vote." Boston mayor Malcolm Nichols, however, voiced his disappointment with the council's actions. "I am very much in favor of Sunday professional baseball," Nichols said following the meeting. "The people of Boston have expressed their desire for this measure and if necessary I will lead the fight to have it approved."[38]

At the next city council meeting slated for December 21, the lack of a quorum prevented any action on the Sunday sports measure. The meeting was adjourned three minutes after its call to order at 12:12, with only 9 council members present and 12 absent. The next meeting was scheduled for December 27.

"Poor little City Councilors, a bunch of orphans!" Mayor Nichols cried sarcastically to the press. "What they want is a Christmas tree and they haven't got one!"[39]

Whether Nichols was in on the behind-the-scenes exchange of words is not known. His comments in retrospect, though, were prescient. The relative anonymity of the Sunday sports law would soon be replaced by acrimonious public debate with charges, and counter charges, of illegal activities to gain its passage.

Chapter 13

BRIBERY SCANDAL SOILED IT

"Adams Urges Early Action By Council" was the seemingly innocuous headline in the December 23, 1928, Sunday edition of the *Boston Globe*. But words contained in the article would set off a firestorm in Boston.

The December 17 and 21 delays by the Boston City Council in acting on the Sunday sports law had stirred concern in Charles Adams, a vice president of the Boston Braves and financial benefactor to Braves owner Judge Fuchs. Adams believed that the council's initial tabling, compounded by the subsequent lack of a quorum four days later, was sufficient evidence that the story that Fuchs had related to Adams about a city councilor soliciting a bribe from him to approve Sunday baseball was seemingly true.

So Adams took the team's case to the newspapers, always a friend of the judge, telling reporters in so many words that it appeared the Braves were being blackmailed to obtain the city council's approval of Sunday baseball.

"We regret to state that it was suggested at that point, it probably would be necessary to pay for the concession of early action, as, if this was not done, the measure might be tabled and remain there indefinitely," Adams remarked in the middle of a lengthy statement to the press. "Our City Council should support and help us, not hinder or unduly oppress," he concluded.[1]

These words launched the Sunday baseball issue into the realm of "bribery scandal." The trip came complete with an intense examination through public hearings, a heavy dose of political intrigue, a startling revelation unrelated to the basic issue as if straight out of a movie script, and bad feelings created all around.

Naturally, the city councilors didn't take Adams' remarks warmly or lightly, particularly coming as they did so near Christmas Eve.

"If he was approached by any member of the City Council, he owes it to the rest of the Council to name the man," the *Boston Globe* quoted

Councilor Herman Bush the next day. "Ask him if he hasn't already paid something to someone to force the matter through the City Council. I don't mean a Councilor." Councilor John Dowd declared that he would not consider giving a permit to the Braves team until Adams has made public the "bribe seeker" and proved the charges true.[2]

The Boston Finance Commission assumed jurisdiction of the inquiry into the bribery allegations. The FinCom, as it was known, was essentially an extension of the Massachusetts legislature. Patrician lawmakers established the FinCom in 1907 out of a general mistrust of how the rising immigrant population in the state's largest city handled the city's fiscal affairs, when elected to office, under the guise that mismanagement would burden the state financially.

Mayor John "Honey Fitz" Fitzgerald, of Irish heritage, had created the FinCom in 1907 "to forestall a more hostile inquiry into city finances by the Republican-dominated state legislature." The state, though, approved appointees to the committee and also provided it with the authority to summon witnesses, enforce their attendance, and administer oaths. The FinCom was so successful investigating the alleged corrupt practices of the Fitzgerald administration, and thus assuaging Yankee concerns about Boston city finances, that the legislature made it a permanent fixture in the city's political landscape. The FinCom still exists today but has far less influence than it once wielded in 1929.[3]

In many ways, the FinCom hearings on the Sunday sports issue were a microcosm of the Yankee-immigrant tussle that had been going on for years and would continue for many more after 1929. Historian James Connolly aptly described the basic mistrust on both sides in his book *The Triumph of Ethnic Progressivism: Urban Political Culture in Boston, 1900-1925*:

> While the Good Government Association saw a handful of greedy Irish politicians conspiring to wrest control of the city from its essentially honest, though deceived, citizenry, [Mayor James Michael] Curley described a handful of Brahmin financiers clinging to power and scheming against the interests of the city's ethnic majority. Curley's depiction triumphed. Even when all but a small remnant of Yankee Boston had fled to the suburbs, and Boston politics was almost entirely an intra–Irish struggle, the image of a Brahmin elite striving to limit the authority of immigrants and their descendants would remain a powerful rhetorical device in the city's politics.[4]

Entering the picture here was John Dowling, who was nominated two weeks earlier by lame-duck governor Alvan Fuller to be chairman of the FinCom. Dowling would swiftly ferret out the many elements of the Sunday baseball bribery allegations.

Adams may have regretted his tactic of going public, as he then immediately clammed up. Dowling launched the FinCom hearings the day after Christmas, not three days following the bribery revelation. Adams refused to testify to the FinCom at that initial December 26 hearing, claiming the organization didn't have the requisite authority to handle the matter.

Silence was a curious position for Adams to take if he really wanted the truth to surface. Dowling put the matter to the courts and two days later on December 28 the Massachusetts Supreme Judicial Court ordered Adams on January 2 to "divulge to the said [Finance] Commission the name of his informant."[5]

Perhaps the strategy backfired on Adams. Maybe he thought the city council would back down to avoid an airing of its dirty laundry. Instead, the council at its December 27 meeting approved Sunday baseball in concept, and the councilors took the opportunity to skewer officials of the Braves and announce that the council would carefully examine how permits would be issued.

"Mid perhaps the fieriest eloquence, charge, counter-charge, innuendo, denunciation that the Boston City Council has perpetrated, and a capacity gallery has listened to, the City Fathers yesterday afternoon passed unanimously an order accepting the Sunday professional sports bill," the *Boston Globe* described the council escapades.[6]

"It is the first time that any such license has come before us for our consideration and we should not hasten our actions," Councilor Henry Parkman Jr. said. "The questions of a fee, the length of time the license will run, the rate of admission, and the price of concessions all must be decided."[7]

Or maybe Adams had a Machiavellian strategy.

Whatever the motive of Adams, the Boston City Council called his bluff. The councilors no doubt knew the allegations would turn out to be weak. It was a classic "He said. He said" that would come down to how credible each side appeared in the debate.

By New Year's Eve, the city councilors had gained the high ground in the debate by first acting indignant at the accusations and then by officially embracing the Sunday sports law. Meanwhile, the courts had to force the accuser to talk further, and John Dowling was running the hearings in a most expeditious manner to commence in earnest following the New Year's Day holiday.

The alleged bribe occurred on November 23, two weeks following voter approval of the Sunday sports ballot referendum, in Judge Fuchs' suite at the Copley Plaza Hotel in Boston. The alleged solicitor of the bribe was City Councilor William Lynch on behalf of a group of 12 councilors.[8]

Charles Adams, vice president of the Boston Braves (far left), testifying at the Boston Finance Commission hearings on Sunday baseball bribery allegations, which were instigated following comments by Adams. (Courtesy of the Boston Public Library, Print Department)

Fuchs had asked Dan Carroll, a boxing manager friendly with Lynch, to stop by his hotel suite that Friday night after attending a boxing match. Lynch accompanied Carroll. Ed Cunningham, secretary of the Braves, was already there when Carroll and Lynch arrived, but he then left to get sandwiches soon after Lynch, Carroll, and Fuchs went into an adjoining room and closed the door to talk privately. The alleged bribe was to have occurred during that private discussion, which was out of range for anyone else to hear.

Burt Whitman, sports editor of the *Boston Herald*, showed up later and was in the suite when the three men emerged from their closed-door conversation. After Cunningham returned to the suite with food, all five persons were in the same room following delivery of the alleged bribe for another three hours until the gathering broke up around 3:00 in the morning.

What was said in that closed-door conversation between Fuchs and Lynch, witnessed by Carroll, was the heart of the matter. In their testimony at the FinCom hearings, the two men didn't agree on the substance of the conversation. They couldn't even agree on whether the door to the room was locked or not (Fuchs said Lynch locked the door; Lynch didn't know whether or not the door was locked).

Fuchs took the witness stand at the FinCom hearings on January 2, 1929, the date Justice Pierce had set for Adams to testify. To accommodate the expected number of spectators, the hearing was moved from the FinCom quarters at 24 School Street to Room 460 at the nearby State House. But the crowd was so large that the hearing was then adjourned to the Gardner Auditorium in the State House.

The testimony of the Braves owner that day was captured in great detail by the more than half dozen daily newspapers in Boston, most with banner headlines on the front page trumpeting the day's major revelation:

> "Fuchs Names City Councilor W. G. Lynch As Bribe Solicitor"—*Boston Globe*, evening edition, January 2
> "Fuchs Names Lynch as Baseball Bribe Seeker"—*Boston Traveler*, January 2
> "Said 13 Councilors Wanted $65,000 for Baseball Vote"—*Boston Post*, January 3
> "13 Councilmen Involved in Bribe Charge by Fuchs"—*Boston Daily Advertiser*, January 3
> "Foley Plans Grand Jury Action at Once as Fuchs Names Council Bloc of 13 Which Demanded $65,000 to Pass Sports Bill"—*Boston Herald*, January 3

The more staid, upscale *Boston Evening Transcript* was the only newspaper not to highly accentuate Fuch's testimony, publishing on January 2 a one-column headline, "Fuchs Tells His Story to the Fin. Com." The afternoon newspaper *Boston American* surprisingly went to press that day without including a story on the Fuchs testimony.

Fuchs said in his testimony that "I did everything I could to see that the Council passed the act as the mandate of the people called for."[9]

As to the bribery solicitation, Fuchs testified that Lynch told him that the members of the block he represented had figured just how many Sundays there would be for baseball, and what the receipts would be, and they had figured that Fuchs should pay $5,000 for each man.

Fuchs then recited the name of 10 councilmen that he said Lynch told him of the 12 contained in the block: Donovan, Murphy, Bush, Ruby, McMahon, Dowd, Sullivan, Motley, Wilson, and Mahoney.

"I informed Lynch that such a proposition was both comical and ridiculous," Fuchs testified, "and that he and the rest of the group he represented were nothing but a jitney chorus of Jesse James boys without horses."

At that point, Fuchs said Lynch told him that the "block" could table the Sunday sports order until he changed his attitude.

"I did not take the thing seriously till the day the resolution was tabled," Fuchs concluded, "and I saw that the very men who voted against it were the ones that had been previously mentioned to me."

Under cross-examination by Joseph Walsh, counsel for Lynch, Fuchs admitted telling Lynch and Carroll that he was under a severe financial strain, and he had come to Boston with a lot of money and it was nearly all gone. He also said one of his worries was the fact that he had arranged for Boston College to use Braves Field for its football games and it had afterward gone to Fenway Park.

Then Walsh asked Fuchs about the refreshments present in the hotel room.

"What did you have besides sandwiches?" Walsh asked.

"We had everything," Fuchs replied.

"Everything!" Walsh exclaimed. "Did you have a little rye?"

"Excluded!" FinCom chairman Dowling shouted.

While Dowling might have thought liquor had no bearing on the case, however, he might also have been protecting "one of his own" from an embarrassing position of charging a bribe solicitation after having overimbibed in illegal spirits during this time of Prohibition.

Fuchs did not come off overly well following his FinCom testimony.

"I say that Judge Fuchs told a pretty good bedtime story," said Councilor William Motley Jr. "It appears that someone talked out of turn and that the Judge has also talked too much." Councilor Dowd said of the Fuchs testimony that it was "a deliberate lie and an attempt to slander a public official who seen fit to do his duty to his constituents." Dowd added, "I will not be blackjacked or hurried in my duties as a public servant."[10]

Adams testified on January 3 and confirmed the judge's account of the incident, but admitted that it was hearsay since he wasn't there that night at the Copley Plaza. Adams did relate a similar incident that involved him, though, a phone call where he thought the voice was that of city councilor Robert Wilson Jr. The call warned him "the Sunday sports bill would be tabled until cobwebbed unless he paid each of the block of 12 or 13 City Councilors $5,000."[11]

Adams thought the voice was Wilson, as he had met him in October to ask him if he were an ally of state senator Bilodeau in opposition to the Sunday sports measure. Adams said that conversation ended his connection to Wilson.

Whitman also testified on January 3 and said Fuchs greeted him as he entered the apartment by saying, "Come in. This is good. This is a fine shakedown. It would be funny if it were not pathetic." But Whitman testified that Fuchs never again mentioned the alleged shakedown. He also said that Fuchs and Lynch were on friendly terms when they parted the room about 3:00 in the morning.

Neither Adams nor Whitman seemed to aid Fuchs. Testimony by Ed Cunningham on Friday, January 4, not only didn't help Fuchs but it also made matters worse.

Cunningham, like Adams, testified that his knowledge of the bribe was secondhand, as related to him by Fuchs. The hearing was rather uneventful until Walsh cross-examined Cunningham. Walsh, Lynch's counsel who had defused testimony by Fuchs two days earlier, this time exposed elements of another dark side to the Sunday sports ballot question, that of how its proponents financed the campaign and targeted certain office holders for political defeat.

"Walsh made an effort to indicate a violation of the corrupt practices act on the part of Braves officials through their connection with the Outdoor Recreation League, which is alleged to have spent $30,000 in a campaign for passage of the Sunday sports referendum," the *New York Times* summarized the day's hearing. "Walsh endeavored to show that the Braves and the Outdoor Recreation League were one, and that the substantial part of the funds of the league, which were used to further the cause of Sunday baseball, were contributed by the Braves."[12]

Cunningham said that he had contributed $200 in cash to the Recreation League fund. When asked why he contributed cash so his name wouldn't be on record, Cunningham replied, "I didn't want any connection with the Braves shown in these contributions."[13]

"A hush fell over the room," following Cunningham's statement, the *Boston Globe* reported.

Cunningham went on to say, "The Lord's Day League was probing everything connected with Sunday baseball just at that time and I didn't want them to trace any contributions that I had got." Cunningham acknowledged that many contributors were Braves employees or connected to Braves Field operations. He ducked questions relating to whether the money for these contributions actually came from Fuchs or the Braves.

Cunningham also admitted that the Braves had issued 5,000 free tickets for ball games with political advertising on the backs in the effort to defeat the re-election of state senator Bilodeau, an ardent opponent of Sunday sports. This would be another violation of the law.

Attorney General Joseph Warner immediately announced that his office would look into the charges brought out in the FinCom testimony of Cunningham.

With the FinCom hearings suspended for three days until the following Tuesday, January 8, the Fuchs camp needed the time to regroup.

The Braves were clearly on the ropes. The focus of the hearings had decidedly shifted from suspected illegalities of public officials to potential improprieties conducted by Fuchs and the Braves.

On Monday, January 7, it was the city council's turn for center stage. The council met and appointed a special committee of five councilors to draft rules and regulations governing Sunday sports.

"It is very fortunate indeed for Boston that certain members of the Council saw fit to hold up the permit for the Braves. Because if they didn't hold it up, the Braves Field people would have had a carte blanche permit to charge anything they wanted to," said Councilor Dowd, who was one of the five appointed to the special committee along with Wilson, Parkman, Edward Gallagher, and Thomas McMahon. "We have the right to tell these gentlemen outside of Boston, who come here thinking that Boston is a hick town and that they can get away with anything, how much they shall charge us. I see no reason why the public should pay Judge Fuchs whatever he wants to charge."[14]

When the FinCom reconvened its hearings on January 8, Ernest Goulston branded the bribe-seeking charges of Fuchs as a "fantastic fairy tale, superinduced by overindulgence in bad liquor."[15]

Dowling couldn't keep the liquor issue out of the hearings forever. The *Boston Post* headlined its story on the day's hearings as "Bad Booze Blamed for Baseball Graft Charges."

Goulston's characterization of Fuchs' testimony came while he told of how he brought together Carroll and Adams for a telephone conversation in an effort to have Adams use his influence to reinstate Carroll's boxers to good standing at the Boston Garden. Adams owned the Boston Garden as well as the Boston Bruins hockey team that played its games there.

Carroll took the stand the next day, January 9, and declared that Fuchs made up the bribery charges to get $100,000 from Adams and keep it due to his financial troubles. Carroll also related the conversation in the hotel room the night of November 23 as he heard it, much to the entertainment of the crowded hall.

"The Judge asked Lynch his age. The Major [as Lynch was called] told him he was 36. Fuchs informed Lynch out of a clear sky that if he voted against the Sunday sports bill in the City Council he would be defeated just as former Senator Bilodeau was," Carroll said. "He had no sooner got the words out of his mouth when the Major jumped up and called him a damn fool and told him he would punch him in the nose. I held them apart while the Judge kept yelling 'wait a minute, wait a minute,' just like that and I finally got the Major seated in one chair and the Judge on the end of the lounge."[16]

Carroll testified that he and Fuchs consumed two pints of rye that night, while Lynch did not have a drink. Carroll also provided financial details that he said Fuchs told him about his finances, including:

- Fuchs had come to Boston with $500,000 and was now broke.
- Fuchs had to "hock" his Braves stock at Atlantic National Bank.
- The Braves dropped $30,000 when Boston College switched its football home games to Fenway Park.
- When Hornsby and manager Jack Slattery didn't get along, Fuchs had to fire Slattery but paid his salary for the year.
- Fuchs was worried about Ku Klux Klan rumors circulating regarding Hornsby and Bruce Wetmore, a Braves director.

The hearings were nearly anti-climatic by the time Lynch testified in his own defense on January 10. But Lynch took the opportunity to dump more innuendo on Fuchs.

"When he [Fuchs] said I was leading the block against the Sunday baseball bill, I thought he was drunk or crazy, because I had come up there to tell him for the third time that I always had been and was absolutely in favor of the bill," Lynch testified.[17]

When asked about Carroll's accusation that Fuchs trumped up the story in an effort to bleed Adams of $100,000, Lynch replied, "My opinion is that Judge Fuchs isn't above it. Fuchs can be proven a racketeer, blackmailer, blackjacker, and he was using this method of forcing the City Council to rush this measure."

Following the hearings, it was learned that Lynch had been referring to Fuchs' representation in New York of Ralph Day, a former prohibition director in 1922. That had resulted in an investigation, but no indictment had been handed down.

With his reputation clearly besmirched in the FinCom hearings, Fuchs issued a statement calling Lynch's testimony "outrageous vilification, slander, and falsehood."

That wrapped up the bulk of the Boston Finance Commission's hearings. But the investigations continued in the office of Attorney General Warner concerning the potential falsification of the contributor list to the Outdoor Recreation League and whether the money actually came from the Braves. The attorney general's office questioned Fuchs for five hours on January 16 and questioned Orris Brusse, treasurer of the Recreation League, on January 21.

In the midst of the numerous FinCom hearings and Boston City Council meetings, Mayor Andrew Casassa of the nearby city of Revere extended an invitation to officials of the Red Sox and Braves to consider an alternative to Boston politics for Sunday baseball. Casassa suggested that the teams establish baseball parks in his city. Casassa, who personally guaranteed a permit for Sunday baseball, pointed out that his beach city was an excellent site for a ballpark, easily accessible by automobile, steam trains, and electric cars with ample parking space.[18]

At the final FinCom hearing on January 23, Adams tried to rehabilitate Fuchs' reputation. Adams appeared with scores of telegrams and letters eulogizing the judge, including one from former New York governor Al Smith, who had just been defeated in the presidential election that November by Herbert Hoover, on the same ballot as the Sunday sports referendum in Massachusetts.

Although the rough-and-tumble politics had reached a completion in the FinCom hearings, the wrangling hadn't yet ended.

On January 28, the city council passed the Sunday sports ordinance by a vote of 12–5, but not without voicing considerable disdain for Fuchs and other New Yorkers.

In its original form, "An Ordinance Concerning Professional Outdoor Sports on the Lord's Day" outlined 12 requirements, most of which focused on finances.[19]

Section Two included restrictions on the sale of concessions or merchandise except at reasonable prices approved by a council vote. The intent of this section, according to Councilor Dowd, was to prevent "the multimillionaire [Harry] Stevens to have a contract to systematically rob the people of Boston."

Section Four required the licensee to furnish free drinking water on the premises as approved by the health commissioner. "It is not always a question of your wanting to buy a bottle of tonic [soda pop], for instance," remarked Councilor Arnold about conditions in the summer at the ballpark. "It is a question of choking to death or paying 15 cents for a bottle of tonic."

Sections Five and Six required that a charge for any seat wouldn't be higher on Sunday than any other day of the week and that a minimum of 35 percent of the seating capacity would at most cost 50 cents. Only 4 percent of the 45,000 seating capacity of Braves Field was available for 50 cents, while more than 25 percent of Fenway Park's 28,000 seating capacity was priced at 50 cents. Dowd remarked that the Braves had not played to a capacity crowd for the past six years and that Fuchs should welcome the opportunity to fill empty seats at 50 cents a ticket.

Section Eight set licensing fees for privately owned parks or fields according to seating capacity. The top fee of $2,500 applied to a 40,000-

plus capacity, with a minimum fee of $100 applicable to capacities less than 10,000. Although the schedule in the ordinance did include fees for fields with a capacity between 10,000 and 40,000, the top and bottom scales pretty much covered the entirety of private ballparks in Boston where Sunday baseball could legally be played.

Councilor Wilson favored high licensing fees because he felt that "90 percent of the voters who comprised the 3 to 1 majority in favor of the Sunday sports law ... so voted because first and foremost they believed they were authorizing Sunday semi-pro ball games on the public parks of the city where collections might be taken." Sunday pro baseball, Wilson said, "was foisted on a gullible public."

After a lengthy and emotional discussion, Sections Two and Six relating to concession prices and availability of 50 cent seating were voted to be struck from the ordinance, due to their dubious constitutional authority.

"The City of Boston had its Sunday Sports Ordinance, local baseball owners had the opportunity to enjoy the profits of broader fan support at games, the workingmen of Boston were now able to suffer the misfortunes of their favorite teams on the Sabbath, and the Boston City Council, having pleasantly exercised its talents, could return to weightier concerns," William Brown concluded in a retrospective article, "Sunday Baseball Comes to Boston."

Mayor Malcolm Nichols signed the city ordinance on January 30, ratifying the Sunday sports bill and granting licenses to the Braves and the Red Sox. The Braves would pay the maximum fee of $2,500.

The shenanigans weren't over just yet, though. The final act, the issuance of a final report on the FinCom hearings, had yet to be played out. The report had been slated for release by February 1, but its release was delayed.

Fuchs filed for a Sunday baseball permit on February 2, three days after the mayor signed the ordinance. With the FinCom report still to be released, the city council tabled the application review at its February 4 meeting and scheduled a public hearing on it for Friday, February 8.

On Thursday, February 7, the FinCom report was released and basically punted the situation to Suffolk County district attorney Foley. The two findings of the report were:

1. There was no evidence presented at the hearing that any of the 12 councilors whose names Lynch is alleged to have given Fuchs authorized him to use their names or to represent them.
2. The name of every city councilor who voted to table the Sunday baseball order at the meeting of December 17 was on the list of names alleged by Adams to have been given him by Fuchs prior to November 30.

13. Bribery Scandal Soiled It

"While the report of the finance commission of its investigation into the Sunday baseball scandal, made public last night, found an 'array of very suspicious characters' it was virtually a whitewash of all accused parties to the controversy by reason of inconclusive findings as to responsibility," the *Boston Herald* reported. "The commission passed the question of future action, if any, to District Attorney William J. Foley."[20]

At the city council's public hearing the next day on a Sunday baseball permit for the Braves, Adams was grilled—essentially one last skewering of the Braves. The Braves finally got their permit approved at the February 11 city council meeting, and the National League could finally issue its official schedule for the 1929 season.

To be able to play Sunday baseball at Braves Field, Judge Fuchs spent nearly a quarter of million dollars to influence voters to approve Sunday sports in Massachusetts. According to Harold Kaese, author of *Boston Braves*, "Fuchs admits he spent close to $200,000 out of his own pocket. A million booklets were printed and four million sample ballots were printed. Placards were placed in every streetcar."[21]

While Fuchs escaped damage at the FinCom hearings, except perhaps to his reputation, the saga was not yet over. Two days after the city council granted the Braves a permit for Sunday baseball, District Attorney Foley issued complaints on February 13 "as to allegations that there were certain inaccuracies in the return of expenses filed by the Outdoor Recreation League that violated the provisions of the corrupt practices act."[22]

The initial hearing, where officials from both the League and Braves needed to answer the charges, was scheduled for municipal court on February 20.

Unlike the politically charged FinCom hearings that precipitated extensive newspaper coverage, the actual court proceedings associated with the resulting legal charges against the Boston Braves barely made a ripple in the news.

The case was concluded on May 12, when Judge Joseph Sheehan imposed a $1,000 fine upon the Boston National League Baseball Company after a plea of nolo contendre to a count charging the expenditure of money to influence the vote of a question submitted to the voters. Brusse of the Outdoor Recreation League also pleaded no contest to the charge of filing a false statement of expenses of a political committee. He was fined $200.[23]

One unanswered question surrounds the FinCom hearings. Why did Adams put the bribery allegations before the public in December 1928 and apparently not try to resolve matters through private channels?

The reason most likely was not the one he gave in his January 3 testimony at the FinCom hearings. There Adams said he did it because it was "his public duty."[24]

Adams, owner of the First National chain of supermarkets as well as the Boston Bruins hockey team, had other possible motivations.

He may have been concerned that without Sunday baseball, Fuchs would have been unable to repay the $250,000 that Adams had invested in the Braves operation earlier in 1928. Public disclosure would exert pressure on Fuchs to run a financially sound business.[25]

Adams may well have been concerned about the impact to his own sports operation, the Bruins hockey team and the new Boston Garden, which opened just weeks earlier on November 14. If the city council could hold up Fuchs and the Braves, at what cost would Adams get a permit for Sunday hockey games at the Garden?

This latter conjecture was a distinct possibility since the Bruins were having a successful 1928–29 National Hockey League season, which culminated in the team winning its first Stanley Cup championship in March 1929.

Since Fuchs had led the fight for acceptance of Sunday baseball in Boston, the Braves were accorded the distinction of hosting the initial Sunday game in Boston for the 1929 season. When the National League schedule was released on February 13, the Braves were slated to play the New York Giants on Sunday, April 21, at Braves Field.

As if the whipping in the FinCom hearings weren't enough, the Braves seemed to be without luck in 1929, as if the Lord's Day Alliance were exacting retribution for the playing of Sunday baseball in Boston by declaring that it rain on Sunday. Not every Sunday, just the ones that the Braves were scheduled to play.

After an all-day soaking the day before, it also rained on Sunday, April 21, to cancel the game with the Giants and ruin the festivities for the first major league game on Sunday in Boston. Thus, the Red Sox had the honor of playing the first Sunday baseball game in Boston the following week on April 28.

"Major league Sunday baseball became a reality in Boston yesterday afternoon," the *Boston Globe* reported, "when upwards of 22,000 fans defied discouraging weather conditions to see the Athletics defeat the Red Sox 7 to 3 at Braves Field in the first scheduled Sunday game between two major league teams ever played in this city."[26]

The Red Sox couldn't play at Fenway Park on Sundays because the new law specified that games weren't permitted within 1000 feet of a church to appease the law's religious opponents. The Church of the Disciples, a Unitarian church, located at 60 Peterborough Street at the corner of Jersey

Street, was within 1000 feet of Fenway Park, prohibiting Red Sox owner Bob Quinn from scheduling Sunday games at his own playing field.[27]

Quinn, however, had little difficulty coming to terms with Fuchs over the use of Braves Field for Sundays, given the pummeling that Fuchs took over the FinCom hearings, and no separate permit was required for the Red Sox by the city council.[28]

"The attitude and behavior of the crowd was a practical demonstration of the fact that a baseball field is a far healthier spot than a street corner or a back room, even if you have to pay Bob Quinn or Emil Fuchs to get there," wrote *Boston Globe* writer Dave Egan of that initial Sunday game. In a satirical column, Egan went on to write about the sin of pocketing a foul ball and how disappointed the "Anti-Enjoyment of Anything League" must have been.[29]

The weather was better for the Braves' true Sunday opener on May 5, although spitballer Burleigh Grimes spoiled the event that Fuchs had worked so hard to achieve, as the Pittsburgh Pirates defeated the Braves before a crowd of 35,000.

Grimes "held the Tribe to seven hits, had the luck commonly associated with the devil, and at any rate hung up a 7 to 2 verdict for the Buccaneers against the still first-place Braves," the *Boston Globe* reported of the 8–3 Braves.[30]

Boston hit into three double plays that day, and the seemingly unusual occurrences plaguing the Braves on Sunday continued as the Braves hit into a weird triple play. With Heinie Mueller on third and Rabbit Maranville on first, Al Spohrer topped the ball to Grimes at the mound. Grimes got Mueller in a rundown between third and home, then Spohrer was nipped trying to make second base on the play. When Maranville tried to score after the Spohrer play, he was thrown out at the plate.

The Braves lost to Cincinnati 9–3 the next Sunday, May 12, before 25,000 fans. And the inauspicious start to Sunday baseball for the Braves continued a week later on May 19 when it rained again, canceling the game with the Phillies. Two of the first four Sunday games on the Braves schedule were rained out; a third rainout occurred two months later on July 14.

One consolation for the Braves was that the team could finally stop making those one-day trips to New York City for a single game on Sunday at Ebbets Field or the Polo Grounds. While the Braves were down to only one such excursion in 1928, to the Polo Grounds on April 29, two other one-day series with the Giants and Dodgers were also piggybacked onto a longer series with the other team (April 19 and July 1) causing a bit more road-trip movement.

Brooklyn was one loser in Sunday baseball arriving in Boston. The

Dodgers had an overbalanced Sunday schedule at Ebbets Field, compared to other National League teams, since Brooklyn was an easy train ride for both the Braves and the Phillies to play Sunday due to their respective home cities not permitting Sunday games. As a tradeoff, the Dodgers did have fewer holiday and Saturday dates. Washington enjoyed a similar treatment in the American League to accommodate Sunday play for the Philadelphia Athletics

With the Braves able to play on Sunday in 1929, Brooklyn had just 18 Sunday dates scheduled for the season, down from 20 Sunday dates in 1928. The Dodgers still enjoyed a slight Sunday imbalance because the Phillies remained unable to play Sundays in Philadelphia.

Because Boston was a two-team major league city at the time, Boston was scheduled to enjoy Sunday baseball every weekend of the 1929 season at the Wigwam, as Braves Field was affectionately referred to.

The Red Sox played .500 ball at Braves Field on Sundays in 1929, with a 7–7 record in their 13 Sunday dates (one was a doubleheader). This was a vast improvement over the team's total record of 58–96, which netted the Sox last place in the American League, 48 games behind the first-place Philadelphia Athletics.

The Braves had a 5–6 record in their nine Sunday home dates played in 1929 (three of the original 12 dates were rained out, two of which were made up as doubleheaders). The Braves, managed by Fuchs himself ostensibly to save a few bucks to recoup expenses from the Sunday baseball battle, also finished in last place, with a 56–98 overall record in the National League, 43 games behind the first-place Chicago Cubs.

Despite their lackluster playing success, both teams attracted large crowds for Sunday games at Braves Field. In fact, Sunday crowds accounted for a significant proportion of season attendance for both teams.

The Red Sox drew 394,600 in 1929, with, if newspaper accounts can be believed, four Sunday crowds (three against the Yankees) representing 26 percent of the total number of fans that paid to see the Red Sox that year. Of the Braves season attendance of 373,300, four Sunday games drew 28 percent of it.[31]

The Red Sox had the advantage of booking the New York Yankees and slugger Babe Ruth for three Sunday games in 1929. Ruth didn't disappoint the Boston fans with his hitting as the Yanks won all three games. On May 26, Ruth went 4 for 5 in a 15–4 rout of the Red Sox, hitting a home run to go with two singles and a double. On June 30, Ruth hit a two-run homer off Sox pitcher Danny MacFayden, which turned out to be the decisive blow in a 6–4 victory. Then on September 1, Ruth hit his 40th home run of the season in another 6–4 win over the Red Sox.

A two-hit shutout by Ed Morris on August 4 against the White Sox was the highlight of the 1929 Sunday season, as the Red Sox won 8–0 for one of Morris' 14 victories in an otherwise bleak season for the Sox.

The Braves were able to make up two of the Sunday rainouts by scheduling Sunday doubleheaders on June 23 and July 21. But with just a four-hour window in the Sunday baseball law (games could only be played between 2:00 and 6:00), finishing the second game sometimes was problematic.

In the June 23 doubleheader, the second game was stopped to comply with the law when 6:00 neared, after the Phillies had batted in the top of the seventh inning. The Braves had staged a late rally to score seven runs in the bottom of the sixth inning to pull ahead of the Phillies 7–5, which was how the game ended. In the July 21 doubleheader, the teams managed to get in nine innings in both games, as the Braves won both from the Cardinals, 4–2 and 4–3.[32]

A 1930 doubleheader, however, raised a ruckus after a rule was adopted to not start any inning after 5:40 to ensure that the game would fairly end by 6:00. On July 13, the Braves won the opener against the Cubs 2–1. Leading 3–0 in the eighth inning of the second game, the Braves stalled considerably trying to get to 5:40 before the ninth inning started. Rabbit Maranville fouled off several pitches with check swings to try to kill time.

But the ninth inning did begin, and the Cubs rallied to score four runs. Knowing that time was running out, the Cubs' Gabby Hartnett allowed himself to be thrown out half-heartedly trying to steal third base, and Footsie Blair purposely struck out to end the half inning.

At 5:55 the Braves went to bat and George Sisler singled. After Buster Chatham fouled off a half dozen balls before finally striking out, Jimmy Welsh doubled to put Braves on second and third with one out when the clock struck 6:00. Police lieutenant McCloskey then took the field and warned the umpires about the Sunday law. Umpire Quigley halted the game and declared the Braves the winner, with the score reverting back to the last complete inning.[33]

Manager Joe McCarthy of the Cubs was a bit miffed at the ruling that negated the four runs scored by his team in the top of the ninth inning, but no one had anticipated that 20 minutes wouldn't be enough time to complete a full inning. That was almost double the usual 12 minutes it normally took to play an inning at that time, according to the umpires interviewed after the game.

The continuing political changes in Massachusetts after the 1928 election enabled the Red Sox to finally play Sunday games in Fenway Park by 1932. The Democrats cut further into the Republican majority in the 1930 state election, including the first Democratic governor in 15 years (Joseph Ely) and 17 additional members of the House of Representatives (now 97 of 240). This made it easier to push through an amendment to the 1000-foot clause of the Sunday sports law regarding proximity to a church.[34]

Although unsuccessful in getting the law changed in 1931, the law was amended in May 1932.

As originally introduced, the bill reduced the required distance from 1000 feet to 750 feet. The legislature modified the bill, however, to make it a special bill just for the Red Sox, permitting Sunday games at Fenway "as now located," lest there be any finagling about moving the park to another location closer to a church.[35]

The last Red Sox Sunday game at Braves Field, a doubleheader with the Philadelphia Athletics, occurred on May 29. "Hereafter, the Red Sox can play their Sunday games at Fenway Park," the *Boston Globe* noted. "They could have played there today, according to law, but for the reason there is a memorial mass late in the forenoon."[36]

The church that forced the Boston Red Sox to play Sunday games at Braves Field from 1929 to 1932, rather than at Fenway Park, since Massachusetts law forbid Sunday games within 1000 feet of a church. Today, the church is the Boston Temple of the Seventh Day Adventist Church; in 1929, it was the Church of the Disciples. (Author's collection)

After a lengthy road trip, the Red Sox returned for a home stand and played at Fenway on Sunday, July 3, against the Yankees. The first-place Yankees pasted the last-place Red Sox 13–2, scoring nine runs in the sixth inning. Boston stood at 14–57 following the first Sunday game at Fenway en route to a horrible 43–111 record for the 1932 season.

The Sporting News was right in its 1928 editorial: Sunday baseball did not guarantee profits for a ball club without a decent product on the field. The Red Sox and the Braves were both miserable ball teams during this period.

In the 11 seasons from 1922 through 1932, at least one of the two teams finished in last place in their respective leagues in 10 of the 11 years. In 1929, the first year of Sunday baseball in Boston, both teams finished in last place. The best finish during those 11 years was a fifth-place finish in 1932 by the Braves, with a 77–77 record. The Braves lost 100 games in a season four times during that 11-year stretch, the Red Sox five years topped by those 111 losses in 1932.

Bob Quinn stopped the financial bleeding by selling the Red Sox in February 1933 to a young millionaire named Tom Yawkey, who refurbished Fenway Park and rebuilt the ball club into a contender. The Red Sox are a team beloved by Bostonians to this day.

After the Braves compiled an ugly 38–115 record in the 1935 season and attracted a meager attendance of just 232,700, Fuchs defaulted on his note to Adams, forfeited his stock in the club, and was ousted as team president. Fuchs filed for bankruptcy in 1936.[37]

The new Braves owners, led by Charles Adams, ironically brought in former Red Sox owner Quinn as the new president of the Braves. Quinn changed the team name briefly to Bees, but the team had little on-field success.

More new owners came in and the Braves won the National League pennant in 1948, but Boston proved to be a tough place to make a buck as a two-team major league town. The Braves moved to Milwaukee for the 1953 season, leaving Boston fans with just one team to follow—the Red Sox—who played Sunday baseball thanks to the efforts 25 years earlier by Judge Fuchs and the Braves.

When Fuchs died in 1961, he was remembered as being "instrumental in bringing Sunday baseball to Massachusetts." But the aftermath continued to follow him as well, as his obituary in the *Boston Post* noted, "In his campaign, which led to a referendum approving Sunday baseball, the judge once charged that 13 Boston City Councilmen tried to hold him up for $5,000 each."[38]

Chapter 14

PHILADELPHIA AT LAST ADOPTED IT

As Boston basked in the euphoria of its first year of Sunday baseball in 1929, Philadelphia was celebrating as the Athletics captured the American League pennant for the first time in 15 years. Connie Mack's team cruised to a 104–46 record, good for an 18-game margin over the second-place Yankees.

In the 1929 World Series, the Athletics defeated the Chicago Cubs in five games. There were two memorable moments for the Athletics in the 1929 World Series. In the fourth game, the Athletics rallied for 10 runs in the seventh inning to overcome an 8–0 deficit to win 10–8. Then in the fifth game, the team mounted a three-run rally in the bottom of the ninth inning for a 3–2 victory to clinch the World Series title.

A less memorable moment for Philadelphia in the 1929 World Series was the inability to play the fifth game on the day following the fourth game that was played on Saturday, October 12. Because the 1794 Sunday law was still in effect in Pennsylvania, Sunday baseball games remained prohibited in the state, and thus the law forced the fifth game of the World Series to be played one day later on Monday, October 14.

It was the first time since 1918 that a Sunday game couldn't be played in the normal course of World Series scheduling. Pittsburgh, ostensibly another potential casualty of the Pennsylvania blue laws, had won the National League pennant in the odd-numbered years of 1925 and 1927 when the American League team was slotted for the middle three games to be played through the weekend. Pittsburgh thus averted the ignominy of a forced open date in the World Series that would have occurred had the Pirates won the National League pennant in an even-numbered year in the latter part of the 1920s.

But the Athletics didn't have as fortunate timing as the Pirates. Not only were the Athletics now the only American League team unable to play home games on Sunday, but that inability had also been spotlighted nationally with a forced open date in the 1929 World Series between the fourth and fifth games in Philadelphia.

With the failure to redress the legal status of Sunday games in Pennsylvania by way of a court decision after the 1926 test game at Shibe Park, Connie Mack and the Shibe family set out in 1930 to pursue a legislative change to permit Sunday baseball in Pennsylvania.

Mack, who usually steered clear of politics, endorsed a candidate that favored Sunday baseball. The Shibes also worked behind the scenes in Democratic circles to build support for a Sunday baseball bill. As Bruce Kuklick remarked in his book *To Every Thing a Season: Shibe Park and Urban Philadelphia*, "The willingness of the franchise to adopt a political stand measured the seriousness of the problem."[1]

Philadelphia citizens were certainly in favor of changing the blue laws to allow Sunday baseball. The *Philadelphia Record* newspaper polled registered voters in Philadelphia in 1930, with the results showing 235,000 for repeal of the blue laws, 12,000 for modification, and 42,000 against any change. The results, wrote the *Record*, were "a clear indication to any one but a blockhead politician that it was time for a change."[2]

The trick was to get the "blockhead politicians" to act.

To apply some political pressure, the Athletics entertained a proposal from the city of Camden, New Jersey, to construct a stadium to seat 50,000 people as the Sunday home of the Athletics. The stadium site would be within 10 minutes of Philadelphia City Hall. The Camden proposal was one of the first instances of an overt threat to use the stadium of a municipality in another state to try to secure favorable in-state legislative treatment.

"The Athletic management is going very slowly in accepting the proposal," said Charles Gartling, attorney for the Athletics. Gartling added, with a touch of bluntness rarely seen today in media relations, that the Athletics were "on the horns of a dilemma whether to encourage the progressiveness of the citizens of Camden at the expense of the backwardness of the citizens of Philadelphia and Pennsylvania."[3]

There was even another test game on August 3, 1930, to pursue the Sunday baseball issue in court. This time, though, two semi-pro teams played the game, as Passon Athletic Association played North Penn Athletic Association at Passon Athletic Field at 48th and Spruce Streets. The issue was whether the teams could take up a collection "to cover the expense of base ball bats, umpires, etc. not for a commercial reason or profits."[4]

In the fifth inning of the game, police arrested the managers of both teams, Malcolm McGowan and Edward Sherman, and the umpire, Ted Voorhees. The charge was disorderly conduct, though, rather than violation of the Sunday law. When, under advice of their attorney, they refused to pay the $10 fine plus court costs as imposed by Magistrate Louis Hamburg, all three were sentenced to 30-day terms in the Moyamensing Prison.[5]

Upon appeal, at a hearing before Judge Edwin Lewis on August 12, Lewis said that he saw no harm in taking up a collection at a Sunday ball game. "It is time the church people and the rest of the citizens of Philadelphia do away with all the rank hypocrisy regarding Sunday amusements," Judge Lewis concluded. "There is no use of us trying to tie up Sunday as it was fifty years ago."[6]

Lewis ruled the arrests illegal because there was no breach of peace and further declared that "collections at Sunday games, when not a disguise for admission fees or an attempt to commercialize the sport, were legitimate and permissible."[7]

With the Lewis ruling opening a crack in the 1794 Sunday law, legislation to authorize professional Sunday baseball seemed to have a greater chance of success.

With the Athletics capturing a second-straight World Series title in 1930, public opinion on its side, and a lobbying effort in the legislature, things looked mildly promising to try to obtain a Sunday baseball law in 1931.

The biggest challenge, though, was a daunting one—no liberalization of the 1794 blue laws had ever made it to a roll call vote in the Pennsylvania legislature. With this more than 125-year-old legacy as a very real impediment to legislative victory, Sunday baseball proponents mounted both front-door and back-door approaches to try to secure a Sunday baseball law in 1931.

Blue law-related bills were inevitably referred to the Law and Order Committee in the Pennsylvania legislature, which meant certain demise for a straightforward Sunday baseball bill. A more innocent modification of the blue laws, therefore, was proposed in the House—to extend the time of Sunday milk deliveries. The Schwartz bill, which provided for an extension of milk deliveries from 9:00 to 10:00 on Sunday mornings, served as the back-door approach for Sunday baseball proponents.

The "true" Sunday baseball bill was the Denning bill, which proposed to let the voters decide the Sunday baseball issue through a local-option referendum vehicle. Local option had been the key to Sunday baseball legalization in New York and Massachusetts. While local option had been introduced in the latter stages of the legislative process in those two states, Sunday baseball proponents in Pennsylvania led with local option.

The Schwartz milk bill, with its seemingly reasonable liberalization of the blue laws, possessed a decent chance to pass the House. What legislator would want to be viewed as denying children increased availability of milk?

As the milk bill passed through committee and reached the House floor, an historic occasion in itself, an amendment was added to provide for baseball on Sunday. Additional milk for children was not enough to overcome long-held Quaker objections to sports on Sunday. On April 21, the House narrowly defeated the blue law amendment by a slim 101–99 margin.[8]

The near victory of the back-door approach encouraged Sunday baseball proponents that a bill through the front door could possibly pass on its own merits. Three weeks later, on May 12, the House passed the Denning bill by a vote of 106–98, one more than the necessary constitutional majority. Supporters, however, admitted that they didn't have the votes in the Senate for the bill to pass the upper chamber of the legislature.[9]

Sure enough, a week later, the Senate Law and Order Committee quashed the Denning bill after a short 15-minute meeting and the bill never left the committee.

"Senate Body Kills Sunday Baseball Local Option Bill" was the headline on the front page of the *Philadelphia Inquirer* on May 20. "No record of the vote was taken," the *Inquirer* reported, "but it was indicated later that only seven of the members of the committee present [of 23 members] favored reporting the measure to the floor. 'Killed.' That was the cryptic announcement of Senator Chauncey W. Parkinson, chairman of the committee, as the lawmakers filed from the meeting room."[10]

Reaction from both sides of the issue was as expected. "It was a wise act on the part of an intelligent committee," said Thomas Mutchler, head of the Lord's Day Alliance. "I believe it meets with the approval of a large percentage of the Senate." Seeing the matter from a different perspective was Philadelphia councilman W. W. Roper, head of a group that had been fighting for a Sunday baseball law, who said, "The adverse action of the committee is, in my opinion, a reflection of only a small part of the sentiment of the people of the State."[11]

The Senate would continue to be a thorn in the side of Sunday baseball proponents in Pennsylvania. Since the Pennsylvania legislature was in session only once every two years, a Sunday baseball bill would have to wait until 1933 for further action.

The Great Depression began to take its toll on Philadelphia in 1931 with increased unemployment among its workers and greater financial concerns among its institutions. One of the latter was the Philadelphia Athletics.

Despite winning a third-straight American League pennant in 1931, the Athletics had fewer patrons at Shibe Park to watch Mack's stars—Lefty Grove, Mickey Cochrane, Jimmie Foxx, and Al Simmons—all future inductees to the Baseball Hall of Fame. Depression-era economics haunted the Athletics team. The team had a heavy payroll with its numerous star players that had brought it on-field success, but unemployed people could ill afford the luxury of paying the admission to Shibe Park.

"During the four years while we were contenders (1925–1928) more people passed through the turnstiles each year than when we were world champions (1929–1930)," Mack lamented in later years. "Figure that out in terms of human nature."[12]

By 1932, the three Pennsylvania teams—Athletics, Phillies, and Pirates—were the only teams left in the major leagues not able to play home games on Sundays. Because of this status, all three teams made frequent trips during their home stands to play in other league cities on Sundays to gain at least the visitor's share of Sunday gate revenue.

The Athletics often made the train trip to Washington to play the Senators on Sunday, with occasional one-day forays to New York to play the Yankees. The Phillies played many weekends in New York, playing the Giants at the Polo Grounds on one day and the Dodgers at Ebbets Field on the other day. The Pirates ventured from Pittsburgh frequently on one-day Sunday excursions to Cincinnati and Chicago.

In 1932, the Athletics made six one-game road trips for Sunday games in Washington. The one-day treks included four games between home games at Shibe Park (April 17, April 24, July 3, and September 4), one game before embarking on a western road trip (June 5), and the last game of the season (September 25).

Games in New York were usually bunched together in two- or three-game sets, but the Athletics did play a solitary Sunday game at Yankee Stadium that year on July 24.

The Athletics also made single-game trips between home games in 1932 to play on Sunday in Cleveland and Detroit. Desperate for revenue from Sunday baseball in the depths of the Great Depression, the Athletics made these lengthy overnight trips not once, but twice to each city in 1932. Single Sunday games in Cleveland were played on May 8 and July 10, while single Sunday games in Detroit were held on May 15 and July 17.

These were not casual excursions for the Athletics. While Washington was a mere 150 miles from Philadelphia and New York just 100 miles away, the trip to Cleveland covered 450 miles and the route to Detroit was 600 miles. The opposing team did travel with the Athletics on one leg of each of these trips, however, playing a series at Shibe Park that either ended on Saturday or began on Monday.

The July 10 game at League Park in Cleveland was a telling example of the financial plight of the Athletics and the toll that these one-game Sunday trips extracted from the team.

Prior to the Cleveland trip, the Chicago White Sox were in Philadelphia for a series at Shibe Park. Due to rainouts earlier in the season, the Athletics and White Sox wound up playing three consecutive doubleheaders on Thursday, Friday, and Saturday. The Athletics faced another doubleheader on Monday with the Indians following the return trip from Cleveland. They played nine games in five days, including a nearly 1000-mile round trip in a hot, stuffy train just to play one of the games — but it was a Sunday game.

To keep expenses down, Mack sent just 11 players to Cleveland for the July 10 game, with a reserve pitcher and catcher the only spare players to the nine-man starting lineup. In hindsight, the Athletics could have used a few more players.

Cleveland pounded Philadelphia starting pitcher Lew Krausse to score three runs in the first inning, so in the second inning Ed Rommel was called upon to pitch in relief. Since Rommel threw a knuckleball, eight innings of relief wouldn't be too much of a burden on his arm. If only Rommel had been so lucky. He needed to pitch 17 innings of relief, a still-standing American League record, as the July 10 game went 18 innings before the Athletics finally won 18–17.

"Rommel's right arm was growing weary after seventeen innings of heart-breaking labor," the *Philadelphia Inquirer* wrote of the pitching effort in relief of the departed Krausse. "Rommel was the only [extra] pitcher with the team and would have been forced to pitch until darkness halted the game had not either team scored."[13]

In addition to yielding 14 runs, Rommel gave up 29 hits to the Indians, including nine by Cleveland shortstop Johnny Burnett who set a major league record for hits made in a single game. Without the quirks of Sunday baseball scheduling in 1932, compounded by Connie Mack's bid to save a buck on transporting players, Burnett would have been just another good ballplayer among the countless forgotten in major league history. Instead, Burnett is the answer to a popular baseball trivia question.

Burnett had six hits in the regulation nine-inning game. He made five hits in his first five plate appearances, rapping out three singles, a double, and another single before striking out in the seventh inning. In the ninth inning, Burnett singled again, and he would have had an excellent, though not fabled, six-for-seven day at the plate had the game not gone into extra innings. Burnett had a double and two singles in the extra frames before flying out in the seventeenth inning in his last at-bat of the game.

The slugfest—both teams combined for 58 hits—should have ended in regulation. In the top of the ninth inning, with Cleveland ahead 14–13 and two outs, Indian first baseman Ed Morgan let Jimmy Dykes' ground ball scoot through his legs for an error to keep Philadelphia in the game. Foxx then singled-in two runs to put the Athletics ahead 15–14. Then in the bottom of the ninth inning, Cleveland scored to tie the game 15–15. With two outs and two men on base, Joe Vosmik hit a line drive to center field that looked like the game-winning hit, but Mule Haas made a running shoestring catch to send the game to extra innings.

After the ninth-inning action, the teams dueled each other for six scoreless innings from the tenth through the fifteenth innings. "Weary Indians and Philadelphians, stiff and creaking, plodded though the long shadows that almost hid the green turf, muttering to themselves," the *Cleveland Plain Dealer* described the lethargy of the extra innings. The teams scored two runs apiece in the sixteenth inning, before Philadelphia finally prevailed in the eighteen inning. At 7:06 that evening, "10,000 fans groaned as Rommel shot a third strike past Eddie Morgan to end the game."[14]

Three days after the 1932 baseball season concluded, on September 28, Philadelphia announced the sale of three players to the Chicago White Sox for the sum of $100,000. Leaving Philadelphia so that Mack could pay the team's bank loans were Al Simmons, Mule Haas, and Jimmy Dykes.

Baseball economics were simple in the 1930s. Income was derived almost solely from game attendance, while expenses were the payroll and park upkeep. Only 400,000 customers trudged into Shibe Park in 1932 to see the second-place Athletics, almost a 50 percent decrease from the 1930 attendance of 720,000. And the players wouldn't take kindly to a salary decrease.

Without the ability to play games on Sunday at Shibe Park, income was down to a level much lower than what was needed to support the expenses of a championship team. With the sale of three popular players, Mack sent a message to the politicians that a Sunday baseball law was required if the city wanted more championship teams at Shibe Park.

Politics were changing due to the Great Depression as well. Since the public blamed the Republican Party for the sad economic times, Democrats ousted Republicans in many jurisdictions. Franklin Roosevelt was elected president in November 1932 and took office in March 1933. Pennsylvania had a new Republican governor, Gifford Pinchot, but one of progressive bent. The Pennsylvania legislature also seated more Democrats than it had during the 1931 session, when a Sunday baseball bill came close to fruition.

Additionally, Maryland passed a Sunday baseball bill in 1932 so that minor league games could be played in Baltimore on Sundays with paid admissions. Since Maryland was an intensely conservative state like Pennsylvania, the change in Sunday baseball attitude there boded well for Pennsylvania.[15]

On February 7, 1933, the Schwartz bill easily passed the House by a vote of 126–76. The Schwartz bill provided for baseball and football games on Sundays between 2:00 and 6:00 in the afternoon at local option. As originally passed by the House, the bill construed local option to mean passage of a licensing ordinance by a municipality, so that Sunday baseball could be played in 1933. Voter referendums could be held later to validate the ordinances; if voters disapproved, the ordinances would become invalid.

The Senate objected to this implementation of the local-option concept and debated the issue for five weeks. Finally, after much back-room discussion, on March 14 the Schwartz bill reached a vote on the Senate floor. Sunday baseball proponents had anticipated a victory but were dismayed to learn that two senators seemingly switched sides on the issue. The bill went down to defeat 26–24.

"A gasp of amazement came from the gallery when Senator McClure of Delaware County voted 'no' when his name was called," one newspaper account described the proceedings. "Senator Owlett of Tioga County likewise had been counted 'safe' by the modificationists."[16]

"To the baseball-minded it appeared that McClure stepped into the razberry balcony of baseball's hall of fame," the *Philadelphia Inquirer* commented on the senator's vote. "He moved into a niche in a section set apart for the worshippers of Casey, who fanned the breeze in Mudville; of Snodgrass, with his $100,000 muff; and of course Merkle, who forgot to touch first base." Continuing with the baseball metaphors, the *Inquirer* added, "McClure, sometimes referred to as the cleanup hitter of the Republican organization, had his chance. And like Casey he took three fast ones and went back to the bench. Had McClure come through with as much as a Texas Leaguer, the jig would have been up."[17]

Sabbatarian groups were obviously happy with the outcome.

"I am very much pleased by the vote, but I cannot understand the attitude of the men who backed this bill," said the Rev. William Forney, head of the Sabbath observance group that fought the measure, about what he considered a tactical blunder. "They brought here Connie Mack and others who stood to benefit financially by its passage."[18]

Mack, who had spoken at the Law and Order Committee hearings in both the House and the Senate, said from the Athletics spring training grounds in Fort Myers, Florida, that the team was going to have a "desperate struggle for existence" without Sunday baseball. "We cannot meet our payrolls playing only on seventy-seven weekdays at home," Mack said. "Last year we ended the season with a big deficit, although finishing in second place, and that's why I had to sell Al Simmons, Jimmy Dykes, and George Haas to get the money to make up for our losses."[19]

Concerned that municipal councils would railroad through a Sunday baseball ordinance where voters would actually disapprove of the notion, Senator McClure wanted the voter referendums to come first before the municipal ordinances did. "I believe the people are entitled to determine for themselves whether they want base ball and foot ball on Sunday," McClure said, adding that he hadn't changed his attitude about Sunday baseball "in the form that it was presented in the Senate." McClure also wanted two referendums, one statewide and the other local. If the majority statewide approved of the issue, then the local referendums would determine the wishes of the community.[20]

On March 20, McClure introduced an amendment to the Schwartz bill in the Senate to provide for the two referendums, which the Senate passed 26–23. The House, however, rejected the Senate amendment without one dissenting vote, since the statewide referendum would eliminate all chance of having Sunday baseball in 1933. With the House and Senate at a stalemate, the Schwartz bill went to a conference committee to resolve the differences.

This was only the beginning of the Sunday baseball soap opera.

Camden, New Jersey, returned with another invitation for the Athletics to play in that state. Unlike the earlier stadium overtures, the Athletics seemed quite serious about the 1933 Camden proposal.

Ever since the 1926 test game at Shibe Park, Camden had been courting the Athletics, once even getting president Tom Shibe to inspect two sites in 1931. The most promising site was adjacent to the Camden Airport in Pennsauken township, which Shibe pronounced "very favorable." Late in March 1933 after the defeat of the Schwartz bill in the Senate, the Camden County Chamber of Commerce enticed John Shibe to visit more proposed playing sites, another near the airport and one at the Crescent Country Club where there was an existing playing field.[21]

Mayor Harry Bacharach of Atlantic City, New Jersey, also offered his city as a possible Sunday site for the Athletics. "They would have huge crowds to draw from here on Sundays," Bacharach postured. "Atlantic City is almost as close to Philadelphia by train as Shibe Park is from West Philadelphia by trolley."[22]

With New Jersey very interested in securing the Sunday games of the two Philadelphia teams, Pennsylvania was still playing hard to get. On the same day that Shibe met with New Jersey officials, the press speculated that should the Schwartz bill pass, Governor Pinchot would veto it.

14. Philadelphia at Last Adopted It

On March 27, the conferees for the House and Senate agreed to eliminate the statewide referendum provision and only have referendums in the individual communities. As with most all compromises, though, there was a "but," and in this case a big "but"—the referendums could not be held until November that year.

Sunday baseball proponents appeared victorious. But there was still no assurance that the Senate would pass this version of the Schwartz bill, nor that Governor Pinchot would sign it into law if the Senate did pass it. What was clear, though, was that Sunday baseball would not occur in 1933. This was not good news for either Philadelphia club, as the Phillies were just as mired in financial difficulties as were the Athletics.

With no possibility of Sunday baseball in Pennsylvania in 1933, the National League finally released its schedule for the 1933 season on the day the compromise was announced. The league had delayed the release six weeks beyond the usual time, hoping that the Pennsylvania legislature would act favorably on the Schwartz bill. The league had drawn up two schedules, one with Pennsylvania Sunday home dates and the other without them, and reluctantly released the latter.

Brooklyn was scheduled for 22 Sunday games in 1933, nearly twice the usual number accorded a team, in order to play both the Phillies and Pirates as often as possible on their vacant Sunday home dates.

The Phillies played five Sundays at Ebbets Field in one-game road trips in 1933, with three such trips to Boston and one to New York. The Pirates played two Sundays in Brooklyn and six Sundays in Cincinnati.

Although the Athletics played four Sundays games in Washington via one-game road trips in 1933, the club generally avoided Sunday opportunities that year while staging home stands at Shibe Park. There were no strenuous scheduling gymnastics to play in Cleveland and Detroit on Sundays, unlike the trips there made in 1932. The last one-game road trip of the Sunday baseball era occurred on October 1, 1933, when the Athletics defeated Washington 3–0 at Griffith Stadium, a game highlighted by the pinch-hitting appearance of 57-year-old Nick Altrock for the Senators.

Both the House and Senate passed the compromise Schwartz bill, the House 140–51 and the Senate 27–22. On April 11, the day before the opening of the 1933 baseball season, the Sunday sports bill was sent to Governor Pinchot for his signature.

Also on April 11, the New Jersey Assembly and Senate passed a home-rule bill for Sunday baseball, which provided for municipal referendums to determine its applicability within the state. This bill set up the situation for Camden to legally allow Sunday baseball within its borders. New Jersey governor Moore promptly signed the bill on April 12, while

Pennsylvania governor Pinchot deliberated signing his state's Sunday baseball bill.

"Sports circles in Philadelphia today watched moves to legalize Sunday athletics in both Pennsylvania and New Jersey and wondered which side of the Delaware River would see the first games," the *New York Times* remarked about the Sunday baseball battle.[23]

Before Mack left to go to Washington for his team's opening day game with the Senators on April 12, he visited Governor Pinchot to urge him to sign the Schwartz bill. Mack left the meeting without any assurances that Pinchot would sign the bill.

The Athletics lost the opener in Washington 4–1 as Franklin Roosevelt threw out the first ball. FDR smiled and posed for pictures with the baseball in his hand and "then suddenly threw it high into the air without rising from his seat," hinting at his disability that was so assiduously hidden from the public during his four terms as president. One of the umpires caught FDR's errant toss.[24]

Pinchot was balancing a number of political issues at the time the Schwartz bill was passed, one of which was creating an unemployment relief program. Even three years deep into the Great Depression, there was great consternation among many citizens (and politicians) about the government using taxpayer dollars to fund aid for the unemployed.

The governor called for a public hearing on the Schwartz bill to be held on April 18, giving him a few more days to decide whether to sign the bill into law. At the public hearing, the Sabbatarians may have overplayed their hand.

C. Burgess Taylor, a member of the Philadelphia Registration Committee, made the observation that "hoodlums flock to the ball yards to see the professional players perform." Taylor's comment would probably have been long forgotten, and not used to ridicule the blue law supporters, had the Rev. William Forney not strayed beyond the usual law and religion arguments for the blue laws in his remarks before the governor at the hearing. "Dr. Forney injected a political note, and by inference, at least, made it plain the foes of the bill would feel they had been betrayed if the governor gives it approval," the *Philadelphia Inquirer* reported. "I want to assure you," Forney told the governor, "that the group here are your friends. They have been your supporters and are with you in your fights."[25]

The *Inquirer* reported that Pinchot had no visible reaction to Forney's statement. Judged by his later actions, though, the governor must have been taken aback, if not shocked, to hear the Sabbatarians overtly hinting at political retribution if he signed the Sunday sports bill. Pinchot could have easily vetoed the Schwartz bill, and the Senate almost assuredly would have upheld the veto. Proponents would have had a daunting task to rustle up seven additional votes, beyond the affirmative votes in the last Senate roll call on the bill, in order to override the veto.

Proponents of the Schwartz bill, after hearing their opponents speak and quite possibly have already turned the tide to their favor, made little attempt to impress the governor with legal or political arguments, and focused their remarks on the need to let voters decide the issue.

"Games are played now on Sunday in defiance of the law. It is far better that these games should be played legally," said Philadelphia councilman W. W. Roper. "We leave this bill with you confident that you will sign it and thereby permit the people themselves to settle the question."[26]

On the day following the public hearing, the Pennsylvania legislature recalled the Schwartz bill to amend it one more time, at the suggestion of the governor. The bill was amended to provide that 10 percent of admission prices to Sunday sports events would go to unemployment funds. With this amendment, Pinchot resolved two political issues at the same time, funding unemployment relief and okaying Sunday baseball.

Pinchot signed the Schwartz bill on April 25, reaching his decision only after "long, anxious, and prayerful consideration," according to his biographer.[27]

"I am emphatically opposed to the commercialization of the Sabbath," Pinchot said in a statement accompanying his signing of the bill. "But in a State which has Sunday trains, Sunday concerts, Sunday golf, Sunday tennis, and a host of Sunday activities of many kinds, the possible addition of baseball and football between the hours of 2 and 6, if the people of any locality vote for it, will not seriously change the present picture. For years anyone with money enough to play golf or tennis on Sunday morning or afternoon has been free to do so — law or no law. This unjust discrimination in favor of the rich and against the poor which has thus existed is one of my strongest reasons for signing this bill." Pinchot went on to conclude, "I have been warned that it will be politically expensive for me to sign this bill. In all probability that is true. But I am not concerned with politics. I am concerned with what I believe to be right — and I believe it is right to sign it."[28]

Pennsylvania voters never did elect Pinchot to another office in the state, although more so for his support of FDR than his signing of the Sunday sports bill. Pinchot unsuccessfully ran for the Republican nomination as U.S. Senator in 1936 and again for governor in 1938. He died in 1947. In honor of his leadership in forestry, the Columbia National Forest in Washington was renamed for Pinchot in 1949. Today the 1.3-million-acre Gifford Pinchot National Forest is best known as the location of the Mount St. Helens National Volcanic Monument.

Although the Schwartz bill was signed into law in April 1933, and Sunday baseball likely would be played in 1934, the damage was already done. The Philadelphia Athletics club continued to be ravaged financially and it needed Sunday baseball in 1933, not 1934, to operate in the black. By October, rumors were flying that the Athletics were going to sell off more players to raise cash.

"Connie Mack again yesterday was called upon to deny the reported baseball deals and sales which would take from this city Lefty Grove, Mickey Cochrane, Max Bishop, Rube Walberg, and George Earnshaw," the *Philadelphia Inquirer* reported early in November. Rumors had Grove going to Boston or Chicago and Cochrane to Detroit as player-manager. "Who are these persons who say I have made deals and will not announce them until after election day?" Mack asked, when queried about holding back information until after Philadelphia voters approved Sunday baseball at the polls.[29]

Mack denied the rumors, but they were indeed true. The deal to send Cochrane to Detroit as player-manager was hatched at the 1933 World Series, where the other deals no doubt were also struck.[30]

Voters who went to the polls on November 7 expecting to save the current Athletics team would be sorely disappointed in the eventual outcome of the ballot question:

> Do you favor the conduct, staging, and playing of baseball and football games regardless of whether an admission charge is made or incidental thereto, or whether labor or business is necessary to conduct, stage, or operate the same, between the hours of 2 and 6 Post Meridan on Sunday?[31]

Philadelphia and Pittsburgh voters overwhelmingly approved the Sunday sports referendum on November 7, as did practically all large cities in the state. Philadelphia approved the measure 370,858 to 57,740 as all 50 wards in the city returned favorable majorities (including the third ward with 2,108 for and just 78 against). Cities such as Altoona, Washington, and Coatsville refused to permit Sunday sports, although Logan township, where Altoona's ballpark was located, did vote "yes." Interior counties such as Union, Blair, Tioga, Snyder, and Mifflin all voted strongly against Sunday sports.[32]

The Pittsburgh City Council hurriedly passed an ordinance immediately after election results were announced to enable the Pittsburgh Pirates and Brooklyn Dodgers to play the first legal Sunday professional sports event in Pennsylvania on November 12 at Forbes Field. The baseball teams came out for a special game in the chilly air of November? No, these were the professional football teams of each city, which possessed the same name as their popular baseball brethren. The Dodgers defeated the Pirates 32–0, as Shipwreck Kelly scored three touchdowns before 12,000 Sunday patrons at Forbes Field.[33]

In Philadelphia, the city council, after some haggling over license fees, also rushed through an ordinance that was signed by Mayor J. Hampton Moore on November 10 to allow a football game that Sunday between the Philadelphia Eagles and the Chicago Bears. The two teams tied 3–3 before 17,850 at Phillies Park.[34]

The Phillies and Pirates would each get 12 Sunday home games on the 1934 National League schedule, which meant fewer such dates for Brooklyn, Cincinnati, and Chicago that had often hosted the two teams on Sundays. In the American League, Sunday games for the Athletics cut back the Sunday schedule in Washington.

Connie Mack, said to be jubilant at the election victory, offered the public these words: "I now want to promise Philadelphia and Pennsylvania that I am going to see to it that what we offer on Sunday can in no way be construed as harmful; rather that it will help make our opportunity for amusement more worthwhile."[35]

Mack's Sunday offering at Shibe Park would indeed "no way be construed as harmful," since he fielded a relatively harmless Athletics team in 1934 and beyond. Waiting a respectable five weeks following the election, Mack finally announced the poorly held secret that he had sold most of his remaining star players on the Athletics team.

"Grove, Cochrane Sold for $200,000" screamed a banner headline on page 1 of the *Philadelphia Inquirer* on December 13. Mack said the sales were necessary to meet bank notes coming due, but "with Sunday baseball a certainty next year, Messrs. Shibe and Mack are convinced that the finances of the club will improve."[36]

The deals were announced at the league meetings in Chicago. Grove went to the Red Sox along with Bishop and Walberg for $125,000. Cochrane went to the Tigers for $100,000 and catcher Johnny Pasek. Earnshaw and Pasek went to the White Sox for $20,000 and catcher Charlie Berry. The only remaining star with the Athletics was Jimmie Foxx, but he too would be gone after the 1935 season in a sale to the Red Sox.

Mack had seemingly duped the voters by withholding information about the sale of the star Athletics to obtain the right to play Sunday baseball. But Mack also had to decimate the team in order to remain financially solvent to continue to field an Athletics team to play on Sundays. It was a cruel resolution to the Sunday baseball issue for the Philadelphia Athletics and their fans.

The first legal Sunday baseball game in Philadelphia was played on April 8, 1934, when the Athletics took on the Phillies in an exhibition game at Shibe Park that was part of their annual pre-season city series. The Phillies won 8–1 before a crowd of 15,000 on a mellow spring day, as the *Philadelphia Inquirer* headlined "Mackmen Lose in First Legal Sabbath Game." The Sunday opener at Phillies Park was a week later on April 15, when the Athletics defeated the Phillies 4–3 before 11,000 to win the city series.[37]

In games that counted in the standings, the Sunday opener for the Athletics occurred on April 22 when it was Louis Schwartz Day at Shibe Park, to honor the man that had championed the Sunday baseball bill through the Pennsylvania legislature. The team gave Schwartz a silver loving cup to recognize his effort before bowing 4–3 to its former Sunday host, Washington, on a chilly day in front of 20,306 fans.

On April 29, the Phillies and Pirates made their Sunday debuts in National League action. The opponents in both games were also former hosts of the teams in one-day Sunday series. The Pirates defeated Cincinnati 9–5 at Forbes Field, while the Phillies lost to Brooklyn 8–7 at Phillies Park.

Philadelphia baseball fans eventually forgave Mack, but big crowds never materialized at Shibe Park for baseball on Sunday. Without a winning club, or even a team with a semblance of a chance for the pennant, the brand of baseball at Shibe Park was decidedly lower quality than the fans were used to with the 1929–1931 championship teams.

Beginning in 1938, Sunday baseball was played at Shibe Park nearly every Sunday when the Phillies became a tenant at the park, as Shibe Park joined Sportsman's Park as the only two-team ballparks in the major leagues.

While the fans may have forgiven Mack the politicians didn't. Mack may have received forbearance on one aspect of the blue laws with Sunday baseball, but the politicians withheld the benefits of further liberalizations of the blue laws as long as they could when it came to selling beer at Shibe Park.

When Prohibition ended in 1933, the Athletics tried unsuccessfully to obtain a beer permit for Shibe Park. The ability to sell beer in Shibe Park was withheld until "the A's had left the city and Connie Mack died," as one writer put it. Not until 1961 could beer be served at Shibe Park (then called Connie Mack Stadium), when beer became part of the plan to build a new stadium. Even then, beer sales were limited to Monday through Saturday. "Indeed, the sale of beer on Sundays did not occur until 1972, when baseball was being played in another park."[38]

After finally being able to play Sunday baseball in 1934, the Athletics stumbled along in the American League for another 20 years before leaving Philadelphia after the 1954 season for Kansas City. The promise of Sunday baseball and blue-law liberalization never quite materialized for the Athletics.

Chapter 15

LEGACY OF SUNDAY BASEBALL

In 1934, at last, all 16 major league teams could play home games on Sunday. There were no more legal battles to be waged over the propriety of playing major league baseball on the Lord's Day. Every Sunday, eight games could be scheduled without regard for the vagaries of whether Philadelphia, Boston, or Cleveland could or could not host such contests.

Beginning on April 22, 1934, every major league team played virtually every Sunday, unless bad weather cancelled the game. Only extraordinary situations prevented teams from engaging in a game on Sunday, such as April 9, 1972, and June 14, 1981, during player strikes and September 16, 2001, in the aftermath of the terrorist attacks.

Large crowds continued to fill major league ballparks on Sunday. Working people craved baseball on the only day many could realistically view a game, excepting holidays. Teams expanded ballparks to accommodate the crowds (no more overflow crowds in the outfield), and new facilities were built to stage the games.

Cleveland's Municipal Stadium, which opened in 1932, became the last Sunday-only ball grounds in 1936. The Indians staged weekday games at League Park and used the cavernous lakeside stadium for Sunday and holiday games (also night games beginning in 1939) until 1947 when the Indians used Municipal Stadium exclusively.[1]

With Sunday home games now legal in all major league cities, Sunday baseball's next greatest legacy was the Sunday doubleheader.

Before 1925, major league clubs rarely scheduled a single-admission doubleheader and only played doubleheaders when necessary to make up postponed games. Teams often did schedule two games on a holiday, but these usually were separate-admission morning and afternoon games.

When weather postponements made doubleheaders necessary, they'd normally be scheduled Monday through Friday, and only on Saturday or Sunday if absolutely necessary. Since the separate admission was lost with the postponement, the second game in essence became a "free" game for the spectators. Originally, in scheduling these doubleheaders, ball clubs sought to avoid hurting their best attendance days, which were Sunday where such games were legal or Saturday otherwise. Gradually, ball clubs saw the second "free" game as an opportunity to maximize incremental attendance on their best days. At worst, the second game was viewed as a desirable substitute for a small crowd attending a weekday game.

Saturday doubleheaders became common in the mid–1920s. Eastern teams that couldn't yet play Sunday baseball were frequent promoters of the Saturday doubleheader. Some of the western teams also held Sunday doubleheaders, particularly against weaker competition or when the eastern teams that couldn't play Sunday home games were in town.

In 1929, when only the Pennsylvania teams couldn't play Sunday baseball at home, Saturday doubleheaders still outnumbered Sunday doubleheaders in the period from July 4 to season-end, when most postponed games were made up.

The economic woes of the Great Depression changed this scheduling pattern, since fewer people could afford to attend baseball games due to the rampant unemployment in the country. When attendance plummeted at the ballparks beginning in 1930, several clubs moved the doubleheader from Saturday to Sunday to try to fill seats on the day that people who did continue to hold jobs could get to the ballpark.

Sunday doubleheaders outnumbered Saturday ones in 1930 during the same July 4 to season-end period. By 1931 half the Sunday schedule was routinely doubleheaders, as Sunday twinbills outnumbered Saturday ones almost two to one. There were even more Sunday doubleheaders in 1932, when for the first time on August 7, six of the eight Sunday dates were played as doubleheaders. On August 27, 1933, seven Sunday doubleheaders were played.

Saturday doubleheaders began to disappear in 1934 in favor of the Sunday doubleheader. The Saturday doubleheader persisted mostly in Philadelphia, Pittsburgh, Detroit, and Washington (the former two cities with the newfound ability in 1934 to play Sunday home games). But even the Pirates and the Phillies joined the Sunday doubleheader parade in 1935.

By 1937, the Saturday doubleheader had all but faded away in most major league cities due to the popularity of the Sunday doubleheader. Even the Philadelphia Athletics tossed in the towel in 1937 and switched from Saturday to Sunday doubleheaders. On Sunday, June 30, 1940, a full slate of eight doubleheaders was played by the 16 teams. Teams now ordinarily played doubleheaders on Sunday, with the single game on the Lord's Day much less common. By 1942, the major leagues also began inserting Sunday doubleheaders on their pre-season schedules rather than rearrange the schedule mid-season due to early-season postponements.

In 1939, aging Ted Lyons of the White Sox began hurling his knuckleball just once a week and gained renown as a "Sunday pitcher."

"By what appears to have been the combination of a matter of chance and an unusual amount of rain along the eastern seaboard, Lyons started games on Sunday, May 21; Tueday, May 30; Sunday, June 4; and Sunday, June 11," one writer described the fortuitous development of Lyons as a Sunday pitcher. "Lyons won all of those games, and moreover, the Sox, who finished in sixth place the year before, were drawing significantly larger crowds whenever the right-hander took the mound." After the 38-year-old Lyons won four more consecutive Sunday starts, "from June of 1939 through his last full season in 1942 Lyons generally started games on Sunday only."[2]

Lyons was 14–6 in 1939. After two more solid seasons, Lyons again posted a 14–6 mark in 1942 as a 41-year-old generally taking the mound just once a week on the Lord's Day. In 13 Sunday games in 1942 Lyons compiled a 10–3 record, all but one game being the first game of a doubleheader. Seven of those 13 Sunday games were home games at Comiskey Park, where Lyons was 6–1. Lyons led the American League with a 2.10 earned run average before entering the military service for the remainder of World War II.[3]

The practice of regular Sunday doubleheaders enabled Lyons to extend his playing career. Because Chicago often played a doubleheader on Sunday in those years, having Lyons pitch just one game a week wasn't a burden for Chicago manager Jimmy Dykes. Lyons didn't disrupt the Chicago pitching rotation, but rather he helped to stabilize it. Lyons was always there to pitch the first game of the Sunday doubleheader, with whoever was next in the regular rotation tapped for the second game.

World War II accentuated the need for the Sunday doubleheader, as workers labored long hours six days a week to support the war effort and many servicemen were stationed stateside. During the four war years, 1942–1945, the Sunday doubleheader became a staple of the major league baseball scene. Nearly every Sunday from May through August, all 16 teams engaged in two games on the Lord's Day to entertain civilians and military personnel and to help take their minds off the war.

Although Sunday laws were liberalized in Massachusetts and Pennsylvania to allow games on the Lord's Day, Sunday laws remained a slight thorn in the side of the major league teams when it came to the increasingly popular Sunday doubleheader. The laws in Massachusetts and Pennsylvania continued to provide for an ending time beyond which Sunday games could not continue, called the "Sunday curfew" by many people.

Originally 6:00 in the evening in both states, the laws were slightly liberalized over the years to permit games to continue until 6:30 and 7:00. And the laws were enforced. When the second game of the May 9, 1948, Sunday doubleheader in Pittsburgh didn't end until 7:40, the city fined the club $100 for violating the Sunday law.[4]

Sunday curfews were a vexing problem, since certain game situations presented the opportunity for teams to practice skullduggery. If a team rallied to take the lead in what would be the final inning, if completed, that team was prone to hurry up by intentionally making outs to get the inning completed and on the books to obtain the victory. Conversely, the team that lost the lead in that situation was prone to stall so that the inning would fail to be completed by the curfew. If the stall was successful, the rally would be negated and the team would escape a loss since the score would revert to the tally at the end of the last completed inning.

In the second game of the September 3, 1939, Sunday doubleheader between the Red Sox and the Yankees at Fenway Park, the game was tied 5–5 after seven innings as the 6:30 Sunday curfew neared. The Yankees rallied for two runs in the top of the eighth inning to make the score 7–5 with less than ten minutes to the curfew.

With two runners on base, Boston pitcher Joe Heving then tried to execute a stall tactic by intentionally walking Babe Dahlgren. Heving threw the first pitch wide, but Dahlgren, trying to execute a hurry-up tactic, swung at the wide serve for a called strike. After Dahlgren also swung at Heving's next wide throw, George Selkirk, the Yankee runner on third base, executed another hurry-up tactic when he "deliberately ran up from third base to be tagged out by catcher Johnny Peacock." On Heving's next pitch, "Gordon repeated the move" for the third out.[5]

Executing another time-proven stall tactic, Boston manager Joe Cronin immediately set to arguing with the umpires about the validity of the two Yankee suicide outs at home plate. As Cronin jawed with the umps, the Boston fans showed their displeasure with New York's hurry-up antics by showering the field with bottles (drinks in paper cups were yet to come). As the curfew arrived, umpire Cal Hubbard declared the game forfeited to New York due to the unplayable field.[6]

Such shenanigans led the Massachusetts legislature to modify the Sunday baseball law in 1943 to provide for the completion of a second game of a Sunday doubleheader, provided the game started before 4:30.

To halt the curfew abuses, the National League adopted a suspended-game rule during the war years when civilian travel restrictions often abbreviated games when one of the teams needed to make train connections. "It eliminated stalling in games about to be halted by Sunday curfew," the *New*

York Times reported in 1949, "but fell out of favor because it also brought about considerable confusion when the schedule became cluttered up with unfinished encounters." A suspended game was resumed at the point the curfew stopped the game when both teams met again in the same place. This was often weeks away, though, since Sunday was usually the last game of a series between two teams.[7]

The leagues went back and forth on the issue. Suspended games were abandoned by the National League after 1946 but reinstated for the 1950 season. The American League adopted a similar rule for the 1952 season, but dropped it after the 1954 season when the issue disappeared due to the transfer of the Philadelphia franchise to Kansas City. The Sunday curfew then only applied to teams based in Pennsylvania, namely the Phillies and the Pirates in the National League.

With games taking longer to complete, more and more second games of Sunday doubleheaders in Philadelphia ended in suspended games, resulting in considerable fan confusion. For instance, the suspended game from the April 28, 1957, Sunday doubleheader between the Philadelphia Phillies and the New York Giants wasn't finished until 16 weeks later on August 16 when the Giants next returned to Philadelphia for a single game (the July 4 date in Philadelphia was already scheduled as a doubleheader).

The Giants were ahead 8–7 in the last of the seventh inning of the April 28 game, with the Phillies at bat and the tying run on second base, when the Sunday curfew under Pennsylvania law stopped the game at 7:00. Needless to say, it was an unsatisfactory finish for Philadelphia fans at the game or listening to it on radio, as well as New York fans since the Giants had lost the first game 11–2 and "at the end, all they had to show for their efforts was the hope of a possible victory some time next August." When the suspended game was finally resumed on August 16, New York pitcher Marv Grissom summarily retired eight straight Philadelphia batters to preserve the 8–7 New York victory, unchanged from the score 16 weeks earlier.[8]

By mid-season 1958, the second game of four of five Sunday doubleheaders in Philadelphia couldn't be completed by the 7:00 curfew and thus resulted in suspended games. Working up an interest in the game once resumed wasn't very appetizing to baseball fans, which one writer likened to "a serving of warmed up leftovers from dinner the night before last."[9]

In 1959, the Pennsylvania legislature finally eliminated the last Sunday curfew in major league baseball, providing for the completion of the game as long as it started before 6:00 in the evening. The House vote was 128–73, with many legislators still uncomfortable with liberalization of the Sunday laws. Governor Lawrence signed the bill on July 31, ending the baseball stoppages to ensure that "an activity not deemed sinful at 3 P.M. doesn't become so at 7:01 P.M." One wag noted that the Sunday curfew "probably did more to provoke sinning in terms of anger and profanity than it ever did to encourage less worldly activities."[10]

In the post-war era, the Sunday doubleheader remained a fixture of major league scheduling for another 25 years. The Sunday doubleheader survived, though, for very different reasons than those that drove its popularity in the 1930s.

"The weekend" became a social institution in the aftermath of World War II, as the normal workweek evolved to five days, creating two consecutive days off for most working people. Suddenly, attending a ball game on Saturday afternoon was a pleasure many more people could enjoy. Saturday at the ballpark became a novelty for working people, just as Sunday had been in the early days of the acceptance of Sunday baseball. Television, an amusement popularized by the greater amount of free time people had, also enhanced the image of Saturday at the ballpark through the televising of the "Saturday Game of the Week."

Night baseball, a novelty in the major leagues before the war, became nearly universal by 1948 as all teams, except the Chicago Cubs, installed lights to play games in the evening. Working people could now also more easily attend games during the week when night games were scheduled.

Sunday lost its special nature, since working people could now attend ball games far more frequently than before the war, either on Saturday afternoon or at night during the week. By 1950, the term "Sunday baseball," once an issue that evoked as much emotion as "abortion" does today, had lost its meaning in society and was all but forgotten. If anything, "Sunday baseball" now meant "Sunday doubleheader." People had discarded memories of the titanic struggle to play major league baseball on the Lord's Day, just as they had forgotten how the ice-cream sundae, now eaten on any day of the week, came to exist as an evasion of Sabbatarian concerns.[11]

On April 18, 1954, the first major league Sunday game in Baltimore, following the relocation there of the St. Louis Browns franchise, was viewed as a natural event even though Sunday baseball with paid admissions had been illegal there as late as 1932, just two decades earlier.

While both the American and National Leagues embraced night baseball, both leagues prohibited night games on Sunday, the last vestiges of special scheduling for the Lord's Day. The availability of artificial lighting installed for night games gave rise to a new set of concerns over completion of Sunday doubleheaders—could the lights be turned on to complete the second game of a Sunday doubleheader?

Intricate rules were devised regarding when lights could and could not be used for a Sunday game. At first, lights could not be used at all on Sunday. This rule created additional Sunday curfews for all teams, and worse, a curfew based on the variable timing of sunset. By the 1954, the general rule in the National League was that lights could be turned on to complete games started in daylight on Sunday, but the second game of a Sunday doubleheader couldn't start under lights after 6:00. But confusion sometimes still occurred.

At the July 18, 1954, Sunday doubleheader in St. Louis between the Phillies and the Cardinals, the first game was delayed by rain in the seventh inning for more than an hour, causing the second game to start after 6:00. There was some confusion as to whether the lights could later be turned on to complete the game; the public address system even announced that the lights wouldn't be turned on. Since the second game had started in daylight, the National League clarified following the game that the lights could have been used if necessary.

With the Phillies ahead 8–1 in the fifth inning of the second game, St. Louis manager Eddie Stanky tried his best to stall, believing that the game wouldn't count if it was called by darkness before the end of the fifth inning (five innings were needed for a suspended game to kick in). In the fifth inning, Stanky brought in two new relief pitchers to kill time. When Stanky waived for Tom Poholsky to come in from the bullpen as a third relief pitcher, umpire Babe Pinelli forfeited the game to the Phillies due to Stanky's antics. At this point, "players on both teams swarmed onto the field swinging, punching, and wrestling in one of the worst riots seen here since the old St. Louis Browns left town," one newspaper reported.[12]

Sunday remained a special day at the ballpark after the war because the doubleheader continued to draw good crowds, despite the fact that baseball competed with other amusement opportunities that baseball fans increasingly pursued, especially now that automobile transportation was so universal. Sunday during the 1950s and the 1960s usually meant a doubleheader at most major league ballparks.

As night baseball during the week gained increasing popularity, and other amusement opportunities siphoned off ballpark patrons during the weekend, baseball clubs gradually viewed the Sunday doubleheader as less-desirable scheduling. Once night baseball completely replaced day games Monday through Friday for most teams, the economic rationale for Sunday doubleheaders virtually disappeared. The "free" second game was less effective at drawing an incremental crowd on Sunday, and there were far fewer poorly attended day games to substitute for.

Sunday crowds, whether for a doubleheader or single game, diminished to normal levels as changing attitudes on Sunday laws increased the opening of commercial establishments on Sunday. Working people could not only indulge in amusements on the Lord's Day, but increasingly they also could shop on Sunday.

By the mid-1970s, the Sunday doubleheader had disappeared from the schedules of successful, big market clubs like the Boston Red Sox and Los Angeles Dodgers. Other teams gradually did away with their Sunday doubleheaders. By 1984, only seven teams had a Sunday doubleheader on the playing schedule—New York, Cincinnati, and San Francisco in the National League and Cleveland, Detroit, Toronto, and Oakland in the American League. Even then, it was just one Sunday doubleheader per season, although the San Francisco Giants did schedule two that year.

One of the last scheduled Sunday doubleheaders in the major leagues occurred on June 9, 1985, when the New York Mets hosted the St. Louis Cardinals for a twinbill at Shea Stadium. The Mets split the doubleheader, winning the first game 6-1 and losing the nightcap 8-2.

With the demise of the Sunday doubleheader came the rise of another Sunday innovation—Sunday night games. Although major league baseball had for many years resisted night games on Sundays, expansion of major league franchises to Texas finally opened up Sunday night play on a limited basis.

The expansion Houston Colts applied to the National League to play Sunday night games at Colt Stadium due to the intense Texas summer heat and received approval to play seven Sunday night games during the 1963 season. The first Sunday night game in the major leagues was played on June 9, 1963, when the Houston Colts defeated the San Francisco Giants 3-0 before 17,437 at Colt Stadium. Temperature at game time was 79 degrees, a drop from the 2:00 temperature of 95 degrees.[13]

When the Washington Senators franchise in the American League transferred to Texas for the 1972 season, the rechristened Texas Rangers immediately took up Sunday night baseball. The team's first Sunday night game was on April 23, a 5-2 victory over the California Angels.

The convergence of Sunday games and night baseball really took off in 1990 when cable network ESPN began nationally televising selected games on Sunday night. As part of the $400 million package to televise major league baseball, ESPN sought to spotlight one baseball game a week on Sunday nights. ESPN hoped to emulate the success that another television network had with Monday night football, which spotlighted one game a week at a time unusual for the sport and conducive to television viewers.

With Jon Miller and Joe Morgan behind the microphone of the ESPN telecasts at 8:00 eastern time each Sunday night, the innovation was slow to catch on. "Although ESPN lost scads of money overall on the [television] contract, the Sunday evening contests turned out to be a popular innovation with the nation's viewers," David Pietrusza wrote in his history of night baseball, *Lights On!* Much like Monday night football became an institution among football fans, the Sunday baseball telecasts on ESPN soon became ensconced in baseball culture.[14]

ESPN brought Sunday baseball full circle. During its infancy in the 1880s and 1890s, Sunday baseball was unique and out of the ordinary. Through its formative years as ball clubs grappled with courts and legislatures to legalize it, Sunday baseball was special. After World War II, when the major leagues routinely played on Sunday—not just one game, but two games—Sunday baseball became commonplace and the term faded from existence. Then in the 1980s even the Sunday doubleheader disappeared from existence. With the ESPN telecasts, baseball on Sunday possessed a unique and special quality once again.

Sunday baseball also re-entered the sport's lexicon due to the ESPN telecasts, albeit with the middle name "night" as part of its appellation. The phrase "Sunday night baseball" now rolls off the tongues of baseball fans across the country, nearly all of whom have no idea how controversial the term "Sunday baseball" once was in baseball history.

Appendix A

SUNDAY BASEBALL FIRSTS IN THE MAJOR LEAGUES

National League—Initial Sunday Home Games (1892–1934)

Team	Regular Grounds	Alternate Site
Baltimore (1892–1899)*	---	---
Boston (1876–1952)	May 5, 1929	September 6, 1903
Brooklyn (1890–1957)*	April 17, 1904[1]	September 18, 1898
Chicago (1876–today)	May 14, 1893	---
Cincinnati (1890–today)*	April 24, 1892	---
Cleveland (1889–1899)*	July 11, 1897	June 12, 1898
Louisville (1892–1899)*	May 1, 1892	---
New York (1883–1957)	August 19, 1917[2]	September 11, 1898
Philadelphia (1883–today)	April 29, 1934	---
Pittsburgh (1887–today)*	April 29, 1934	---
St. Louis (1892–today)*	April 17, 1892	---
Washington (1892–1899)*	---	---

* Team transferred from the American Association, may have previously played Sunday home games in that league.
1. Game at Washington Park; first Ebbets Field game was July 1, 1917, and first legal game was May 4, 1919.
2. First legal game at Polo Grounds was May 4, 1919.

National League—Initial Sunday Road Games (1892–1903)

Team	Away Game
Baltimore (1892–1899)*	May 1, 1892
Boston (1876–1952)	June 14, 1903
Brooklyn (1890–1957)*	July 9, 1893

Team	Away Game
Chicago (1876–today)	April 30, 1893
Cincinnati (1890–today)*	Home Game Earlier
Cleveland (1889–1899)*	May 8, 1892
Louisville (1892–1899)*	Home Game Earlier
New York (1883–1957)	May 22, 1898
Philadelphia (1883–today)	June 7, 1903
Pittsburgh (1887–today)*	April 17, 1898
St. Louis (1892–today)*	Home Game Earlier
Washington (1892–1899)*	May 1, 1892

* Team transferred from the American Association, may have previously played Sunday road games in that league.

American League—Initial Sunday Home Games (1901–1934)

Team	Regular Grounds	Alternate Site
Baltimore (1901–1902)	———	———
Boston (1901–today)	July 3, 1932	April 28, 1929
Chicago (1901–today)	April 28, 1901	———
Cleveland (1901–today)	May 14, 1911	June 8, 1902
Detroit (1901–today)	August 18, 1907	April 28, 1901[3]
Milwaukee (1901)	May 5, 1901	———
New York (1903–today)	June 17, 1917[4]	July 17, 1904
Philadelphia (1901–1954)	August 22, 1926[5]	———
St. Louis (1902–1953)	April 27, 1902	———
Washington (1901–1960)	May 19, 1918	———

Note: All American League teams played Sunday road games in their first year in the league.
3. Game at Springwells, Michigan; first neutral-site game was May 24, 1903.
4. Game at Polo Grounds; first legal game at Polo Grounds was May 11, 1919; first Yankee Stadium game was April 22, 1923.
5. First legal game at Shibe Park was April 22, 1934.

American Association—Initial Sunday Home Games (1882–1891)

Team	Regular Grounds	Alternate Site
Baltimore (1882–1889, 1890–1891)	———	———
Boston (1891)	———	———
Brooklyn (1884–1889, 1890)	———	May 2, 1886
Cincinnati (1882–1889, 1891)	May 11, 1884	August 25, 1889[6]
Cleveland (1887–1888)	———	August 21, 1887
Columbus (1883–1884, 1889–1891)	May 6, 1883	———
Indianapolis (1884)	———	May 18, 1884
Kansas City (1888–1889)	April 22, 1888	———
Louisville (1882–1891)	May 7, 1882	———

Team	Regular Grounds	Alternate Site
Milwaukee (1891)	September 13, 1891	————
New York (1883–1887)	————	September 11, 1887
Philadelphia (1882–1891)	————	June 10, 1888[7]
Pittsburgh (1882–1886)	————	————
Richmond (1884)	————	————
Rochester (1890)	————	May 11, 1890
St. Louis (1882–1891)	June 4, 1882	————
Syracuse (1890)	————	May 18, 1890
Toledo (1884, 1890)	May 4, 1890	————
Washington (1884, 1891)	————	————

Note: All American Association teams played Sunday road games in their first year in the league.

6. Game in Hamilton, Ohio, stopped in the fourth inning.
7. Game disallowed by Association president; first official game was on August 5, 1888.

Union Association—Initial Sunday Home Games (1884)

Team	Status	Regular Grounds
Altoona	Disbanded	————
Baltimore	Full Season	————
Boston	Full Season	————
Chicago	Transferred	May 11, 1884
Cincinnati	Full Season	April 27, 1884
Kansas City	Replacement	July 27, 1884
Milwaukee	Replacement	September 28, 1884
Philadelphia	Disbanded	————
Pittsburgh	Replacement	————
St. Louis	Full Season	April 20, 1884
St. Paul	Replacement	————
Washington	Full Season	————
Wilmington	Replacement	————

Note: All Union Association teams except Pittsburgh and Wilmington played Sunday road games in its only year of existence.

Federal League—Initial Sunday Home Games (1914–1915)

Team	Status	Regular Grounds
Baltimore	Both Years	————
Brooklyn	Both Years	————
Buffalo	Both Years	————
Chicago	Both Years	April 26, 1914
Indianapolis	1914 Only	April 26, 1914

Team	Status	Regular Grounds
Kansas City	Both Years	April 19, 1914
Newark	1915 Only	April 18, 1915
Pittsburgh	Both Years	---
St. Louis	Both Years	April 19, 1914

Note: All Federal League teams except Brooklyn played Sunday road games in the league.

Appendix B

SIGNIFICANT COURT DECISIONS ON SUNDAY BASEBALL

State v. Chris Von der Ahe, Missouri, 1887*

OPINION OF JUDGE NOONAN

The defendant is prosecuted under section 1578 of the Revised Statutes, which reads as follows:

> Every person who shall either labor himself or compel or permit his apprentice or servant or any other person under his charge or control to labor or perform any work, other than household offices of daily necessity, or other work of necessity or charity, or who shall be guilty of hunting game or shooting on the first day of the week, commonly called Sunday, shall be deemed guilty of a misdemeanor and fined not exceeding fifty dollars.

The evidence introduced in behalf of the State at the trial was in substance as follows. That the defendant was President and Superintendent of the base ball club known as the "St. Louis Browns"; that he permitted and caused them to play on his private premises on Sunday, July 10, 1887; that they had been playing there for many years on Sundays, and were never arrested before; that he charged a fee to see the game; that many people went there; that good order prevailed and did when he was arrested.

The evidence for the defendant so far as it affects this case was that he allowed and caused a game of base ball to be played on his private premises on Grand avenue, near the Fair Grounds, in the City of St. Louis, on the 10th day of July, 1887, the same being Sunday. That the place where

---

*Source: *St. Louis Post-Dispatch*, July 15, 1887, p. 1

the said ball game was played was a large square, fenced in by a high board fence, and with buildings erected facing the square for the accommodation of those who witness the games of ball players there; that it is remote from any place of worship or any religious sect or denomination; that it has been used as a base ball park since 1868, and that base ball has been played there on Sunday afternoons between the hours of 3 and 6 o'clock since that time under defendant's control and superintendence, and that he has never been molested or arrested by any authority for so doing prior to July 10, 1887; that the game of base ball has been known and played in many parts of the country as recreation and entertainment many years; that it has never been regarded as labor or work, as that word is understood and commonly used; that since defendant has allowed base ball to be played in his private premises as aforesaid, hundreds of thousands of citizens of St. Louis, as well as of all classes both male and female on week days and Sundays have witnesses the same for recreation and entertainment; that good order and propriety has always been maintained and observed there; that the people in the immediate vicinity of said premises of defendants' grounds testify that they are in no way disturbed in their peace and refuse by any disturbance or noise emanating therefrom while the game of base ball is going on; that Sunday, July 10, 1887, when the defendant was arrested, was no exception to the good order and propriety that has prevailed there before.

To understand the policy and scope of the Sunday laws on our statute books, it is necessary not only to look at the section under which this prosecution is carried on and which only prohibits "labor or work" by any person or by his servant or any one under his control (other than the household offices of daily necessity, or other works of necessity or charity), or hunting game or shooting on Sunday, but we must look at sections 1580 and 1581 in connection with it.

Section 1580 reads as follows: "Every person who shall be convicted of horse-racing, cock fighting or playing cards or games of any kind on the first day of the week, commonly called Sunday, shall be deemed guilty of a misdemeanor, etc."

Section 1581 reads: "Every person who shall expose to sale any goods, wares or merchandise, or shall keep open any ale or porter house, grocery or tippling house, or shall sell or retail any fermented or distilled liquor on the first day of the week, commonly called Sunday, shall, upon conviction, be adjudged guilty of a misdemeanor, etc." Section 1582 continues section 1581 as follows: "The last section shall not be construed to prevent the sale of any drugs, medicines, provisions or other articles of immediate necessity."

Taking all these sections together, we see section 1578 prohibits work and labor of a servile character, or manual work or labor, and hunting and shooting on Sunday. Section 1580 prohibits horse-racing, cock fighting or playing at cards or games of any kind on Sunday. "Games of any kind" following the special words "playing at cards" means playing at any game of cards, dice or games of alike character. In a word, it means gambling games, not games like base ball. *City of St. Louis vs. Laughlin*, 47th Mo. Bishop on Written Laws, s. s. 245 and 246.

Section 1581 prohibits the exposure to sale of any goods, wares or merchandise, etc.

In none of these sections do we find recreation or entertainment, such as the evidence shows the game of base ball as conducted by the defendant in this case, prohibited. On the contrary, the fact that some pleasures, sports and games are prohibited, and base ball is not, is an intimation by the Legislature that there was no intention to prohibit the game. If any recreation or entertainment, even of a moral tendency, was carried on or conducted in a loud or disorderly manner on Sunday it would be illegal, but the evidence in this case shows that no disorder or disturbance was committed, but that the best of order prevailed, and the neighborhood was not annoyed or disturbed.

The *People vs. Wm Dennis*, 42 Supreme Court Reports of New York, page 327, was a case where the defendant was arrested for playing base ball on Sunday. There the statute is much broader than ours. The statute under which he was prosecuted reads as follows: "All shooting, hunting, fishing, horse-racing, gaming, or other public sports, exercises, pastimes, or shows upon Sunday, and all noise disturbing the peace of the day are prohibited." There servile labor, trades, manufactures and mechanical employments and public traffic are prohibited likewise. The evidence shows that the base ball playing was in private grounds, and no noise disturbing the peace of the neighborhood resulted therefrom, and the Court decided that the defendant committed no offense under the statute in playing base ball and discharged him.

Our Supreme Court in 1876 decided that hunting game on Sunday was not a work or labor within the statute and discharged the defendant, who had been convicted of hunting under the Sunday laws. *State vs. Carpenter*. Since that case was decided our Legislature has made hunting game a violation of the Sunday law. But they have not prohibited either expressly or by construction base ball carried on decently, orderly and quietly on Sunday.

I might say in addition to this that the game was a reasonable sport and use of nature's powers, and while the evidence showed that money was taken and money paid to the players, it in my mind is not within the meaning of this statute any more than would be the paying of any piano player or singer that might come into the home of a citizen on Sunday to contribute to his entertainment.

I therefore find the defendant, under the laws and the evidence, not guilty and discharge him.

State v. Powell, Ohio Supreme Court, 1898*

OPINION OF JUDGE MINSHALL

John Powell, with others, was prosecuted in the police court of the city of Cleveland, on an information charging him, in one count, with having on Sunday, May 16, 1897, participated in playing baseball, and, in a second count, with having exhibited a game of baseball playing, on certain grounds in the city, a charge for admittance having been made. The case was tried to a jury on a plea of not guilty. He was found guilty on both counts, and after a motion for a new trial made and overruled, was sentenced to pay a fine and costs of prosecution. The case was taken to the court of common pleas on error, where the judgment was reversed, and the defendant discharged, on the ground that the section of the Revised Statutes (7032a) under which the conviction was had is unconstitutional. This section, among other things, makes it an offense, punishable by fine and imprisonment, for any one on the first day of the week, commonly called Sunday, to participate in, or exhibit to the public in any "building" or on any "ground" in this state, "any baseball playing." A bill of exceptions was taken by the prosecuting attorney to the ruling of the judge, and, on application, leave was given by this court to file the same. The question presented by the bill is the validity of our Sunday laws. After so many years of acquiescence in their adoption, and, I might say, of almost unquestioned validity, these laws are now assailed on the ground that they violate the guaranties of personal and religious liberty contained in the first and seventh sections of our bill of rights. These questions may be better considered in their reverse order.

The seventh section secures to every citizen of the state the fullest liberty of conscience in matters of religion. No one can be compelled to support or observe any form of worship against his consent. If the observance of Sunday as a day of rest and abstinence from all secular pursuits had for

---

*Source: 58 Ohio St. 324, 50 N.E. 900 (April 19, 1898).

its object the enforcement of a religious requirement, there are few lawyers or judges that would undertake to sustain the statute as a valid enactment. It would clearly contravene the section of the bill of rights just referred to. But that they are secular in purpose, and not made to enforce any particular form of religious observance, is sustained by a consensus of opinion in the discussions of the courts of this country, rarely found upon any other subject. Indeed, there is not to be found a decision of a court of last resort to the contrary, except that of the state of California, which has since been overruled by the same court. *Ex parte Newman*, 9 Cal. 502, overruled in *Ex parte Andrews*, 18 Cal. 679. And though the day adopted for the observance of rest may coincide with the religious persuasion of a large part of the people, but not with all, this is not regarded as infringing upon the rights of the latter, since no religious observance of any kind is enjoined. Those who desire can devote the day to religious observances. Others may do as they see fit, so that they do not engage in such secular pursuits as, in accordance with the policy of the law, are prohibited. The policy of Sunday laws is based upon the observed fact, derived from long experience and the custom of all nations, that periods of rest from ordinary pursuits are requisite to the well-being, morally and physically, of a people. If there were no such regularly occurring periods, there is reason to believe that the masses would become morbid in body and mind, crime would multiply, and degeneracy likely ensue. Rest recuperates the mind and body, gives new life and hope to the people, and cheerfulness and health attend renewed labor; and, as has been well observed, more under these circumstances, can be accomplished in six days than would otherwise be accomplished in seven. This is the foundation and policy of all statutes regulating the observance of a day of rest; and whether the day selected is one consonant to the religious views of a portion of the people or not does not affect the validity of the regulation, where no religious observance is enjoined. Religious liberty does not consist in the right of any sect to oppose its views to the policy of a government. Such a claim would end in simple intolerance of all not in accord with the sentiments of the particular sect. Those who, as a matter of religious faith, observe the seventh day of the week, are not prohibited from doing so; but they cannot insist that others shall do so, nor refuse to observe the day fixed by the state for secular reasons. There are sects who believe in polygamy, and adopt it as part of their religion. But, however conscientitious they may be in entertaining such notions, if one of them should come into Ohio, and bring with him his wives, his religious scruples would not protect him on an indictment for bigamy.

The question, however, is not an open one in this state. In *Bloom v*

Richards, 2 Ohio St. 387, decided in 1853, the whole subject was fully considered. While holding that the making of a contract is not within the meaning of the term "common labor," the statute, as thus construed, was sustained as a secular regulation, that in no way interferes with any one's rights of conscience. Thurman, J., in delivering the opinion, said that "acts evil in their nature, or dangerous to the public welfare, may be forbidden and punished, though sanctioned by one religion and prohibited by another; but this creates no preference whatever, for they would be equally forbidden if all religions permitted them. Thus, no plea of religion could shield a murderer, ravisher, or bigamist; for community would be at the mercy of superstition, if such crimes as these could be committed with impunity, because sanctioned by some religious delusion." "We are then," he said, "to regard the statute under consideration as a mere municipal or police regulation, whose validity is neither strengthened nor weakened by the fact that the day of rest it enjoins is the Sabbath day. Wisdom requires that men should refrain from labor at least one day in seven, and the advantages of having the day of rest fixed, and so fixed as to happen at regularly recurring intervals, are too obvious to be overlooked. It was within the constitutional competency of the general assembly to require the cessation of labor, and to name the day of rest. It did so by the act referred to, and in accordance with the feelings of a majority of the people, the Christian Sabbath was very properly selected. But, regarded merely as an exertion of legislative authority, the act would have had neither more nor less validity had any other day been adopted." He then cites a number of cases, particularly *Specht v. Com.*, 8 Pa. St. 312, and *City Council v. Benjamin*, 2 Strob. 508, which fully support his opinion as to the secular character of Sunday laws and the policy on which they rest. Among the cases that may be cited sustaining the enactment of Sunday laws, in addition to those already referred to, are the following: [ten case citations omitted]. They are also fully collected and well considered in the opinion of Fisher, J., in *Ex parte Newman*, 9 Cal. 518, since the decision of the majority in this case was overruled by an unanimous decision in the subsequent case of *Ex parte Andrews*, 18 Cal. 679; and the law of that state "for the better observance of the Sabbath," sustained, though the same constitutional objections were urged against it that are made in this case, the provisions of their bill of rights being in this regard substantially the same as our own.

But it is further claimed that the statute violates the guaranty of personal liberty contained in the first section of the bill of rights. This, though one of the great maxims of our form of government, has never been regarded as limiting the power of the legislature in the enactment of such good and wholesome laws as are required to secure the peace, health, and good order of society. The learned Sedgwick, in his work on *Statutory and Constitutional Construction* (page 153) commenting on the provisions usually contained in the bill of rights of our American constitutions, says: "They are of no little value as safeguards against error and injustice; but I think they must be regarded rather as guides for the political conscience of the legislature than as texts of judicial duty. Important as they are, still they are expressed in such general terms as necessarily to admit of great and prominent exceptions. As to the enjoyment of life and liberty, property, and the pursuit of happiness, all these rights are daily interfered with by the legislature, without scruple, for the common welfare. I suppose it must be admitted that, in a judicial sense, these clauses could not easily be made available." Liberty, as understood in this country, is not license, but liberty regulated by law. The personal liberty of every man is subject to such reasonable regulations as, in the wisdom of the legislature, are regarded necessary to promote, not only the peace and good order of society, but its well-being. This objection to the law is well answered in the clear and forcible language of Justice Field, in the dissenting opinion before referred to. "If," he says, "it be admitted that the legislature possesses the right to restrain each one in his freedom of conduct only so far as is necessary to secure protection to all others, from every species of danger to person, health, and property, no inference can be drawn against the validity of the act under consideration. The character and mode of protection, and what is dangerous to the person or to health and property, must necessarily be left to its determination; and in the first section of the constitution no inhibition to the exercise of its power in this respect can be found. The prohibition of secular business on Sunday is advocated on the ground that by it the general welfare is advanced, labor protected, and the moral and physical well-being of society promoted. The legislature has so considered it, and the judiciary cannot say that the legislature was mistaken, and therefore the act is unconstitutional, without passing out of its legitimate sphere, and assuming a right to supervise the exercise of legislative discretion in matters of mere expediency," and which he proceeds to say cannot be done.

We have carefully considered the able argument of counsel for the judge whose ruling is under review. The gist of his argument is that the purpose of the act is to enforce the observance of Sunday as a religious requirement, and calls attention to the claims and views of those most zealous in its enforcement. No doubt, many who advocate Sunday observance, particularly the Christian ministry, do so from the persuasion that our Sunday laws are designed as religious observances only, and insist that they should be more rigidly enforced, that the people may be more accessible to the influences of the Christian pulpit. However desirable this may be from the Christian standpoint, it is certain that it is not in the power of the legislature to accomplish this by any direct legislation, so long as religious liberty is guaranteed, as it is, in our bill of rights. This was settled by the case of *Bloom v. Richards*, supra. The fact, however, that such views are entertained of the purpose of the law, and may have controlled the votes of many who supported it in the legislature, cannot affect its real character and proper construction. The purpose and object of a law are to be determined by the language applicable to its subject matter. Speaking to the same point, Baldwin, J., in *Ex parte Andrews*, 18 Cal. 685, said: "The act itself, in the body of it, explains in what manner the day was to be observed, and shows that the object of it was only to require duties purely civic or secular." A law enacted for sufficient reasons of a secular nature, as the public health, cannot be held invalid because there is a variety of religious notion upon the subject. Nor can the state be prevented from adopting certain civil regulations, recommended by a wise public policy, simply because they are found to be in accord with the teachings of some religion. There is probably no religious observance that could not be enforced as a secular duty, without violating the guaranty of religious liberty, where there are sufficient secular reasons for doing so, independent of what is ordained as a matter of religion. In general, where there are secular and religious reasons for the same observance or law, the observance or law may be adopted as a civil regulation by the legislature for the attainment of the secular purposes; and, when enforced for these purposes alone, no one can complain of it simply because the observance or law finds support in the precepts of some religion. It is enjoined for secular, and not religious reasons. It might be questioned whether the Jewish Sabbath was prescribed purely as a religious observance, and without any regard to the temporal welfare of the people. It must be remembered that the Jewish government was in the nature of a theocracy, and its precepts were given without much regard to what was of a spiritual nature, and what was secular and related to the temporal government of the people alone. Exceptions sustained.

People v. Poole, New York, 1904*

Opinion of Justice Gaynor

In the case of Rath and others which was recently before me on the writ of habeus corpus, the complaint was simply that the defendants played

---

*Source: 89 N.Y.S. 773 (June 18, 1904).

a game of baseball on Sunday. There was no allegation that the game was a public one, or that it disturbed the peace of the day by noise. The complaint presented nothing but the case of ordinary private games of baseball or of golf on Sunday, which have long been allowed unmolested in the open fields in the outskirts of this city, and throughout the State, and which are not prohibited by the statute, as will presently be seen.

The present case is different. The complaint is of a public game of baseball: i.e., of a game held out to the public, i.e., of a game to which the public were invited, and to which an admission fee was charged. Is such a game prohibited by statute? I think it is.

The various penal Sunday statutes were collected together, and re-enacted as a chapter in revised form in our Penal Code, which was passed in 1881. Those curious on the subject may trace them through the colonial statutes of 1685 and 1695, the Revised Laws of 1813 and the Revised Statutes of 1829.

Section 259 of the Penal Code is as follows:

> The first day of the week being by general consent set apart for rest and religious uses, the law prohibits the doing on that day of certain acts hereinafter specified, which are serious interruptions of the repose and religious liberty of the community.

This section is sort of a preamble; and it is noteworthy that the "general consent" of the community in observing Sunday is given by it as the reason and basis of our Sunday laws. The wishes of the community, therefore, should have much to do with their enforcement, as is the case with all laws which depend for their vigor on public opinion.

Section 262 summarizes under general heads the acts so prohibited, the second head being in the words "Public sports and shows." This word "public" excludes private sports and shows. This section was repealed in 1883, but reference to it is still necessary in getting at the intention and scope of the whole chapter.

Section 265 enumerates the acts embraced under this head, and is as follows:

> All shooting, hunting, fishing, playing, horse racing, gaming or other public sport, exercises, pastimes or shows, upon the first day of the week, and all noise disturbing the peace of the day, are prohibited.

Here, again, the prohibition seems to be against public acts only. The enumeration of the specific things prohibited is followed by the general clause, "or other public sports, exercises, pastimes or shows." This general clause is not only expressly limited to public sports, etc., but is a continuation of the same category of acts, and not the introduction of a new category. But it suffices for the present case that the general clause is limited to public sports, etc., for unless it embraces baseball, golf and all other games not specified by name in the section, they are not prohibited at all. And a public sport, game, show or entertainment is one held out and given to the public. In 1883 this section was amended by dropping the word "pastimes."

Such is the interpretation of the statute without the aid of any side light. But if we go outside of the statute, and resort to the Holy Scriptures and to Christian rules, as some insist must be done, to aid in getting at its color and scope, and into the intention of the Legislature, the interpretation must remain the same. Physical exercises and games are not forbidden on the Sabbath in the Ten Commandments. Only work is there prohibited. "Six days shalt thou labor and do all thy work, but the seventh day is a sabbath unto the Lord thy God; in it thou shall not do any work" (Revised Version). Moreover, this commandment relates to the seventh day of the week, and not the first. In the New Testament there is no Sunday law at all. And in the Christian church there never have been any rules prohibiting physical games and exercises on Sunday. Those who say the contrary only speak at random, and from lack of education. Not long ago a complaint was made to the Archbishop of Canterbury that Mr. Balfour, the prime minister of England, played the game of golf on Sunday. The Archbishop's official response in writing was that "it is certain that the Christian church has never laid down detailed directions affecting the actions of individuals in this matter. Each of them is responsible to God for so using the Lord's day as to fit him best for the working days that follow." It is not to be understood that the Legislature meant to be stricter than the divine law of the Hebrew scriptures, or than the rules of the Christian church, excepting the extent to which it has expressly gone.

And if we view the statute as a health law, we shall still not perceive any intention in it to prohibit all out-of-door games and exercises on Sunday, for to prevent them, especially in the cities, would injure the health of the community and materially increase the death rate. The prohibition is only against public games and exercises, namely, those to which the public are invited, because the statute presumes that they interrupt the repose of the community; and that is the case against these defendants.

Our judicial reports furnish only three cases on the criminality of games or sports on Sunday, owing, no doubt, to the fact that the people of this State have not been prone to meddle with how their neighbors spend Sunday. In the Case of Dennin, 35 Hun, 327, the conviction of the defendant for playing baseball on Sunday was reversed on appeal in the Supreme Court, because the game was not one held out to the public, although played in public view, and there was no evidence that it interrupted the repose of the community. The Case against Moses, 140 N.Y. 214, 35 N.E. 499, was for fishing in a stream on Sunday, and the defendant was convicted. Three judges of our highest appellate court voted that the offense was made out by the mere act of fishing, regardless of whether it interrupted the repose of the community. Three judges dissented from this view. The remaining judge of the seven voted to uphold the conviction on the ground that there was sufficient evidence to show that the repose of the community had been interrupted. The decision was therefore indecisive of the question whether the mere act itself constituted a criminal offense, three judges out of the seven being squarely against that view, and another being unwilling to join in it. The Rupp Case, 33 App. Div. 468, 53 N.Y. Supp. 927, was an application to remove a police commissioner for not causing the arrest of persons playing a game of baseball habitually in the same place on Sundays. The evidence there was that the game was a public one, an admission fee being charged, and also that it interrupted the repose of the community; and it was therefore held that the game was a criminal offense. The construction which I give to the statute is in harmony with these decisions.

The motion is denied.

Commonwealth v. American Baseball Club of Philadelphia, Pennsylvania Supreme Court, 1927*

OPINION OF JUSTICE SCHAFFER

Defendant, a corporation of the second class and therefore organized for profit, was incorporated under the General Act of April 29, 1874, P.L. 73, and its supplements, for the purpose of organizing and maintaining a team or club for the playing of baseball. It holds a franchise as a member of the American League of professional baseball clubs and owns a baseball park known as Shibe Park, situated in the City of Philadelphia. All its players are paid and it charges the public an admission fee to see the games. In the summer of 1926, appellant announced that it intended playing professional baseball at its park on Sundays, and on Sunday, August 22, it did play a game of professional ball with another team of the American League,

*Source: 290 Pa. 136, 138 Atl. 497 (June 25, 1927)

to which the public was admitted on payment of an admission fee. Thereafter the attorney general on behalf of the Commonwealth filed the suggestion for the writ of quo warranto in this proceeding, his averment being that the playing of the game of baseball on Sunday violates the Act of April 22, 1794, 3 Smith's Laws 177, and that the appellant is without the power or authority of law, under the letters patent granted to it, to play baseball on Sunday. The answer of the defendant denied that the playing of baseball on Sunday is a violation of the Act of 1794 or that it is without authority to play the game on that day and averred that the writ of quo warranto would not lie against it because the sole penalty for its so doing is the payment of the sum of four dollars as provided in the act. The attorney general having demurred to the answer, the court below after hearing sustained the demurrer and entered a judgment that defendant be ousted from any right, privilege or authority to maintain or conduct upon its grounds any game of professional baseball on Sunday and directed that a perpetual injunction issue restraining it from so doing; from the judgment and decree thus entered defendant brings to us this appeal.

The questions we are asked to pass upon may be thus summarized: (1) Is the playing of professional baseball on Sunday as defendant played it a violation of the Act of 1794? (2) Is the act unconstitutional for uncertainty? (3) Is quo warranto the proper remedy and the judgment entered a proper one?

As to the first and main question we fail to see how, when the language of the act is called to mind and account is taken of what the defendant is and what it actually did, it can be affirmed that the statute was not violated. To hold otherwise would mean that the words do not have their ordinary meaning. The statute says "If any person shall do or perform any worldly employment or business whatsoever on the Lord's Day, commonly called Sunday, works of necessity and charity only excepted and be convicted thereof, every such person so offending shall, for every such offense, forfeit and pay four dollars, to be levied by distress; or in case he or she shall refuse or neglect to pay the said sum he or she shall suffer six days imprisonment in the house of correction of the proper county." The word "worldly" as here used means "concerned with the enjoyments of this present existence, secular," [and] "not religious, spiritual or holy." Chief Justice Lowrie, speaking for the court in *Com. v. Nesbit*, 34 Pa. 398, 409, said "Very evidently, worldly is contrasted with religious, and the worldly employments are prohibited for the sake of the religious ones." We cannot imagine in this sense anything more worldly or unreligious in the way of employment than the playing of professional baseball as it is played today. It is not only worldly employment which is forbidden, but business. There are businesses which are not trade or commerce: *Hooper v. California*, 155 U.S. 648. Can anyone hope to successfully contend that today's professional baseball enterprises are not business? It was taken for granted by the Supreme Court of the United States that they are. "The business is giving exhibitions of baseball": *National League v. Federal Baseball Club*, 259 U.S. 200. We think no one would argue that conducting a circus is not a business or running a theater is not and yet there is no difference between them and playing professional baseball. In all three the participants are hired to give the exhibition and the public is admitted for a price. Pertinent to this line of thought is what was said by Mr. Justice Strong in *Sparhawk v. Union Passenger Ry. Co.*, 54 Pa. 401, 409, "Many might be found, doubtless, who would affirm on oath that theatrical representations are conducive to mental and bodily health, and that such recreation as they afford is a necessity. Such a construction of the statute would make it but an empty sound. It would be losing sight entirely of the objects sought to be secured, the observance of a day of rest for the community, thereby enabling every one to worship God according to the dictates of his conscience, without distraction, and without disturbance, and thus giving a check to vice and immorality. A construction that leads to such an absurdity must be erroneous."

The claim here made—the right to play baseball on every day of the week notwithstanding the Act of 1794—is the same that was made for the licensees of taverns in *Omit v. Com.*, 21 Pa. 426, and in the opinion in that case completely answered. In *Com. v. Naylor*, 34 Pa. 86, the question presented was whether a sale of liquors on Sunday by a licensed innkeeper was an indictable offense, at that time there being no statute covering Sunday selling. In answering the query as to whether the license authorized its holder to sell liquor on Sunday, it was said (p. 88): "Certainly not; because the Act of Assembly of 1794 forbids any worldly employment on Sunday." It would be a difficult matter to state a satisfying reason why the sale of liquor on Sunday is a worldly employment and the sale of admission to see a baseball game is not. In that case the license from the Commonwealth gave the right to sell liquor; in the one at bar the charter is the privilege of conducting games of ball, but neither privilege from the State can override its laws. This same principle is announced in *Johnston v. Com.*, 22 Pa. 102. The Superior Court in *Com. v. Coleman*, 60 Pa. Superior Ct. 380, decided that the playing of professional baseball on Sunday was a violation of the Act of 1794, even though no admission be charged. Nothing brought to our attention leads us to otherwise conclude. In that case it was conceded that had an admission fee been charged it would have been a worldly employment.

Christianity is part of the common law of Pennsylvania (*Updegraph v. Com.*, 11 S.&R. 393) and its people are christian people. Sunday is the holy day among christians. No one we think would contend that professional baseball partakes in any way of the nature of holiness and when contrasted with things which do, it is bound to be categorized as worldly. Great emphasis is laid upon the fact, in appellant's brief, that the baseball game was conducted without undue noise, that there were no disturbances, and altogether in a manner not to annoy in the slightest those living in the neighborhood of the ball park or to interfere with religious worship. It is not necessary that one, in carrying on a worldly employment on Sunday, should do any of these things before being guilty of a violation of the act, nor is it essential that there should have been a breach of the peace: *Com. v. Foster*, 28 Pa. Superior Ct. 400. Our conclusions must be that the defendant, a corporation existing for profit, in doing the acts against which the Commonwealth complains, was engaged in and performing a worldly employment and business on Sunday and therefore violating the Act of 1794.

On appellant's second proposition that the act is unconstitutional for uncertainty, we think very little is required to be said. See 37 Cyc. 541; 12 C.J. 1275. It has been on the statute books for 133 years and has been the subject of much judicial consideration. When its language is given its ordinary not a strained construction, its meaning we think is plain. It may be that those who do not wish to understand or abide by its provisions find them uncertain; surely those who wish to follow the custom of our people in Sunday observance do not so find the interdictions of the statute. We can see no basis whatever for the argument that the act violates the 14th Amendment to the federal Constitution.

This brings us to the third question presented by appellant, the one most stressed in oral argument and in printed brief: Is quo warranto the proper remedy and the judgment entered a proper one? In passing upon this question, it is important at its threshold to consider who brought the proceeding. It was initiated by the attorney general, the chief law officer of the Commonwealth and necessarily has behind it the approval of the State's highest executive officer, the Governor. The people's mandate to him in their fundamental law (Constitution, article IV, section 2) is "The supreme executive power shall be vested in the Governor, who shall take care that the laws be faithfully executed." This proceeding was brought to the end that this mandate should be fulfilled.

Appellant does not contend that a corporation may not be ousted of all its franchises for willful misuser. If it may be ousted from all of them, certainly it may be of part. A corporation may be ousted from the exercise of powers not granted and powers forbidden to be exercised (Act June 14,

1836, section 11, P.L. 621; 22 R.C.L. 672; High's Extraordinary Legal Remedies (3d ed.) Sections 647, 648; *Com. v. Delaware & Hudson Coal Co.*, 43 Pa. 295; *Com. ex rel. v. Northeastern Elevated Ry. Co.*, 161 Pa. 409) and the way to oust it is by writ of quo warranto: *Kishacoquillas Turnpike Road Co. v. McConaby*, 16 S.& R. 140. It is especially the province of the attorney general to sue out such writ in cases of public wrong: *Murphy v. Farmers' Bank of Schuylkill Co.*, 20 Pa. 415.

Appellant argues that its charter gives it express power to play baseball. This may be admitted and yet there be no denial of the right to the writ which is one of inquiry: By what warrant are the acts done of which complaint is made? It does not avail to say to the Commonwealth, you granted me the privilege to do this thing, if it appears that what is being done under cover of the charter is unlawful. If all that was being carried on was unlawful, then there would be no warrant for its doing and no question of the propriety of the writ; if part of what was being carried on was lawful and part was not, then there would be warrant only for that which was lawful; what was unlawful, not being justified, would have to cease. It would seem to be well nigh ridiculous to hold that by its writ of quo warranto the Commonwealth may interdict that which is entirely unlawful but cannot lop off that part which is not within the law. The use of quo warranto to inquire into particular acts of private corporations alleged to be unlawful is adverted to in High's Extraordinary Legal Remedies, sections 677b and 677c. It was said in *Com. v. Banks*, 198 Pa. 397, that quo warranto would be a proper remedy to restrain a business school, not having authority to confer degrees, from unlawfully claiming to be a "university." It is argued that under its charter defendant has the express power granted to it to play professional baseball and nowhere therein is it prohibited from conducting this undertaking on Sunday. Neither was the innkeeper in the case heretofore cited prohibited in his license from selling liquor on Sunday, yet this court denied him the right. It would be an unthinkable proposition that the Commonwealth would create organizations to break its own laws. Every corporation which it calls into existence by letters patent takes its charter subject like natural persons to the rule of and obedience to law. Its charter is a grant of lawful privileges, not a warrant to violate any law. Violation of the Act of 1794 is a crime: *Com. v. Eyre*, 1 S.&R. 347; *Com. v. Wolf*, 3 S.&R. 48; *Com. v. Smith*, 266 Pa. 511; *Com. v. Coleman Co.*, 60 Pa. Superior Ct. 380; *Com. v. Shields*, 50 Pa. Superior Ct. 194. "Whenever the attorney general shall have reason to believe that any corporation has exercised any power, privilege or franchise, not granted or appertaining to such corporation, it shall be his duty to file a suggestion [for a writ of quo warranto] and to proceed thereon for the determination of the matter": Act June 14, 1836, P.L. 621. We can think of no instance in which the attorney general can move with greater propriety to fulfill his duty under this requirement than in such an instance as the one before us, where one of the State's creatures, a corporation of its creation, avows its right and power to nullify a criminal statute. If appellant's argument in this respect were to be upheld, then by the same token every merchandising corporation granted the privilege under its charter to sell its wares could open its doors for trade on Sunday and the day as it has been observed in the United States since the arrival of the first immigrants would be at an end and secular doings would be the same as on other days of the week. There is and could be no implied power in a corporation to violate an Act of Assembly. "The doctrine of implied powers is not to be stretched to permit that to be done by a corporation which the legislature has previously said shall not be done": *Pittsburgh Rys. Co. v. Pittsburgh*, 226 Pa. 498, 502. We said in *Kenton v. Union Passenger Ry. Co.*, 54 Pa. 401, 454, that "The company's violation of the Sunday law can be redressed only by enforcing the statutory penalty, or by a proceeding on behalf of the Commonwealth against the company for misuse or abuse of their charter."

We agree, and have so announced, that courts should act with extreme caution in proceedings which have for their object the forfeiture of corporate franchises (*Com. v. Monongahela Bridge Co.*, 216 Pa. 108) but it has been our policy from a very early date not to limit the use of quo warranto proceedings. "The remedy by quo warranto is by statute, and is special; and as the statute is remedial it is to be so construed and administered as to advance, that is, to render effective, the remedy. This is the rule of all remedial statutes": *Com. v. Dillon*, 61 Pa. 488, 490. See also, *Com. ex rel. v. Stevens*, 168 Pa. 582, 587, and High's Extraordinary Legal Remedies (3d ed.) section 622.

The argument that the Act of 1794 provides the sole penalty for its violation cannot be made in this proceeding where the Commonwealth itself through the attorney general seeks to call one of its creatures to account. "There can be no doubt that a corporation may be proceeded against by quo warranto for a misuse of perversion of the franchise conferred upon it by the State, notwithstanding its officers and agents may at the same time be amenable to the criminal law for offense committed by them in the perversion of such franchise": *State ex rel. Hadley v. Delmar Jockey Club*, 200 Mo. 34, 92 S.W. 185; 9 A.L.R. 106. Speaking through Mr. Justice Simpson, in *Com. ex rel. v. Wilkins*, 271 Pa. 523, we made it clear that a penalty provided in a penal statute for those who refuse to enforce it did not mean that that is the exclusive "remedy"; certainly it should not be that the presence in a penal statute of a penalty for individuals who break it should preclude the attorney general from proceeding against a corporation, not by way of imposing a penalty but with a view to prohibit the misuse of a franchise granted by the State. We do not understand that anything said in *Com. v. Smith*, 266 Pa. 511, is at variance with this view; that was a proceeding in equity.

As to appellant's contention that "The sentence of corporate death cannot be imposed for minor infractions which do not go to the essence of the corporate franchise nor inflict injury upon the public generally," while we are not prepared to say there is no public injury by a willful violation of a criminal law, it would seem that all necessary to be said is that the corporation is not under sentence to death; the court has ousted it only from any right, privilege or authority to maintain or conduct any game of professional baseball on Sunday.

The judgment and decree of the court below are affirmed at the cost of appellant.

Appendix C

MASSACHUSETTS BALLOT INITIATIVE, 1928*

To vote on the following, mark a Cross X in the Square at the right of YES or NO:

Law Proposed by Initiative Petition

Shall the proposed law which provides that it shall be lawful in any city which accepts the act by vote of its city council and in any town which accepts the act by vote of its inhabitants, to take part in or witness any athletic outdoor sport or game, except horse racing, automobile racing, boxing or hunting with firearms, on the Lord's Day between 2 and 6 P.M.; that such sports or games shall take place as may be designated in a license issued by certain licensing authorities; that no sport or game shall be permitted in a place other than a public playground or park within one thousand feet of any regular place of worship; that the charging of admission fees or the taking of collections or the receiving of remuneration by any person in charge of or participating in any such sport or game shall not be prohibited; that the license may be revoked; and that in cities and towns in which amateur sports or games are permitted under existing law such amateur sports or games may be held until the proposed law is accepted or the provisions of the existing law fail of acceptance on resubmission to the people, which law was disapproved in the Senate by a vote of 9 in the affirmative and 22 in the negative, and in the House of Representatives by a vote of 93 in the affirmative and 110 in the negative, be approved?

YES ☐
NO ☐

*Source: *Boston Globe*, November 5, 1928, p. 15

Notes

Chapter 1

1. *Indianapolis Journal*, May 19, 1884.
2. *Sporting Life*, July 2, 1884.
3. *Rochester Herald*, July 21, 1890; *Sporting Life*, July 26, 1890.
4. *Cincinnati Enquirer*, August 26, 1889.
5. *Sporting Life*, June 13 and 20, 1891.
6. *Chicago Tribune*, January 14, 1896.
7. *Cleveland Plain Dealer*, May 17, 1897.
8. *Cleveland Plain Dealer*, July 10, 1897.
9. *State v. Powell*, Ohio Supreme Court decision, April 19, 1898, 58 Ohio St. 324, 50 N.E. 900.
10. *People v. Poole*, 89 N.Y.S. 773, June 18, 1904.
11. *Cleveland Plain Dealer*, May 17, 1897.
12. *Brooklyn Daily Eagle*, June 18, 1906.
13. *New York Times*, June 18, 1906.
14. *Brooklyn Daily Eagle*, June 18, 1906.
15. *New York Times*, August 22, 1917.
16. Lyman Abbott, "Letters to Unknown Friends," *The Outlook*, January 25, 1913.
17. Julius Ward, "The New Sunday," *Atlantic Monthly*, April 1881.
18. Dulles, *A History of Recreation*, p. 4–5.
19. Daniels, *Puritans at Play*, pp. 166–67.
20. Ibid., pp. 165–66.
21. Ibid., p. 165.
22. Dulles, *A History of Recreation*, p. 9; Abbott, *The Outlook*, 1913.
23. Daniels, *Puritans at Play*, pp. 166–67.
24. Ibid.
25. McCrossen, *Holy Day, Holiday*, p. 10.
26. David Laband and Deborah Hendry Heinbuch, *Blue Laws: The History, Economics, and Politics of Sunday-Closing Laws* (Lexington, Mass.: Lexington Books, 1987), p. 31.
27. Betts, *America's Sporting Heritage*, p. 228.
28. McCrossen, *Holy Day, Holiday*, p. 8.
29. Witold Rybczynski, *Waiting for the Weekend* (New York: Viking Penguin, 1991), p. 132.
30. *St. Louis Globe-Democrat*, May 21, 1877.
31. Ward, "The New Sunday."
32. McCrossen, *Holy Day, Holiday*, pp. 58–62, 68–71.
33. Ibid., p. 14.
34. Hofstadter, *The Age of Reform: From Bryan to FDR*, p. 150.
35. McCrossen, *Holy Day, Holiday*, p. 140.

36. Ibid., p. 101.
37. Rybczynski, *Waiting for the Weekend*, pp. 133–34, 141–42.
38. Edward Reilly, "Religion," *Baseball: An Encyclopedia of Popular Culture* (Santa Barbara, Calif.: ABC-CLIO, 2000).
39. Steven Riess, *Touching Base: Professional Baseball and American Culture in the Progressive Era* (Westport, Conn.: Greenwood Press, 1980), p. 13.
40. Ibid., pp. 7–8.
41. Seymour, *Baseball: The Golden Age*, p. 361.
42. Philadelphia *Evening Bulletin*, November 8, 1933; unidentified newspaper clipping dated July 30, 1969, in the "Sunday Baseball" vertical file at the Urban Archives in the Paley Library at Temple University.
43. Rybczynski, *Waiting for the Weekend*, p. 143.
44. *St. Louis Post-Dispatch*, July 15, 1887.
45. Correspondence dated April 7, 2002, to author from Darryl Brock, author of "How Many Games Did the 1869 Red Stockings Win?" published in the 1987 *Baseball Research Journal*.
46. *St. Louis Globe-Democrat*, May 24, 1875.
47. *St. Louis Globe-Democrat*, May 17, 24, and 31, 1875.

Chapter 2

1. Voigt, *American Baseball*, p. 64; "The History of Major League Baseball," *Total Baseball*, 2nd ed. (New York: Warner Books, 1991), p. 10.
2. Seymour, *Baseball: The Early Years*, p. 91; Riess, *Touching Base*, p. 27.
3. National League Constitution, *Spalding Guide*, 1877.
4. *New York Clipper*, February 12, 1876.
5. *Chicago Tribune*, February 4, 1876.
6. *Spalding Guide*, 1878, p. 33.
7. Ibid., p. 36.
8. *Lowell Courier*, June 21, 1877.
9. Melville, *Early Baseball*, p. 94.
10. *St. Louis Globe-Democrat*, July 8, 1877.
11. *St. Louis Globe-Democrat*, June 11, 1877.
12. National League Constitution, *Spalding Guide*, 1878.
13. *New York Clipper*, December 15, 1877; *Chicago Tribune*, December 7, 1877.
14. Melville, *Early Baseball*, p. 113.
15. Seymour, *Baseball: The Early Years*, p. 91.
16. *Cincinnati Enquirer*, July 29, 1880.
17. *Worcester Spy*, July 23, 1880.
18. *Worcester Spy*, July 10, 1880.
19. *Cincinnati Enquirer*, July 29, 1880.
20. *Chicago Tribune*, August 15, 1880.
21. *Spalding Guide*, 1881. pp. 85–87.
22. Ibid.
23. Seymour, *Baseball: The Early Years*, p. 92.
24. *New York Clipper*, December 18, 1880.
25. Lee Allen, *The National League Story: The Official History*, (New York: Hill & Wang, 1965), p. 32.
26. Ibid.
27. *Chicago Tribune*, August 22, 1880.

Chapter 3

Seasonal attendance figures prior to 1901 are from "Nineteenth Century Major League Attendance," compiled by Robert Tiemann in an unpublished document housed in the Society for American Baseball Research lending library. Attendance figures from 1901 forward are from "Major League Attendance" in *Total Baseball*, 4th ed. (New York: Viking, 1995), pp. 105–109.

1. Nemec, *The Beer and Whisky League*, p. 22.
2. Voigt, *American Baseball*, pp. 212–14.
3. November 1881 letter from Hulbert to McKnight in the records of the Chicago Base Ball Club at the Chicago Historical Society, referenced in Melville, *Early Baseball*, p. 132.
4. *St. Louis Globe-Democrat*, July 25, August 1, and August 15, 1881.
5. *Louisville Courier-Journal*, May 8, 1882.
6. *Cincinnati Enquirer*, July 3, 1882.
7. Melville, *Early Baseball*, p. 133.
8. *Sporting Life*, May 13, 1883.
9. *Sporting Life*, May 20, 1883.
10. *Columbus Dispatch*, May 8, 1883.
11. *Sporting Life*, July 8, 1883.
12. *Sporting Life*, July 15, 1883.
13. Voigt, *American Baseball*, p. 138; Nemec, *The Beer and Whisky League*, p. 30.
14. Voigt, *American Baseball*, p. 138; Nemec, *The Beer and Whisky League*, p. 97.
15. Voigt, *American Baseball*, p. 139.
16. *St. Louis Globe-Democrat*, April 21, 1884.
17. *Boston Herald*, October 20, 1884.
18. *Indianapolis Journal*, May 19, 1884.
19. *Cincinnati Enquirer*, May 19, 1884.
20. *Indianapolis Journal*, May 20, 1884.
21. *Cincinnati Enquirer*, May 20, 1884.
22. *Columbus Dispatch*, June 30, 1884.
23. *New York Times*, June 17, 1884.
24. *New York Times*, June 23, 1884.
25. *Sporting Life*, July 2, 1884.
26. *New York Times*, June 23, 1884.
27. *New York Times*, June 24, 1884.
28. *Sporting Life*, July 2, 1884.
29. *Columbus Dispatch*, June 24, 1884.
30. *Columbus Dispatch*, June 28, 1884.
31. *Ex Parte Carroll, on Habeas Corpus*, 1884 WL 4674 (Ohio Com. Pl.).
32. *Columbus Dispatch*, June 30, 1884.
33. William McMahon, "Frederick Herbert Carroll," *Baseball's First Stars* (Cleveland: Society for American Baseball Research, 1996), p. 22.

Chapter 4

1. Nemec, *The Beer and Whisky League*, p. 72.
2. *Sporting Life*, March 4, 1885.
3. *Sporting Life*, March 11, 1885.
4. *Brooklyn Union*, referenced in *Sporting Life*, March 18, 1885.
5. *Sporting Life*, March 18, 1885.
6. *Sporting Life*, May 13, 1885.
7. *Sporting Life*, April 15, 1885.
8. *Brooklyn Daily Eagle*, May 2, 1886.
9. *Sporting Life*, May 12, 1886.
10. *Sporting Life*, August 10, 1887.
11. Ridgewood Park was located on Myrtle Avenue between Decatur and Weirfeld Streets.
12. *Brooklyn Daily Eagle*, July 26, 1886.
13. *Brooklyn Daily Eagle*, June 4, 1888.
14. *Brooklyn Daily Eagle*, August 23, 1886.
15. *Brooklyn Daily Eagle*, September 6, 1886.
16. *Sporting Life*, September 15, 1886.
17. David Zang, *Fleet Walker's Divided Heart* (Lincoln, Neb.: University of Nebraska Press, 1995), p. 51.
18. Ibid.
19. *Cincinnati Enquirer*, July 5, 1886.
20. *Sporting Life*, July 21, 1886.

21. *Cincinnati Enquirer*, July 12, 1886.
22. *Brooklyn Daily Eagle*, July 12, 1886.
23. *Cincinnati Enquirer*, July 12, 1886.
24. *Sporting Life*, July 21, 1886.
25. *Brooklyn Daily Eagle*, July 12, 1886.
26. *St. Louis Globe-Democrat*, October 18, 1885.
27. *Sporting Life*, May 20, 1885.
28. *Sporting Life*, April 6, 1887.
29. *St. Louis Post-Dispatch*, July 9, 1887.
30. Ibid.
31. Ibid.
32. *St. Louis Post-Dispatch*, July 11, 1887.
33. *St. Louis Post-Dispatch*, July 15, 1887.
34. Ibid.
35. *St. Louis Globe-Democrat*, July 16, 1887.
36. *St. Louis Post-Dispatch*, July 15, 1887.
37. Ibid.
38. Ibid.
39. Ibid.
40. Harlan Hatcher, *The Story of New Connecticut in Ohio* (Kent, Ohio: Kent State University Press, 1991), p. 4.
41. *Sporting Life*, July 20, 1887.
42. *Sporting Life*, August 24, 1887.
43. *Cleveland Plain Dealer*, August 22, 1887.
44. *Cleveland Plain Dealer*, August 26, 1887.
45. Ibid.
46. *Sporting Life*, April 27, 1887.
47. *St. Louis Globe-Democrat*, September 5, 1887.
48. *Brooklyn Daily Eagle*, September 5, 1887.
49. *St. Louis Globe-Democrat*, September 5, 1887.
50. *Brooklyn Daily Eagle*, September 12, 1887.
51. *New York Times*, September 12, 1887.
52. Nemec, *The Beer and Whisky League*, p. 138.
53. Dean Sullivan, "Faces in the Crowd: A Statistical Portrait of Baseball Spectators in Cincinnati, 1886–1888," *Journal of Sports History*, Winter 1990.
54. *Sporting Life*, May 23, 1888.
55. *Sporting Life*, May 30, 1888.
56. *Philadelphia Inquirer*, May 21, 1888.
57. Ibid.
58. *Philadelphia Inquirer*, June 11, 1888.
59. *The Sporting News*, June 16, 1888.
60. *Sporting Life*, July 18, 1888.
61. *Cleveland Plain Dealer*, July 22–23, 1888.
62. *Cleveland Plain Dealer*, July 30, 1888; While major league baseball never returned to Geauga Lake, the Aurora, Ohio, area did flourish as a popular site for amusement parks. Geauga Lake Park operated for 110 years until 2000, when it was renamed Six Flags Ohio. In 2001, the park merged with the neighboring Sea World of Ohio attraction to form the Six Flags Worlds of Adventure amusement complex.
63. *Sporting Life*, June 27, 1888; *Cleveland Plain Dealer*, July 16, 1888; the Malleables defeated the Graphics, 8–2.
64. *The Sporting News*, August 11, 1888.
65. *Cleveland Plain Dealer*, September 3, 1888.
66. *Cleveland Plain Dealer*, September 10, 1888.
67. Blair bill, S.2983 in the 50th Congress (CR 19), 1888, referenced in McCrossen, *Holy Day, Holiday*, pp. 146–47.
68. McCrossen, *Holy Day, Holiday*, pp. 145–46.
69. Ibid., pp. 146–47.

Chapter 5

1. George Gipe, "They Tried to Throw the Rascals Out," *Sports Illustrated*, May 20, 1974, p. E7.
2. *Brooklyn Daily Eagle*, May 6, 1889.
3. *Sporting Life*, September 18, 1889.
4. *Brooklyn Daily Eagle*, September 8, 1889.
5. *Brooklyn Daily Eagle*, September 9, 1889.
6. *Cincinnati Enquirer*, September 9, 1889.
7. *Brooklyn Daily Eagle*, September 15, 1889.
8. *Brooklyn Daily Eagle*, September 15, 1889; The Grand Jury process then was much less secretive than today. Names of the grand jurors were even printed in the newspaper.
9. Riess, "Professional Sunday Baseball."
10. *Brooklyn Daily Eagle*, October 7, 1889.
11. *Brooklyn Daily Eagle*, October 21 and 28, 1889.
12. *Cincinnati Enquirer*, August 12, 1889.
13. *Cincinnati Enquirer*, August 16-18, 1889.
14. *Brooklyn Daily Eagle*, August 26, 1889.
15. *Cincinnati Enquirer*, August 26, 1889.
16. *Brooklyn Daily Eagle*, September 2, 1889.
17. *Cincinnati Enquirer*, August 26, 1889.
18. Ibid.
19. Ibid.
20. David Ball, "John Good Reilly," *Baseball's First Stars* (Cleveland: Society for American Baseball Research, 1996), p. 135.
21. *Sporting Life*, October 30, 1889.
22. New Jersey court ruling mentioned in *Sporting Life*, April 24, 1889.
23. *Sporting Life*, April 26, 1890.
24. *Sporting Life*, May 3, 1890.
25. *Rochester Herald*, May 5, 1890.
26. *Rochester Herald*, May 12, 1890.
27. *The Sporting News*, May 3, 1890.
28. *Sporting Life*, May 18, 1890.
29. *Sporting Life*, May 31, 1890.
30. *Sporting Life*, June 21, 1890.
31. Ibid.
32. *Rochester Herald*, June 10, 1890.
33. *Sporting Life*, June 28, 1890.
34. *Sporting Life*, June 21, 1890.
35. *Washington Post*, June 9, 1890.
36. Gipe, "Throw the Rascals Out."
37. Washington was dropped from the National League along with Indianapolis to make room for the Brooklyn and Cincinnati teams from the Association.
38. *Washington Post*, June 16, 1890.
39. *Washington Post*, June 30, 1890.
40. *Sporting Life*, July 12, 1890.
41. *Sporting Life*, July 5, 1890.
42. *Rochester Herald*, July 21, 1890.
43. Ibid.
44. *Sporting Life*, July 26, 1890.
45. *Rochester Herald*, July 21, 1890.
46. *Sporting Life*, July 26, 1890.
47. *Rochester Democrat and Chronicle*, July 22, 1890.
48. *Rochester Democrat and Chronicle*, July 23, 1890.
49. *Rochester Democrat and Chronicle*, July 25, 1890.
50. *Rochester Herald*, July 26, 1890.
51. *Rochester Herald*, July 28, 1890.
52. *Rochester Democrat and Chronicle*, July 28, 1890.
53. *Sporting Life*, August 2, 1890.
54. *Rochester Herald*, August 4, 1890.
55. *Sporting Life*, August 9, 1890, and *Rochester Democrat and Chronicle*, August 4, 1890.
56. *Brooklyn Daily Eagle*, May 19 and 26, 1890.
57. *Brooklyn Daily Eagle*, July 28, 1890.
58. *New York Times*, July 28, 1890.

59. *Reach Guide*, 1891, p. 5.
60. *Philadelphia Inquirer*, October 13, 1890.
61. *Cincinnati Enquirer*, April 27, 1891.
62. Marty Appel, *Slide, Kelly, Slide*, (Lanham, Md.: Scarecrow Press, 1996), p. 161.
63. *Sporting Life*, May 2 and 9, 1891.
64. *Sporting Life*, June 20, 1891.
65. *Sporting Life*, May 16, 1891.
66. *Cincinnati Enquirer*, May 24, 1891.
67. *Sporting Life*, May 23, 1891.
68. *Sporting Life*, May 16 and 23, 1891, and *Cincinnati Enquirer*, May 25, 1891.
69. *Cincinnati Enquirer*, June 3, 1891.
70. *Sporting Life*, June 13, 1891. All material concerning the trial of Willie Mains in the succeeding paragraphs is from this source.
71. James D. Smith III, "Willard Eben Mains," *Baseball's First Stars* (Cleveland: Society for American Baseball Research, 1996), p. 99.
72. *Sporting Life*, June 13, 1891.
73. *Sporting Life*, June 20, 1891.
74. Ibid.
75. Ibid.
76. Ibid.
77. *Milwaukee Sentinel*, October 5, 1891.
78. McCrossen, *Holy Day, Holiday*, p. 146.
79. Ibid., p.147.
80. Ibid., pp. 147–48.

Chapter 6

1. Nemec, *The Beer and Whisky League*, p. 235.
2. Seymour, *Baseball: The Early Years*, p. 294.
3. *Sporting Life*, November 18, 1885.
4. *Spalding Guide*, 1891, p. 38.
5. *The Sporting News*, July 10, 1897.
6. *Boston Post*, May 9, 1892.
7. *Boston Herald*, May 9, 1892.
8. *Boston Post*, May 10, 1892.
9. *The Sporting News*, December 24, 1892.
10. Riess, "Professional Sunday Baseball."
11. *The Sporting News*, December 24, 1892.
12. *Brooklyn Daily Eagle*, as quoted in *Sporting Life*, May 27, 1893.
13. *Sporting Life*, May 27, 1893.
14. *Sporting Life*, June 17, 1893. Darby O'Brien died a week later on June 15.
15. *New York Times*, April 25, 1904.
16. *Brooklyn Daily Eagle*, July 10, 1893.
17. *Sporting Life*, July 15, 1893.
18. Ibid.
19. *Louisville Courier-Journal*, July 9, 1893.
20. *Sporting Life*, October 7, 1893.
21. Ibid.
22. *Fremont Daily News*, August 7, 1893.
23. *Chicago Tribune*, August 7, 1893. All material concerning the train accident in the succeeding paragraphs is from this newspaper article.
24. William McMahon, "James E. Ryan," *Nineteenth Century Stars* (Kansas City: Society for American Baseball Research, 1989), p. 112; Stephen Holtje, ed., "Jimmy Ryan," *The Ballplayers: Baseball's Ultimate Biographical Reference* (New York: Arbor House/William Morrow, 1990), p. 952.
25. *Sporting Life*, June 24, 1893.
26. Riess, "Professional Sunday Baseball."
27. *Chicago Tribune*, August 6, 1894.
28. *Sporting Life*, August 18, 1894.
29. *Sporting Life*, August 25, 1894.
30. *Sporting Life*, September 1 and 8, 1894.
31. *Chicago Tribune*, June 24, 1895.
32. *Chicago Tribune*, January 14, 1896.

33. Murphy, "Pros and Cons of Sunday Baseball."

Chapter 7

1. *Sporting Life*, August 19, 1895.
2. *Sporting Life*, January 25, 1896.
3. Reed Browning, *Cy Young: A Baseball Life* (Amherst, Mass.: University of Massachusetts Press, 2000), p. 52.
4. *Sporting Life*, May 16, 1896.
5. *Sporting Life*, June 20, 1896.
6. *Cincinnati Enquirer*, July 20, 1896.
7. *The Sporting News*, March 6, 1897.
8. *The Sporting News*, March 27, 1897.
9. *The Sporting News*, April 24, 1897.
10. *The Sporting News*, May 15, 1897.
11. *Cleveland Plain Dealer*, May 17, 1897.
12. *Sporting Life*, February 13, 1897.
13. Ibid.
14. *Cleveland Plain Dealer*, May 17, 1897.
15. Ibid.
16. Ibid.
17. Ibid. Arrested from the Cleveland team were Burkett, Sockalexis, Tebeau, McKean, Powell, Wallace, Blake, Zimmer, and Wilson. Arrested from the Washington team were Brown, Selbach, DeMontreville, Farrell, O'Brien, Cartwright, Abbey, German, and Reilly.
18. *Cleveland Plain Dealer*, July 10, 1897.
19. *State v. Powell*, Ohio Supreme Court decision, April 19, 1898, 58 Ohio St. 324, 50 N.E. 900.
20. *Cleveland Plain Dealer*, July 10, 1897.
21. Ibid.
22. Stephen Holtje, ed., "Jack Powell," *The Ballplayers: Baseball's Ultimate Biographical Reference* (New York: Arbor House/William Morrow, 1990), p. 880.
23. *Cleveland Plain Dealer*, July 12, 1897.
24. *State v. Powell*, Ohio Supreme Court decision.
25. *Sporting Life*, April 30, 1898.
26. *Cleveland Plain Dealer*, June 12, 1898.
27. *Cleveland Plain Dealer*, June 13, 1898.
28. *Cleveland Plain Dealer*, June 18, 1898.
29. *Cleveland Plain Dealer*, June 20, 1898.
30. *Cleveland Plain Dealer*, June 27, 1898.
31. *The Official Directory of Collinwood for 1899*, in the Special Collections of the Cleveland State University Library available online at the Cleveland Digital Library. Hall's picture was on page 3, his business ad on page 18, and his street listing on page 36. Collamer Street has been renamed East 152nd Street on today's maps while Manchester Avenue is now Aspinwall Avenue. Collinwood was annexed to Cleveland in 1910.
32. *Sporting Life*, September 3, 1898.
33. *Rochester Herald*, August 27, 1898.
34. *Rochester Herald*, August 29, 1898.
35. *Rochester Democrat*, August 29, 1898.
36. *Pittsburgh Post*, April 18, 1898.
37. *Sporting Life*, May 5, 1900.
38. Ibid.
39. *Sporting Life*, May 28, 1898.
40. *Chicago Tribune*, May 1, 1899.
41. Ibid.
42. *Sporting Life*, September 2, 1899.
43. *Sporting Life*, September 9, 1899.
44. *Chicago Tribune*, October 16, 1899.
45. *Sporting Life*, August 25, 1900.

Chapter 8

1. The other two 20,000-plus Sunday crowds were 22,484 on June 19, 1898, and 24,421 on June 25, 1899.
2. *Detroit Free Press*, May 1, 1899.
3. *Detroit Free Press*, June 12, 1899.
4. *Sporting Life*, June 24 and July 1, 1899.
5. *Detroit Free Press*, June 22, 1899.
6. Burns Park is long gone, but on today's map it would be located within the city of Detroit at the intersection of Dix Avenue and Waterman Street near the railroad tracks (*Green Cathedrals*, 1986 edition, p. 51); The town of Springwells became a city in the 1920s after the nearby River Rouge plant of the Ford Motor Company created a population surge due to the influx of factory workers. Springwells became the city of Fordson in 1925, which then merged in 1929 with the city of Dearborn (Dearborn Historical Society).
7. *Detroit Free Press*, May 7, 1900.
8. *Boston Globe*, July 22, 1901.
9. *Chicago Tribune*, April 29, 1901.
10. *Detroit Free Press*, April 21 and 28, 1901.
11. *Sporting Life*, May 18, 1901.
12. *Milwaukee Sentinel*, June 3, 1901.
13. *Boston Globe*, June 3, 1901.
14. *Sporting Life*, May 17, 1902.
15. *Cleveland Plain Dealer*, June 16, 1902.
16. *Sporting Life*, February 7, 1903.
17. Anthony Papalas, "Frank Navin," *American National Biography* (New York: Oxford University Press, 1999), Vol. 16, p. 253.
18. *Sporting Life*, March 14, 1903.
19. *Sporting Life*, April 18, 25, and May 2, 1903.
20. *Detroit Free Press*, May 25, 1903.
21. *New York Times*, April 11, 1904.
22. Wendy Knickerbocker, *Sunday at the Ballpark: Billy Sunday's Professional Baseball Career, 1883–1890* (Lanham Md: Scarecrow Press, 2000), pp. 1 and 3.
23. Murray Polner, *Branch Rickey* (New York: Atheneum, 1982), photo between pp. 52–53.
24. Ibid., p. 38.
25. Ibid., p. 42.
26. Ibid., p. 69.
27. *New York Times*, February 1, 1920; Ray Robinson, *Matty* (New York: Oxford University Press, 1993), p. 52.
28. Robinson, *Matty*, pp. 93–94.
29. *New York Times*, February 1, 1920.
30. *Boston Post*, June 15, 1903.
31. *Philadelphia Inquirer*, June 7, 1903.
32. *Boston Post*, September 7, 1903.
33. *New York Times*, October 5, 1903.

Chapter 9

1. *Brooklyn Daily Eagle*, April 11, 1904.
2. *Brooklyn Daily Eagle*, April 12, 1904.
3. *New York Times*, April 17, 1904.
4. *Brooklyn Daily Eagle*, April 18, 1904.
5. *New York Times*, April 19, 1904.
6. Ibid.
7. *New York Times*, April 23, 1904.
8. Ibid.
9. *New York Times*, April 25, 1904.
10. Ibid.
11. Ibid.
12. *New York Times*, May 2, 1904.
13. *Brooklyn Daily Eagle*, May 3, 1904.
14. *New York Times*, May 30, 1904.
15. *People v. Poole*, 89 N.Y.S. 773 (1904).
16. Lately Thomas, *The Mayor Who Mastered New York: The Life & Opinions of William J. Gaynor* (New York: Morrow, 1969), pp. 174–75.
17. Ibid., p. 91.

18. *New York Times*, August 12, 1894.
19. Thomas, *The Mayor Who Mastered New York*, pp. 467–68.
20. *Brooklyn Daily Eagle*, June 27, 1904.
21. *New York Times*, May 29, 1905.
22. *New York Times*, May 30, 1905.
23. *Brooklyn Daily Eagle*, June 9, 1906.
24. *New York Times*, April 30, 1906.
25. *Brooklyn Daily Eagle*, June 8, 1906.
26. *Brooklyn Daily Eagle*, June 9, 1906.
27. *New York Times*, June 9, 1906.
28. *New York Times*, June 11, 1906.
29. Ibid.
30. *Brooklyn Daily Eagle*, June 18, 1906.
31. *New York Times*, June 18, 1906.
32. *Brooklyn Daily Eagle*, June 18, 1906.
33. *Sporting Life*, October 20, 1906.
34. Sanborn, "The Pros and Cons of Sunday Baseball."
35. *Sporting Life*, July 28, 1906.
36. *Boston Globe*, August 20, 1907, and *Providence Journal*, August 26, 1907.
37. *Chicago Tribune*, August 26, 1907.
38. *Bridgeport Post*, August 19, 1907.
39. *Chicago Tribune*, August 19, 1907.
40. *Bridgeport Post*, August 19, 1907.
41. *Sporting Life*, August 24, 1907.
42. *Detroit Free Press*, August 19, 1907.
43. *Sporting Life*, September 14, 1907.
44. *Detroit Free Press*, August 15, 1907.
45. Papalas, "Frank Navin," *American National Biography*.
46. *Sporting Life*, September 14, 1907.
47. Zane Grey, *The Shortstop* (Chicago: A. C. McClurg, 1909; New York: William Morrow and Company, 1992), pp. 162 and 176.
48. *Sporting Life*, March 22, 1902.
49. *Sporting Life*, March 11, 1911; the Indiana case overturned the conviction of Indianapolis manager Charlie Carr in the minor league American Association.
50. *Sporting Life*, March 18, 1911.
51. *Sporting Life*, March 11, 1911.
52. Ibid.
53. *Sporting Life*, April 29, 1911.
54. *New York Times*, May 9, 1911; *The Sporting News*, May 11, 1911.
55. *Cleveland Plain Dealer*, May 15, 1911.

Chapter 10

1. Robert Slayton, *Empire Statesman: The Rise and Redemption of Al Smith* (New York: The Free Press, 2001), p. 67.
2. Ibid.
3. Jeffrey Krossler, "Baseball and the Blue Laws." *Long Island Historical Journal*, Vol. 5, No. 2; *Sporting Life*, July 28, 1884.
4. *Sporting Life*, September 5, 1891.
5. Krossler, "Baseball and the Blue Laws."
6. McCrossen, *Holy Day, Holiday*, p. 49.
7. Riess, "Professional Sunday Baseball."
8. Lane, "The Critical Situation in Sunday Baseball."
9. Ibid.
10. William Kirk, "Shall We Have Sunday Baseball?" *Baseball Magazine*, July 1908.
11. Rev. William Sunday, "Keep the Sabbath Undefiled," *Baseball Magazine*, August 1908.
12. Rabbi Charles Fleischer, "Sunday Baseball the Crying Need," *Baseball Magazine*, August 1908.
13. *New York Times*, April 16, 1907.
14. *New York Times*, April 27, 1910.

15. Ibid.
16. *New York Times*, March 15, 1911.
17. *New York Times*, March 24, 1911.
18. *New York Times*, July 13, 1911.
19. *New York Times*, April 8, 1911.
20. McCrossen, *Holy Day, Holiday*, p. 101.
21. *Sporting Life*, March 28, 1914.
22. Ibid.
23. *Sporting Life*, February 27, 1915.
24. Bob Golon, "Newark's Harrison Field" *The National Pastime*, 1996.
25. Marc Okkomen, *The Federal League of 1914-1915: Baseball's Third Major League* (Garrett Park, Md.: Society for American Baseball Research, 1989), p. 17.
26. Irwin Chusid, "The Short, Happy Life of the Newark Peppers" *Baseball Research Journal*, 1991.
27. *New York Times*, March 18, 1915.
28. Ibid.
29. Seymour, *Baseball: The Golden Age*, p. 245.
30. *Brooklyn Daily Eagle*, July 2, 1917.
31. *New York Times*, June 18, 1917.
32. *New York Times*, July 2, 1917.
33. *Brooklyn Daily Eagle*, July 2, 1917.
34. *Brooklyn Daily Eagle*, July 6, 1917.
35. Ibid.
36. Ibid.
37. *Brooklyn Daily Eagle*, September 24, 1917.
38. Ibid.
39. Ebbets, "A Defense of Sunday Baseball." Ebbets' comments in the next two paragraphs are also from this article.
40. *New York Times*, July 31, 1917.
41. *New York Times*, August 22, 1917.
42. Ibid.
43. Senate Bill Nos. 866, 1281, 1402 introduced on March 5, 1918, referenced in "Letters, Comments and Editorials Endorsing Sunday Baseball," April 1918.
44. New York *Evening World*, July 19, 1917, reprinted in "Letters, Comments and Editorials Endorsing Sunday Baseball," April 1918, p. 39.

45. *New York Times*, April 5 and 13, 1918.
46. Riess, *Touching Base*, p. 134.
47. Whitman's obituary in *New York Times*, March 30, 1947.
48. *New York Times*, May 4 and May 5, 1918.
49. *Brooklyn Daily Eagle*, July 29, 1918.
50. *Washington Post*, May 15, 1918.
51. *New York Times*, April 20, 1919.
52. *New York Times*, May 5, 1919.
53. *Brooklyn Daily Eagle*, May 5, 1919.
54. *New York Times*, May 12, 1919. The first Sunday home game for the Yankees that counted in the American League standings was played on June 8 when the Yankees defeated the Chicago White Sox 4–0.
55. Neil J. Sullivan, *The Diamond in the Bronx* (New York: Oxford University Press, 2001), pp. 18 and 28.
56. The July 25, 1920, Sunday games were: National League—Pittsburgh at Brooklyn, Philadelphia at Chicago, New York at Cincinnati, Boston at St. Louis. American League—Chicago at Cleveland, St. Louis at Detroit, Boston at New York, Philadelphia at Washington.
57. *New York Times*, April 21, 1924.
58. Marshall Smelser, *The Life That Ruth Built* (New York: Quadrangle, 1975), p. 270.
59. *New York Times*, October 26, 1923, p. 9.
60. Seymour, *Baseball: The Golden Age*, p. 364.
61. Slayton, *Empire Statesman*, p. 298.
62. *New York Times*, September 7, 1928.

Chapter 11

1. Lucas, "Unholy Experiment."
2. Ibid.

3. Philadelphia *Evening Bulletin*, May 23, 1917.
4. Philadelphia *Evening Bulletin*, April 30, 1918.
5. Philadelphia *Evening Bulletin*, May 1 and May 3, 1918.
6. Philadelphia *Evening Bulletin*, May 9, 1920.
7. Philadelphia *Evening Bulletin*, April 28, 1924.
8. Hofstadter, *Age of Reform*, pp. 279–80.
9. Heywood Broun, "A Bolt From the Blue," *The Nation*, July 31, 1920, referenced in Lucas, "Unholy Experiment."
10. U.S. Census, 1870–1890.
11. Sanborn, "The Pros and Cons of Sunday Baseball."
12. Outdoor Recreation Bureau flyer in "Sunday Baseball" vertical file at the National Baseball Library in Cooperstown, New York.
13. Letter dated May 7, 1925, to August Herrmann, president of Cincinnati National League Baseball Club, from Clyde Stern, managing director of the Outdoor Recreation Bureau, in "Sunday Baseball" vertical file at the National Baseball Library in Cooperstown, New York.
14. *New York Times*, July 24, 1926.
15. Philadelphia *Evening Bulletin*, August 5, 1926.
16. *The Sporting News*, August 26, 1926.
17. *New York Times*, August 7, 1926.
18. Philadelphia *Evening Bulletin*, August 5 and 11, 1926.
19. *New York Times*, August 20, 1926.
20. Ibid.
21. *New York Times*, August 22, 1926.
22. *Philadelphia Inquirer*, August 23, 1926.
23. Ibid.
24. *New York Times*, August 23, 1926.
25. Philadelphia *Evening Bulletin*, April 7, 1934.
26. *Philadelphia Inquirer*, August 23, 1926.
27. *Philadelphia Inquirer*, October 29, 1926. The material in the next three paragraphs is also from this source.
28. Philadelphia *Evening Bulletin*, April 12, 1927.
29. *Philadelphia Inquirer*, June 26, 1927.
30. *Commonwealth v. American Baseball Club of Philadelphia*, 290 Pa. 136, 138 Atl. 497, June 25, 1927. Material in the next three paragraphs is also from this source.
31. *Literary Digest*, "Pennsylvania Bans Sunday Baseball as Unholy," July 30, 1927.
32. *Commonwealth v. American Baseball Club of Philadelphia*.
33. Ibid.
34. Philadelphia *Evening Bulletin*, August 10, 1927.
35. *New York Times*, October 16, 1927.
36. *Literary Digest*, "Pennsylvania Bans Sunday Baseball as Unholy."
37. *Worcester Telegram*, September 30, 1927.
38. Jim Kaplan, *Lefty Grove: An American Original* (Cleveland: Society for American Baseball Research, 2000), p. 108.
39. *Worcester Telegram*, October 1, 1927.

Chapter 12

1. *Boston Herald*, May 23, 1887.
2. *Worcester Spy*, June 5, 1888.
3. *Boston Globe*, June 24, 1910, p. 5.
4. Stephen Hardy, *How Boston Played: Sport, Recreation, and Community 1865–1915* (Boston, Northeastern University Press, 1982), p. 60.
5. *Boston Globe*, April 9, 1914.
6. *New York Times*, April 16, 1918.
7. *Boston Globe*, May 26, 1918.

8. Seymour, *Baseball: The Golden Age*, p. 359.
9. Murphy, "The Pros and Cons of Sunday Baseball." The quotations attributed to Murphy in the following two paragraphs are also from this source.
10. *Boston Globe*, March 12 and April 3, 1920.
11. *Boston Globe*, evening edition, April 2, 1920.
12. Ibid.
13. *New York Times*, February 4, 1922.
14. *Boston Post* and *New York Times*, October 27, 1923.
15. *Boston Globe*, February 6, 1925. All remarks concerning the hearing in subsequent paragraphs are from this source.
16. *Boston Post*, August 4, 1925.
17. *Boston Post*, February 14, 1926.
18. *The Sporting News*, October 26, 1926, and *Boston Globe*, April 4, 1928.
19. *Boston Post*, May 10, 1926.
20. *Boston Post*, May 16, 1926.
21. *Boston Herald*, March 10, 1927.
22. *Boston Herald*, March 17, 1927.
23. *New York Times*, February 5, 1928.
24. *New York Times*, February 1, 1928.
25. *Boston Globe*, April 5, 1928.
26. *Boston Globe*, July 16, 1928.
27. *Boston Globe*, August 13, 1928.
28. Joseph Huthmacher, *Massachusetts People and Politics* (Cambridge: Harvard University Press, 1959), p. 260.
29. Richard Brown and Jack Tager, *Massachusetts: A Concise History* (Amherst, Mass.: University of Massachusetts Press, 2000), p. 272.
30. Ibid., pp. 242–46.
31. Ibid., p. 272.
32. *The Sporting News*, November 1, 1928.
33. The five players coming to the Braves in the Hornsby transaction were second basemen Fred Maguire; pitchers Percy Jones, Bruce Cunningham, and Harry Seibold; and catcher Doc Legett.
34. *Primaries and Elections, 1928* (Boston: Office of the Secretary of the Commonwealth, 1929).
35. *The Sporting News*, November 15, 1928. The 16 states that didn't allow Sunday baseball at the time were Arkansas, Delaware, Florida, Georgia, Iowa, Maine, Maryland, Mississippi, New Hampshire, North Carolina, Pennsylvania, South Carolina, South Dakota, Vermont, Virginia, and West Virginia.
36. *Literary Digest*, "Lifting the Ban on Sunday Sports," December 1, 1928.
37. *The Sporting News*, November 15, 1928.
38. *Boston Globe*, December 19, 1928.
39. *Boston Globe*, evening edition, December 21, 1928.

Chapter 13

The Boston Finance Commission hearings that examined the Sunday baseball bribery allegations were covered extensively by the Boston newspapers of the day. Material for this chapter was drawn predominantly from two major Boston newspapers, the *Boston Globe* and the *Boston Post*, as well as the *New York Times*, which carried abridged summaries of the hearings. The *Boston Herald* was not used as a source because its sports editor, Burt Whitman, was involved in the proceedings.

1. *Boston Globe*, December 23, 1928.
2. *Boston Globe*, evening edition, December 24, 1928.
3. James Connolly, *The Triumph of Ethnic Progressivism: Urban Political Culture in Boston, 1900-1925* (Cambridge: Harvard University Press, 1998), p. 86.
4. Ibid., p. 188.
5. *Boston Globe*, December 27 and 29, 1928.

6. *Boston Globe*, December 28, 1928.
7. *Boston Globe*, January 1, 1929.
8. The summary of the bribery allegation contained in this paragraph and the next three paragraphs was drawn by the author based on all the material sourced in this chapter.
9. Material on the January 2 hearings is from *Boston Globe*, *Boston Post*, and *New York Times* editions of January 3, 1929.
10. *Boston Globe*, January 3, 1929.
11. Material on the January 3 hearings is from *Boston Globe*, *Boston Post*, and *New York Times* editions of January 4, 1929.
12. *New York Times*, January 5, 1929.
13. Material on the January 4 hearings is from *Boston Globe*, *Boston Post*, and *New York Times* editions of January 5, 1929.
14. *Boston Globe*, January 8, 1929.
15. Material on the January 8 hearings is from *Boston Globe*, *Boston Post*, and *New York Times* editions of January 9, 1929.
16. Material on the January 9 hearings is from *Boston Globe*, *Boston Post*, and *New York Times* editions of January 10, 1929.
17. Material on the January 10 hearings is from *Boston Globe*, *Boston Post*, and *New York Times* editions of January 11, 1929.
18. *Boston Globe*, January 18, 1929.
19. Material on the January 28 Boston City Council hearing is drawn predominately from the William Brown article, "Sunday Baseball Comes to Boston," in the 1994 *The National Pastime*, since it elaborates richly on the newspaper coverage of the hearing.
20. *Boston Herald*, February 8, 1929. Full text of the FinCom report was contained on page 24 of that newspaper issue.
21. Harold Kaese, *Boston Braves* (New York: G. P. Putnam's Sons, 1948), p. 207.
22. *Boston Globe*, February 14, 1929.
23. *Boston Globe*, May 13, 1929.
24. *Boston Globe*, January 4, 1929.
25. Robert Fuchs and Wayne Soini, *Judge Fuchs and the Boston Braves* (Jefferson, North Carolina: McFarland & Company, 1998), p. 58.
26. *Boston Globe*, April 29, 1929.
27. *Boston Globe*, May 20, 1932, and *Boston City Directory, 1929*.
28. *Boston Globe*, February 20, 1929.
29. *Boston Globe*, April 29, 1929.
30. *Boston Globe*, May 6, 1929.
31. The four Red Sox games were the April 28 inaugural Sunday game (22,000 attendance) and Yankees games on May 26 (27,000), June 30 (25,000), and September 1 (30,000). The four Braves games were its May 5 inaugural Sunday game (35,000 attendance), May 12 (25,000), June 23 (20,000), and July 21 (25,000).
32. *Boston Post*, June 24 and July 22, 1929.
33. *Boston Post*, July 14, 1930.
34. Huthmacher, *Massachusetts People and Politics*, p. 213.
35. *Boston Globe*, May 20, 1932. The Church of the Disciples was built in 1904. By 1941, the Unitarian congregation had dwindled to just a few members, so the church was sold to the Boston Temple of the Seventh Day Adventist Church, which continues to own the building. The church's address is now 105 Jersey Street.
36. *Boston Globe*, May 29, 1932.
37. Kaese, *Boston Braves*, p. 233.
38. *Boston Post*, December 6, 1961. History treated Charles Adams more kindly. After Adams died in 1947, his obituary noted, "He took the ailing Boston National League baseball team when it was floundering around in the cellar of the National League and almost bankrupt and built it into the

valuable property it is today" (*Boston Herald*, October 3, 1947).

Chapter 14

1. Bruce Kuklick, *To Every Thing a Season: Shibe Park and Urban Philadelphia, 1909-1976* (Princeton, N.J.: Princeton University Press, 1991), p. 71.
2. *Literary Digest*, "Pennsylvania Changes Ancient Blue Laws," November 25, 1933.
3. *New York Times*, August 3, 1930.
4. Philadelphia *Evening Bulletin*, August 2, 1930.
5. Philadelphia *Evening Bulletin*, August 4, 1930.
6. Philadelphia *Evening Bulletin*, August 13, 1930.
7. *Philadelphia Record*, August 23, 1930.
8. *New York Times*, April 22, 1931.
9. *New York Times*, May 13, 1931.
10. *Philadelphia Inquirer*, May 20, 1931.
11. Ibid.
12. Charlie Bevis, *Mickey Cochrane: The Life of a Baseball Hall of Fame Catcher* (Jefferson, North Carolina: McFarland & Company, 1998), p. 101.
13. *Philadelphia Inquirer*, July 11, 1932.
14. *Cleveland Plain Dealer*, July 11, 1932.
15. *New York Times*, May 8, 1932.
16. *New York Times*, March 15, 1933.
17. *Philadelphia Inquirer*, March 15, 1933. The *Inquirer* writer seemed to be unaware that "Merkle's Boner" occurred when Fred Merkle, a runner on first base, failed to touch *second* base after Al Bridwell stroked the apparent game-winning hit in a late September 1908 game.
18. *New York Times*, March 15, 1933.
19. Ibid.
20. Philadelphia *Evening Bulletin*, March 16, 1933.

21. Philadelphia *Evening Bulletin*, March 28, 1931, and March 27, 1933.
22. Philadelphia *Evening Bulletin*, March 17, 1933.
23. *New York Times*, April 12, 1933.
24. *New York Times*, April 13, 1933.
25. *Philadelphia Inquirer*, April 19, 1933.
26. Ibid.
27. M. Nelson McGeary, *Gifford Pinchot: Forrester, Politician* (Princeton, N.J.: Princeton University Press, 1960), p. 325.
28. *Philadelphia Inquirer*, April 26, 1933.
29. *Philadelphia Inquirer*, November 1, 1933.
30. Bevis, *Mickey Cochrane*, pp. 108-109.
31. *Philadelphia Inquirer*, April 12, 1933.
32. Philadelphia *Evening Bulletin*, November 8, 1933, and *Philadelphia Inquirer*, November 9, 1933.
33. The football Pirates changed their team name to Steelers for the 1940 season. The football Dodgers disbanded after the 1943 season. Pro football teams parroting their city's baseball team name were a common occurrence in the early days of the National Football League, to create interest in the fledging league. The best-known example is the New York Giants, although the Cincinnati Reds and Cleveland Indians were also football teams at one point. Parallel names have survived longer, as witnessed by the Detroit Lions (vs. baseball Tigers) and Chicago Bears (vs. baseball Cubs). For more, see the author's article "Diamond Names for Gridiron Teams" in the 1996 *Baseball Research Journal*.
34. Philadelphia *Evening Bulletin*, November 9, 1933. License fees, originally set at a flat fee of $50, were finalized as a graduated schedule: $50 where attendance capacity is 5,000 or more; $10 for capacity ranging from 2,500 to

5,000; $5 for those ranging from 1,000 to 2,500; and $1 for less than 1,000.

35. Philadelphia *Evening Bulletin*, November 8, 1933.

36. *Philadelphia Inquirer*, December 13, 1933.

37. *Philadelphia Inquirer*, April 9, 1934.

38. Kuklick, *To Every Thing a Season*, pp. 72–73.

Chapter 15

1. Bob Boynton, "One Team, Two Fields," *The National Pastime*, 1995.

2. Thomas Karnes, "The Sunday Saga of Ted Lyons," *Baseball Research Journal*, 1981.

3. Lyle Spatz, "Ted Lyons's Complete Season of 1942," *The National Pastime*, 1995.

4. *New York Times*, May 11, 1948. Not disappointing the crowd of 40,797 to see the Pirates defeat the Dodgers 10–8 was certainly the reason for the "confusion" over whether the 7:00 curfew was on standard time and could be advanced an hour to 8:00 for daylight savings time. Pittsburgh promised not to play past 7:00 again.

5. *New York Times*, September 4, 1939.

6. American League president Will Harridge backed up umpire Hubbard and ruled the playing statistics would stand for seven innings, with those of the eighth inning tossed out. So Heving never officially pitched in that game and Peacock had two less career putouts since the suicide outs at home plate by Selkirk and Gordon never officially occurred.

7. *New York Times*, December 13, 1949.

8. *New York Times*, April 29 and August 17, 1957.

9. Unidentified newspaper clipping dated July 30, 1958, in the "Sunday Baseball" vertical file at the Urban Archives in the Paley Library at Temple University.

10. Unidentified newspaper clippings dated July 24 and July 31, 1959, in the "Sunday Baseball" vertical file at the Urban Archives in the Paley Library at Temple University.

11. The ice cream sundae was created to evade a Sunday blue law that forbade serving ice cream sodas on the Lord's Day. An enterprising proprietor, in obeying the law, served his customers ice cream with syrup, but without the soda. The popular soda-less soda became the Sunday soda. After Sabbatarians objected to the dish's name, which they felt disrespected the Lord's Day, the "y" was changed to an "e" for the treat to be called the sundae.

12. *New York Times*, July 19, 1954, and unidentified newspaper clipping dated July 20, 1954 in the "Sunday Baseball" vertical file at the Urban Archives in the Paley Library at Temple University.

13. *New York Times*, January 25 and June 10, 1963.

14. David Pietrusza, *Lights On!* (Lanham, Md.: Scarecrow Press, 1997), p. 223.

BIBLIOGRAPHY

Betts, John. *America's Sporting Heritage: 1850-1950*. Reading, Mass.: Addison-Wesley, 1974.

Daniels, Bruce. *Puritans at Play: Leisure and Recreation in Colonial New England*. New York: St. Martin's Press, 1995.

Dulles, Foster Rhea. *A History of Recreation*. New York: Appleton-Century-Crofts, 1965.

Ebbets, Charles. "A Defense of Sunday Baseball: Why I Believe Major League Baseball Ought to Be Permitted in the Eastern Cities." *Baseball Magazine*, September 1917.

Hofstadter, Richard. *The Age of Reform: From Bryan to FDR*. New York: Alfred A. Knopf, 1956

Lane, F. C. "The Greatest Problem in the National Game: The Critical Situation in Sunday Baseball." *Baseball Magazine*, October 1911.

Lucas, John A. "The Unholy Experiment: Professional Baseball's Struggle Against Pennsylvania Sunday Blue Laws 1926-1934." *Pennsylvania History*, No. 38, 1971.

McCrossen, Alexis. *Holy Day, Holiday: The American Sunday*. Ithaca, New York: Cornell University Press, 2000.

Melville, Tom. *Early Baseball and the Rise of the National League*. Jefferson, North Carolina: McFarland & Company, 2001.

Murphy, Charles. "The Pros and Cons of Sunday Baseball." *Baseball Magazine*, June 1919.

Nemec, David. *The Beer and Whisky League: The Illustrated History of the American Association, Baseball's Renegade Major League*. New York: Lyons & Burford, 1994.

Riess, Steven. "Professional Sunday Baseball: A Study in Social Reform, 1892-1934." *Maryland Historian*, No. 4, 1973.

Sanborn, Irving. "The Pros and Cons of Sunday Baseball." *Baseball Magazine*, October 1926.

Seymour, Harold. *Baseball: The Early Years*. New York: Oxford University Press, 1960.

———. *Baseball: The Golden Age*. New York: Oxford University Press, 1971.

Voigt, David. *American Baseball: From Gentleman's Sport to the Commissioner System*. Norman, Okla.: University of Oklahoma Press, 1966.

Baseball Periodicals

New York Clipper
Reach Guide
Spalding Guide

Sporting Life
The Sporting News

General Newspapers

Boston Globe
Boston Herald
Boston Post
Brooklyn Daily Eagle
Chicago Tribune
Cincinnati Enquirer
Cleveland Plain-Dealer
Columbus Dispatch
Detroit Free Press
Indianapolis Journal
Louisville Courier-Journal

Milwaukee Sentinel
New York Times
Philadelphia *Evening Bulletin*
Philadelphia *Inquirer*
Pittsburgh Post-Gazette
Rochester Democrat and Chronicle
Rochester Herald
St. Louis Globe-Democrat
St. Louis Post-Dispatch
Washington Post
Worcester Spy

INDEX

Abbey, Charlie 6, 299n
Adams, Charles 228, 230, 231p, 233, 237, 239–240, 245, 305n
Alexandria Driving Park 87
Allegheny (AA) *see* Pittsburgh (AA)
Altrock, Nick 255
American Association: adopted Sunday baseball 34–35; bad image 57–58, 67; decline 81–82, 100; expanded Sunday baseball 51–52, 66–73; merger with National League 101–102; required Sunday home games 82
American League: adopted Sunday baseball 138–139; all teams played on a Sunday 143; minor league Sunday play 136–138; special Sunday rules 265, 267
Ames, Red 147
Anderson, Fred 189
Angus, Sam 144
Anson, Cap 6, 110, 112, 114
arrests of players (amateurs): Boston 214–215; Brooklyn 158; New York 153, 155, 176; Philadelphia 247–248
arrests of players (professionals): Baltimore 86, 87; Brooklyn 6, 8, 9–10, 46–47, 79, 155, 159, 162, 187; Chicago 7, 114; Cincinnati 5–6, 7, 9, 10, 45, 78–79, 94–98, 162, 189; Cleveland 7, 9, 65, 121–122, 127; Columbus 6, 46–48; Detroit 137; Indianapolis 5–6, 44–45; New York 10, 189; Philadelphia 9, 155; Rochester 6–7, 88–89; St. Louis 6, 60–61; Washington 87, 96–97, 121–122.
Athletic (AA) *see* Philadelphia (AA)
Ayers, Doc 193

Baldwin, Kid 79
Baltimore (AA): first Sunday road game 37; left league 82; other Sunday games 52, 60, 70, 73; re-entered league 92; transfer to National League 102
Baltimore (AL) 140, 266
Baltimore (minor league) 86, 87
Baltimore (NL) 105, 134
Barnie, Billy 52, 86, 87
Berry, Charlie 259
Beville, Charlie 141
Beyerle's Park 72–73
Bishop, Max 258, 259
Blair, Footsie 243
Blair, Henry 73
Blake, Harry 299n
Blong, Joe 27
Boston (AA) 98–99
Boston (AL): exhibition games on Sunday 150, 217; first Sunday game at Fenway Park 245; first Sunday home game (Braves Field) 240–241; first Sunday road game 140–141; one-game road trips on Sunday 222; other Sunday games 242, 243, 264
Boston (NL): bribery scandal 228–240; exhibition games on Sunday 149, 165, 222; first Sunday home game 240–241; first Sunday road game 149; holdout on Sunday play 104, 131, 135, 142, 148–149, 204, 215; one-game road trips on Sunday 196, 222, 241; other Sunday games 153, 241, 242; Rocky Point games 149, 165
Boston (UA) 44
Bracken, Jack 140
Braves Field 237, 240
Bridgeport, Connecticut 164, 165–166
Briggs, Grant 91
Broad Ripple, Indiana 44
Brooklyn (AA): arrests of players 6, 46–47, 79; crowds 54, 66, 68, 75–76; exhibition

games on Sunday 77; first Sunday home game 52–53; first Sunday road game 46; one-game road trips on Sunday 68–69; other Sunday games 57, 66; replacement team 91–92; stoppage of Sunday play 54–55, 66, 77; use of Sunday-only ball grounds (Ridgewood Park) 52–55
Brooklyn (FL) 182, 184
Brooklyn (NL): arrests of players 8, 9–10, 155, 159, 162, 187; exhibition games on Sunday 107, 150, 182; first Sunday home game 153–154; first Sunday home game at Ebbets Field 186–187; first Sunday home game (legal) 194–195; first Sunday road game 108; holdout on Sunday play 104; one-game road trips on Sunday (host) 196, 241–242, 250, 255, 259; other Sunday games 129–130, 197; schemes to play Sunday games 153–163; threat to play in Newark 192
Brooklyn, Maryland 86
Brown, Tom 299n
Browning, Pete 36
Bruce Grounds 44–45
Brush, John 154, 157
Burkett, Jesse 6, 9, 111, 119, 122, 299n
Burnett, Johnny 251–252
Burns, George 189
Burns, Jim 137, 144, 168
Burns Park 137–138, 139–140, 300n
Burns, Tom 112
Byrne, Charlie 51–52, 68, 76

Calihan, Will 84
Canton, Ohio 143, 145
Carman, George 93
Carpenter, Hick 79
Carr, Charlie 301n
Carroll, Dan 231, 235–236
Carroll, Fred 6, 46, 48–49, 49p
Cartwright, Ed 299n
Cedar Avenue Driving Park 64–65
Charlotte, New York 129
Chatham, Buster 243
Check, Charlie 9, 162
Chicago (AL): crowds 154; exhibition games on Sunday 224; first Sunday home game 139; other Sunday games 209, 263
Chicago (NL): arrests of players 7, 114; crowds 135, 154, 163; disasters related to Sunday play 110–111, 113; exhibition games on Sunday 165–166; first Sunday home game 107; first Sunday road game 106; one-game road trips on Sunday (host) 110, 173, 259; other Sunday games 132, 133, 161, 243; position on Sunday play 104, 106; as Sunday baseball capital 135–136, 163
Chicago (UA) 43
Church of the Disciples 240–241, 244p, 305n
Cincinnati 1869) 21
Cincinnati (AA): arrests of players 5–6, 7, 45, 78–79, 94–98; disorderly crowds 56–57; first Sunday home game 42; first Sunday road game 37; one-game road trips on Sunday 56; other Sunday games 56–57, 69; replacement team 93–99; stoppage of Sunday play 78–80; suspension of Sunday play 55–56; transfer to National League 81
Cincinnati (NL, pre-1890): banishment from league 31–33, 36; Sunday games 28–31
Cincinnati (NL, 1890+): arrests of players 9, 10, 162, 189; crowds 119; fines for Sunday play 104; first Sunday home game 104–105; one-game road trips on Sunday (host) 173, 250, 259; other Sunday games 133
Cincinnati (UA) 42, 44
Clark, Bob 57
Clark, Ed 56–57
Clarke, Fred 132–133
clergy: Berry 127; Clark 113; Conrad 221, 224; Forney 208, 253, 256; Hawes 131; Sunday 146, 178
Cleveland (AA): arrests of players 7, 65; first Sunday home game at alternate site 64–65; impact of 1885 court decision 55; transfer to National League 73; use of Sunday-only ballparks 64–65, 71–73
Cleveland (AL): first Sunday home game 172; neutral-site Sunday games 143–145; one-game road trips on Sunday 140, 144, 167, 172–173; one-game road trips on Sunday (host) 173, 205, 250, 255; other Sunday games 193, 251–252; position on Sunday play 140, 142, 169, 170
Cleveland (NL): arrests of players 9, 121–122, 127; dropped from league 134; first Sunday home game 120–121; first Sunday road game 105; neutral-site Sunday game 129–130; one-games road trips on Sunday 105–106, 117; other Sunday games 124, 133; stoppage of Sunday play 127–128; suspension of Sunday road games 116–119; transfer to St. Louis

119–120, 130; use of Sunday-only ballpark 126; *see also State v. Powell*
Cochrane, Mickey 205, 250, 258, 259
Collins, Bill 108
Collins, Jimmy 141, 143
Collinwood, Ohio 126–128; 299n
Columbian Exposition 16, 100, 106–107, 206
Columbus (AA): arrests of players 6, 46–48; disruption of Sunday play 39; dropped from league 50; first Sunday home game 38; re-entry to league 75; stoppage of Sunday play 48–49
Columbus, Ohio 143, 145
Comiskey, Charlie 40, 76
Commonwealth v. American Baseball Club of Philadelphia 211–212, 285–291
Coney Island, New York 51–52
Continental Sabbath 11, 14, 40, 59
Cooley, Duff 149
court proceedings: Brooklyn 77, 156, 157, 162–163, 187–188, 203, 282–285; Chicago 113–114; Cincinnati 79, 94–97; Cleveland 55, 122–123, 142, 203, 278–282; Columbus 47–48; Detroit 137; Indianapolis 45; New York 189–190; Philadelphia 207–212, 285–291; Rochester 89–90; St. Louis 61–62, 275–278
Crane, Ed 94
Crawford, George 93
Cronin, Joe 264
Croul, Frank 144, 169
Cunningham, Ed 231, 234
Cuppy, George (Nig) 105, 141

Dahlgren, Babe 264
Daily, One Arm 43
Daly, Joe 93
Davidson, Claude 1, 224
Dayton, Ohio 143
Decker, George 111, 113
DeMontreville, Gene 132–133, 299n
Detroit (AL): first Sunday home game at alternate site 139; first Sunday home game at Bennett Park 167–169; minor league Sunday history 136–138; neutral-site Sunday games 145; one-game road trips on Sunday 167, 222, 250; other Sunday games 159; use of charitable donations 137, 168; use of Sunday-only ballpark (Burns Park) 137–140, 144–145
Dillon, Pop 140
Doe, Fred 220, 221

Dorner, Gus 145
Dowd, Tommy 140–141
Dreyfuss, Barney 133, 204
Duffy, Hugh 9, 155
Dykes, Jimmy 252, 263

Earnshaw, George 258, 259
Eason, Mal 9, 162
Ebbets, Charlie 10, 152–154, 156, 160–162, 187–189, 192, 197
Eclipse (AA) *see* Louisville (AA)
Eclipse Park 37, 108–109, 132
Ecorse, Michigan 136
ESPN 268–269
Esterbrook, Tom 49
Euclid Beach Park 126

Farrell, Duke 99, 299n
Federal League 182–185
Fenway Park 237, 240–241, 243–244
Ferguson, Bob 79
Field, Jim 46
Foley, Curry 27
Fort Wayne, Indiana 143
Foxx, Jimmie 205, 250, 252, 259
Fraser, Chick 9–10, 162, 166–167, 166p
Frazee, Harry 196, 217
Freeman, Buck 140–141, 145
Fuchs, Emil 219–220, 226, 228–240, 245
Fultz, Dave 145–146

Gardner, Jim 127
Geauga Lake, Ohio 71–72, 126
Geier, Phil 159
German, Les 299n
Gilbert, Billy 140
Gloucester, New Jersey 69–71, 82, 99
Gordon, Joe 264
Grand Avenue Park 21, 27–28
Grand Rapids, Michigan 145
Greenwood, Bill 46, 47, 89
Grey, Zane 170
Griffin, Mike 130
Griffith, Clark 139, 159
Grimes, Burleigh 241
Grissom, Marv 265
Grove, Lefty 205, 209, 213, 250, 258, 259

Haas, Mule 252
Hallman, Bill 140, 141
Hamilton, Ohio 78–79
Hanlon, Ned 9, 162
Harkness, Spec 172
Harrison Park 183–185, 192–193

Index

Hart, Jim 106, 133–114
Hartnett, Gabby 243
Hauck, John 55, 56
Heving, Joe 264
Hoboken, New Jersey 20, 149, 150, 156, 164
Hornsby, Rogers 226, 236
Houston (NL) 268
Hulbert, William 22, 25–26, 29–31, 35–36, 103

Indianapolis (AA): arrests of players 5–6, 45; dropped from league 50; first Sunday home game 44–45; use of Sunday-only ballpark (Bruce Grounds) 44–45
Indianapolis (NL) 29
Iron Pier, New York 90–91
Irondequoit, New York 83, 85–86, 88–89

Jacklitsch, Fred 6, 155, 159
Johnson, Ban 138, 142, 168
Johnson, Tom 17, 170
Jones, Fielder 130
Jones, Oscar 159
judges: Gaynor 8–9, 153, 156–158; Gregg 95–96; Hargest 209; McQuade 10, 189–190; Noonan 60, 62; Ong 8, 123; Schaffer 211; Smith 207, 208; Wylie 48
justices of the peace: Coy 86, 88, 89; "Squire" Drummond 87; history of 175

Kansas City (AA) 68
Kansas City (UA) 43, 44
Keefe, John 91
Keefe, Tim 39, 49
Kelley, Joe 146
Kelly, Mike "King" 6, 7, 93–94
Kennedy's Kids 91
Kentucky Sunday game sites: Covington 95, 97; Ludlow 78; Parkland 108–109
Keokuk (NA) 22
Kilfoyl, John 169
Kittridge, Malachi 110–111
Knell, Phil 117
Knickerbocker Club 20
Knox, Andy 93
Krausse, Lew 251
Kuehne, Willie 46

Lajoie, Nap 143
Law and Order Societies: Cincinnati 78; Cleveland 64; Columbus 46; Irondequoit 85–86, 88–89
laws prohibiting Sunday games: admission fees 160, 218; "blue laws" 13–14; breach of peace 158, 160; day of rest 11, 14–15, 214; historical perspective 11–20; labor 45–48, 59–62, 81–82, 201; Massachusetts history 14, 214–219; New York history 175–176; Ohio history 63–66; Pennsylvania history 202–202; public sport 122, 155, 157, 160; Puritan attitudes 11–13
Leach, Tommy 132
League Park 121, 171
Lee, Joseph 215
legislation for Sunday baseball: ballpark in another city as leverage 192, 236–237, 247, 254; church proximity restrictions 171, 218, 240–241, 244; hours of play restrictions 171, 191, 218, 253, 258, 264; local option concept 19, 171, 181, 191, 218, 227, 253, 258; Massachusetts 216–219, 220–224, 243–244, 264; New York 174, 179–182, 185, 190–194; Ohio 125, 171–172; Pennsylvania 247–257, 264–265; voter referendum 220, 223–226, 253, 255, 258, 272; Washington, D.C. 193
Lindsey, Ohio 110
Liquor League (Cleveland) 120–121
Long Island Grounds 92
Louisville (AA): first Sunday home game 36; one-game road trips on Sunday (host) 37–38; other Sunday games 67, 90–91; transfer to National League 102
Louisville (NL, pre-1892): 25, 26, 28
Louisville (NL, 1892+): dropped from league 134; first Sunday home game 105; one-game road trips on Sunday 110, 133; Parkland disagreement 108–109
Lowell, Mass. (minor league) 27
Lucas, Henry 41
Lynch, William 230–232, 235, 236, 238
Lyons, Denny 71
Lyons, Harry 89
Lyons, Ted 263

MacFayden, Danny 213, 242
Mack, Bill 165
Mack, Connie 207, 247, 250, 251, 253–254, 256, 258, 259, 260
Mack, Denny 36
Mains, Willie 7, 95–96, 97p
Maranville, Rabbit 241, 243
Maspeth, New York 92
Mathewson, Christy 10, 147, 189
mayors: Dick (Hamilton, Ohio) 79; Hall (Collinwood, Ohio) 128, 299n; Kendrick (Philadelphia) 202, 206–207; McKisson

(Cleveland) 120–121, 125; Mosby (Cincinnati) 94–95; Nichols (Boston) 227, 238
McAdoo, William 153–156, 160
McBride, John 93
McCarthy, Joe 243
McCormick, Harry 37
McGill, Willie 110
McGinnis, Jumbo 38, 39
McGinnity, Joe 132, 147
McGraw, John 10, 147, 151, 189
McGunnigle, Billy 77
McKean, Ed 65, 299n
McKnight, Denny 35, 58
McTamany, Jim 92
Merkle, Fred 147, 253
Metropolitan (AA) *see* New York (AA)
Milwaukee (AA) 99–100
Milwaukee (AL) 140–142
Milwaukee (NL) 29
Milwaukee (UA) 43, 44
minor league adoption of Sunday baseball 1, 55, 86–87, 98, 136–138, 164, 177, 179, 200, 224, 252–253
Morgan, Ed 252
Morris, Cannonball 46, 48
Morris, Ed 243
Mowrey, Mike 187
Mueller, Heinie 241
Mullane, Tony 36, 37
Murphy, Charles 115
Murphy, Morgan 99

National Association 21–23
National League: all teams play on Sunday 195; banned Sunday games 24–33; expanded Sunday games 106–107, 130; permitted Sunday games 101–104; policy against Sunday games 59, 81, 103–104; special Sunday rules 264–265, 267
Navin, Frank 144, 168, 169
neutral-site Sunday games: Cleveland 129, 143, 145; Detroit 145; strategy 129, 144, 163
New Jersey Sunday game sites: Atlantic City 254; Bayonne 150; Camden 247, 254; Fairway 131; Gloucester 69–71, 82, 99; Hoboken 20, 149, 150, 156, 164; Jersey City 156, 177; Newark 153, 156, 159, 177, 183, 192–193; Weehawken 66–67, 132
New York (AA): first Sunday home game at alternate site 66–67; first Sunday road game 67; left league 67; other Sunday games 39, 64
New York (AL): crowds 195, 197; exhibition games on Sunday 152, 154, 161, 182; first Sunday home game at alternate site 159; first Sunday home game (Polo Grounds) 186; first Sunday home game (legal) 195; first Sunday home game at Yankee Stadium 198; one-game road trips on Sunday 192; one-game road trips on Sunday (host) 205, 222, 250; other Sunday games 199, 242, 264; position on Sunday play 154; threat to play in Newark 192
New York (NL): doubleheaders 265, 268; exhibition games on Sunday 107, 131, 150, 153, 154, 182; first Sunday home game at alternate site 131–132; first Sunday home game 189; first Sunday home game (legal) 194; first Sunday road game 131; one-game road trips on Sunday 192, 250; other Sunday games 157, 160; position on Sunday games 104, 154, 157; use of New Jersey ballpark 131–132; threat to play in Newark 193
New York Sunday game sites: Iron Pier 90–91; Long Island Grounds 92; Maspeth 92; Ontario Beach 129–130; Ridgewood 52–55, 66, 77, 91–92, 152, 153, 155, 183; Three Rivers 83; Windsor Beach 83, 90
Newark (FL) 183–185
Newburgh, Ohio 72–73, 142

O'Brien, Darby 107, 298n
O'Brien, John 299n
O'Connor, Jack 124, 130
Ohio Sunday game sites: Geauga Lake 71–72; Hamilton 78–79; Newburgh 72–73, 142
one-game road trips on Sunday: first instance 56; last instance 255; use by teams 68–69, 105–106, 110, 117, 148, 167, 172–173, 184, 196, 204, 205, 250, 255, 260
O'Neil, Ed 93
Ontario Beach Grounds 129–130
Outdoor Recreational League 204–205, 224, 226, 234, 236, 239

Parent, Fred 141
Parkland, Kentucky 108–109
Pasek, Johnny 259
Patterson, Roy 140
Peacock, Johnny 264
People v. Poole 8–9, 157, 158, 282–285
Pettit, Bob 100
Philadelphia (AA): first Sunday home game at alternate site 70–71; first Sunday road game 37; other Sunday games 56–57,

94–95; stoppage of Sunday play 92–93; use of Sunday-only ball grounds (Gloucester, New Jersey) 69–71
Philadelphia (AL): Camden proposals 247, 254; doubleheaders 262; exhibition games on Sunday 156, 161, 201; first Sunday home game 11, 207–209; first Sunday home game (legal) 260; first Sunday road game 140; one-game road trips on Sunday 173, 205, 250, 255; other Sunday games 199, 251–252
Philadelphia (NL): doubleheaders 262, 265, 267; first Sunday home game 260; first Sunday road game 149; holdout on Sunday play 104, 131, 135, 142, 148, 149, 204; one-game road trips on Sunday 196, 242, 250, 255
Pinchot, Gifford 256–257
Pittsburgh (AA): 37, 58
Pittsburgh (NL): doubleheaders 262, 264; exhibition games on Sunday 165; first Sunday home game 260; first Sunday road game 130–131; position on Sunday games 104, 125; one-game road trips on Sunday 173, 204, 250, 255
players refusing to play on Sunday: Fultz 145–146; Mathewson 147; Radford 146; Rickey 146–147; Young 117
Players League 81, 90, 91, 101
Poholsky, Tom 267
Polo Grounds 182, 195, 196–197
Poole, Ed 8, 155, 157, 282–285
Poorman, Tom 70
Powell, Jack 7–8, 122–124, 123p, 127, 130, 278–282
Powers, Pat 6, 88–90, 164, 177, 183
Puritans 11–13, 214

Radford, Paul 146
Reidy, Bill 141
Reilly, Charlie 299n
Reilly, John 6, 79–80, 80p
Reipschlager, Charlie 65
Richmond, John 46
Rickey, Branch 146–147
Ridgewood Park 52–55, 66, 77, 91–92, 152, 153, 155, 183
Ritter, Lew 155, 157
Rixey, Eppa 187
Robertson, David 189
Robinson, Wilbert 10, 187
Robison, Frank 63, 64, 71–73, 116, 125–130
Rochester (AA): arrests of players 6–7, 88–89; first Sunday home game 83–84;
other Sunday games 83–86, 88–90; stoppage of Sunday play 88–89; use of Sunday-only ball grounds (Windsor Beach Grounds) 83
Rochester, New York 129
Rocky Point, Rhode Island 149, 164–165
Rommel, Ed 251–252
Roth, Frank 9, 155
Ruppert, Jake 192, 196
Rusie, Amos 131
Ruth, Babe 195, 196, 197, 198, 199, 242
Ryan, Jimmy 110–112, 112p, 113

Sabbatarians: in 1880s 44, 45, 58, 59, 73, 74, 75; in 1890s 6, 81, 85, 100, 108, 131, 266; in 1900s 17–18, 19, 156, 176–177, 178; Boston 219, 221, 234; Brooklyn/Queens 54, 77, 154–155; Chicago 106–107, 113–114; Cincinnati 55, 78; Cleveland 120; Lord's Day Alliance 219, 224, 234, 240, 249; New York 176–177, 181; Philadelphia 206, 208, 249, 253, 256–257; see also Law and Order Societies; Reverends
St. Louis (AA): arrest for Sunday play 6, 60–61; championships 58, 59; crowds 59, 68; exhibition games on Sunday 58–59, 67; first Sunday home game 37; impact of Sunday baseball 40–41, 59; other Sunday games 36, 38, 39, 76; transfer to National League 102; see also Von der Ahe, Chris
St. Louis (AL) 141
St. Louis (NA) 22
St. Louis (NL, pre-1892): 25–28, 58–59
St. Louis (NL, 1892+): decline in Sunday influence 136; first Sunday home game 104; other Sunday games 133, 154, 267
St. Louis (UA) 41–42
St. Louis, early Sunday games 21, 22, 27–28, 36
Scheffler, Ted 84
Selbach, Kip 299n
Selkirk, George 264
Sesquicentennial Exposition 206–207
Seward, Ed 70, 71
Shaw, Dupee 44
Sheckard, Jimmy 130, 165
Shibe, John 206, 207
Shibe, Tom 254
Shibe Park 199, 205, 260
Shoch, George 100
Siever, Ed 140
Simmons, Al 205, 250, 252
Sisler, George 243
Slattery, Jack 236

Smith, Al 179, 192, 193–194, 198–199, 224–225, 237
Smith, Aleck 132–133
Smith, Elmer 79
Smith, Pop 46, 47
Sneed, John 92
Sockalexis, Louis 299n
Sommers, Joe 55
Spalding, Albert 103–104, 106
Spohrer, Al 241
Sportsman's Park 40, 42
Springwells, Michigan 137, 300n
Stafford, Bob 93
Stanky, Eddie 267
State v. Chris Von der Ahe 61–62, 275–278
State v. Powell 8, 125, 171, 278–282
Stengel, Casey 186
Sterling, John 93
Stern, Aaron 79
Stivetts, Jack 94
Stovall, George 172
Stovey, Harry 70, 76
Stricker, Cub 6, 65–66, 65p
Sullivan, Dan 36
Sullivan, Mike 70
Sunday 11–20, 74, 100, 130, 203, 223, 267–268
Sunday, Billy 146, 178
Sunday baseball, ruses: annexation of land 109; charitable donations 137, 168; contribution boxes 160–162; patriotic concerts 186; scorecard prices 151, 153, 154, 159, 160
Sunday baseball, term 5, 20, 266, 269
Sunday baseball, ways to play where illegal *see* neutral-site Sunday games; one-game road trips on Sunday; Sunday-only ball grounds
Sunday games: all teams play on Sunday 197; charity benefit games 161, 182; crowd size 37, 39, 40, 54, 66, 68, 119, 132, 135, 139, 140–141, 154, 157, 160, 163, 164, 194, 195, 197, 199, 242, 260, 261; curfews 243, 263–264; disorder 56–57, 67; doubleheaders 133, 147, 185, 199, 243, 261–263, 265–269; first ever 36; first game by each major league team 271–274; forfeits 76, 92, 264; ground rules 54, 139, 143, 145; military benefit games 186, 189, 201, 217; night games 266–267, 268–269; odd occurrences 53, 92, 100, 130, 132–133, 145, 243, 251–252, 264, 265; profitability 58, 68, 98, 113–114, 226–227; scheduling 68, 69, 105, 112, 148, 163, 167, 184, 194– 196, 240, 255, 261, 266; tragedies 110–111, 113, 165–166
Sunday-only ball grounds: Baltimore 86–87, 99; Brooklyn 52–55, 68–69, 92; Chicago 106; Cincinnati 78; Cleveland 64–65, 71–73, 126, 261; Detroit 136–138; Indianapolis 44–45; Philadelphia 69–71, 99; Rochester 83; Syracuse 83, 90; Washington 87, 99; *see also* Rocky Point, Rhode Island
Sunday pitcher 263
Sunday Rest Day Bill 73–74, 75, 100, 103, 221–222
Supreme Court appeals 8, 11, 124, 125, 134, 171, 210–212, 278–282, 285–291
Sweeney, Charlie 44
Sweigert, Hampton 93
Syracuse (AA): first Sunday home game at alternate site 84–85; stoppage of Sunday play 90–91; use of Sunday-only ballpark (Three Rivers, Iron Pier) 83, 90

Tannehill, Jesse 131
Tebeau, Patsy 117, 130, 299n
Terry, Adonis 46, 47, 57
Texas Rangers (AL) 268
Thatcher, Grant 155
Three Rivers, New York 83
Titcomb, Ledell 89
Toledo (AA) 83
Toledo, Ohio 145

Umpires: Bradley 57; Ferguson 67; Goldsmith 76; Haskell 140; Holland 76; Hubbard 264; Peoples 92; Pinelli 267
Union Association 41–44

Von der Ahe, Chris 6, 40–41, 60–61, 67, 76–77, 81, 82, 102, 130, 275–278
Vosmik, Joe 252

Walberg, Rube 258, 259
Walker, Ed 145
Walker, Fleet 42–43, 55
Walker, Jimmy 193–194, 198
Walker, Oscar 46, 47
Wallace, Bobby 299n
Washington (AA): 96–97, 102
Washington (AL): first Sunday home game 193; first Sunday road game 140; one-game road trips on Sunday 173; one-game road trips on Sunday (host) 193, 250, 255, 259; other Sunday games 198
Washington (minor league) 87

Index

Washington (NA) 22
Washington (NL): arrests of players 121–122; dropped from league 134; first Sunday road game 105
Weehawken, New Jersey 66–67, 132
Welch, Curt 76
Welsh, Jimmy 243
West Side Grounds 106–107, 113–114
Whitman, Burt 231, 233–234
Whitman, Charles 189, 191, 192
Wiedenmeyer's Park 159
Willis, Vic 149
Wilmot, Walt 7, 110, 113, 114
Wilson, Zeke 122, 299n
Windsor Beach Grounds 83, 90

Worcester (NL) 29–31
workweek 14–15, 18, 20, 203, 263, 266
World Series: exhibition games on Sunday during series play 58–59, 77–78, 150; Sunday games 163–164, 169, 197, 246–247
World's fairs 16, 100, 106–107, 206–207
Wright, Harry 21, 35

Yankee Stadium 197, 198
Yawkey, Bill 167, 169
Young, Cy 106, 117, 118p, 119

Zimmer, Chief 149, 299n

www.ingramcontent.com/pod-product-compliance
Ingram Content Group UK Ltd.
Pitfield, Milton Keynes, MK11 3LW, UK
UKHW041923140426
5217IPUK00014B/294